Managing Coastal Tourism Resorts

ASPECTS OF TOURISM

Aspects of Tourism is an innovative, multifaceted series which will comprise authoritative reference handbooks on global tourism regions, research volumes, texts and monographs. It is designed to provide readers with the latest thinking on tourism world-wide and in so doing will push back the frontiers of tourism knowledge. The series will also introduce a new generation of international tourism authors, writing on leading edge topics. The volumes will be readable and user-friendly, providing accessible sources for further research. The list will be underpinned by an annual authoritative tourism research volume. Books in the series will be commissioned that probe the relationship between tourism and cognate subject areas such as strategy, development, retailing, sport and environmental studies. The publisher and series editors welcome proposals from writers with projects on these topics.

Other Books in the Series

Music and Tourism: On the Road Again
 Chris Gibson and John Connell
Tourism Development: Issues for a Vulnerable Industry
 Julio Aramberri and Richard Butler (eds)
Nature-based Tourism in Peripheral Areas: Development or Disaster?
 C. Michael Hall and Stephen Boyd (eds)
Tourism, Recreation and Climate Change
 C. Michael Hall and James Higham (eds)
Shopping Tourism, Retailing and Leisure
 Dallen J. Timothy
Wildlife Tourism
 David Newsome, Ross Dowling and Susan Moore
Film-Induced Tourism
 Sue Beeton
Rural Tourism and Sustainable Business
 Derek Hall, Irene Kirkpatrick and Morag Mitchell (eds)
The Tourism Area Life Cycle, Vol. 1: Applications and Modifications
 Richard W. Butler (ed.)
The Tourism Area Life Cycle, Vol. 2: Conceptual and Theoretical Issues
 Richard W. Butler (ed.)
Tourist Behaviour: Themes and Conceptual Schemes
 Philip L. Pearce
Tourism Ethics
 David A. Fennell
North America: A Tourism Handbook
 David A. Fennell (ed.)
Lake Tourism: An Integrated Approach to Lacustrine Tourism Systems
 C. Michael Hall and Tuija Härkönen (eds)
Codes of Ethics in Tourism: Practice, Theory, Synthesis
 David A. Fennell and David C. Malloy

For more details of these or any other of our publications, please contact:
Channel View Publications, Frankfurt Lodge, Clevedon Hall,
Victoria Road, Clevedon, BS21 7HH, England
http://www.channelviewpublications.com

ASPECTS OF TOURISM 34
Series Editors: Chris Cooper (*University of Queensland, Australia*),
C. Michael Hall (*University of Canterbury, New Zealand*)
and Dallen Timothy (*Arizona State University, USA*)

Managing Coastal Tourism Resorts

A Global Perspective

Edited by
Sheela Agarwal and Gareth Shaw

CHANNEL VIEW PUBLICATIONS
Clevedon • Buffalo • Toronto

Library of Congress Cataloging in Publication Data
Managing Coastal Tourism Resorts: A Global Perspective / edited by Sheela Agarwal and Gareth Shaw.
Aspects of Tourism: 34
Includes bibliographical references and index.
1. Seaside resorts–Management. 2. Sustainable development. 3. Tourism.
I. Agarwal, Sheela II. Shaw, Gareth. III. Title.
TX911.3.M27C63 2007
647.94068–dc22 2007020002

British Library Cataloguing in Publication Data
A catalogue entry for this book is available from the British Library.

ISBN-13: 978-1-84541-073-5 (hbk)
ISBN-13: 978-1-84541-072-8 (pbk)

Channel View Publications
An imprint of Multilingual Matters Ltd

UK: Frankfurt Lodge, Clevedon Hall, Victoria Road, Clevedon BS21 7HH.
USA: 2250 Military Road, Tonawanda, NY 14150, USA.
Canada: 5201 Dufferin Street, North York, Ontario, Canada M3H 5T8.

The policy of Channel View Publications is to use papers that are natural, renewable and recyclable products, made from wood grown in sustainable forests. In the manufacturing process of our books, and to further support our policy, preference is given to printers that have FSC and PEFC Chain of Custody certification. The FSC and/or PEFC logos will appear on those books where full certification has been granted to the printer concerned.

Typeset by Datapage International Ltd.
Printed and bound in Great Britain by MPG Books Ltd.

Contents

Illustrative Material

Tables

Figures

Plates

Preface and Acknowledgements

Surprisingly, despite the fact that coastal tourism resorts are an immensely important tourist space and are dealt with in most postgraduate and undergraduate tourism courses, there are few books which focus solely upon them, and there has been limited critical assessment of their evolution, planning, development and management. Moreover, the majority of academic research undertaken in this area has been completed within Northern and Southern Europe at the expense of a wider global consideration, and is overly descriptive in nature, consisting of a collection of theoretically unconnected case studies. This book addresses this research vacuum by adopting a thematic framework in which to examine coastal tourism resorts in a selected range of environments across the globe. It incorporates a detailed analysis of a range of economic, sociocultural, political and environmental issues that are being experienced, to differing extents, by coastal tourism resorts that are at different life-cycle stages of development. By doing so, this book is more than a mere amalgamation of existing literature, as it aims to advance conceptual understanding of resort evolution and change. It is therefore aimed at undergraduate and postgraduate courses in tourism in which students are introduced to the importance of coastal tourism resorts and to issues that affect their planning, development and management.

The inspiration for this book may be traced back to my doctoral studies and to Professors Gareth Shaw (University of Exeter) and Allan Williams (London Metropolitan University), who nurtured and developed my interest in coastal resorts. Since completing this initial piece of research, the dynamics of coastal resorts have continued to remain a source of enormous fascination for us both. Gareth and I are deeply grateful to a great many people who together have enabled this book to come to fruition. First and foremost, of course, we are extremely indebted to the book's chapter contributors for volunteering to participate in this project, and for providing much interesting material. I would like to thank Bill Bramwell at Sheffield Hallam University for his insightful conversations, which enabled me to maintain enthusiasm for the book, and for his continued support. In addition, Gareth and I would like to express our appreciation to Helen Jones at the University of Exeter, who skilfully and quickly produced the figures in Chapters 1, 7, 8 and 13. Finally, we would like to thank Channel View Publications for their support with this project.

Sheela Agarwal
University of Plymouth

Gareth Shaw
University of Exeter

The Contributors

Sheela Agarwal is a Senior Lecturer in Tourism at Plymouth University's Business School (Drake Circus, Plymouth PL4 8AA, UK. E-mail: sagarwal@plymouth.ac.uk). Since completing doctoral research on the restructuring of English coastal resorts, in 1995, she has written and co-authored numerous journal articles and book chapters relating to various aspects of coastal resort tourism, including the impact and consequences of globalisation, economic restructuring and social exclusion. Her research interests include discourses of globalisation, economic restructuring, conceptualisation of space and place, local governance and social exclusion.

Bill Bramwell is Professor of International Tourism Studies at Sheffield Hallam University's Centre for International Tourism Research (Sheffield S1 1WB, UK. E-mail: w.m.bramwell@shu.ac.uk). He co-edits the *Journal of Sustainable Tourism*, and he has edited books on tourism's relationships with partnerships, sustainability in Europe, rural development and coastal areas in Southern Europe. His research interests include connections between tourism and environmental politics, discourses of sustainability, governance arrangements, actor perspectives on political economy and cultural change.

Kobi Cohen-Hattab is a Lecturer at the Department of Land of Israel Studies and Archaeology, Bar Ilan University (Ramat-Gan, Israel, 52900. E-mail: cohenko@mail.biu.ac.il). His PhD thesis examined the development of tourism infrastructure in Jerusalem during the British rule (1917–1948). He conducted his postdoctoral research at the Department of Geography, York University, Toronto (2001–2002). His main research interests are historical geography of tourism, tourism in historical towns and the development of seaside resorts.

Tim Coles is Senior Lecturer in Management in the Department of Management at the University of Exeter, where he is Co-Director of the Centre for Tourism Studies (E-mail: t.e.coles@exeter.ac.uk). From 2002 to 2004, he was University Business Research Fellow funded by the Southwest of England Regional Development Agency. Based on work with business and policy-makers during this secondment, he has been developing research on the role of property markets in tourism enterprises and their implications for destination sustainability.

Tim Gale is Senior Lecturer in Tourism Geography in the Faculty of the Built Environment at the University of the West of England, Bristol. His research interests include the relationship between late 20th-century processes of economic restructuring and cultural change and the built environment of cold-water resorts, new forms of tourism production and consumption (e.g. cyber- and eco-tourism), and environmental sustainability and tourism development. He is particularly interested in the potential for new knowledge creation, with regards to each of these areas of enquiry, offered by the so-called 'mobilities turn' in tourist studies and critical realism as a philosophy of, and for, the social sciences.

Dr Alison Gill is a Professor with a joint appointment in the Department of Geography and the School of Resource and Environmental Management at Simon Fraser University in Vancouver, Canada. She is currently serving as the Associate Dean in the Faculty of Arts and Social Sciences. Her primary research focus is on community development and planning issues in tourism environments. She has published extensively on change in mountain resort environments and has more recently also begun work in coastal tourism areas.

Joan C. Henderson is an Associate Professor at Nanyang Business School at Nanyang Technological University in Singapore, where she has worked since 1997. Prior to this, she lectured in Travel and Tourism in the UK after periods of employment in the public and private tourism sectors there. Her PhD thesis, completed at the University of Edinburgh, was on the subject of social tourism and she also holds an MSc in Tourism and a BScEcon (Hons) in Politics and History. Current research interests include tourism in the Asia-Pacific region, heritage as a tourist attraction and crisis management and tourism.

Brian King is Professor and Head of the School of Hospitality, Tourism and Marketing at Victoria University, Australia. The university has won the Australian Tourism Award in the Education and Training category on three occasions. His strong engagement with the tourism sector has included management roles in tour operations, resorts and airlines. He has consulted to a range of international agencies in the areas of tourism marketing and human resource development. His book publications include: *Creating Island Resorts, Tourism Marketing in Australia and Asia-Pacific Tourism: Regional Planning, Co-operation and Development*. He is Joint Editor-in-Chief of the international journal *Tourism, Culture and Communication*.

Joan Carles Llurdés is Senior Lecturer in the Department of Geography at the Universitat Autònoma de Barcelona, where he teaches in both the Departments of Geography and Humanities, and in the School of Tourism and Hotel Management. He is also Tutor for Tourism Studies in the Universitat Oberta de Catalunya (Open University). His teaching interests focus on Cartography and Photo Interpretation, and the Geography of Tourism. Specific topics of research experience include: tourism planning; industrial heritage tourism; environmental risks; climatic change and tourism. He has published many papers in regional, national and international journals and has participated in the production of several multiauthor books.

Catherine Oelofse is a Lecturer in the School of Environmental Sciences at the University of KwaZulu-Natal, where she is engaged in research on issues of environmental management in relation to coastal development at various locations along the South African coastline.

Robert Preston-Whyte is Professor Emeritus at the University of KwaZulu-Natal in South Africa. His recent research activity has focused on issues of coastal tourism in KwaZulu-Natal as well as the impact of climate and environmental change on tourism in Southern African.

Gerda K. Priestley is a Bachelor and Master graduate of Queen's University, Belfast and Bachelor and Ph.D. graduate of the Universitat Autònoma de Barcelona (UAB), where she is a Senior Lecturer in the Department of Geography. Her roles include the Director of International Relations, Research and Postgraduate Education at the UAB School of Tourism and Hotel Management. Her research experience focuses on projects in the field of tourism, including: the sustainable development of natural areas; the evolution, impact and sustainable management of golf tourism; rural tourism in Spain; cultural tourism; and leisure and tourism in urban areas. She is the author of numerous publications related to her research interests and on more general topics such as: regional tourism planning and sustainability in tourism.

Richard Sharpley is Professor of Tourism at the University of Central Lancashire. Since commencing his academic career some 15 years ago he has developed his research interests in a number of areas, including rural tourism, the sociology of tourism, tourism and sustainable development, and island tourism, the latter with a particular focus on Cyprus. He is the author of a number of tourism textbooks, including the widely used *Tourism, Tourists and Society*, and has also published numerous chapters and journal papers.

Gareth Shaw is a Professor of Retail and Tourism Management in the Department of Management at the University of Exeter, where he is Co-Director of the Centre for Tourism Studies (Exeter, EX4 4RJ. E-mail: g.shaw@exeter.ac.uk). He has published numerous papers on tourism and co-authored or co-edited the following books including: *The Rise and Fall of British Coastal Resorts* (Cassell, 1997); *Tourism and Economic*

Development (3rd edn, Wiley, 1998); *Critical Issues in Tourism* (2nd edn, Blackwell, 2002); and *Tourism and Tourism Spaces* (Sage, 2004). His research interests include tourism entrepreneurship and small firms, tourism and innovation, and tourism, disability and social exclusion.

Noam Shoval is a Lecturer at the Department of Geography of the Hebrew University of Jerusalem (Jerusalem 91905, Israel. E-mail: noamshoval@huji.ac.il). He conducted his postdoctoral research at the Department of Geography, King's College, University of London (2000–2001). He was the recipient of the Lord Goodman Chevening Post-doctoral fellowship (2000) and a Fulbright postdoctoral award (2000). His main research interests are: tourism and culture as tools for urban regeneration, models of hotel location, spatial activity of tourists and tourism management in heritage cities.

David Weaver is Professor of Tourism Management at the University of South Carolina, where he specialises in ecotourism, sustainable tourism and destination life-cycle dynamics. He has held previous positions in the USA, Australia and Canada and is the author or co-author of more than 70 refereed journal papers and book chapters as well as several textbooks. He is the editor of the Encyclopedia of Ecotourism (CABI) and sits on the editorial boards of seven international refereed tourism journals.

Erin Welk completed a Master of Arts degree in Geography at Simon Fraser University which focused on power and politics in tourism development. She has a BA (Honours) in Geography from the University of Calgary. Her research interests include coastal community development and planning, tourism policy and the politics of development.

Atila Yüksel is a Lecturer (BA in Tourism and Hotel Management, Dokuz Eylul University; MSc in Tourism Management, the University of Wales; PhD at Sheffield Hallam University. E-mail: ayuksel@adu.edu.tr) is a Lecturer in the Faculty of the School of Tourism and Hospitality Management, Adnan Menderes University. He has published articles, book chapters and conference papers on tourist satisfaction and complaint management, destination planning and marketing, and tourism research in prestigious scientific journals, including *Annals of Tourism Research, Tourism Management, Journal of Hospitality and Tourism Research, Journal of Travel and Tourism Marketing, Journal of Vacation Marketing, the Cornell Hotel and Restaurant Administration Quarterly*, and the *Journal of Travel and Tourism Research*.

Fisun Yüksel (BA in Tourism and Hotel Management, Dokuz Eylul University; MSc in Tourism Management, Sheffield Hallam University, PhD at Sheffield Hallam University. E-mail: fisunyuksel@yahoo.com) is in the Faculty of the School of Tourism and Hospitality Management,

Mersin University. She has published papers on destination management, planning and marketing, tourist satisfaction and complaint management, and tourism research in prestigious scientific journals, including *Annals of Tourism Research, Tourism Management, Journal of Hospitality and Tourism Research, Journal of Travel and Tourism Marketing, Journal of Vacation Marketing*, and the *Journal of Travel and Tourism Research*. Her recent research is in the field of actor-network relationships.

Chapter 1

Introduction: The Development and Management of Coastal Resorts: A Global Perspective

GARETH SHAW and SHEELA AGARWAL

Introduction: The Coastal Resort a Neglected Tourism Environment

Despite the fact that coastal resorts are still the main tourism destinations for many holidaymakers, academic interest in such environments has been limited compared with other forms of tourism. Certainly, within the tourism literature, with the exception of a handful of studies that have focused on specific coastal resorts (Agarwal, 1999, 2002; Gale, 2005; Pollard & Rodriguez, 1993; Priestley & Mundet, 1998; Shaw & Williams, 1997a; Smith, 2004), these environments have either been neglected, subsumed within analyses of coastal tourism regions (Coccossis & Parpairis, 1996; Goytia Prat, 1996; Jordon, 2001; Knowles & Curtis, 1999; Twining-Ward & Baum, 1998; Zanetto & Soriani, 1996) or viewed in relatively narrow economic and historical perspectives (Beatty & Fothergill, 2004; Clegg & Essex, 2000; Soane, 1992; Tunstall & Penning-Roswell, 1998; Urry, 2002; Walton, 1997, 2000). For example, with regards to the latter, within the British context, seaside resorts have been seen as old forms of tourism, catering for a Fordist form of consumption based around mass tourism. Indeed, Urry's (2002) discourse on the decline of the British resort epitomises such views, claiming seaside resorts have not shared in the growth of tourism. More tellingly, he argues that 'seaside resorts have also become less distinct because of the de-industrialisation of many towns and cities' (Urry, 2002: 36). This has occurred in contrast to other environments, which have become new leisure spaces, re-fixing the tourist gaze so that resorts 'are no longer extraordinary' (p. 36). In part however, such ideas are contested by Walton (2000: 196), who argues that instead of discussing resort decline, 'we should be trying to explain the British seaside's survival'.

Part of the literature on coastal resorts is therefore concerned with the failure or decline of such environments. This in turn is also often linked with the so-called Butler life-cycle or resort life-cycle model (Butler, 1980;

see Agarwal (2002) for a recent review and Butler (2005) for a much broader perspective). In this context, the resort is often viewed almost as an attachment to the mechanisms of the model in its different variations. Often what such studies have exposed is how little is known in detail about the functioning of coastal resorts due to inadequate levels of information at the resort level (Agarwal, 2005; Cooper, 1990; Prideaux, 2000; Shaw & Williams, 2002). In contrast, early tourism studies gave much more emphasis to coastal resorts, focussing especially on their layout and morphology, resulting in a range of structural models (see Pearce, 1995 for a review). Such representations however have focused mainly on physical features and land use patterns, neglecting the sociocultural aspects of coastal resorts or indeed details of development processes.

Based on the existing literature, our contention is that coastal resorts have received somewhat inadequate attention and have largely been neglected, relative to other tourism destinations. To date, surprisingly few books have been published that focus on coastal tourism resorts and consequently there has been little critical assessment of their development and management. Moreover, the majority of academic research undertaken in this area has very largely been completed within Northern and Southern Europe, at the expense of a wider global consideration. Given this lacuna, our aim is to readdress the balance by providing a global perspective on aspects of coastal resort development and management. In this chapter, we start by considering the growth and diffusion of the coastal resort, along with the development of international competition and the resort as a global tourism product, before going on to outline possible management issues and the organisation of this book.

The Development and Diffusion of the Coastal Resort: The Growth of International Competition

The historiography of the coastal resort has been relatively well researched despite the claims of Walton (2000). Lencek and Bosker (1998) have provided a general perspective on the development of the coastal resort, whilst Shaw and Williams (2004) and Gale (2005) have set such growth within a more socioeconomic framework. According to Walton (2000), the origins of coastal resorts may be traced back to Britain, when during the latter part of the 18th century, more organised and fashionable sea-bathing developed in England, thereby marking the institutionalisation of the beach. The creation of distinctive coastal resorts centred around the royal patronage given to Brighton on the south coast of England was confirmed by the completion of the Royal Pavilion in 1820 (Gilbert, 1954). This signalled a process of the 'architecturalisation' of the seaside (Lencek & Bosker, 1998: 90), creating new public leisure spaces including the promenade.

Despite Walton's (2000) claims that British coastal resorts were a 'cultural export', in the absence of concrete evidence, combined with the proliferation of inland spas across Continental Europe, it seems likely that the ideas behind the coastal resort diffused rapidly across Northern Europe at similar times. This resulted in the creation of a range of English resorts and, equally importantly, numerous Continental equivalents. Resorts began to appear on the French Channel coast and into what became Belgium and the Netherlands by the late 18th century. By the early 19th century, coastal resorts were developing in Normandy and Southwest France, along the North German coast and in parts of Scandinavia. The early 19th century also witnessed the creation of resorts in North America, notably along Florida's Gold Coast (for example, Miami and Fort Lauderdale) and in New Jersey, with Newport (Rhode Island) and Cape May in New Jersey catering for the wealthier classes (Lewis, 1980). Later, in the mid-19th century, seaside resorts began to be developed on the Spanish Atlantic coast and along the French and Italian Riviera; Rimini and Ostia were among several Italian coastal resorts that developed during this period, along with an increasing German and Austrian presence. By the end of the 19th century, coastal resorts were being created along the Adriatic coastline and in parts of the colonies, especially on South Africa's Western Cape (for example, Simonstown, St. James and Mulzenberg) and on the coast of Queensland in Australia. In Sydney, for example, the development of a new pier at Coogee Beach in the 1920s epitomises the Victorian seaside era (Walton, 2000). It was also during this time that coastal resorts developed in Latin America and the Caribbean, with the creation of Costa Rica's San Jose, the Dominican Republic's Puerto Plata and Argentina's Mar del Plata.

The transformation of coastal resorts from the preserves of the wealthy to mass holiday centres took place in the second part of the 19th century and continued into the early 20th century. This democratisation of leisure travel and holidaymaking, according to Walton (2000), stemmed from aspects of industrialisation along with the creation of 'new modes by which pleasure was organised and structured' (Urry, 2002: 17). Across Northern and Southern Europe and North America, a combination of factors helped transform these resorts into centres of mass pleasure. Such factors as improved access, via rail travel, improvements in social access to leisure time and the recognition of new investment opportunities in creating these coastal resorts, produced a series of inter-related movements (Walton, 1983). The trends are summed up by Lencek and Bosker (1998: 115), who claimed that coastal resorts were 'children of cities'.

The creation of such centres of mass pleasure also involved the construction of new forms of 'high' and 'low' entertainment (Urry, 2002), including theatres and opera houses, Punch and Judy shows, minstrel shows, end-of-pier shows, beach entertainers and military and German 'oompah' bands (Walton, 2000). At Coney Island near New York for example, between 1897 and 1904, three large-scale amusement parks were built at a cost of $5 million (Snow & Wright, 1976). According to Lewis (1980: 48), 'this was the "New Coney Island" with lavish display and family entertainment', the aim of which 'was to manufacture a carnival spirit and offer fast-moving elaborated children's play' (the words of Thompson in 1908, the developer of Luna Park quoted in Lewis, 1980). Similar features were developed, albeit on a smaller scale, in many European resorts, reaching a larger scale in Blackpool in Northwest England, Southend-on-Sea in Southeast England and Berck in Southwest France, with the development of 'pleasure palaces' (Walton, 2000).

Coastal resorts also took different pathways to development seeking, to some degree, differing segments of the holiday market, or what Walton (2000) terms social tone. In Britain, such variations in social tone reflected the relationships between patterns of land ownership and attractive scenery (Perkin, 1976; Travis, 1992; Urry, 2002). This produced a complex hierarchy of coastal resorts that by the 20th century 'satisfied a wide range of aesthetic preferences . . . and catered for almost a complete cross section of society' (Walton, 2000: 27). Within North America such differences of social tone were also very visible as a 'world of difference separated the beach experience of urban workers from that of the wealthy entrepreneur' (Lencek & Bosker, 1998: 149). Thus, the very wealthy visited resorts such as Newport and Rhode Island, whilst places such as Atlantic City, initially created for the wealthier people of Philadelphia, was, by the late 19th century, appealing to a more classless market (Towner, 1996). Within Continental Europe, meanwhile, the casino and the grand hotel began to redefine the resorts for the wealthier classes, especially along the French Riviera. Nice and Cannes, along with other Riviera resorts, very largely designed themselves after high-class spa towns such as Vichy and Aix-les-Bains (Towner, 1996). In the case of Nice, development was rapid as visitor numbers grew from just 5000 in 1861 to 150,000 by 1914 (Rudney, 1980). More generally, Towner (1996) has attempted to draw together the early development of resorts in Germany, France, Spain and America, providing one of the few comparative studies. This gives some limited perspectives and shows that across these cultures, the variations in the 'social tone' of resorts or resort type was a common feature.

The growth of resorts within Europe and North and Latin America up to the mid-20th century was very much based on the exploitation of domestic holiday demand. There were exceptions, such as the wealthy British visitor who 'came to the Mediterranean to cast their net of affluence around the pleasure ports of the French Riviera' (Lencek &

Bosker, 1998: 131). In essence the resort systems that had evolved competed largely at the national level for domestic tourists. The most significant shift has been the strong and rapid growth of competition from international resorts since the 1960s. Urry (2002: 36) puts such changes within the context of 'the globalisation of contemporary tourism', which is a key theme of this book. The growth of the price-driven package holiday of the 1960s and 1970s has had a major impact on the traditional resorts of Europe and North America.

Indeed some of the earliest impacts of competition and resort decline are to be found in North America, where some of the older resorts on the northeastern seaboard had begun to lose their appeal by the 1950s, resulting in a declining share of the holiday market. Atlantic City, for example, lost much of its main tourist market to the growing Miami Beach – a completely planned and manufactured resort. Not only were its facilities more modern but it had a climatic advantage of being in Southern Florida. Within Britain, the percentage of people taking overseas holidays grew from 7.4% in 1955 to 16.7% by 1975 (British Tourist Authority, 1976). Similarly, consumer spending on domestic holidays grew by 80% between 1951 and 1968, but on overseas holidays spending increased by a massive 400% over the same period (Page, 2003). One of the major destination areas were the resorts of the Spanish Costa's and Spain's share of the British overseas holiday market grew from 6% in 1951 to 30% by 1968 (Page, 2003). Spain witnessed the growth of new purpose-built, mass coastal resorts offering affordable holidays based around the economics of the package tour (Barke & France, 1996; Bramwell, 1997a; Laws, 1997). Such resorts were not only created physically by the economics of mass tourism and the requirements of tour operators, but these organisations help shape the tourists' images of such places (Shaw & Williams, 2004).

Throughout the coastal resorts of the Mediterranean, there has been an increasing orientation of resorts as different market segments have been exploited in the face of increasing global competition. To a large extent the marketing of coastal resorts has mainly been controlled by the major tour operators selling some destinations to the youth market and others to families, along with the growing importance of the retirement market. Such activities have increasingly been characterised by the internationalisation of the coastal resort as part of the process of the globalisation of tourism.

The Coastal Resort as a Global Tourism Product

We argued in the previous section that coastal resorts and tourism practices switched to a more concentrated level of international growth after the 1960s. Within the context of the demands within the UK market, Evans and Stabler (1995) have identified three phases of growth:

(1) An introductory phase from the 1950s to around the mid-1960s, characterised by limited growth of new destination opportunities mainly for a few affluent tourists.
(2) A growth phase from the mid-1960s until the end of the 1980s, which saw the rapid development of mass tourism based around the inclusive package holiday. These changes were based on the growing power of tour operators that stimulated the growth of coastal resorts in a range of new destinations especially in parts of the Mediterranean.
(3) A so-called mature phase from the early 1990s, which witnessed the start of more flexible tourism products catering for changing market demands. In part, these have been signified by the transition from Fordist forms of consumption to post-Fordist ones, reflecting a move from the mass package holiday to more flexible patterns.

In terms of such phases, some commentators imply that the switch to post-Fordism forms of consumption is based on new forms of tourism away from the beach holiday (Urry, 2002). However, in a mature tourism market such as the UK, the evidence does not point to such a declining interest in the 3 S (sea-sun-sand) holiday product. Research suggests that in 2000 over 12 million UK tourists took a beach-based holiday (Mintel, 2001). More significantly, the market trends in beach holidays show a number of important features, including:

- an above average growth in tourist travel to long-haul destinations, with the top 20 of such destinations offering beach holidays;
- an increase in speciality market segments such as luxury all-inclusive resorts, with some specialising in weddings and honey-moons;
- the development of combination holidays in which the beach component is linked with some element of special interest tourism. (Meyer, 2003; Mintel, 2001)

In effect, such changing demands are part of globalisation trends in tourism and more particularly the development of the coastal resort as a global product. To understand such trends we need to examine two main inter-related processes. The first concerns the nature of tourism globa-lisation, whilst the second is associated with the impacts of the former on the development of coastal resorts.

The nature of tourism globalisation

Much confusion still surrounds the debates on tourism globalisation, especially in recognising the term and the processes associated with it, and in ascertaining its meaning for tourist destinations (Agarwal, 2005). Within the tourism literature, the globalisation of tourism has been represented by what Mowforth and Munt (1998: 12) view as 'an ever tightening network of connections which cut across national boundaries'. These connections operate in terms of a growing globalisation of consumer demand, which Levitt (1983) first identified as a 'global-village'. In general terms, such ideas represent a trend towards increased homogeneity, with consumer demand across different national markets becoming similar. In addition, Mowforth and Munt's (1998) interconnections are represented economically through global flows of capital, the activities of transnational companies and increased levels of competition (Shaw & Williams, 2004). In more general economic contexts, some organisations have constructed a globalisation index based around such key variables as foreign direct investment, capital flows, trade and levels of international travel and tourism (Foreign Policy, 2003). However, as the authors of the index explain, such 'key indicators only scratch the surface of globalization's complexity' (Kearney and Foreign Policy, 2001: 2).

In an attempt to uncover such complexity, Yip (1992) made an early conceptualisation of so-called key globalisation drivers. These covered four main aspects, namely:

- Market drivers including the homogeneity of consumer demand at a global level, transferable marketing techniques and brands.
- Cost globalisation drivers including: global scale economies (covering product development, financing and procurement), variable operational costs across different economies, e.g. transnational hotel groups have utilised such geographical variations, steep experience curves favouring global companies when good practices and knowledge can be shared across different economies; of course this is contingent on organisational structures that allow knowledge to be transferred effectively (Gupta & Govindarajan, 2000).
- Competitive drivers including: interdependence of countries, which tends to stimulate greater globalisation; the presence of global competitors acts to pressure other organisations to operate globally; higher levels of international development trends produce globalisation tendencies as in the rapid growth of international tourism.
- Government drivers including: state policies encouraging large-scale tourism developments, such as in Mexico (see Brenner & Aguilar, 2002; Clancy, 2001), and favourable global trading conditions through the activities of the World Trade Organization.
- (modified from Evans *et al*., 2003; Yip, 1992).

Yip (1992), along with others (e.g. Campbell & Verbeke, 1994; Porter, 1986; Stonehouse *et al.*, 1999), has provided general perspectives on globalisation, but it is Yip's framework that permits a flexible view of global–local differences. This stresses that there may be some aspects of an industry that are global whilst other components are more local in their orientation. More specifically, Shaw and Williams (2004) have attempted to outline some of the key relationships in the globalisation of tourism. These include some of the 'drivers' identified previously, as well as migration, which generates increasing levels of visiting friends and relatives tourism (VFR) at an international level.

One key global force within tourism and part of Yip's cost globalisation driver is the activities of tour operators and transnational hotel corporations. In terms of the latter, four main companies had operations across 80 countries in 2000 (Shaw & Williams, 2004). Furthermore, Page (2003) estimates that almost 30% of all world hotel stock is controlled by transnational companies. Their recent competitive advantages have been enhanced by technological advances such as Global Distribution Systems (GDS) and links with the internet (Buhalis, 2003). Another key advantage is the increasing importance of brand identity, a strategy that transnational hotel organisations have fully utilised (Sharpley, 2005). This is part of transferable marketing, representing the degree 'to which . . . brand names and promotions can be used globally' (Evans *et al.*, 2003: 307).

The other major force in the globalisation of tourism has been through the activities of tour operators, especially the promotion of package holidays. Changes in demand and increased levels of competition have combined to change the characteristics of the package holiday, making the product more flexible in nature. To a degree such changes are contingent on shifts in tourism consumption towards a greater demand for new holiday experiences and destinations. The generality of such trends has been codified as a shift from Fordist forms of production and consumption through to post-Fordist ones along with more recent neo-Fordist patterns. Closer inspection of tourism consumption however reveals a duality of capitalist regimes, as complex and highly segmented markets coexist, embracing all forms of tourism (Torres, 2002).

Such trends are highlighted within the UK market for international tourism. For example, whilst long-haul travel was initially very often organised independently, in recent years package holidays have increased in importance within this market, growing from 15.4 million in 1997 to around 19 million by 2001. Moreover, the distribution of such packages varies across destination regions and by product type. Thus, across North Africa, Central and South America, and the Caribbean, inclusive packages are dominant, especially in coastal holidays. Of course the market is highly segmented and at the lower end of the market for the 3S product, demand is highly price sensitive. The relationship between tour operators and the shaping of the market for global tourism is complex and embraces many of the global drivers previously outlined. Major European-based operators such as My Travel plc and TUI plc typify these large international groups. In the case of the former, international expansion took place after 1994 when the organisation acquired the Scandinavia Leisure Group, followed by Sunquest Vacations, giving it a larger presence in Northern Europe and North America. They also created a cruise product – Sun Cruises – centred around Mediterranean resorts and those in the Caribbean (Evans *et al.*, 2003). Similarly, TUI (the largest German-based tour operator, as well as the key player in the UK market) has a massive global reach, operating in 70 countries, owning 3700 travel agencies, along with 81 tour operators and 285 hotels, with a turnover in 2001–02 of around €22 billion (Civil Aviation Authority, 2005; Meyer, 2003).

The impact such transnationals have on the coastal resort product in developing countries is in part shown in Table 1.1. This indicates how transnationals have promoted and developed the beach holiday in their holiday programmes. The global competitive processes (drivers) exercised by these tour operators produce unequal relationships within destination areas. This was recognised by the UNCTAD (1998: 3), which stated 'many suppliers of tourism services in developing countries (hotels, tourist guides, land-transport providers) are hampered by their weak bargaining position ... which often results in unfavourable contractual conditions'. Such inequalities in power relationships, together with intense competition with other transnationals, results in what the OECD (1999) and Souty (2002) have described as an abuse of buying power operated by predatory pricing strategies (OECD, 1997a). Within tourism these are used by large companies who dominate particular destinations such as coastal resorts. Indeed, Souty (2002: 26) terms this the 'Greek squeeze', after a situation in the 1980s when major tour operators continually reduced the prices they paid to hotels in Greece. Despite the fact that tourist numbers increased in that country from 5.5 million in 1981 to 8 million by 1989, the real value of receipts from tourism fell by 20% due to the activities of tour operators. Greek hoteliers continue to face pressures from tour operators in what Koutoulas (2006: 103) terms 'a situation of oligopoly with just one company [TUI] supplying 29% of their clientele from the twelve largest source markets'. As the United Nations (UN) (1999: 19) explains, such situations demonstrate how an economy dependent on mass tourism but caught in intense competition with other destinations 'at the low end of the value chain can face shrinking revenues when confronted by powerful tour operators'.

Table 1.1 Examples of destinations in three developing countries featured in the 'mainstream' beach holiday programmes sold by the three largest tour operators in the UK (2003–04)

Tour operator	*Holiday programmes*	*Developing countries included in the mainstream summer sun/winter sun 2003/4 programme*	*Other developing countries featured but in specialised holiday packages*
TUI (UK)	Examples from: Thomson Holidays (summer and winter programmes, 2003/04), Portland Holidays (summer and winter programmes, 2003/04), Tropical Places (summer and winter programmes, 2003/04), Thomson World Wide (summer and winter, 2003/04)	Antigua and Barbuda, Bahamas, Barbados, Borneo, British Virgin Islands, Cuba, Dominican Republic, Dubai, Egypt, Gambia, Grenada, Grenadines, India, Indonesia, Jamaica, Kenya, Malaysia, Maldives, Mauritius, Mexico, Morocco, Peru, Seychelles, South Africa, Sri Lanka, St. Kitts and Nevis, St. Lucia, Vietnam, Tanzania and Zanzibar, Thailand, Tobago, Tunisia, Turkey, Turks and Caicos Islands	Botswana, Nepal, Cambodia, Cook Islands, French Polynesia, Myanmar, Namibia, Reunion, Samoa, Zambia, Zimbabwe
My Travel	Examples from Direct Holidays (summer sun 2003), and Tradewinds (2003/04)	Antigua, Bahamas, Barbados, Brazil, Cuba, Dominican Republic, Dubai, Egypt, Gambia, Grenada, Indonesia, Jamaica, Kenya, Malaysia, Maldives, Mauritius, Mexico, Morocco, Seychelles, South Africa, Sri Lanka, St. Lucia, Tanzania, Thailand, Tobago, Tunisia, Turkey, Vietnam	Cambodia, Costa Rica, India, Myanmar, Oceania, UAE

Table 1.1 (*Continued*)

Tour operator	*Holiday programmes*	*Developing countries included in the mainstream summer sun/winter sun 2003/4 programme*	*Other developing countries featured but in specialised holiday packages*
First Choice	Examples taken from: Main summer sun/winter sun brochure 2003/4	Antigua, Aruba, Bahamas, Barbados, Cuba, Dominican Republic, Egypt, Gambia, India, Jamaica, Kenya, Malaysia, Maldives, Mexico, Morocco, South Africa, Sri Lanka, Thailand, Tunisia, Turkey	Belize, Bhutan, Bolivia, Borneo, Botswana, Cambodia, China, Costa Rica, Ecuador, Eritrea, Ethiopia, Ghana, Guatemala, Indonesia, Iran, Jordan, Ladakh, Madagascar, Malawi, Mali, Mozambique, Namibia, Nepal, Pakistan, Peru, Sudan, Syria, Tanzania, Tibet, Zimbabwe

Source: Modified from Meyer (2003)

Impact of globalisation on the development of coastal resorts

The globalisation of tourism services, as outlined in the previous section, leads to a consideration of how such forces have impacted on the coastal resort, at the regional and local scale. Gormsen's (1981) attempt to construct a centre–periphery model of international resort development gives one perspective. Within this context he recognised so-called first and second peripheries of coastal resorts which encompassed developments in Northern and Southern Europe. The third periphery includes North Africa, whilst the fourth covers resorts within the Caribbean, West Africa, parts of the Pacific and India Oceans, South East Asia and South America (see also Pearce, 1995). The model also postulates about the relative importance of external capital, especially in the more peripheral areas. Similarly, Britton's (1982) work highlights the dominance of external developers and in part gives a slightly clearer picture of the development process.

More recent studies have also drawn attention to the geography of resort growth (Clancy, 2001; King, 1997a, 2001). King (2001), building on earlier work by Turner and Ash (1975), has viewed the new resort developments as constituting a pleasure periphery, which in part fits with Gormsen's ideas. The creation of purpose-built resorts, comprising large hotel complexes and holiday villages, in many developing countries has produced a massive transformation of the environment, which Ayala (1991) has described as an international mega-trend.

Against this background there are two aspects that need further discussion, namely the process of resort development and the influence of place image-making at the resort level. In terms of the first aspect, a few generalised early models of resort development exist, including those by Miossec (1976) and Oppermann (1993). The former postulates a four-stage model, namely:

Stage 1: Development of pioneer resort attracting international tourists.
Stage 2: A multiplication of clone-like resorts with more infrastructural developments.
Stage 3: Restructure and reorganisation.
Stage 4: Resort specialisation is a dominating feature with increased tourism pressures.

However, as Brenner and Aguilar (2002: 503) point out, the model ignores the fundamental question of 'who builds the resort'. In part, Oppermann's work (1992) tackles this with his identification of two different but interconnected forms of international tourism: formal mass tourism developed around high levels of global investment and large-scale facilities, and 'drifter tourism' based on more local, small-scale investments. Even so, the details of the development process are still somewhat hidden. A more recent study instigated through the UN Environment Programme in 2001 (Hawkins *et al*., 2002), based on trends in 12 different resorts in various ecosystems, has attempted to outline the resort development process (Fig. 1.1). Of course such a generalisation still misses the detail, but nevertheless it highlights some key stages and stakeholders, which include:

- local investors,
- international developers and partners such as tour operators and/ or cruise carriers, and
- national governments.

As we argued previously, such processes need to be understood in the broader context of globalisation drivers. Within such a context, a number of authors have drawn attention to what Hudson (2001: 71) terms the 'hollowing out' of the state with regard to its role in regulation. Shaw and Williams (2004) and Agarwal (2005) observe such tendencies within tourism, but both argue that within this context 'the death of the state is a gross overstatement'.

Certainly there are many examples of resort development where the state has played a leading role in the development process as well as in regulating the nature of development (Sadi & Henderson, 2001). Within

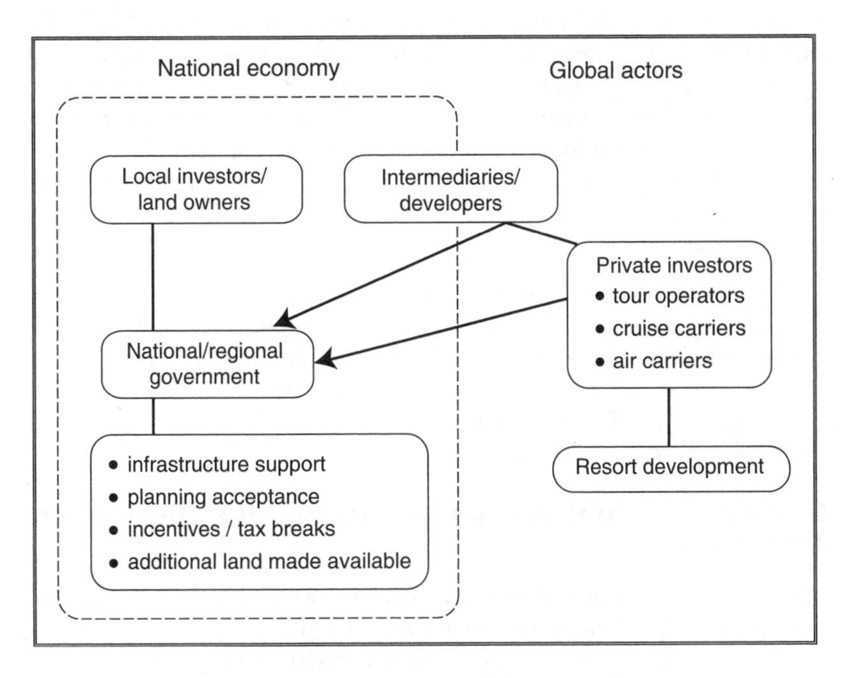

Figure 1.1 Key actors in the development of international resorts

the UK for example, Agarwal (1999, 2002, 2005), Gale (2005) and Morgan and Pritchard (1999) discuss the role of the local government in developing many English coastal resorts, particularly highlighting the variability of success in its efforts at restructuring. Meanwhile, Clancy (2001) and Brenner and Aguilar (2002) detail the role of the government in initiating resort development in Mexico. However, what has tended to happen is that the state has played the role of facilitator (see Fig. 1.1) and appears to have neglected its regulatory or management role in many instances. Certainly, the Mexican government has been strongly criticised in its lack of planning and development control in Cancún (Weiner, 2001).

The success of state intervention in coastal resort development is clearly variable but there appears to be two main reasons for the relative failure of state regulation and management over resort development. One is associated with the increasing calls by transnationals and their trade associations within tourism for self-regulation, which as Mowforth and Munt (1998: 117) explain is 'regulation by global capital'. The second reason is more complex but certainly related to the first and is associated with intense global competition. This competition is played out at two levels: globally amongst the large tour operations and regionally between different resort destinations. At the resort level, increasing attention is given to image creation and its role within the marketing system. More specifically, it is the creation of an image, which, whilst emphasising 'placeness' (Ayala, 1991) along with the lure of the beach, also links with different tourist experiences or what some authors are terming the 'experience-scape' (O'Dell & Billing, 2005). This relates to notions of theming (Shaw & Williams, 2004) and reflects the increasing trend for resort developers and tour operators to use particular settings in order to create product differentiation. In this context, King (2001) has outlined a basic typology of resorts based on their characteristics and degree of specialisation. These include:

- sport and beach-orientated resorts
- theme-park and golf resorts (Pleumaron, 1992)
- so-called 'mangrove resorts' (Thomas & Fernandez, 1994)
- large-scale, water-park resorts (Turner, 1996)
- mega-resorts (Clancy, 2001)
- boutique resorts (Meyer, 2003)

Managing Coastal Tourism Resorts and the Organisation of the Book

Given the long history of the coastal resort and its main phases of development, it is hardly surprising that a range of management issues exist. These include managing decline and restructuring, the problems of environmental impact, aspects of sustainability and socioeconomic impacts. One of the difficult issues of tourism management in the context of coastal resorts concerns the dimensions of the management function. In much of the literature, tourism management is often focussed on the business itself (Page, 2003) and certainly in many resorts local economies are structured around fragmented small- and medium-sized enterprises (SMEs). However, to make sense of management issues within coastal resorts, we need a broader perspective, which is partly provided by Middleton and Hawkins (1998: 84), who define tourism management as: 'strategies and action programmes ... to control and influence supply and visitor demand in order to achieve defined policy goals'. As both Doswell (1997) and Mason (2003) point out, the dividing line between tourism management and planning is unclear. Indeed the two closely fit together, as viewed by Hall and Page (1999), who argue that tourism management can be seen as a concurrent process involving strategic planning.

It is against this definitional background that issues of coastal resort management are considered in this book. At this juncture it is important to note that within the confines of this book, it is not possible to comprehensively cover coastal resort developments across the globe. Our intention is thus to provide a flavour of global coastal resort developments through the inclusion of numerous case studies across a variety of geographical regions. Moreover, the broad scope of interlinkages between planning and management, what Mason (2003: 80) calls a complex and practical relationship 'taking place simultaneously in a given context', involves key decisions from managers as well as viewing planning as a central process of management. Our context is of course the coastal resort in all its stages of development and its variations. Thus, this book aims to draw attention to the diversity of coastal resorts, to the variety of planning and management issues being experienced and to the conceptual and theoretical complexities that surround their study on a global scale. To reflect this, the book is structured around five main themes: (1) coastal resorts in transition; (2) the diversification and sustainable development of coastal resorts; (3) the pleasure periphery and managing the postmodern coastal resort; (4) coastal resort structures: variation versus standardisation; and (5) state intervention and the planning and management of coastal resorts.

Part 1, 'Coastal Resorts in Transition', examines the causes and consequences of broad structural economic and cultural forces of change for the 'cold water' (Cooper, 1997) post-mature coastal tourism resorts of Britain and Northern Europe. These resorts represent early examples of seaside development and the key management issues of many of these resorts tend to revolve around strategies of economic restructuring. However, as the three chapters in this section highlight, the problems facing these resorts are varied, a point that is reflected in the variety of management solutions that are suggested. Chapter 2 (Gale) provides an account of the recent fortunes and contemporary condition of post-mature resorts in Northern Europe, and by drawing on a critical realist perspective, identifies the causes and consequences of the decline of selected resorts. In contrast, Chapter 3 (Shaw and Coles) presents an overview of current trends in British resorts, highlighting the changing role of the tourism product as well as the increasing complexity of the resort economy. Meanwhile Chapter 4 (Agarwal) assesses the capacity of resorts to respond to global forces and highlights the importance of locally determined factors in influencing the extent and effectiveness of local action.

Aspects of sustainability are key aspects of the chapters in Part 2 – 'The Diversification and Sustainable Development of Coastal Resorts'. Whilst mass tourism has undoubtedly brought sustainable economic rewards to many mass tourism coastal resorts, it has often been accompanied by negative economic, environmental and sociocultural impacts, particularly in Southern Europe where tourism in coastal environments was characterised by rapid and uncontrolled growth. In response to the problems that mass tourism has created, tourism planners and managers are now seeking to diversify away from the attractions of 'sun, sea and sand', which are typical of mass tourism, into alternative tourism that is characterised by higher spending patterns, lower volumes of visitors and niche markets. However, Bramwell's (Chapter 5) study of resorts in Malta emphasises the potential complexity of management issues within sustainable strategies, by highlighting the difficulties of understanding cause and effect relationships. In contrast, Priestley and Llurdes (Chapter 6) analyse the present along with the future sustainability of state planning initiatives and assess their implications for selected Spanish coastal resorts. Chapter 7 takes up a similar theme, as Sharpley, in his comparative study of resorts in Cyprus and Tenerife, raises issues of sustainability and resort redevelopment in the face of intense international competition.

Part 3, 'The Pleasure Periphery and Managing the Postmodern Resort', draws on the ideas of global competition and the development of what King (1997a, 2001) highlighted as postmodern structures, by examining, in depth, the growth of coastal tourism resorts into the pleasure periphery in a range of environments. It discusses the influence and consequences of deeper underlying structural sociocultural changes that are allegedly occurring in society on coastal tourism resorts. The challenges of planning and managing these forces of change in postmodern resorts are examined, particularly with regard to local communities and environments. Thus, King's (Chapter 8) review of Australian resorts serves to emphasise the growing development pressures on coastal areas along with the need for management strategies that can sustain both global tourism demands and domestic pressures. Meanwhile, Henderson's chapter (9) on resort management in Malaysia in part highlights the problems of unplanned and uncontrolled growth, but at the same time contrasts the management issues associated with planned, integrated resorts. She notes that although the environmental impacts of both types of development are wide-ranging, from harmful sedimentation discharges impacting on coral reefs through to water shortages, religious tension is also a worrying undercurrent that is affecting most of Malaysia's coastal resorts. In contrast Gill and Welk's (Chapter 10) study of Tofino, a coastal resort located on the west coast of Canada, highlights how engagement with the pleasure periphery has led to the commodification of the natural heritage and to subsequent problems that are arguably irresolvable.

Part 4, 'Coastal Resort Structures: Variation versus Standardisation', adds another dimension to management issues. It is derived from the fact that coastal resort structures differ greatly as some may be tightly packed, mass tourism landscapes, compared with some that may be carefully managed, low-density developments in traditional building styles, whilst others may be 'mega' ghetto-like structures (Bramwell, 1997a). This section aims to explore the global diversity of coastal resort structures and its implications for the coastal resort product. The alleged shift in the post-Fordist resort product is contested in that increasing evidence suggests that the resort experience is still strongly engineered and somewhat standardised. These ideas are explored in three different contexts. Preston-Whyte and Oelofse (Chapter 11) emphasise the different forms of coastal tourism development in South Africa together with the management implications. In contrast, Weaver (Chapter 12) utilises dependency theory to examine the structural characteristics of resorts in South Carolina and Antigua. Within this context he identifies four key management issues, namely 'interiorisation', global impacts, tourism and non-tourism developments (a theme also highlighted by King in Chapter 8), and the role of protected areas. Then Agarwal and Shaw, in Chapter 13, explore the tensions created by the coexistence of mass tourism and eco-tourism resorts in Mexico and their management implications.

Part 5, 'State Intervention and the Planning and Development of Coastal Resorts', brings the discussion back to the context of tourism management. It demonstrates how the nature and extent of state intervention in tourism planning and management varies greatly between coastal resorts globally. In doing so, it attempts to account for this variation and considers implications for coastal resort planning, development and management. Attention is directed at contrasting systems of governance and how this translates to the planning and management of resorts. Thus, Chapter 14 (Shoval and Cohen-Hattab) discusses the role of the state in the creation and management of Egypt and Israel's Red Sea coastal resorts. Yuksel and Yuksel (Chapter 15) then highlight how clientelism has impacted on the development of selected Turkish resorts. Finally, Agarwal and Shaw (Chapter 16), in the concluding chapter, review the key themes highlighted throughout the book and place these in a wider management context.

Part 1

Coastal Resorts in Transition

Chapter 2

The Problems and Dilemmas of Northern European Post-mature Coastal Tourism Resorts

TIM GALE

Introduction

This chapter is concerned with 'first-generation' European coastal tourism resorts (Knowles & Curtis, 1999: 89), which emerged in the north of the continent from the late 18th century onwards. Their decline, with the exception of a few large and diverse or small and distinctive destinations, has been endemic since the late 1970s (Agarwal, 2002), thanks in part to the sale of affordable package holidays to the Mediterranean and other pleasure-peripheries bestowed with virtually guaranteed sunshine. The proliferation of alternative places to visit within the countries of Northern Europe such as urban areas, the countryside, theme parks and holiday villages has also had a marked impact, as has the deteriorating quality and unsuitability of resort amenities and accommodation that were built for visitors of the late 19th and early 20th centuries. Local authorities, often in conjunction with other public agencies and the private sector, have responded to these challenges by implementing a range of measures designed to rejuvenate tourism. These include constructing wet-weather facilities, conference venues and heritage centres, conserving the historic built environment, and refurbishing accommodation. However, such interventions have met with limited success in attracting holidaymakers back to these coastal resorts (Agarwal, 1999, 2002; Gale, 2005). Consequently, an increasing number are now faced with thinking the unthinkable: whether they should exit the tourism industry (Baum, 1998, 2006).

The aim of this chapter is to examine the problems and dilemmas common to all such destinations, which, as a rule, are in the post-stagnation phase of the tourist area life-cycle (TALC) (Butler, 1980, 2005a,b). Accordingly, an assessment is undertaken of the causes and consequences of their decline that is consistent with a realist philosophy of Social Science. This is argued to be a more satisfactory means, compared with conventional positivistic and hermeneutic approaches to tourism research, of understanding the rise and fall of these destinations

(Gale & Botterill, 2005). It should be noted that there is an emphasis in the early part of this chapter on English and Welsh seaside resorts purely because 'it was Great Britain ... which witnessed the earliest, comprehensive evolution of maritime resorts and leisure towns as an integral cultural element of a rapidly urbanizing society' (Soane, 1992: 13). However, the experience of resorts elsewhere in Northern Europe is not overlooked and is dealt with in the latter part of this chapter.

Causes and Consequences of Northern European Resort Decline

Agarwal (2002: 39–40) suggests that the 'causes of [resort] decline are difficult to disentangle from its consequences' and it is possible to note a tendency to confuse the former with the latter in earlier, generally descriptive accounts of the threats facing cold-water coastal resorts in Britain and Northern Europe in the post-war period (see Middleton, 1989 for an example). However, Gale (2005: 90) implies that this is something of a false dichotomy for, regardless of whether they explain or are the things to be explained, these threats 'are bound up in simple, yet compelling, cause and effect relationships that occupy a surface ontology, which much of the debate on the contemporary condition of cold-water resorts has failed to penetrate'. Thus, it is possible to distinguish, in reverse order, between *symptoms* of cold-water resort decline, their immediate or apparent causes which, after Agarwal (2002), may be divided into *external threats* and *internal problems*, and the deep-seated *structural changes* or *universal processes* that underpin these cause–effect relationships.

Symptoms of decline

Studies of the recent history of Northern European resorts have tended to focus on what Agarwal (2002: 33) terms the 'symptoms of decline' (see Table 2.1). Based on the earlier work of Cooper (1990), many of these symptoms appear to have persisted although, as will be demonstrated later, some have been tackled and perhaps now constitute less of a problem than they were a couple of decades ago. For example, many English seaside resorts have invested heavily in the provision of wet-weather facilities and out-of-season activities, in improving the quality of accommodation and amenities, and in ensuring that appropriate market research is undertaken (Agarwal, 2002). Despite this, it is still possible to appreciate the severity of the problems that many English seaside resorts are experiencing with reference to one particular statistic of significance, namely visitor nights. In England alone, these fell from 193 million in 1973, or 27% of the UK total, to 104 million in 1998, or 13%

Table 2.1 Symptoms of decline experienced by Northern European post-mature coastal tourism resorts

• Declining tourist arrivals
• Dependence on long-holiday markets
• Diminishing share and volume of domestic holiday market
• Growth in low-status, low-spend visitors and day-trippers
• Outdated, poorly maintained accommodation and amenities
• Lack of wet-weather facilities and out-of-season activities
• Highly seasonal flow of visitors
• Low proportion of first-time visitors
• Poor information and interpretation provision
• Low budgets for marketing and promotion
• Lack of professionalism and experienced staff
• Low priority given to strategic thinking
• Shortage of market information and limited quality control

Source: Adapted from Agarwal & Brunt (2006: 667), and based on the earlier work of Cooper (1990)

(English Tourism Council, 2001a). More specifically, evidence at the local scale (see for example Clegg & Essex, 2000 for a detailed discussion of the decline of Torbay, located in Southwest England) points to two critical periods of decline in the recent history of English resorts, namely the late 1970s to the mid-1980s and the early 1990s, which coincided, respectively, with the 'wholesale' switching of domestic with foreign long holidays, and a downturn in the economic cycle that affected core and periphery alike (see Chapter 1 for a fuller discussion of the globalisation of the tourism product).

However, tourism data are not always easy to come by given the failure of resorts, historically, to capture information that might be of assistance in decision-making. This difficulty in itself is arguably a factor that has contributed to their decline. Hence, it is often necessary to look to the supply side and to indicators such as labour market statistics (Beatty & Fothergill, 2004), commercial property values (Coles & Shaw, 2006; Gale, 2005) and planning application data (Clegg & Essex, 2000), where these are available. Other alternatives include qualitative indicators of stagnation and decline/rejuvenation, such as additions to and deletions from a resort's portfolio of visitor attractions, commentary in guidebooks and other literature, and photographic evidence of changes in the resort landscape.

External threats and internal problems

Arguably the most significant, or at least obvious, dilemma facing many Northern European resorts is the diminished volume and value of the domestic long holiday market (i.e. 4+ nights), due to the emergence of competition from overseas 'sun, sea and sand' resorts initially in the Western, then Eastern Mediterranean, and subsequently throughout the pleasure-peripheries of the Caribbean and Latin America, southern Africa and Southeast Asia (see Chapters 9 and 13 for a fuller discussion). This has been facilitated by the development of faster, larger and more fuel-efficient aircraft, and the widespread availability of easy-to-book and comparatively inexpensive package holidays or inclusive tours that are organised, distributed and promoted by vertically integrated tourism operations such as TUI and Thomas Cook. Their role should not be underestimated for, as 'gatekeepers' to resorts in other countries, they 'have created new icons of holiday experiences whereby the foreign holiday – no matter how tightly packaged and culturally sanitized – has become an indicator of style, fashion and status' (Williams & Shaw, 1997: 5).

In resigning oneself to the inevitability of Northern European resort decline as an outcome of the internationalisation, and now globalisation, of tourist and associated information flows, brought about by innovations such as the jet engine and computerised reservations systems, it is possible to overlook the causal factors that lie closer to home. Therefore, there is a need to acknowledge developments in and adjacent to (international) traveller-generating regions, as distinct from tourist destinations (Leiper, 1990). One such development is the recent and exponential growth in short breaks (1–3 nights) and day trips, which was expected to provide some compensation to resorts for the reduction in long holidays. For example, despite an increase in the number of short breaks to the English seaside, from 4.8 million trips in 1993 to 8.8 million in 1999, which occurred alongside a decrease in long holidays, from 3 million to 2.5 million, much of this growth has been captured by the ever-expanding range of competing attractions and activities within the interiors of source countries themselves, not least the post-industrial spaces of town and country (English Tourism Council, 2001a). Significantly, these also appeal to foreign visitors in a way that traditional seaside resorts do not, for example in respect of their built and natural heritage and perceived higher standards of service.

Gordon and Goodall (2000) identify three factors that might explain this trend: (1) private motorisation and, in parallel, the scaling-down of public transport networks as demonstrated by the closure or downgrading of rail/bus termini in several British seaside resorts in the 1950s and 1960s; (2) a convergence in the locational requirements of much tourist activity and other service and information industries; and (3) shifting attitudes to urbanism encompassing 'a heightened demand for rurality and a positive taste for the metropolitan' (Gordon & Goodall, 2000: 296). Another recent development of significance has been the advent of the low-cost carrier (e.g. easyJet, Ryanair), supported by online booking systems that help keep costs to an absolute minimum and manage yield.

In addition to these adverse competitive conditions, resource depletion has undermined the competitiveness of Northern European resorts. There are two aspects to this, namely:

- The depreciation of, and disenchantment with, resort amenities and infrastructures dating back to previous rounds of investment (most notably in the late 19th and early 20th centuries), due to a combination of age and the exposure of structures to bleaching from the sun and excessive abrasion and corrosion from windblown sand and salt water, coupled with insufficient or nonexistent maintenance regimes. Other contributory factors include changing expectations with regards to hospitality and entertainment, and the failure of public authorities to adequately provide for the needs of travellers in the immediate aftermath of modal changes in transport to/from and within resorts (e.g. adequate car parking).
- A 'loss of tourism function' manifested in the closure of unprofitable visitor attractions and a reduction in serviced, and some self-catering, accommodation stock as hotels, guest houses and holiday apartments are converted to other uses, sometimes at odds with the image that the resort in question is trying to project (e.g. houses in multiple occupation), or abandoned altogether. As a result, some resorts such as New Brighton in Northwest England are contemplating a new future as dormitory towns and places of recreation for commuters working in nearby conurbations or, sometimes, for migrants with no work at all (e.g. retirees and socially excluded persons of working age).

These problems are compounded by local politics, especially with respect to the creation through local authority reorganisation of new, larger municipal areas which also serve rural hinterlands and whose constituents may have competing agendas. In addition, entrepreneurial structures also exacerbate the problems experienced by many English seaside resorts, most notably the typically high proportion of family-owned and operated businesses at the seaside with neither the expertise of managing change nor the capital for reinvestment. Moreover, it is important not to forget the challenges of spatial fixity and seasonality which work against good governance and the involvement of 'big business' in the tourist trade. Examples of such challenges include the investment of emotions, as well as finance, in constituent products such as piers, theatres, holiday camps, and bed and breakfast establishments, which might get in the way of some tough but necessary decisions concerning the future direction of a particular resort, and the understandable reluctance of profit-oriented organisations to commit capital to a highly seasonal, not to mention volatile, industry.

On the face of it, competition and resource depletion seem somewhat predictable challenges for any post-mature coastal tourism resort. Therefore, it should come as no surprise that they have been awarded explanatory status in two not so recent, but seminal attempts at modelling resort development, by Brougham and Butler (1972) and Butler (1980). The former model implies a process of class succession emanating in this context from Northern Europe (Fig. 2.1), with tourists at the top end of the market discovering a resort ('A', of the same country). Then, as time-space compression makes it accessible to lower-order market segments and vulnerable to excessive levels of development, these tourists move on to other, less developed resorts ('B', then 'C') located further away from their point of origin. Brougham and Butler (1972) conceived this shift as occurring within the same general location

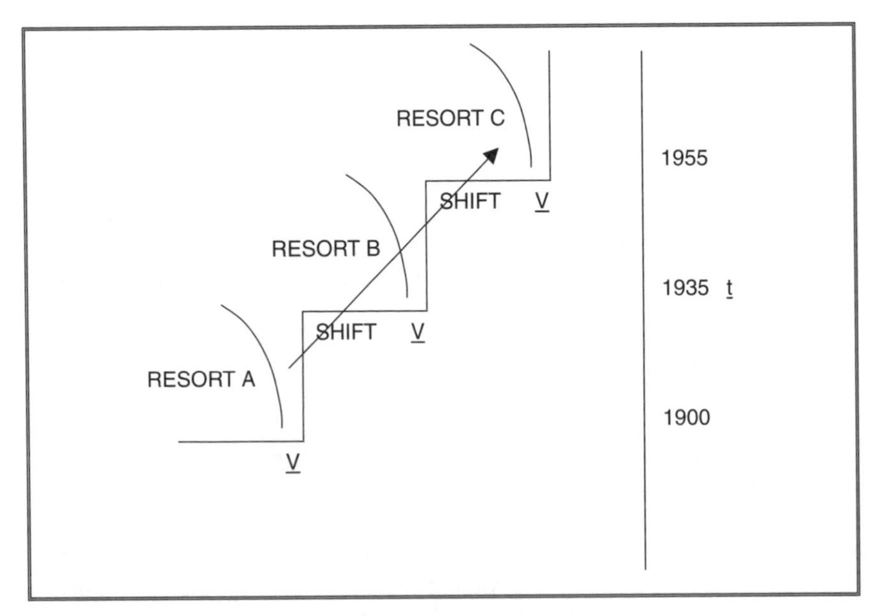

Figure 2.1 Destination shift in resort development over time.
Source: Modified from Brougham and Butler (1972)

or region as the original tourist development. The irony is that, in attempting to maintain exclusivity, these wealthier tourists simply render such resorts desirable to those wishing to emulate them. So, assuming that accessibility is further enhanced through continuous improvements in transport and communications, together with rising incomes and more generous entitlements to paid leave amongst the population at large, the process by which the first tourists to a resort are displaced to more remote, exotic and unspoilt destinations is repeated until there is little left in the world to be discovered and commoditised for tourist consumption, extreme environments excepted. Hence, the original model may be updated by adding at least two further shifts in the pleasure periphery (Prosser, 1999; Turner & Ash, 1975), taking in the mega-resorts of the Caribbean and Pacific Rim, for example Cancún (see Chapter 13 for a fuller discussion) and Goa, and also emerging destinations such as The Gambia, which were developed for mass tourists in the 1970s and 1980/90s, respectively.

If the first of these models affords greater attention to competition from up-and-coming resorts as a mitigating factor and how this is mapped out in space and time, the second – the oft-quoted and debated TALC – does the same for resource depletion in reminding us of tourism's self-destructive tendencies in a given locality (Fig. 2.2). Discounting, for the moment, the possibility of rejuvenation, the 'boom and bust' sequence advanced by the TALC (whereby tourist arrivals at a given destination increase, slowly at first and then more rapidly, before stabilising and then, in the absence of remedial action, declining) may be seen as the logical outcome of a number of transformations: from year-round natural and relatively enduring to highly seasonal and ephemeral man-built attractions; from small-scale integrated to large-scale non-integrated developments; from embedded local to footloose external capital; from allocentric/wanderlust to psychocentric/sunlust tourists; and from euphoric to antagonistic host attitudes towards tourism (Doxey, 1976; Gormsen, 1981, Plog, 1974; Young 1983). Fundamental to the TALC is the idea that a resort will continue to develop through a number of stages until it reaches its carrying capacity, defined by Pearce (1989: 169) as 'the threshold of tourist activity beyond which facilities are saturated ... the environment is degraded ... or visitor enjoyment is diminished'. Thereafter the net impact of further tourism development on the environment and, in due course, the local economy becomes negative as conceptualised by Wolfe (1982). Accordingly, these transformations result from particular carrying capacities being exceeded, namely biological, infrastructural, economic, psychological and social, in that order, not forgetting the physical carrying capacity of a resort (Baud-Bovy & Lawson, 1998). These types of carrying capacity vary in their tolerance to unsustainable development (depending on the structure and

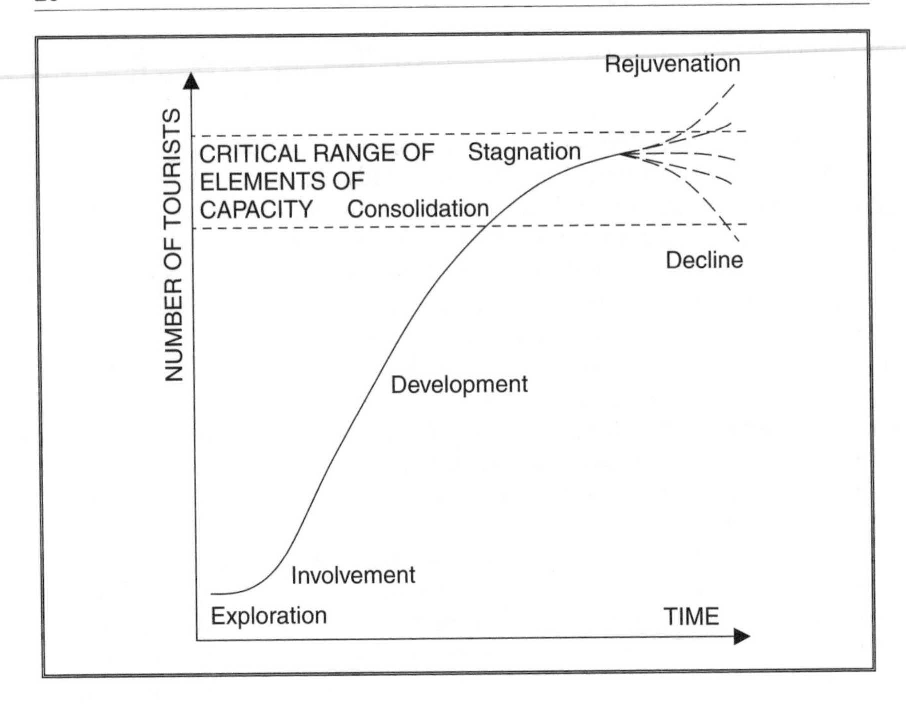

Figure 2.2 The tourist area life-cycle.
Source: Modified from Butler (1980)

fragility of the resort's tourism resource base and the types of tourist staying in the resort and the activities undertaken), therefore Butler (1980: 7) refers to a 'critical range of elements of capacity' in which the least tolerant type is the first to be surpassed followed, in succession, by the remainder (all things being constant).

Where the TALC has been applied to individual tourist resorts or regions, it has often been with a view to articulating their historical development rather than as a forecasting tool for resource managers, as demonstrated by Agarwal's (1997a) study of Torbay. If the model has a role to play in predicting change, as advocated by Butler (2004), Manente and Pechlaner (2006) and Berry (2006), then it must surely be in respect of highlighting the capacity of resorts, or to be precise those individuals and institutions with a stake in them (see Chapter 4 for a fuller discussion of the institutional capacity of resorts to respond to change), to contest a downward trajectory of development via appropriate product development and market repositioning initiatives (see Agarwal, 2002: 37 for some specific examples; Smith, 2004). Of course, the success of responses to decline, whether proactive or reactive, is one factor that differentiates resorts, as will be seen later in this chapter.

Notwithstanding the above, the TALC has come in for some criticism in recent years (see Haywood, 1986 in particular), largely with regards to the shape of the curve and the sequence of stages (the 'asymptotic' development trajectory being one of several possibilities), the representativeness of the model as the level of abstraction increases (thus encompassing products, market segments or sectors of the local economy whose own life cycles may be at odds with the overall picture) and the critical incidents that mark the end of one stage and the beginning of another (which are poorly defined, leading to a reliance upon best guesses when attempting to apply the model to individual destinations). To a greater or lesser extent, these criticisms have been addressed in subsequent works (see Butler, 2005a,b).

Of greater importance, however, is the hitherto unanswered charge that explanations for resort decline based on competition from other tourism places and/or the existence of a resort life-cycle invariably fail to 'sufficiently interrogate changes in fashion, style and taste which have transformed British [or Belgian, Dutch, French, German, etc] social life in the past few decades' (Urry, 1997: 103). These changes, in turn, have occurred alongside but are not reducible to a shift in the regime of accumulation in advanced capitalist societies (Ioannides & Debbage, 1997), from Fordism (characterised by mass production and consumption, standardisation and large-volume sales with attendant economies of scale) to neo-Fordism (characterised by flexible/smaller-scale production, increased market segmentation and more individualised consumption). In short, unilinear models of resort development such as the TALC overlook those structural changes or 'universal processes' (Cooke, 1987; cited in Agarwal, 1997b: 139) that are ultimately responsible for the rise and fall of destination areas, primarily economic restructuring and cultural change.

Structural changes/universal processes

The role of structural changes and/or universal processes in contributing to the problems and dilemmas facing many Northern European resorts is discussed by Agarwal (2002) and Gale (2005). Concerning economic restructuring, Agarwal (2002) points to four processes associated with post-Fordism, namely the: (1) search for capital accumulation as embodied in the internationalisation and globalisation of tourism; (2) consumption changes favouring bespoke and niche forms of leisure travel; (3) shifts in production mode in response to the above; and (4) a flexibility of production made possible by new technologies. It is these processes, she contends, that have influenced the creation of new, and previously inaccessible and undeveloped destinations, a preference for independent and special interest holidays in non-resort environments (e.g. cultural, eco- and adventure tourism), an increase in the popularity of rural and urban areas (as places in which to reside as well as to visit) along with substitutes for the touristic experience (e.g. online gaming in one's home or at an Internet cafe), and the opportunity to customise products to a differentiated clientele (thus threatening the appeal of standardised, rigidly packaged and mass-marketed holidays).

Meanwhile, on the subject of cultural change, Gale (2005) speaks of five processes related to postmodernism and the dedifferentiation of tourism from other social practices such as 'hobbies, sport, shopping, television, film and eating' (Urry, 1994: 235–236, based on the earlier work of Harvey, 1989). These are: (1) the visualisation of culture due to the 'mediatisation' of the material and symbolic properties of a given way of life and the ease with which they may be mechanically and electronically reproduced for the visual consumption of others, as in the hyper-real landscape of Las Vegas; (2) the emergence of instantaneous time (e.g. the so-called 'three-minute culture' advanced by the video cassette recorder and satellite/cable television); (3) the formation of identity through consumption and play instead of the once-dominant influences of occupation and the home; (4) the reconfiguration of production and consumption to a post-Fordist pattern, leading to the dissipation of communal work and leisure practices and a distaste for mass-produced products; and (5) resistance to globalisation and homogenisation through localisation (e.g. the reassertion of vernacular built form, and the development of themed environments such as cafe and cultural quarters in city centre and waterfront locations). As a consequence, contemporary social life takes on a certain 'nomadic' quality marked by a curiosity for distant places and peoples. Pleasure/delight and pain/despair are no longer concentrated in appointed and highly circumscribed sites, as evidenced by the high levels of deprivation in some seaside wards and electoral districts in England (Agarwal & Brunt, 2006) and, on the flipside, the seemingly endless number of post-industrial towns and cities that 'model themselves on tourist resorts and generate a kind of holiday atmosphere all year around' (Franklin, 2003: 79).

From the above analyses, it is possible to conclude that economic restructuring and cultural change, as generative mechanisms salient to the decline of Northern European resorts have a number of features in common:

- They are revolutionary, not evolutionary. In other words, the economic and cultural transformations of the late 20th century were, by and large, unintended and unexpected, and have brought about the decline of purpose-built tourist destinations such as the seaside resorts of Northern Europe by weakening those very agglomeration (Gordon & Goodall, 2000) and demarcation (Rojek, 1995) processes in tourism that gave rise to and sustained them.

- They interact with, and are modified by, indigenous social structures and local actors, thereby manifesting themselves in subtly and sometimes radically different ways from one resort to the next.
- They are hidden from the gaze of the casual observer and cannot be tested empirically and, therefore, are commonly overlooked in conventional positivistic analyses of cold-water resort decline.
- They are difficult to substantiate and are, therefore, highly contested. For example post-Fordism/post-tourism is challenged by the McDonaldisation/McDisneyisation thesis of Ritzer and Liska (1997), which maintains that people continue to want highly predictable, efficient, calculable and controlled holidays (thereby suggesting that little has changed since the origins of mass participation in tourism).

When viewed alongside the symptoms of decline and external threats and internal problems discussed earlier, these structural changes/universal processes enhance understanding of the causes and consequences of resort decline.

Towards a deeper understanding of cold-water resort decline?

Much emphasis thus far has been placed on the apparent causes and consequences of seaside resort decline in England and Wales, and underpinning structural changes or universal processes. When illustrated (Fig. 2.3), this resembles the three-tiered ontological structure championed by critical realists, comprising the domains of 'the empirical', 'the actual' and 'the real' (Bhaskar, 1978: 13). The first is exemplified by surface or experiential knowledge, as in the claims made by various practitioners to the effect that the least competitive resorts lack sufficient en-suite accommodation and/or wet-weather facilities. The second relates to events that happen whether we perceive them or not, for example the adverse effects of competition and resource depletion upon tourist arrivals to a given resort, enshrined in unilinear models of tourism development such as the TALC. Finally, the third encompasses nonobservable generative mechanisms such as economic restructuring and cultural change, which give rise to events in the world and 'whose powers may exist unexercised or be exercised unrealised, that is with variable outcomes due to the variety of intervening contingencies which cannot be subject to laboratory closure' (Archer, 1998: 190).

Examining cold-water resorts in this way can permit a greater depth of understanding of the problems and dilemmas that many of them are experiencing. However, it is important not to generalise about Northern European resort decline and overlook the fact that the resorts in question

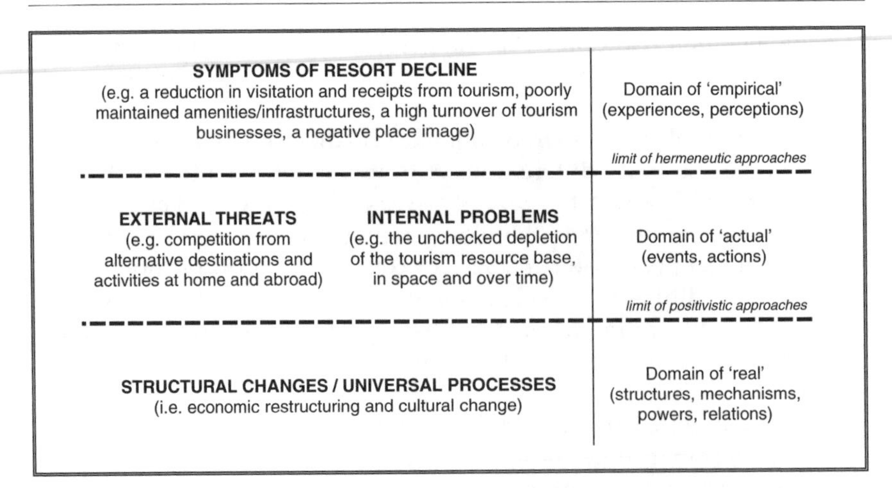

Figure 2.3 The association between symptoms of resort decline, their immediate causes and underpinning structural changes/universal processes (with reference to the stratified model of social reality advocated by critical realists)

are at various stages of development (Fig. 2.4). As has been discussed in Chapter 1, England's seaside resorts developed rapidly in the mid-19th century following the arrival of the railways and, with the exception of the World Wars, boomed until the 1970s. In the Netherlands, seaside resort development began in the early 19th century with investment in a bath-house in Scheveningen in 1819. Despite suffering a number of setbacks to development such as the building of the Atlantic Wall and the demolition of many of its buildings during the Second World War, its seaside resorts remained popular throughout the 1960s. But, as in England, they started to lose their visitor share in the 1970s, and many became characterised by a deteriorating environment (Mason & Studsholt, 2001). In contrast, although beginning in the early to mid-19th century, the Swedish and Danish resorts developed at a much slower rate throughout the 20th century, and currently exhibit few indicators of decline (Mason & Studsholt, 2001).

Moreover, it is not appropriate to speak of Northern European resorts *per se* as being in decline, a point emphasised by Agarwal (2005: 354), who highlights the 'spatial unevenness' of resort decline by drawing on the examples of Bournemouth and Scarborough. Rather, we should seek to explain why some Northern European resorts succeed and others fail when all are subject, more or less, to the same set of challenges.

Clearly, no two cold-water resorts are the same; indeed, we are talking of a place 'with as many variations as a hawkweed or burnet-moth' (Walton, 2000: 22). There is a diversity of experience, with a variety of

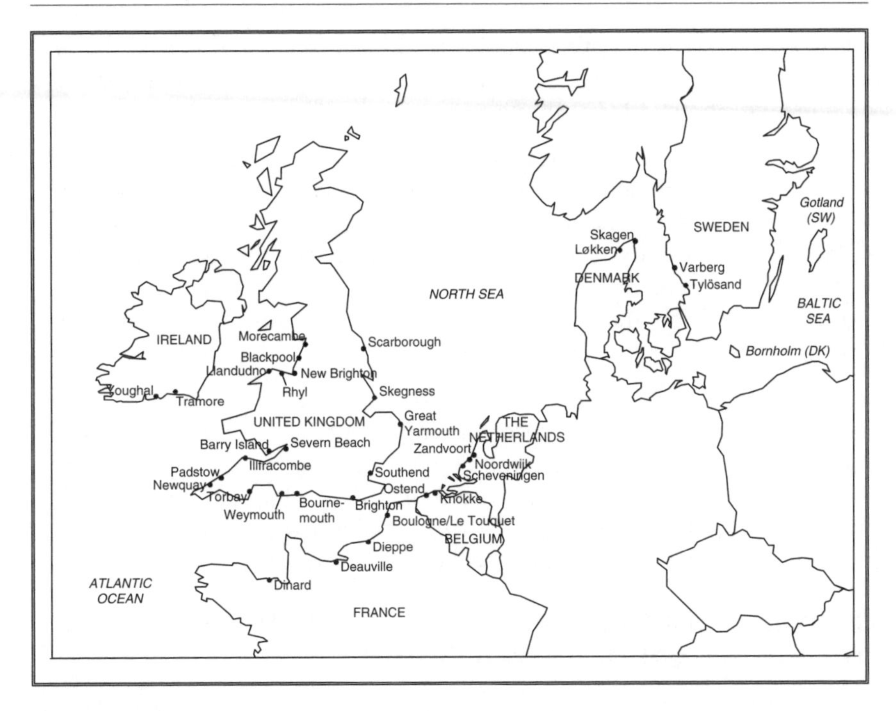

Figure 2.4 Location of Northern European coastal tourism resorts named in this chapter

factors such as institutional capacity (Agarwal, 2005; see Chapter 4 for a fuller discussion), past patterns and rates of development (Cooke, 1990), and geography (scale and location) influencing a resort's ability to tackle its problems. Compare, for example, the resorts of Llandudno and Rhyl on the North Wales coast, the relative remoteness of the former in relation to the heavily populated and industrialised regions and source markets of Lancashire, Merseyside and the West Midlands (as against the proximity of the latter), insulating it from development of the lowest common denominator (Fletcher, 1993). This 'friction of distance' might also explain why Dinard 'was considered socially superior to Dieppe' (Soane, 1992: 18), at least by Parisians of the early 20th century. Variations in social tone are evident within individual resorts, too, whose recreational business districts (RBDs) often contain one sector which outperforms the other. For instance, the Sun Centre on Rhyl's East Parade was one of Wales' most popular visitor attractions at a time when the resort was haemorrhaging bed-spaces along its West Parade, the equivalent of Blackpool's 'Golden Mile' (Gale, 2005).

It would therefore appear that resort decline is influenced by a complex interplay of the global and the local. This is highlighted by Williams and Shaw (1997: 13), who state that:

> The reason why one resort prospers and another is in crisis is due to the complex interaction of global and national shifts in culture and the economics of the tourism industry, and the way that these interact with the local dimensions of culture, class images, the built environment created by previous rounds of investment, and the capacity of both the local state and private investors to adapt to change.

This synthesis of the global and the local is, of course, what makes a Northern European seaside resort unique, but yet recognisable as a distinctive kind of town (Agarwal, 2005). With this in mind and given that most emphasis has so far been placed on English resorts, the remainder of this chapter explores the variable experience of non-UK Northern European post-mature coastal tourism resorts.

Variability in the Experience of Non-UK Northern European Post-mature Coastal Tourism Resorts

The differential economic performance of Northern Europe's seaside resorts is reflected in a number of recently completed projects. For example, since 1996, the European Commission has been working to identify and promote measures to remedy the deterioration of its coastal zones, and operated a demonstration programme on Integrated Coastal Zone Management. This aimed to provide concrete technical information about the factors and mechanisms that either encourage or discourage the sustainable management of coastal zones and to stimulate a broad debate and exchange of information among the various actors involved in planning, management or use of Europe's coastal zones, including resorts. Another example is NORCOAST (1998–2001), financed by the INTERREG IIc programme for the North Sea region. This project aimed to investigate and promote good practice in integrated coastal zone management through the study of planning methods and exchange of experience. In particular, it focused on the decline of the North Sea's seaside resorts, concentrating on those located on England's Northeast Yorkshire and Lincolnshire coasts, in Denmark's North Jutland, in the Netherlands and in Sweden's Halland coastal area.

However, establishing the stage of development that the resorts in each of these locations have reached is problematic as data sets for the period 1970 to early 1990s are either unavailable or are severely limited (Mason & Studsholt, 2001). In Halland (Sweden), the first research of the economic importance of tourism was completed in 1991, whilst in

Denmark, data for North Jutland is available from 1996 onwards, and in the Netherlands data run from the early 1990s (Mason & Studsholt, 2001). The lack of resort-specific data is not a problem that is confined to these specific locations, as Agarwal (1997a, 1999, 2002) and Gale (2005) note a series of data limitations relating to other English and Welsh seaside resorts. Moreover, differences within data sets and definitions of tourism across Northern European countries make it difficult to integrate data and to determine similar trends across countries for comparative studies. Given such difficulties, it is only possible to provide a flavour of the variability of economic performance amongst non-UK Northern European seaside resorts, and an insight into the different issues faced by such resorts.

Belgium and the Netherlands

Owen (1990) suggests that English resorts could learn much from their counterparts on the continent, citing Scheveningen in the Netherlands and Knokke-Heist and Ostend in Belgium as examples of good practice. These resorts generally boast clean and well maintained beaches that are accessible to wheelchair users, a variety of seafront cafes and restaurants offering *al fresco* dining, traffic-free promenades and year-round events programmes. In addition, there has been investment in upscale amenities such as marinas, casinos and boutiques, thereby making these resorts more attractive to the image- and status-conscious service classes, which have increased significantly in size in the last few decades to the point where they now collectively constitute the mass market in most, if not all, Northern European countries (Geddes, 2002). Of course, some of this infrastructure is the product of cultural and political contingencies operating almost exclusively on the 'other' side of the English Channel, as it were, which might be why seaside resorts in Britain have been slow to catch up with their continental cousins. For example, it is still not clear, at least at the time of writing, whether the UK Government's recent review of gambling will lead to the development of Las Vegas-style casino hotels in Blackpool and other large British seaside resorts.

Scheveningen, as the leading Dutch resort, is an interesting case in point. By the early 1960s, and despite the construction of a new, modernist pier between 1959 and 1961, it was showing signs of stagnation and decline as a holiday destination, notably a surplus of serviced accommodation, even in the high season. The response of the local state was to produce a master plan for the resort in partnership with a consortium of investment companies, the implementation of which commenced in 1973 with the acquisition of a 12-hectare site at the heart of the resort stretching for some 500 m along the seafront. Envisaging a place that was attractive to both tourists and residents regardless of social class, that functioned in all seasons, and in which people would want to live and work as well as play, the municipality/consortium set about revitalising Scheveningen with the redevelopment of the area surrounding the former Grand Hotel (to include a variety of housing and a large car park), followed by the renovation of the historic Kurhaus ('Cure House') as a five-star hotel with conference facilities and a casino/nightclub, together with the construction of a new square and adjacent shops, bars and restaurants.

Buoyed by the response to these developments, namely a doubling in the number of visitors from around 3 million in 1978 to 6.5 million in 1981 (van de Weg, 1982), the authorities secured the addition of a shopping mall and an indoor 'surfpool' to the product mix complete with saunas, solaria and sports facilities. Visitor numbers subsequently rose to 9.1 million in 1996. Bergen aan Zee, in the Netherlands, is another example of a traditional seaside resort whose facilities were also in need of updating. Funded by the INTERREG IIc Quality of Coastal Towns project, steps have recently been taken to update facilities for tourism and at the same time improve the quality of Bergen aan Zee itself, based on the consideration of the surrounding landscape and natural values. Unfortunately, the success of this particular initiative is not known, although Mason and Studsholt (2001) comment that the regeneration of the Netherlands' seaside resorts generally has attracted a new generation of visitors, and as a result has reversed their downward trend.

However, despite regeneration in Knokke-Heist (Belgium) during the late 1980s, visitor numbers continued to decline, triggering a European Union-financed Integrated Quality Management programme focusing on improving product service quality. In 1996, 1.26 million overnight stays were recorded, with domestic tourism accounting for 89.7% of arrivals. Although its market share has remained stable for long-stays (7+), its market share for medium and short stays 4–6 and 1–3 fell between 1991 and 1996. Turnover from tourism correspondingly fell by 35% over the same period (European Commission, 2000). This is in contrast to Ostende, which has established itself as one of the leading maritime festivals, attracting over 100 historic and heritage ships. Visitor numbers have varied between 250,000 in 2001 and 165,000 in 2003.

Notably within the Netherlands, the regeneration of its seaside resorts is ongoing and is being addressed by the production of a joint action plan, 'A Sea of Culture' (Toerisme Recreatie Nederland, 1997), which advocates linking the coast with culture and urban heritage and ensuring the provision of a quality product (Mason & Studsholt, 2001). But a lack of co-operation and co-ordination within and between the public and private sectors is also highlighted as being a major obstacle to successful regeneration (see Chapter 4 for a fuller discussion). Indeed within 'A Sea of Culture' it is stated that 'our limited cohesion is a bigger threat to the future of our tourism/recreational product than the growing competition from our neighbours' (cited in Mason & Studsholt, 2001). This in turn has also had the effect of weakening the voice of the tourism industry throughout the levels of government, limiting public interest in tourism and leaving tourism low on the political agenda, all problems that have also been found to occur in English seaside resorts (Agarwal, 2005; Shaw & Williams, 1997a; see Chapters 3 and 4 for a fuller discussion).

Denmark and Sweden

In contrast to Britain, Belgium and the Netherlands, Denmark and Sweden's seaside resorts along the more developed coasts of North Jutland and Halland, and the Baltic Islands of Bornholm and Gotland, have experienced less of a decline (Mason & Studsholt, 2001). Many resorts such as Skagen (Denmark) and Skummerslöv, Tylösand and Olosfsbo (Sweden) have continued to remain popular (Mason & Studsholt, 2001). In contrast, some holiday centres, particularly in North Jutland (Denmark), such as Molle and Hirtshals, are in decline. This is partly because they have not been modernised due to a lack of financial resources combined with the difficulty of changing their bombastic architecture (Mason & Studsholt, 2001). Thus, within these centres over the past 25 years many hotels and boarding houses have changed use and been converted into timeshare flats, resulting in the deterioration of the buildings.

However, despite the fact that decline is less of an issue within Denmark and Sweden's seaside resorts, the built environment of many is in need of improvement to reduce the possibility of a downturn in visitor arrivals in the future, as is their market image (Mason & Studsholt, 2001). These resorts are further distinguished by the Scandinavian tradition of second-home ownership, which, due to its spatial and temporal concentration, has impacted on the environment and frustrated attempts to spread the season. The emphasis, therefore, in the coastal resorts of Denmark and Sweden is on conserving the best of what they have to offer and adding value through product- and market-oriented initiatives that are relatively small in scale, at least compared to the comprehensive regeneration schemes of the above-mentioned countries. Notable examples include the renovation of some of the older hotels and summer houses in Løkken alongside attempts to counter its 'rowdy' image by targeting the family market. There have been planning interventions also in Skagen designed to maintain the resort's distinctive appearance as it is well known for its painted houses, and to manage tourism development in Tylösand within existing carrying capacity constraints. This has been achieved, for example, by strictly limiting car parking space which, in turn, has helped to maintain its status as an upscale destination (Mason & Studsholt, 2001). In addition, community pressure in Varberg to safeguard its spa facilities has resulted in their purchase and restoration by the municipality as the centrepiece of a privately managed health resort.

France and Germany

It has already been noted that seaside resorts in Britain would do well to emulate those on the continent, at least according to Owen (1990) and Tuppen (1998). Included in the list of examples Owen (1990) gives in support of this argument are the French resorts of Dieppe, Le Touquet and Deauville. The latter two, in particular, have much in common with their counterparts in Belgium and the Netherlands, not least in respect of checking down-market drift. Indeed, the sun and the sand continue to be a popular attraction, notably within many French resorts. For example, in Brittany's resorts of La Trinite, Locmanaquer and Vannes, in 1994 approximately 2,042,000 visitors were received, 85% of which were from France, and tourism has grown at a rate of 3–4%/year since 1991 (European Commission, 2000). Consequently, the focus of more recent regeneration efforts is less on product improvement and market repositioning and more on the management and conservation of the environment (European Commission, 2000).

In addition to maintaining and increasing visitor numbers, many resorts within France and Germany, such as Heligoland and Damp (Germany), have developed all-year-round visitation by successfully courting the health tourist, offering spa facilities and various forms of therapy. For example, according to the European Commission (2000), Damp averages 90,300 visitors a year, 96% from Germany and 4% from Scandinavia, and in 1997, generated €120 million, whilst Heligoland received 485,432 day visitors and 45,400 tourists in 1998. In addition, all-year-round visitation has also been achieved within resorts including Le Touquet and Deauville (France) by attracting cultural or heritage tourists to the large villas on the periphery of both resorts commissioned in the late 19th and early 20th centuries by wealthy visitors from Paris and England and designed by some of the leading architects of the day. Deauville is also well known for its American Film Festival, now in its 32nd year, which attracts some of the world's leading actors and directors. Moreover, many have been attracting the sports tourist with an interest in golf, horse racing and water-based activities. Le Touquet, for example, is famous for 'Enduro', an annual quad- and motor-bike race that takes place along its beach.

Conclusions

The aim of this chapter has been to produce not a mere review of relevant literature, useful as that may be, but rather an account of the recent fortunes and contemporary condition of post-mature coastal tourism resorts in the countries of Northern Europe. In particular, it has sought also to provide a flavour of the variability of decline amongst seaside resorts, emphasising the fact that due to the slower pace of development, those in Sweden and Denmark generally have experienced less decline than those resorts in Belgium, the Netherlands, France, Germany, England, Wales and Ireland. The focus of regeneration therefore differs among these countries, with current attempts in Sweden and Denmark being more concerned with the preservation and conservation of the built and natural environment. In contrast, regeneration of seaside resorts in England, Wales, Ireland, the Netherlands and Belgium has involved primarily product updating and development.

In addition, the intention of this chapter was also to succeed, firstly, in separating the causes of decline in Northern European seaside resorts from the consequences and, secondly, in alerting the reader to economic restructuring and cultural change in the late 20th century as more fundamental, and hitherto neglected, causal structures (or, in realist parlance, 'generative mechanisms'). It does this by proposing a tiered ontology of cold-water resort decline comprising the domains of 'the empirical', 'the actual' and 'the real'. It is important to note that the first of these domains represents the limit of most hermeneutic or interpretative approaches, these being unconcerned with nondiscursive practices, and the second the limit of positivistic or deductive approaches, which make no provision for the existence of underlying mechanisms. In this respect, the above account satisfies one of the chief philosophical tenets of critical realism (Bhaskar, 1978, 1979), that is, a differentiated and stratified ontology in which 'the domain of the real is greater than or equal to the domain of the actual, which is greater than or equal to the domain of the empirical' (Collier, 1994: 44). Hence, the chapter doubles as an argument for tourism researchers to take seriously the possibilities of realist tourism research (Botterill, 2003; Gale & Botterill, 2005).

Chapter 3

The Resort Economy: Changing Structures and Management Issues in British Resorts

GARETH SHAW and TIM COLES

Introduction: The Death of the Seaside Resort?

Under the newspaper headline 'No, we don't like to be beside the seaside', Girling (2006: 16) argues that 'the seaside has been written off more times than the English novel, and just as often has been reinvented'. Certainly, media coverage over the last decade has largely portrayed the seaside resort as a residual tourism destination with limited potential, frequented by fewer visitors. Such a perspective is also seen in the academic literature, which has viewed the British resort as a tourist experience that 'lacked competitiveness in the face of new products' (Williams & Shaw, 1997: 9). As a touchstone indicator of such a decline, Girling (2006) takes the number of visitors to Southend Pier, where there was a peak of 7 million visitors in 1950 compared to just 331,306 in 2005. More accurate and extensive pictures of the loss of visitors are given by Cooper (1997) and Walton (2000).

The aim of this chapter is not to examine the trends marking out the decline of the seaside resort, but rather to focus much more detailed attention on its current state along with potential strategies for survival. In doing so it is important to recognise two key points from the outset. The first is that a plethora of difficulties beset British seaside resorts which are related to both internal and external issues (see Chapter 2 for a fuller discussion). The second point is that the seaside resort is a complex tourism space and one that is extremely variable. In other words, to compare the issues in a large resort such as Blackpool with those of smaller resorts within Southwest England is difficult. As Marsden (2003: 54) argues, 'one size fits all is a motto you apply at your peril to seaside and coastal resorts'. Marsden is commenting not as an interested academic but as the local MP for Blackpool and chair of the British Resort and Destination Association, and a member of a number of influential pressure groups working for the restructuring of seaside resorts.

It is therefore difficult to 'generalise about the trajectories of resort development' given the differing types of destinations (Smith, 2004: 17). This is hardly remarkable given that previous work has recognised the gap between large, medium and small resorts (British Resorts Association, 1989; Shaw & Williams, 1997a). In this context, the large resorts such as Blackpool, Bournemouth and Torbay show very different structures than that of the smaller resorts of which a good number have less than 1000 letting rooms. Gordon and Goodall (2000: 295), from an economic perspective, also argue that the 'largest of the seaside resorts had already become substantially diversified economies by the 1970s'. The variability in resort types is also recognised in terms of the types of tourism environments on offer from a marketing standpoint (English Tourism Council (ETC), 2001a; Shaw & Williams, 2004). In terms of the latter perspective, limited, as well subjective evidence by the now defunct ETC (2001), classified English resorts into 'Picturesque, Traditional, Family, Lively and Fun' (see also Shaw & Williams, 2004; Smith, 2004). The fact that these subjective labels clearly overlap is just one of the problems with such a typology. Moreover, the complexity of the seaside resort as a tourism product is further complicated by its relative neglect in both political and economic terms.

Given the complexities of British resorts, it is therefore worthwhile examining their current health in terms of tourism demand. Are they in terminal decline reaching the final stages of death as significant tourism spaces? Urry (1997: 112) was in little doubt a decade ago when he commented that: 'Our contemporary social practices are not so organised around ... spatial and temporal regularities. They are pleasures of the new, the fickle, the unexpected; and resorts are weakly placed to attract many visitors since they lie near the bottom of ... the consumption spaces hierarchy'. Increasingly, resorts have been associated with Fordist forms of tourism production and consumption based around the mass holiday as compared with the postmodern tourist trends as described by Urry (1997) and others (Agarwal, 2002; Shaw & Williams, 2004). In contrast to this, official figures collated by the British Resorts and Destinations Association (2006) show that domestic tourists take 25.5 million seaside holidays in the UK, spending around £4.7 billion. In addition to these overnight stays, there were an estimated 270 million day trips made to coastal destinations, generating a £3.1 billion spend. Data from the UK Day Visits Survey (2002–03) suggest that the average length of trip was 3.9 hours usually by parties of between 3 and 4 people, although 24% of day trips were taken by people travelling alone (TNS Travel & Tourism, 2004). As Table 3.1 shows, the majority of activity was based around English resorts, but in terms of relative importance, coastal holidays in Wales accounted for 44% of all holiday nights in that economy, compared with 27% in England.

Table 3.1 The dimensions of seaside tourism in the UK (2002–03)

	Staying visitors			*Day visits*	
	(m) visits	*(£ billion) spend*	*% of all holiday trips*	*(£ billion) Spend*	*(m) visits*
UK	25.5	4.7	–	3.1	270
England	19.1	3.5	27	2.5	200
Wales	3.7	0.6	44	0.2	25
Scotland	2.0	0.35	19	0.3	42

Source: TNS Travel & Tourism (2004)

Table 3.2 Major trends conditioning tourism consumption in the UK

Socioeconomic changes
An ageing population
More single-person households
Increasing gap between rich and poor
Consumption changes
Growth of experience economy, increasing importance of purchasing 'an experience'
Increasing interest in the environment and sustainable products
A growing interest in individual well-being
Increasing fragmentation of leisure demands, importance of particular segments
Increasing importance of tribing in terms of consumption groups
Technology changes
Increasing importance of e- and m-marketing
Continual impact of low-cost airlines

Source: Modified from VisitBritain (2005b)

Unfortunately, the information in Table 3.1 fails to reveal the full extent of the recent forces acting on the tourism economy of seaside resorts. This is because a combination of factors underpin shifts in tourism consumption, as shown in Table 3.2. Of particular note are the changing social and demographic structure of the domestic market and the coming of age of what Pine and Gilmore (1999) termed the experience economy. In terms of the former, one in every five people in the UK are over 65. Furthermore, the healthy life expectancy of this group is increasing, which has helped to explain the growing levels of holiday consumption from this consumer group. This group, on average, takes 1.5 million overnight domestic holiday trips, whilst recent research by MORI predicts an increase in the number of short-break holidays taken by retired people (VisitBritain, 2003). Of course how many of these visits will be to seaside resorts is open to question and much depends on the quality of experience such places can offer. What is known is that short breaks and day visits have played increasingly important roles in the visitor pattern to UK resorts. However, expenditure by day visitors averages £18.50 in seaside resorts compared to £31 in trips to urban areas (VisitBritain, 2005a). Nevertheless, the value of the short-break market has increased since the late 1990s and such visits to seaside resorts accounted for 25% of all short breaks in England in 2003. Moreover, surveys conducted on this market have shown that amongst people over the age of 50 there is a much greater interest in visiting seaside locations (VisitBritain, 2006).

In addition to these indicators of the visitor economy, some coastal resorts are also witnessing a continual increase in population through migration. This in itself is complex, but two strands appear to be dominant, namely: (1) the migration of young people often with low skills in search of work; and (2) the movement of middle-age or older couples seeking new lifestyles. These highlight different sets of migration factors but are also another measure of the attractiveness of coastal resorts. All these forces add to the complexity and changing structures of British seaside resorts, which we give more detailed attention to in the first part of this chapter. This is then followed by a review of the key management issues and development strategies set within a policy context, which emerge from these issues.

Mobility Issues and the Changing Structure of Seaside Resorts

Before examining the complexity and variations between resorts, it is worthwhile establishing some general indicators of their changing economic and social structure. As we have seen from Table 3.1, seaside resorts still account for substantial numbers of holidaymakers, even though these are far less than in the period before the early 1970s. In addition, they also continue to attract large number of in-migrants and as a consequence the 43 largest resorts, those with populations of 8000 plus in 1971, accounted for just over 3 million inhabitants by 2001 (Beatty & Fothergill, 2003).

Beatty and Fothergill's (2003) research is of particular importance as it provides one of the first detailed analyses of the changing employment structure of seaside resorts. In doing so it starts to challenge some of the popular myths about the changing nature of coastal resorts. Their study of change between 1971 and 2001 shows a number of interesting trends. Perhaps most remarkable given the constant image of resort decline is that, in the 30 years since 1971, the number of jobs in such locations has grown by 317,000. In contrast, levels of recorded unemployment showed a relatively low increase of just 19,000 over the same period.

In economic terms, as measured by the growth of jobs, the seaside towns in Beatty and Fothergill's study exhibit none of the obvious signs of stagnation or decline. Such dichotomy represents the complexity of resort economies which in the past have either been ignored or treated in a somewhat simplistic fashion. As Gordon and Goodall (2000) argue, the share of employment in accommodation and catering activities does not adequately reflect the importance of tourism. Whilst Gordon and Goodall (2000) could only provide employment data for a limited number of activities for 1971–97 at the scale of official Travel to Work areas, the research by Beatty and Fothergill (2003) allows a more accurate picture of employment structures to be gained for seaside resorts. As Table 3.3 shows, whilst the hotel, catering and distribution sector is dominant, accounting for almost a third of all jobs, public sector employment is also significant and 4 percentage points above the national average. Of equal importance are the changes in employment calculated for the period 1981–2001, which shows that (with the exception of manufacturing, agriculture and fishing) all of the other key economic sectors recorded an increase in jobs. The largest shifts occur in financial services, the accommodation, distribution and catering sector and construction, all of which relate to aspects of the tourism economy.

Table 3.3 Employment trends in major seaside towns: 1981–2001

	Seaside towns		*National*	*% change*
Sector	*Jobs (000)*	*%*	*%*	*1981–2001*
Agriculture and fishing	5	0.3	2	– 68
Energy and water	9	0.7	0.6	– 49
Manufacturing	131	10	14	– 21
Construction	92	7	6	+ 37
Distribution, hotels and restaurants	413	32	25	+ 45
Transport and communications	56	4	6	– 11
Banking, finance, insurance	196	15	20	+ 65
Public admin, education, health	341	26	22	+ 42
Other services	64	5	5	No data
Total	1306	100	100	+ 29

Source: Modified from Beatty and Fothergill (2003) based on Census of Population and Annual Business Inquiry (with adjustments to include self-employed)

Of course there are temporal variations in employment in terms of seasonal demand and economic recessions, both of which are important within seaside economies. Tourism employment is often characterised by low wages, part-time work and seasonal patterns (Williams & Shaw, 1988). Such features tend to be at their more extreme in seaside resorts given their higher dependence on seasonal patterns of demand. According to Beatty and Fothergill (2003: 13), 'An annual cycle of claimant unemployment is still evident'. They also found that unemployment was much more seasonal in smaller resorts and greater for men than women. Similarly, in seaside resorts there is a high level of reliance on part-time employment, which accounted for 18% of all male employment and 54.2% of all female jobs (recalculated from Beatty & Fothergill, 2003: 37). In terms of total employment, 38.4% of all jobs in seaside towns are part-time compared with a national average of 30%. In the context of economic cycles and recessions, Clegg and Essex (2000) have examined the response of accommodation providers in the major South Devon resort of Torbay, especially during the 1990–92 recessions. They highlight a number of strategies adopted by the accommodation sector in response to falling demand, but few involved reductions in staff, perhaps in part because many smaller businesses rely on family labour.

Recessions appear to have a complex impact on resort economies and they appear to do so through changes in business start-ups. Clegg and Essex (2000) found in Torbay that 33% of serviced accommodation businesses and 30% of those in self-catering within their sample came into being between 1990 and 1995. In other words many small- and medium-sized enterprises were being created during part of the recession corresponding to a downturn in the property market. Coles and Shaw (2006) have investigated such links further and found potential relationships between the wider aspects of the property market, perceptions of future property values and the activities of small-scale entrepreneurs in seaside economies.

A second important feature of these resort economies is the pattern of increased migration. According to Beatty and Fothergill's (2003: 28) findings, 'the net in-migration to seaside towns tended to accelerate as the period progressed', i.e. towards 2001. The increase in population of seaside towns grew by 12% or 340,000 between 1971 and 2001, compared to 6% nationally. In part this is due to the employment opportunities within the resort economies, although most of the in-migration was amongst people over 35 years old and those over 65. The main reason for the high levels of in-migration is lifestyle preferences – people want to live by the coast. In this context there are two distinct groups of in-migrants. The first are those who initially seek employment – although according to Beatty and Fothergill only 20% cited work-related reasons for moving. The second main group comprise those wanting to become self-employed and establish a tourism business (Shaw & Williams, 2003) and those wanting to retire. The latter group has become of growing significance in economic terms due to their influence on the local property markets in seaside towns. This has manifested itself through a rapid rise in residential property prices as migrants seek either to move permanently to seaside resorts, or purchase second homes for individual use or as investment opportunities.

Such mobility flows are reshaping the social ecology of resorts and creating much more divided communities as well as a series of difficulties. These relate to an increase in social care problems, a transient, low-skilled population and housing difficulties, along with a growing elderly population. The dimensions of these socioeconomic problems and the patterns of social exclusion have been highlighted by the Government Committee of inquiry into coastal towns (Agarwal & Brunt, 2006; Office of the Deputy Prime Minister, 2006), with the latter outlining the general socioeconomic characteristics of the seaside resorts in England and Wales.

Many of the difficulties appear to relate to patterns of migration and the low wage economy associated with many parts of the tourism sector. In this context, a number of intersecting problems can be recognised. First, the profile of in-migration shows both a large proportion of retired people, who together with the low-skilled migrants put increased pressure on social care facilities. Secondly, it has produced a mismatch between the 'affordability ratio of earnings against house prices' (Office of the Deputy Prime Minister, 2006: 6). Thirdly, past periods of low investment in terms of the residential environment have produced a situation where, on average, resorts have over 50% of their housing stock classified as 'non-decent' or 'unfit' (English House Condition Survey, 2001). Furthermore, the decline in the traditional bed-and-breakfast and guesthouse market has led to many of these properties being converted to housing in multiple occupations, which has also attracted low-income, low-skilled migrants. This may be illustrated by just one example, the town of Thanet, where the qualifications of younger local residents where shown to be well below the national average (Table 3.4). Poor housing conditions tend to be exacerbated by the higher level of private renting (on average 20%), which is almost twice the rate as elsewhere (Office of the Deputy Prime Minister, 2006: 6). Beatty and Fothergill (2003) argue that such conditions have led to a large group of people who are marginal in the resort economy, many of whom are claiming sickness benefit and not recorded as unemployed. Consequently, they argue that the real level of unemployment is closer to 10% rather than the officially recorded figure of 4%. More generally, Agarwal and Brunt (2006) have attempted to demonstrate the full scale of multiple deprivation and social exclusion within many seaside resorts.

Table 3.4 Comparative levels of qualifications in the working population of Thanet

Locations	*% below NVQ2*
Thanet	41.7
Kent and Medway	39.1
Southeast England	32.5
Nationally	36.4

Source: Local Futures (2005) cited by the House of Commons (2005–06)

There is however another dimension to the social structure of such resorts, which many recent reports have tended to ignore. This concerns the increasing migration of retired, semi-retired and second-home owners who are drawn from more affluent groups. These are also attracted for lifestyle and environmental reasons either to establish small family businesses, as documented by a plethora of studies (see Shaw & Williams, 2003), or just simply to retire. The interaction between these social groups and the resort economy has produced a different set of changes. These in recent years are marked out by an increasing demand for high-quality residential units, which has seen property prices at favoured resorts increase well above the national average (Table 3.5). Furthermore, in some resorts hotel properties are being sold for redevelopment into private rented apartments, as these are in greater demand.

Variations in Resort Restructuring

Seaside resorts are therefore complex socioeconomic environments that are being restructured by different forces, many of which relate to broader aspects of mobility, as well as those changes related to the tourism economy. Some of the common, if complex, processes acting on resorts have also led to significant variations at the local level, as these economies have reacted in different ways. Earlier studies had sought to explain differences in terms of resort size, identifying the seven large resorts (these being Blackpool, Bournemouth, Brighton, Great Yarmouth, Scarborough, Torbay and Newquay) as having very different prospects than medium and smaller ones (Shaw & Williams, 1997b). Certainly, official perspectives were clear that the very small resorts had specific difficulties regarding their tourism products (English Tourist Board (ETB), 1991). Interestingly, the study by Beatty and Fothergill (2003) ignored such smaller resorts, as have other recent discussions (House of Commons, 2005–06).

Table 3.5 Retirement population and house prices to income ratio in selected Devon resorts

Resort	*% pop. over 60*	*Average house prices (2004)*	*Average income*	*Ratio prices to income*
Ilfracombe	24.5	174,141	22801	7.6
Teignmouth[a]	30.7	177,577	26,176	6.8
Dawlish[a]	33.2	189,083	24,864	7.6
Westward Ho	38.3	191,427	26,479	7.2
Seaton[b]	46.3	176,933	22,311	7.9
Salcombe[b]	39.5	396,844	23,448	16.9
Exmouth[a]	28.1	180,803	24,299	7.4
Sidmouth[b]	45.3	273,635	26,821	10.2
Budleigh Salterton[b]	49.1	259,334	28,967	9.0

Source: Compiled from House of Commons (2005–06: 110–112)
[a]These are also commuter settlements for Exeter; [b]major retirement areas.

Nevertheless, some recent studies do provide a fresh insight into the varying fortunes of different seaside resorts. Thus, the British Resorts and Destination Association (House of Commons, 2005–06 along with Beatty & Fothergill, 2003) identify location and accessibility as key variables in explaining variations in resort development, claiming 'size seems not to be a key factor' (Beatty & Fothergill, 2003: 43). Of course the last statement can be contested given that smaller resorts were omitted from Beatty and Fothergill's study and therefore the overall influence of resort size would not be fully measured. Acknowledging such a limitation, their results show that location by region appears to be significant, as shown in Table 3.6. As their data demonstrate, the resorts of Southwest England have seen proportionately larger increases in employment and in-migration. Similarly, resorts in the Greater Southeast region have witnessed high growth rates. This is largely associated with the impact of London, certainly in terms of those resorts that can act as commuter towns. Those further away, such as Bournemouth, have benefited by a diversification of their economy, especially through the growth of education and language schools. Within Southwest England, the growth has been related to a series of factors including the retirement industry (particularly in resorts such as Sidmouth in Devon), together with fashionable second home locations and the perception of better lifestyle environments.

Of course such regional patterns also hide variations between resorts at the intraregional level, and the Southwest is a good example of this. Thus, the major resort of Torbay sees itself as having high levels of multiple deprivation and suffering from what it calls a 'Benefit economy', where there are a high number of claimants having 'a disproportionate impact on the general economy' (House of Commons, 2005–06: 149). In contrast, other smaller South Devon resorts such as Budleigh Salterton and Sidmouth have relatively large numbers of fairly affluent retired people.

Management Issues and Policy Responses

British seaside resorts have undergone a complex series of changes in recent years that have resulted in a range of management issues, as summarised in Table 3.7. Of course these are related to issues of tourism globalisation and the changing structure of tourism demand, as previously outlined (see Chapters 1 and 2). In addition, there are a range of other challenges to resort economies that in part relate to the tourism economy but also have their origins in wider social trends within British Society. These have long remained neglected issues as seaside towns fail to gain much political recognition for their problems. This is slowly changing, as is evident from the House of Commons report on Coastal Towns (House of Commons, 2005–06).

Table 3.6 Variations in the growth of seaside resorts by region: 1971–2001

	Net in-migration (working age)[a]		*Employment change*	
Region	***Number***	***1971 pop.***	***Number***	***1971 pop.***
South West	66,000	37	61,000	34
Greater South East[b]	222,000	29	189,000	24
Wales	14,000	18	12,000	15
North West	37,000	18	28,000	14
East Coast	16,000	12	16,000	12

Source: modified from Beatty and Fothergill (2003)
[a]As a percentage of 1971 working age population; [b]this includes Clacton, Southend and Bournemouth as well as resorts in the Southeast.

Table 3.7 Key issues facing seaside resorts

Key issues
Shifts in tourism demand and the growth of tourist subcultures (see Table 3.1)
High rates of in-migration
High proportions of retired in-migrants
High rates of younger people, many with low skills
A growing 'benefit culture' associated with transient population
High levels of multiple deprivation indicators
High rates of house price increases
Low wage rates and seasonal employment
Peripheral locations and weak transport links

Source: Modified from Memorandum by the Office of the Deputy Prime Minister (2006)

Attempts to tackle the problems of the tourism product offered by seaside resorts have a slightly longer history, with a series of reports that initially highlighted the problems of coastal resorts before turning to potential solutions. Shaw and Williams (2004) argue that the perspectives on resort regeneration, certainly with an English context, have moved through three key phases, to which now can be added a fourth phase. In part these have been reflected in a series of key reports (Table 3.8).

During the first phase in the 1980s early emphasis was on the use of public funding to assist tourism development, particularly through Section 4 Grants. These were used in resort areas to help improve

Table 3.8 Key reports on the redevelopment of coastal resorts in England

Report	*Source*	*Date*
Perspectives on the Future of Resorts	British Resorts Association	1989
The Future of England's Smaller Seaside Resorts	English Tourism Board	1991
Making the Most of the Coast	English Tourism Board	1993
Revitalizing the Coast	English Tourism Board	1995
Sea Changes: Creating World-class Resorts in England	English Tourism Council	2001
Coastal Towns	House of Commons	2005–06

Source: Modified from Shaw and Williams (2004)

facilities in hotels. Unfortunately these were often applied without any policy focus and consequently were not targeted according to need. They were abolished in England in 1989 partly because of misuse and mainly due to government cutbacks. During this phase state intervention also operated through public–private partnerships in the form of Tourism Development Action Programmes (TDAPs), along with Local Area Initiatives and Strategic Development Initiatives (Bramwell, 1990; Bramwell & Broom, 1989). All these measures were widely applied and as such, resorts did not receive any special treatment, although a number did have TDAPs. However, as Agarwal (1999) has pointed out, their success in halting the decline of tourism in coastal resorts was on the whole disappointing (see also Tourism Research Group, 1989).

The second phase of state interest in coastal economies occurred from the late 1980s into the 1990s. This was marked by the demise of TDAPs due to further changes in government spending and the publication of a series of reports on seaside resorts (Table 3.7). These drew attention to the need for resorts to change in the face of significant shifts in tourism demand. A particular emphasis was given to a refocusing on the history and heritage aspects of seaside resorts. This was not surprising given the great increase in heritage tourism during the 1990s. There was also recognition of the problems of very small resorts and also the limitations of many small-scale entrepreneurs. Unfortunately, there was little in the way of direct help or possible solutions. The recognition of the importance of the physical environment did lead to an implementation of town centre management schemes in seaside resorts in a belated effort to improve the visitor experience.

From the late 1990s, increasing recognition was given to the seaside product itself, with reports from various agencies stressing the need to differentiate such a product to target different market segments (ETB, 1993, 1995; ETC, 2001; Shaw & Williams, 2004). Of course it should also be added that some resorts have been able to tap into the Single Regeneration Budget during this phase. Moreover, although this was not specifically for the tourism industry, it has helped to improve the overall attractiveness of some seaside environments. More recently the interest in coastal towns has drawn a more wider ranging inquiry into their socioeconomic conditions in addition to the nature of the tourism industry (House of Commons, 2005–06), as discussed earlier in the chapter, and this represents the fourth phase of state interest.

Set against all these different reports is the fact that the state has increasingly withdrawn financial support from the tourism industry in coastal resorts. Moreover, in England the closure of the England Tourism Council left a strategic management gap in terms of tourism development. The creation of marketing emphasis in the shape of both 'VisitBritain' and 'VisitEngland' has done little to fill the vacuum. At the regional level, the increased influence of Regional Development Agencies and the relative decline or in some cases the closure of Regional Tourist Boards has also weakened the tourism industry. The creation of the Tourism Alliance in 2002, which is now the self-proclaimed voice of tourism, has attempted to set out strategy documents to influence government thinking (Tourism Alliance, 2003). In their first review they draw attention to the plight of seaside resorts, highlighting the fact that many of these economies still need access to regeneration funds (Tourism Alliance, 2003). Equally significant was their recognition that 'government funding for tourism remains woefully small in relation to the sectors turnover and employment growth potential' (Tourism Alliance, 2003: 7). Such problems are particularly marked in English seaside resorts, as is evident by the fact that one of the major domestic tourism regions, Southwest England, only received £13.19 per head of population in state tourism funding compared with £221.91 per head for Wales (Tourism Alliance, 2003).

Where do such changes in state funding and the loss of a key voice for tourism at government level leave seaside resorts? It would appear that future policy remains fragmented and under New Labour, strategies will be derived at the regional/local level. As the report by the Office of the Deputy Prime Minister (2006: 4) states 'given the varied needs [of seaside towns]... a national programme to address these issues may not be the best way forward, given the importance the Government attaches to regional and local strategies and decision-making'. Much of the activity will therefore be within the strategies of the Regional Development Agencies. The complexity in terms of policy and strategy is however exacerbated by the activities of other national, regional and local agencies.

Certainly at the resort level there are still many policy gaps between, for example, regional-based strategies and those being formulated by local authorities. Indeed, as the English Regional Development Agencies state, they do 'not operate a specific coastal area programme [but will consider particular factors] in delivering wider programmes of development' (House of Commons, 2005–06: EV15). As part of this complex of policy there have been significant flows of capital from Heritage Lottery Fund grants into many coastal resorts, which have funded a variety of activities including tourist attractions. This encompasses some £234 million of funding covering 517 projects in 79 different coastal locations (information collated from the Office of Deputy Prime Minister, Memorandum 2006: 1). In some cases it has been the funding of tourism projects away from seaside resorts that has had the most significant impact on such economies. This is certainly the case with the Eden Project in Cornwall, which received Millennium Funding (Shaw & Williams, 2004). This major attraction has helped reshape part of the visitor market for seaside resorts such as Newquay. In this case, the resort has seen a growth in short-break packages with visitors staying two nights in Newquay but mainly wanting to visit the Eden Project. Work commissioned by the Eden Project (Jasper, 2002) claims some 2 million visitors between 2001 and 2002, generating a direct economic impact of £155 million.

There are also examples of attempts to co-ordinate policy initiatives at the subregional level, with a growing number of partnership schemes, such the East Kent Partnership. This brings together stakeholders from the district councils, national and regional public sector organisations and local businesses. In terms of strategic issues its focus is to optimise investment opportunities (House of Commons, 2005–06: CT22). In this instance funding is provided by the RDA, although at the time of writing the partnership had only made modest improvements, and appealed for greater 'co-ordination and co-operation between government departments and agencies in terms of bending mainstream funding to address the needs of our coastal towns' (House of Commons, 2005–06: EV46).

Conclusion

This chapter has attempted to highlight the changing nature of seaside towns both in terms of their economic, social and environmental problems and in terms of policy responses. In doing so it recognises that these resorts are complex spaces and that such complexity reflects macro level changes in the nature of tourism demand, and in particular the increasing importance of the tourist experience. Furthermore, these relate to broader changes in the way lifestyles are constructed and how those impact on consumption patterns. This is not new but we would argue that the trends are now much more visible and intensive than in the late 1990s. Trends in tourism consumption are more complex and dynamic and much more segmented in terms of particular markets (Shaw, 2006). These patterns are changing the way in which seaside resorts are perceived and used. In turn the changing nature of migration to such resorts has brought both fresh impacts and challenges, especially regarding their social ecology.

Such trends have in part been reflected in the changing management issues of resorts in terms of policy initiatives and the role of the state. Since the 1980s the difficulties of the tourism product in resorts has been recognised. However, a series of policy initiatives during the 1990s did little to turn around the product on offer. The latest government review of coastal resorts has highlighted a far more wide-ranging set of issues, but as yet few solutions have been formatted. The British seaside resort is not in terminal decline but rather continuing to experience a shift in its role.

Chapter 4

Institutional Change and Resort Capacity: The Case of Southwest English Coastal Resorts

SHEELA AGARWAL

Introduction

The meaning of the 'local' and the 'global', the relationships between the concepts involved, and the ways in which these relationships are structured in space have been explored extensively (Beck, 2000; Castells, 1989; Crang, 1999; Featherstone, 1990; Hirst &Thompson, 1999). Recent theorisations of globalisation have emphasised its relational, nonlinear and nonscalar nature (Amin, 2002; Massey, 1999; Thrift, 1999), and have postulated the mutual constitution of the 'global' and the 'local', which produces specific processes and outcomes, or particular geographies of development. Despite recognition of the significance of the local and of the need to understand local settings in the context of global processes (Bagguley *et al*., 1990; Massey, 1978; Urry, 1987), within the tourism literature research of local mediation of global forces is a relatively recent phenomenon (Chang, 1999; Cooke, 1989; Milne & Ateljevic, 2001; Sorkin, 1992; Teo & Li, 2003; Urry, 1996; Yeoh & Teo, 1996). Consequently, there is a paucity of research of this issue.

Within this context, this chapter examines the capacity of coastal resorts in Southwest England to respond to global forces, by drawing on a survey of key local authority personnel's perceptions of, and attitudes to, local action in those resorts that are situated in their authority's administrative area. In the first part of the chapter, the impact of global forces on English coastal resorts is detailed, followed by an outline of the management implications for England's coastal resorts. In the second part of the chapter, the study's methodology is presented, followed by analysis and discussion of the main survey results. This study makes a theoretical contribution to understanding resort restructuring by highlighting the implications of global forces for the management of coastal resorts. In addition, this study has practical value, as although it is set in a Southwest English context, it highlights some generic obstacles and some locally determined factors that may influence the effectiveness of resort restructuring in other European mass tourism coastal resorts.

The Impact of Globalisation on English Coastal Resorts

Although the nature and meaning of globalisation for English coastal resorts, particularly in relation to the alleged emergence of a 'new' form of globalisation, is unclear, the contention that the global and the local are mutually constituted has been gaining ground (Dicken, 1998; Giddens, 1999). In light of this, global forces are increasingly no longer viewed as being unilateral, hegemonic and all-encompassing. For English coastal resorts, what this now means is that specific outcomes or particular geographies of development may be produced, a notion that Agarwal (2005) has utilised to account for their differential economic performance. Thus, the author argues that change may be viewed as an outcome of global–local interactions, with globalisation impacting upon local action, and with local action mediating the influence of global processes.

However, it is not only the trajectories of resorts that globalisation has influenced. While it is important not to overstate its consequences (Davies, 2001; Gibbs *et al.*, 2001), within the UK it is widely accepted that global forces have contributed to an altering of the regulatory framework within which resorts are managed. According to Fuller *et al.* (2004), Jessop (1997) and Jones (2001), this has involved profound changes in state intervention, resulting in the rescaling and reterritorialisation of national state capacities. New state organisations operating on a range of spatial scales have been created and added to the two existing tiers of local government (county and district/borough councils) that are responsible for their economic development. Furthermore, the roles for state bodies have also been reconfigured (Fuller *et al.*, 2004), from a system of local government to one of local governance; the former is associated with narrow responsibilities for service provision, whilst the latter involves a broader range of activities involving contracting, regulating, enabling, problem-solving, networking and leadership (Brookes, 1989; Stoker, 1995, 1999; Thomas & Thomas, 1998). Local authorities now have a responsibility to address a wide range of problems, with cross-departmental and interorganisational public, private and voluntary sector co-operation and collaboration being defining features (Thomas & Thomas, 1998). For Massey (1978), Amin and Thrift (1994) and MacLeod (2001), these changes are even more significant, despite the fact that the 'real' role of the state is contentious, as outlined in Chapter 1. This is because such changes provide a framework within which local institutions may influence the outcome of global forces.

Local management and resort capacity

Within English coastal resorts, there is widespread evidence that local areas are impacting on global forces through the implementation of local development strategies and initiatives. In studies of coastal resorts in Southwest and Northwest England, Agarwal (1997b, 1999, 2002) cites numerous examples of regeneration programmes and restructuring strategies. These management approaches have been aided by local governance, which encourages institutional flexibility and cross-institutional co-operation. For English coastal resorts, flexible management mechanisms are imperative given the diverse range of economic, social and environmental problems being experienced (Agarwal & Brunt, 2006; Dinan, 2002), combined with the fact that their amelioration requires the involvement of multiple organisations, institutions and agencies.

However, whilst institutional changes in the UK allegedly encourage more 'joined-up' policy intervention, enabling the English Regional Development Agency and a multitude of subregional partnerships to play a key role in development (Roberts & Benneworth, 2001), in reality it has led to the proliferation and increased importance of different levels of government which operate at different sociospatial scales, resulting in the development of complex multigovernance arrangements (Breener, 1999; Fuller *et al.*, 2004). What this now means for economic development is that decisions have to be made, and resources need to be shared across a range of public, quasi-public and non-public agents (Pierre & Peters, 2000). Thus the potential for duplication, inertia and financial wastage is high. Nevertheless, given the limited powers and reduced financial resources available to English local authorities, subregional partnerships involving the English Regional Development Agencies are important to coastal resort restructuring as they have been granted enhanced funding. Therefore they have the potential to help resorts design and implement regeneration plans, and to fund major projects.

Local and subregional partnerships are clearly essential to economic development, however several factors have been identified, albeit in the contexts of local and regional economic development, which influence the capacity of resorts to respond to global forces (Agarwal, 1997b; Amin & Thrift, 1994; Cheshire & Gordon, 1996; see also Chapter 1). These factors are collectively known as institutional capacity or 'Institutional Thickness' (Amin & Thrift, 1994: 14), a term that emphasises the existence of, and interaction between, different institutions and agencies, all or some of which can provide a basis for the growth of particular local practices and collective representations. Their relevance to English coastal resort capacity is summarised in Table 4.1. Moreover, Agarwal (2005) notes the importance of place characteristics such as scale, location and/or past patterns of development, and some locally determined factors such as central–local and regional–local relations as influencing the capacity of resorts to mediate global forces. Within many English coastal resorts, although the presence of all of these factors is problematic, according to Agarwal (2005: 365), 'it is important to note that the presence of a

Table 4.1 Factors influencing English coastal resort capacity

Factors influencing the resort capacity	*Evidence of relevance to English coastal resort capacity*
The failure to appreciate the nature, influence and consequence of global forces	Although resort decline has been endemic since the 1970s, action has been belated (English Tourism Council, 2001). This is perhaps because there is a lack of specialist tourism expertise (Cooper, 1997) and because there is poor understanding of resort dynamics (Agarwal, 2002). Furthermore, the appropriateness of local action has been questioned by Agarwal (2002), who contends that it focuses on the symptoms rather than the causes of decline.
The degree to which there is public sector commitment to tourism	Cooper (1997) argues there has been a major civic commitment to resort restructuring, however, Agarwal (1997) revealed a marked variation in policy response in an analysis of the treatment of tourism in county structure and borough and district local plans along the South coast of England.
The existence of shared economic interests and trust	This is problematic in English coastal resorts due to the fragmented structure of the tourism industry, the involvement of a large number of decision-makers (Cooper, 1997) and a weak culture of trust amongst firms (Coles & Shaw, 2006; Shaw & Williams, 1997a).
Strong institutional presence	Despite the existence of numerous public and private sector organisations and agencies responsible for tourism, English coastal resorts tend to be characterised by a weak institutional presence. This is because coastal tourism has a low profile amongst national, regional and local government departments (Dinan, 2002; English Tourism Council, 2001), and because of local government reorganisation in 1996, which amalgamated many independent resorts with surrounding residential and industrial hinterlands, thereby transferring political interests away from resorts (Cooper, 1997).

Table 4.1 (*Continued*)

Factors influencing the resort capacity	*Evidence of relevance to English coastal resort capacity*
High levels of contact, co-operation and information exchange	There is a tradition of poor co-operation, particularly between the public and private sectors in English coastal resorts. According to Cooper (1997), the private sector has traditionally held a short-term tactical view of tourism and has been poorly disposed to all-embracing attempts to co-ordinate the industry.
The existence of collective representations that serve to minimise costs and control rogue behaviour	This is lacking in English coastal resorts as there is a long tradition of poor investment and co-operation between the public and private sectors (British Resorts Association, c.2000; Dinan, 2002; English Tourism Council, 2001).
The development of mutual awareness amongst institutions that they are involved in a common cause	According to Cooper (1997), in the case of English coastal resorts, the tourism industry rarely speaks (or lobbies) with one voice, as it is highly fragmented, dominated by small firms and ill-defined in as much as it includes traders who do not solely depend on tourism.

Source: collated from Agarwal (1997b, 2002), British Resorts Association (c.2000), Coles & Shaw (2006), Cooper (1997), Dinan (2002), English Tourism Council (2001a)

favorable conjunction of material, institutional and cultural factors and, in particular, institutional thickness, does not necessarily equate to resort success'. However, the extent to which each of these factors influences the capacity of English coastal resorts to mediate global forces is largely unknown.

Therefore, the remainder of this chapter is concerned with investigating such issues in Southwest England through an examination of key local authority personnel's perceptions of, and attitudes to, local action that is occurring within the coastal resorts for which they are responsible. Coastal tourism within the Southwest of England is of immense importance, accounting for 40% of the 20.5 million trips taken by UK residents to the region in 2004 (United Kingdom Tourism Survey, 2005).

Methodology

Data collection involved the implementation of a postal questionnaire targeted at key local authority representatives in Southwest England with responsibilities for tourism in coastal resorts. The questionnaire took a structured format and contained a mix of open-ended, closed and Likert-scale questions. This mix of questions were devised to gain knowledge of the respondents' general understanding (closed-ended questions), but as it is easy for a respondent who does not know the answer to a question to answer randomly (Bailey, 1987), the open-ended questions required the respondents to recall information, thereby providing an indication of conceptual understanding (Lee & Balchin, 1995). The Likert-scale questions were used to assess respondents' attitudes, as it is possible to obtain a direct measure of attitudes by asking respondents to rate an object on a given scale (Fishbein & Ajzen, 1975). Respondents were therefore asked to rate the strength of their opinion, by selecting one of the following options: 'strongly agree', 'agree', 'no opinion', 'disagree' and 'strongly disagree'.

Given that this study aimed to ascertain the views and attitudes of key informants, theoretical purposeful sampling was undertaken. This was achieved by identifying all the county, borough and district councils that encompass Southwest England. Then, drawing on the *Municipal Yearbook 2003* (Hemming Information Services, 2003), which contains the names and addresses of all local authority department heads, those representing the departments which were deemed to be involved with coastal resorts were noted. For the most part, for each county, borough and district council, the names of those heading-up economic development, urban regeneration, tourism, planning, environmental services, marketing and town centre management were sent a questionnaire. Although these individuals will have their own strategic viewpoint, it can be argued that they are in a uniquely strong position to provide an informed view of resort capacity.

In total, 70 respondents were identified. The questionnaire was mailed out during mid-2003, with one follow-up. In total 37 questionnaires were returned, however three were returned incomplete and were therefore unusable, resulting in a response rate of 49%. Of those that were returned, 8 were from county council representatives, 21 were from district councils and 5 were from borough council representatives. The small sample size means that interpretation must be treated with caution. The assessments are the subjective or perceptual views of the respondents, with the main emphasis in this assessment being the relative frequency of views in different types of local authority area. Assuming of course that the Southwest's resorts are representative of other regions, this allows a survey of individual perception to be generalised as a comment for English coastal resorts as a whole. In order to ascertain the opinions and attitudes of key local authority personnel in relation to local action within coastal resorts, the questionnaire specifically aimed to ascertain their views on institutional change and how this has impacted upon local action. In particular, their perceptions of the factors that were perceived to influence its extent and effectiveness were elicited.

Perceptions of institutional change

In terms of perceptions of institutional change, the majority of respondents (88.2%) stated that their role had changed substantially over the last five years, with most citing characteristics that have been associated with local governance. For example, 85.3% stated that they engaged more in partnership-working, and 82.3% said they worked more closely with other public sector institutions and/or agencies. Meanwhile, 76.5% said that they now worked more closely with the private sector and were responsible for tackling a wider range of problems. Fulfilling a 'greater co-ordinating role' received only 5.9% of responses. There also appeared to be evidence of cross-agency working, another alleged characteristic of local governance as many respondents indicated that they represented more than one department, with most representing 'Tourism' (22), followed by 'Economic Development' (16) and then 'Planning', and that they had contact with other departments; planning and the environment were the departments that respondents tended to have most contact with, closely followed by leisure/recreation, transport and economic development. Surprisingly, tourism and urban regeneration received the fewest responses. Perhaps this may be explained by the fact that not all English county and local borough and district councils have these specific departments within their organisation.

The respondents were probed further on the issue of partnership working and working more closely with other public sector institutions and/or agencies. Of the 34 respondents who completed this questionnaire, 79.4% stated they worked closely with Southwest Tourism, one of England's regional tourist boards and 73.5% with the Southwest Regional Development Agency. 70.6%, however, also stated they worked closely with the Local Hoteliers Association and with the resorts' town councils; 64.7% stated that they worked with the Local Chambers of Commerce, another organisation that represents local businesses, and 79.4% stated that they worked closely with Local Tourism Associations. These findings suggest that the private and public sectors are, at least on the surface, working together, and further evidence of this was revealed when the respondents were asked about the frequency of meeting with public sector organisations on coastal tourism. 37.5% stated that they met 'more than twice a year', 31.2% stated that they met 'monthly' and a handful of respondents stated they met either 'twice a year' (6.3%), 'once a year' (6.3%), 'weekly' (6.3%) or quarterly (3.1%). Meanwhile, 6.3% stated that they never met, while 3.1% said that the frequency of meeting was variable depending on the organisation. Their commitment to cross-sector working was also investigated, with 82.3% stating that they provided human and/or financial resources.

Effectiveness of local action

Views relating to the effectiveness of local action were elicited through a series of statements against which the respondents rated the strength of their agreement (Table 4.2). Although 74.7% agreed and strongly agreed with the statement that the public sector is strongly committed to tourism, surprisingly only 32.3% agreed and 2.9% strongly agreed with the statement that 'local responses to increased competition have overall been very effective'; 17.6% disagreed and 41.2% had no opinion. More interestingly, it appears that three problems that have traditionally been associated with ineffective local action, namely: (1) a lack of co-operation and contact amongst public sector organisations; (2) a lack of co-operation and trust amongst the public and private sectors; and (3) limited political representation of local tourism issues and/or matters (Coles & Shaw, 2006; Cooper, 1997; Shaw & Williams, 1997a), were not perceived by the majority of respondents to have negatively affected local action, eliciting responses of 38.2%, 41.2% and 47% respectively.

Withstanding the respondents' obvious reluctance to be critical of the public sector, perceptions of the effectiveness of local action may be explained by the fact that the majority, 76.4%, perceived it to be limited by a lack of funding. In addition, 70.6% viewed the barriers and obstacles hindering local action to be insurmountable. Moreover, other factors that

Table 4.2 Respondents' strength of agreement to statements relating to resort capacity

N=34	***Strongly agree***	***Agree***	***No opinion***	***Disagree***	***Strongly disagree***
Global forces of change have adversely affected the competitiveness of coastal resorts in Southwest England	5.9% (2)	29.4% (10)	23.5% (8)	32.2% (11)	2.9% (1)
It is extremely important to counter and engage with global forces of change		52.9% (18)	29.4% (10)	11.8% (4)	
There is a lack of understanding of the external dynamics of resort change	11.8% (4)	35.3% (12)	26.5% (9)	23.5% (8)	
Local action is limited by a lack of funding	38.2% (13)	38.2% (13)		11.8% (4)	
Local action is hindered by a lack of co-operation and contact amongst public sector organisations	5.9% (2)	32.3% (11)	26.5% (9)	29.4% (10)	2.9% (1)
Local action is hindered by a lack of co-operation and collective action amongst local tourism businesses	11.8% (4)	38.2% (13)	32.3% (11)	2.9% (1)	
A strong unified vision and/or common interest is present	2.9% (1)	44.1% (15)	29.4% (10)	17.6% (6)	2.9% (1)
There is a lack of trust amongst the public and private sectors	5.9% (2)	35.3% (12)	26.5% (9)	26.5% (9)	2.9% (1)
Political representation of local tourism issues and/or matters is limited		14.7% (5)	44.1% (15)	44.1% (15)	2.9% (1)

Table 4.2 (*Continued*)

N=34	*Strongly agree*	*Agree*	*No opinion*	*Disagree*	*Strongly disagree*
A strong ethos of collective action exists		14.7% (5)	38.2% (13)	38.2% (13)	2.9% (1)
The public sector is strongly committed to tourism	14.7% (5)	50% (17)	11.8% (4)	14.7% (5)	2.9% (1)
There is a mutual awareness amongst public sector institutions that they are involved in a common cause	5.9% (2)	44.1% (15)	23.5% (8)	14.7% (5)	5.9% (2)
Local responses to increased competition have overall been very effective	2.9% (1)	32.3% (11)	41.2% (14)	17.6% (6)	–
The barriers/obstacles which hinder local action is/are insurmountable	2.9% (1)	5.9% (2)	14.7% (5)	41.2% (14)	29.4% (10)

Rows do not add up to 34, as some respondents failed to provide a response.
Source: Author's survey

a substantial proportion of the respondents perceived to influence the effectiveness of local action included the lack of mutual awareness amongst public sector institutions that they are involved in a common cause (50.0%), the fact that local action is hindered by a lack of co-operation and collective action amongst local tourism businesses (49.6%), and the absence of a shared unified vision and/or common interest (53.0%) and a spirit of collective action (58.6%).

Interestingly, while there appeared to be recognition of the importance of global forces (52.9%), a large proportion of the respondents (47.1%) indicated that they had little understanding of resort dynamics and of the relevance of global forces to the competitiveness of resorts. However, despite these perceptions, several examples of restructuring strategies were cited that have been identified previously by Agarwal (2002), including diversification, market repositioning and professionalism. These are considered by some to be the most appropriate response to globalisation (Debbage & Ioannides, 1998). In light of this, it therefore appears, at least tentatively, that as Cooke (1989) and Amin and Thrift (1994) suggest, globalisation is encouraging proactivity in an attempt to capture competitiveness, and that local action is shaping the course of economic evolution (Cheshire & Gordon, 1996) in English coastal resorts. Local action is, as Amin and Thrift (1994) suggest, structuring responses to processes of globalisation and in doing so, it has become part of the process, thereby reinforcing the notion of the mutual constitution of the global and the local.

The respondents were also asked specifically about the existence of obstacles and/or barriers that they perceived to negatively influence resort capacity. Overall, 73.5% stated that there were barriers/obstacles in existence, and 14.7% perceived there to be no barriers/obstacles in existence. 67.6% stated that these barriers/obstacles were local, 52.9% perceived there to be regional barriers, while 50.0% stated that there were national barriers. A wide variety were identified, but overall, the lack of available funding was again the most cited, eliciting 14 responses, while the lack of local consensus on action was identified by five respondents and a lack of local authority co-operation was cited by four respondents. Other responses include social problems, inflexible planning legislation, lack of dedicated staff, lack of understanding of local and national problems, traffic congestion and a lack of understanding of major projects by elected members. The wide-ranging nature of the identified barriers and/or obstacles perhaps reflects either the diverse problems that many coastal resorts are experiencing or different levels of perception by different types of local authority. When asked about the type of action required to overcome the identified barriers and/or obstacles, 18 of the 34 respondents stated that more funding was required, 14 out of 34 said that there needed to be increased co-operation between the public and private sectors and between public sector organisations and agencies, while 13 out of 34 said that there needed to be increased co-operation amongst the private sector. Furthermore, two respondents thought more staff resources were required and one thought that co-operation needed to be increased amongst local residents.

Resort institutional capacity

When taken together, the statements ascertaining the effectiveness of local action provide a crude indication of the institutional capacity of each local authority area. Indicators of high capacity include the presence of a strong unified vision, the presence of a shared local economic vision, the existence of a strong ethos of collective action, strong public sector commitment to tourism and the existence of a mutual awareness amongst public sector institutions that they are involved in a common cause. In contrast, indicators of low capacity include limited political representation of local tourism issues, a lack of trust amongst the public and private sectors, and a lack of co-operation between the public and private sectors and amongst tourism businesses. The responses from each of the councils, with the exception of counties, as there were too few responses to provide meaningful results, were collated and a point system was devised ('Strongly agree' (SA) = 2; 'Agree' (A) = 1; 'No opinion' = 0; 'Disagree' (D) = -1; and 'Strongly disagree' (SD) = -2). Each local administrative area within each of the four Southwest English counties (Cornwall, Devon, Dorset and Somerset) was then graded in terms of high and low capacity (Table 4.3).

Overall, no one Southwest county had more than two of its local administrative areas scoring highly in terms of high institutional capacity and no more than one scored highly with respect to low institutional capacity. This suggests that there is a good degree of institutional thickness in the majority of local areas within each Southwest county. A more in-depth analysis revealed, however, that although some factors that contribute to institutional thickness are perceived to be present in each of the Southwest's local administrative areas, such as a common interest and/or vision, the institutional capacity of their coastal resorts was perceived to be limited again by a lack of co-operation within and between the public and private sectors.

Furthermore, despite the fact that most local authority areas were perceived to be institutionally thick in terms of sharing a strong interest and common vision, most local authority officers perceived their administrative areas to lack four key elements of thickness. These were: (1) co-operation and collective action amongst local tourism businesses, (2) a strong ethos of collective action, (3) co-operation and contact amongst public sector organisations and (4) trust amongst the

Table 4.3 Southwest local administrative areas' scores of high and low institutional capacity

High capacity	*High (scored 6–9)*	*Mid (scored 2–5)*	*Low (scored -3 to 1)*
Cornwall	1	3	2
Devon	2	1	2
Dorset	1	0	2
Somerset	2	0	1
Low capacity			
Cornwall	1	2	3
Devon	0	1	4
Dorset	0	2	1
Somerset	1	2	0

Source: Author's survey

public and private sectors. Whilst the first and second of these elements reinforce earlier findings that the lack of co-operation and collective action amongst local tourism businesses and the absence of a strong ethos of collective action are issues that are perceived to hinder local action, the other two elements, although not perceived by the majority of respondents to be problematic, are worryingly viewed, albeit to a greater or lesser extent, to be present within all local borough and district council areas.

Co-operation and trust are particularly important to engender as they facilitate agencies coming together and co-operating, and their perceived absence is surprising particularly in light of the emergence of local governance. However, there are a number of possible explanations for this finding, as it may point to the failure of local governance to foster a culture of collective action that was originally envisaged (Stoker, 1995, 1999). Given the continuing importance of central government in 'local' partnerships (Davies, 2001), local governance often varies in the extent to which it has been operationalised (Stoker, 1999). Another possible explanation may be sought from Newman (2001), who highlights a possible dissonance between local authorities and other organisations, because they operate in different strategic contexts, and relate to different priorities, spatial boundaries, organisational cultures and partnership-working attitudes. Alternatively, due to a greater emphasis on public accountability and assessments against predetermined targets (Fuller *et al.*, 2004), there may have been a reluctance on the part of the respondents to admit that local action was perhaps not being as effective as it could be.

Overall however, this study's results highlight the importance of the institutional context for effective and successful economic development (Amin & Thrift, 1994; Jones & MacLeod, 1999). However, determining the extent to which it provides an effective framework for economic development requires knowledge and understanding of a complex network of relationships between central, regional, subregional and local organisations. This implication is of course not new as it has already been rehearsed within studies of urban and regional development in recent years by a number of scholars who have heralded and enthusiastically embraced a new institutional perspective or 'institutional turn' (Amin & Thrift, 1994; Healey, 1997). There is now a flourishing of strong institutionalist accounts which seek to place local processes firmly within a global context (Peck, 2000), and the institutional context in which economic development takes place has thus become an area of increasing academic and policy interest. But within tourism, there is a dearth of research of the institutional context of tourist destinations, and it is an area of study that requires more than a mere cataloguing of local economic development organisations. Rather, it should seek to elucidate the conditions and framework required for effective public–private sector encouragement of, and involvement with, tourism development and resort restructuring.

This study also draws attention to the fact that resort capacity was perceived to be hindered by generic obstacles, such as lack of funding, and by some locally determined factors. One notable problem was the lack of co-operation and trust within and between the public and private sectors. For English coastal resorts, although the development of mutual awareness of a common cause and shared goals amongst institutions is critical, it is of little use if the public and private sectors do not act together to achieve this. It is also important to note that while these factors are specific to English coastal resorts, given the fragmented structure of the tourism industry it is not inconceivable that they may also occur in other European mass tourism coastal resorts. Indeed, Sadler (2004) notes a lack of public sector co-operation in Northern Cyprus's resorts whereas Tosun *et al.* (2004) state that a lack of public–private co-operation has contributed to the widening of regional inequalities in Turkey's coastal resorts. In light of this, the study highlights the urgent need for the mechanisms that connect institutions with coastal resort development to be reviewed and for capacity-building strategies to be devised that encourage greater co-operation and trust.

Conclusion

This chapter has examined the capacity of English coastal resorts to respond to global forces and highlights the occurrence of some generic obstacles and locally determined factors that influence resort capacity. In particular, the lack of co-operation and trust within and between the public and private sectors is perceived to limit the capacity of coastal resorts in Southwest England to respond to global forces. If economic development generally, and resort restructuring specifically, are to be successful, then considerable energy must be devoted to effectively managing the relationships between all relevant actors. When taken together, these study findings raise some important questions concerning the extent to which the institutional landscape of English coastal resorts is helping or hindering resort restructuring. Resort restructuring requires institutional flexibility and cross-institutional co-operation, but according to Fuller *et al*. (2004), the institutional changes that have occurred in recent years have produced few changes in how economic development occurs or how local government operates. This is because the multilevel governance arrangements now characterising the UK have increased rather than diminished the complexity and fragmentation of institutions responsible for economic development (Fuller *et al*., 2004). This view is reinforced by the Audit Commission (1999: 12), who state that 'fragmentation and duplication on the ground still persists, underpinned by a maze of strategies, partnerships and organizational configurations'. However, due to a lack of research, the extent to which such contentions are applicable to English coastal resorts and other mass tourism coastal resorts elsewhere in Europe is difficult to ascertain. Thus, in order to enhance knowledge and understanding of mass coastal tourism resort restructuring, there is an urgent need for more in-depth resort-based investigations of their capacity to respond to change.

Note

1. This chapter presents some of the findings from a project, 'Global–Local Interactions in English Seaside Resorts', which was funded by the British Academy.

Part 2

The Diversification and Sustainable Development of Coastal Resorts

Chapter 5

Complexity, Interdisciplinarity and Growth Management: The Case of Maltese Resort Tourism

BILL BRAMWELL

Introduction

Policy makers increasingly recognise the potential to manage the tourism industry so as to secure destination growth objectives. This chapter argues that attempts to manage tourism growth in a destination need to recognise the full complexity of the relationships and issues that are involved. There is a discussion of the sources of this complexity, and then some of these are examined for the case of resort tourism in the small state of Malta in the central Mediterranean. Much tourism development in the Maltese islands has been concentrated in a few resorts and there are many difficult decisions to be made about the levels, types and locations of future tourism growth in these resorts and also elsewhere in these small islands. The sources of some of the complexities involved in these growth management decisions are discussed and evaluated. The chapter also looks at the implications of the identified complexities for tourism research and for the practice of tourism planning and management. It is contended that these implications point to the need for more holistic and integrative frameworks, the overcoming of narrow academic disciplinary boundaries, recognition of nonlinearity of tourism impacts, and planning as an adaptive and collective learning process.

Complexity and Growth Management

Attempts can be made by policy makers to alter three aspects of tourism growth: the quantity or amount of development, its types and quality, and its geographical distribution or dispersal (Bosselman *et al*., 1999; Gill, 2004). The first of these approaches relates to the tourism industry's size and the volume of tourist arrivals, and it is often associated with concerns to keep development within what are considered an area's carrying capacities or limits to acceptable change. The second approach involves alterations to the types of development, with this often intended to attract higher spending tourists so as to maximise economic yields and to retain a destination's status and attraction. And, third, there are policies to affect the industry's geographical dispersal, and these involve intentions to secure benefits from either concentrating or dispersing tourism activity. Destination management in particular places usually combines aspects of these three approaches.

Tourism growth management may seem to be a relatively simple process. It can appear deceptively straightforward if it is depicted largely as a technical or managerial process that is likely to succeed as long as scientific rationality and scientific management are applied consistently, perhaps including formal planning steps, systems engineering and quantitative modelling (Coccossis & Mexa, 2004; Reid, 2003). An implied ease and simplicity might also result from the view that tourism planning is just an applied management discipline. But such perspectives can seriously underestimate tourism's complexity and can 'flatten' the complications resulting from this industry's diverse relationships, the difficulties of nonlinearity and unpredictability related to changes in society and nature, and the issues of values, power, contestation and governance.

This chapter suggests that the notion of complexity can help us to understand tourism growth management and to improve the practical approaches to it that may be adopted. The idea of complexity has gained increased prominence in social science research, and this concept is often associated with a relational perspective that is based on the idea that entities do not have separate and distinct essences (Bramwell & Meyer, 2007; Bramwell & Pomfret, 2007; Yeung, 2005). From a relational perspective, complexity is considered to result from there being a wide array of actors and of networked or circulating relationships in society, from the varied interactions between social systems and environmental processes, and from these relationships being implicated within contexts at different spatial scales. Not only are there numerous elements in social and natural systems, but the interactions between them are complex and rich and they involve multiple negative and positive feedback loops. It is necessary, therefore, to recognise the diverse and dialectical connections between tourism growth management and the social and natural worlds and to consider how these complicate growth management activity. Just some examples of the varied complexities associated with tourism growth management are summarised in Table 5.1.

One complexity is that predicting the outcomes of tourism growth strategies is often very difficult due to the diverse impacts and nonlinearity of the changing relationships. In part, this is because the industry has a range of physical and social effects that sometimes have little or no immediate or obvious linkage with tourism (Weaver, 2004). Cause and effect relationships are hard to know, with few cases where a

Table 5.1 Complexity in tourism growth management

Types of complexity
Diversity of impacts
Nonlinearity of relations
Actors' responses to impacts
Trade-offs between impacts
Diversity of local contexts
Connections between spatial scales
Selection of tourism types
Mix of tourism types and elements
Combining the mix of tourist types, quantity and location
Effects of interests and values on decisions
Effects of power and influence on decisions
Capital flows and relations
Governance and democracy
Commitment, resources and co-ordination for implementation
Multiple influences on change
Holistic integration, notably for sustainable development

simple increase or decrease in one input will produce a clearly predictable output. With tourism's consequences for humans there are the complexities related to people's values, social networks and subjectivity. Another complication is that actors vary in their personal responses to tourism and their reactions are also multifaceted. Thus, some people distinguish between tourism's consequences for themselves personally as distinct from their implications for other people, while others may not make this distinction. People also vary in the trade-offs they make between tourism's diverse social, environmental and economic impacts.

Assessments of the potential merits of growth policies are also difficult because they are likely to vary geographically between specific local contexts, such as according to the amount of prior development and the resilience and uniqueness of local resources (Hunter, 1997). Linked to this, there is the complication that development policies often spill over spatially between destinations at various spatial scales, so that places should not be considered in isolation (Weaver, 2004). There are further difficulties because of the need to consider the value for a destination of different tourism types – such as resort tourism, adventure tourism and rural tourism – and also of the combination of tourism types, the mix of accommodation and other facilities, and the mix of tourist activities. These issues also need to be integrated with decisions about the quantity and location of tourism.

Other difficulties arise because of the range of affected actors who have varied interests, values and policy preferences, and these actors have differing capacities to influence the policy decisions. Decision-making about tourism growth is also influenced by governance arrangements, including the extent to which the affected actors are encouraged to participate in decision-making. It must also be noted that there are underlying pressures, such as from capital accumulation and globalisation, which can result in more emphasis being given, for example, to economic priorities, even when this has adverse social or environmental consequences (Bianchi, 2004). Further complications surround the implementation of growth management policies. Here the relevant government agencies may lack commitment or resources, or they may encounter obstacles in securing action from, and co-ordination between, the many organisations that need to adopt an active role.

Further, the success of growth management is often mediated by numerous changes that originate outside the tourism sector or outside the destination and across spatial scales, such as from global economic recessions (Faulkner & Russell, 2001). There is also the tricky question of ensuring that growth management for the tourism sector supports the holistic and integrative objectives of sustainable development, which embrace economic, social, cultural and political concerns, and societal and ecological well-being. Finally, there is a suspicion that growth management policies for tourism are focused too often on the future of the tourism industry, when that is actually only one part of the much bigger picture of sustainable development.

In sum, tourism growth management is difficult because it brings together nature and human activity in contexts characterised by dialectical relations, complexity, uncertainty, underlying pressures, inequalities, trade-offs and political decisions (Farrell & Twining-Ward, 2005). These characteristics are not always fully appreciated by policy makers and academic researchers, which means that they can make their favoured policy prescriptions seem to be obvious and clear cut, when this is misleading. As a result, there is a need for new approaches to studying the management of tourism growth. These approaches would focus on diverse and dialectical connections, contextual differences, nonlinearity, underlying pressures, diverse impacts and integration. They would adopt a broad view of sustainable development and consider issues of power, politics and equity. In this context, policy prescription would emphasise integrative and adaptive approaches, with management seen as a continuous and broadly drawn process, incorporating constant review and revisions as well as wide participation and mutual learning (Farrell & Twining-Ward, 2004; McLain & Lee, 1996; Reed, 2000).

The breadth and complexity of growth management also highlights the need for interdisciplinary thinking (Coles *et al*., 2005). Both practical and theoretical work in this field needs to place tourism in, rather than abstract it from, wider social relationships, environmental processes and more holistic frameworks. There is a requirement for research to be framed within social science theory and the webs linking human society with nature, and for it to draw on interdisciplinary as well as multi-disciplinary approaches.

The chapter will now illustrate some of the complexities of decision-making about tourism growth policies in the case of the Mediterranean micro-state of Malta. Just a few key examples can be evaluated in this review, relating to three broad approaches used in tourism growth management: managing the quantity, quality and location of tourism.

Context of Resort Tourism

The Maltese islands have a land area of only 316 km^2 and a population of almost 400,000, giving it one of the highest population densities of any country. In addition to the main island of Malta, the smaller island of Gozo has an area of only 67 km^2 and it has a population of about 30,000 inhabitants (Fig. 5.1). Tourism to these islands has developed since the 1960s and by 2003 the number of tourist arrivals reached 1,126,601 (Malta Tourism Authority, 2004). The combination of the restricted physical space and large number of tourists compared to the resident population means that tourism is a major issue and concern in Maltese society.

Malta's tourism industry was largely socially constructed as a sun and sea product, and much tourism development has been concentrated in a few coastal resorts (Lockhart, 1997). One cluster is in the resorts of Sliema and St Julian's, which are near the main city of Valletta, and these combine substantial resort functions with being desirable residential towns. Here ranks of high-rise hotels and holiday apartment blocks tower over narrow residential streets that are home to middle-class residents. Further to the north is another concentration of resort facilities at Buġibba and Qawra, which form a sprawling resort town of apartments, self-catering blocks and hotels built at great speed in the 1970s and 1980s and largely unregulated by planning controls. Such resorts have been built to a high density and parts are characterised by poor-quality townscapes and inadequately maintained public spaces. Further to the northwest there is a different form of coastal tourism,

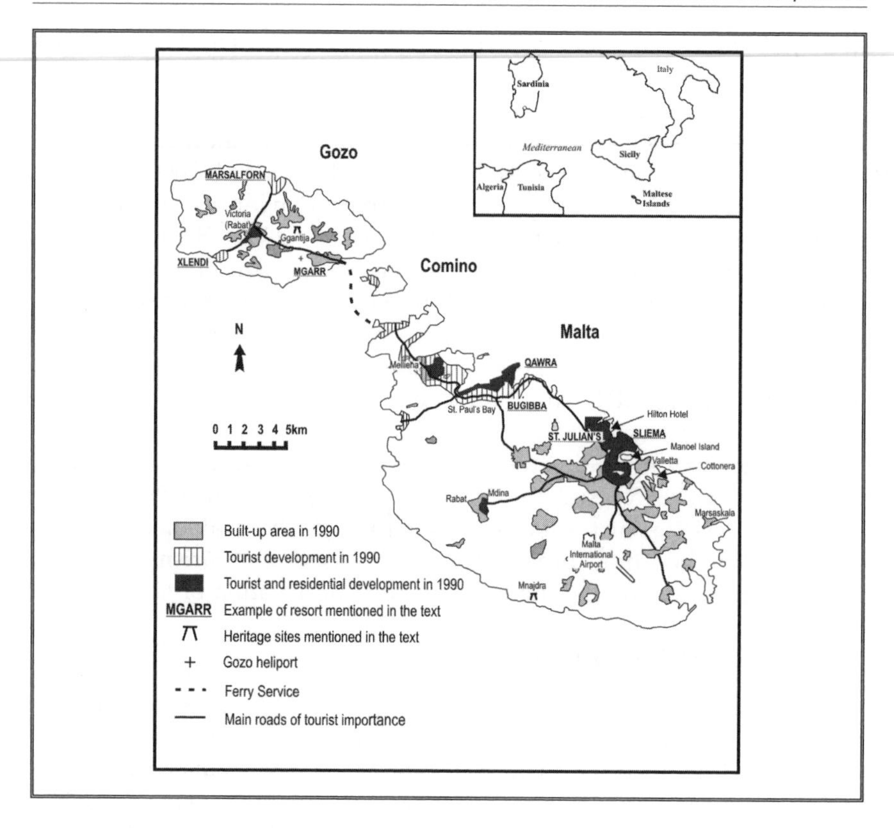

Figure 5.1 The Maltese islands

consisting of a small number of isolated, large hotels. This form of development resulted from early government policies for tourism that gave coastal land to hotel developers on 99-year leases, provided free utility services and favoured self-contained resort hotels. On the much smaller sister island of Gozo, the coastal zone has largely escaped substantial resort development, but there are small-scale exceptions, notably Marsalforn and Xlendi. These geographically uneven patterns of previous investment in the islands' resorts add to the complexity of choices about future development.

Growth management of these resorts must be considered in the context of the whole Maltese islands. The author has argued previously that 'resorts should be considered in their wider regional contexts because such contexts are usually affected by resort-related socio-economic activities in varied ways' (Bramwell, 2004b: 4). In terms of the Maltese archipelago, while some tourism impacts are contained within the resorts, many others spill across other parts of the islands.

This is influenced by the tiny size of these islands, with even the largest island of Malta being only 27.3 km long and 14.5 km wide, and by the major importance of the industry for the Maltese economy, with an estimated 27% of full-time equivalent employment stimulated by tourists' initial spending (Chapman & Cassar, 2004; Ministry of Tourism, 2001). Many of tourism's environmental pressures often also affect other parts of the islands, such as from the demand for ground water and sites for desalination plant, and from the spread of waste disposal sites. And – while perhaps overstating the case – a study of the islands' carrying capacity concluded that 'a visitor travels throughout the whole island and is not restricted to a resort. This makes the islands a country destination and not simply a resort destination' (Ministry of Tourism, 2001: 9). This assessment therefore considers growth management policies for resort tourism in the context of the whole Maltese islands.

Managing Quantity

The Ministry of Tourism in Malta has led a carrying capacity study to identify an appropriate level of future tourism development in the Maltese islands, and it endorsed the study's recommendations in 2001. The timing of the study reflected a growing awareness that, while the islands' economy depends crucially on tourism, very substantial additional development might exert unacceptable pressures on the society and environment (Bramwell, 2003a). It also coincided with a period when there were planning approvals for a rapid expansion in the stock of hotel bedrooms, and when previous growth in this stock was being blamed for many hotels experiencing reduced financial returns. The study considered the various potential benefits and costs of future tourism development. It also examined a range of growth options from 'free development' without any restrictions, to more limited development, and to an 'upmarket' scenario involving attracting 'upmarket' tourists to fill a reduced number of tourist beds (Ministry of Tourism, 2001: 6, 15). The option finally endorsed in the study was a 'limited growth' option.

The carrying capacity study illustrates the complexity of identifying tourism's potential impacts at differing future levels of development and also of deciding on trade-offs between those impacts. The assessment claimed to consider tourism's diverse sociocultural, environmental and economic impacts, with the stated intention being 'the harmonization of the overall local tourism context with national interests, whilst respecting the limitations posed by environmental, socio-cultural and economic constraints' (Ministry of Tourism, 2001: 1). It was also asserted that the study 'aims to set out the islands' tourism development strategy within a framework of sustainability' (Ministry of Tourism, 2001: 2). But it will be shown that in practice it was based on a less than extensive assessment of all potential impacts, and in deciding on trade-offs it gave much prominence to economic considerations. Thus, it is suggested that it reflected a rather restricted view of sustainable development. The carrying capacity study highlights the need to consider the complex political economy and governance issues that lie behind tourism growth management policies, and also the requirement to reflect on the full implications of these policies across diverse and variously connected economic, social and environmental domains.

One problem was that the study evaluated relatively limited information on the potential impacts of different growth scenarios (Ministry of Tourism, 1999, 2001). The range of data collected for the study was a considerable advance on that provided for earlier work on these issues, and it included surveys of residents' views and tourists' opinions of their experiences at popular locations. The study also made use of a separately produced State of the Environment Report for the Maltese islands. But, while data were collected on aspects of the attitudes of the Maltese and of tourists, and on ecology and land-use, relatively much more data were assembled on the economic importance of tourism and on the occupancy levels of hotels. Also, in the study these data were not related in detail to each of the differing tourism growth scenarios, so that selection of the preferred growth option seems not to have been based on detailed evaluations of trade-offs. In reality the data requirements for a full assessment of trade-offs between various impacts for different growth scenarios are very demanding, and this involves considerable resources.

A second difficulty was that decisions about a favoured growth option seem to have been more concerned about economic and business considerations than social and environmental impacts, but this priority in trade-offs is not always stated overtly in the study. The logic used to determine the ceiling to growth gave considerable priority to retaining economically viable occupancy rates for the islands' hotels, and seems much influenced by concerns about the oversupply of tourist accommodation and the related business difficulties of hoteliers. This might help to explain why more consideration was not given to the option of reducing tourism development, or even maintaining the existing level, and attracting fewer but higher spending tourists. The balance in the trade-offs led one participant in the group undertaking the study to complain that the proposed growth limit 'does not take into account that sustainable tourism needs to be based on longer term approaches and not focused on short term aims and driven by economic aims' (Pollacco, 2003: 294).

The carrying capacity study also highlights how growth management can be influenced in complex ways by issues of power and governance. This study was commissioned, steered and endorsed by the Ministry of

Tourism and it was developed by a small group of actors largely made up of tourism industry professionals. In effect it was a classic corporatist arrangement between government and tourist industry representatives. Thus, only a very restricted group of actors debated the trade-offs involved with the competing growth scenarios, with no representatives from, for instance, community or environmental interest groups. Given tourism's importance in Malta, it can be argued that there ought to have been a national debate and wide consultation about the various scenarios and also about tourism's future importance relative to other economic activities and uses of scarce resources. While overall growth management frameworks are potentially very helpful for the objectives of sustainability, they may be rather intangible and abstract for people to comprehend and take a great interest in. The general public and some interest groups, such as environmental groups, are more likely to become actively engaged in debates about the trade-offs involved in specific, individual development proposals.

Despite its official endorsement by the Maltese government, the study also illustrates how there can be major doubts about the implementation of growth policies. Since the assessment's endorsement in 2001, one cannot point to a single specific decision to restrict or halt tourism construction that was due to this policy framework. It may end up largely as a paper exercise and some might argue it serves simply to obscure the lack of real action. Since the study was developed, tourist arrivals have fallen behind expectations and there has been an over-supply of tourist accommodation, but the government's past record suggests that in future it may well regain its enthusiastic support for new tourist accommodation construction, especially if tourist demand picks up again. This is because the government puts a very high priority on tourism's economic importance for Malta's economy, and because of the continued potential of such development to create jobs. The government also focuses on the volume of tourists as a symbol of the nation's economic strength and its own success, and it considers that this volume influences their electoral support from the public. And no doubt Maltese investors and developers will continue to exert considerable pressure on politicians and the planning system for further tourism-related property development. Yet limiting the quantity of tourism would clearly seem to be a fundamental prerequisite of sustainable development in the Maltese islands.

Managing Quality

Growth management often involves selecting certain types of tourism, and this selection is fraught with complexity. Malta illustrates how it is not at all easy to determine the relative merits of developing different tourism products and combinations of such products. The islands' tourism industry relied in the past on a fairly low-cost beach tourism product, but since 1989 the official policy has been to encourage higher-quality development. This is to retain competitiveness when the islands cannot easily compete on price, to secure an improved image for the islands, and to respond to rising tourist expectations. It does appear to be very sensible to seek a greater yield from each tourist in order to secure more economic returns from fewer tourists, especially because of the islands' limited resources, including its restricted space for development. Yet investment in 'higher-quality' products does not necessarily always provide a better development path than low-cost beach tourism. 'Quality tourism' is sometimes thought to be beneficial due to assumptions that can be taken to be self-evident rather than propositions to be demonstrated through careful assessment. Instead, there is a need to identify for specific circumstances the sociocultural, environmental and economic impacts and related benefits and costs of both cheaper coastal resort tourism and 'quality tourism', and to undertake a detailed evaluation of the balance of costs and benefits between them, including the opportunity costs. These requirements are indicated by some commentators who have questioned the merits of Malta developing certain products that cater for higher-spending tourists.

One trend in Malta's tourism development since the early 1990s has been the building of new, large-scale up-market tourist facilities, such as five-star hotels, luxury apartment complexes and marinas, and proposals to build golf courses. Thus, from 1988 government policy has been to approve new hotels only of 4- or 5-star quality (Cleverdon, 2000; Horwath & Horwath, 1989). This restriction has applied in the resorts and elsewhere, but there has also been a strong policy preference for new hotel construction to be located within existing resort areas, and the result has been a substantial increase in bedrooms in higher-quality hotels (Planning Authority, 2000). Also, large marinas have been completed or are under construction at the Hilton hotel (in the resort of Sliema), Manoel Island (between Sliema and the capital city of Valletta) and Cottonera (a historic harbour area opposite Valletta) (Malta Environment and Planning Authority, 2002a; Planning Authority, 2000). Malta's planning authority has considered detailed Environmental Impact Assessments for new golf course proposals, and it has stated that perhaps two new golf courses may be required 'in order to sustain growth of the dedicated golfer package market segments' (Planning Authority, 2000: 46; Markwick, 2000).

In the case of the large, high-quality hotels, their construction has encouraged increased tourist expenditures, an expansion in lucrative business and conference tourism, and helped to improve Malta's image as a tourist destination. But Ioannides and Holcomb (2001, 2003) contend that this type of hotel has had some adverse environmental consequences for Malta. This is because many are sited in prominent coastal locations, and they consume relatively more energy, due to facilities such as central heating and air conditioning, along with more water, due, for example, to their larger baths, more swimming pools and more frequent linen changes. To this could be added the problem that, while most of Malta's hotels are owned by Maltese, the increased representation of large, high-quality hotels has reduced the opportunities for smaller-scale Maltese investors and many of the large new hotels have management contracts with international hotel groups.

It can also be contended that for a small island where space is at a premium it would be much better to concentrate on upgrading existing hotels rather than building new ones on virgin sites. Building new hotels on undeveloped sites reduces the open land area and fails to reduce the number of lower-quality hotel bedrooms. But the upgrading of existing hotels saves valuable land and, if carefully controlled, can reduce the surplus of lower-quality bedrooms while also not adding to the total bed stock.

There has been much controversy about the proposed development of golf courses in Malta. In the case of a proposed golf course on farmland at Rabat, the arguments made in support were largely economic, related to new jobs and increased financial returns, together with a reduction in the tourism industry's seasonality. By contrast, there was much criticism of the scheme from diverse interest groups in relation to environmental and social issues. It was contended that the project would use up a substantial land area, damage the area's landscape qualities, require substantial amounts of water for irrigation purposes, and threaten the quality of groundwater due to the use of fertilisers and pesticides. This upmarket project was also criticised for undermining the livelihoods and ways of life of traditional farmers (Bramwell, 2003b; Markwick, 2000).

Many would argue that the construction of numerous large, upmarket tourism projects – luxury hotels, marinas and golf courses – is likely to be a highly unsustainable use of Malta's scarce resources, especially when resources in this small island are much scarcer than in many competitor destinations and when the resources might be used in much better ways. There is an increasing feeling among the Maltese that these luxury projects are using up scarce national resources. Boissevain and Theuma (1998: 99) argued in the late 1990s that 'Recent public protest about threats to Malta's environment have *all* concerned new projects aimed at attracting up-market tourists'.

Malta's government also wants to promote tourism related to the islands' rich heritage and cultural resources, again in part because this is expected to attract higher-spending tourists. Many layers of history and cultural influences have given the islands an unusually rich heritage, including the ancient temples of Mnajdra and Ggantija, and the city of Valletta built in the 16th century by the Knights of St John, which are all World Heritage Sites. Heritage tourism offers many important potential advantages for Malta but it must not be assumed that necessarily it will always offer a better alternative to coastal resort tourism. The positive and negative features of both forms of tourism need careful evaluation and comparison.

Among the potential benefits of heritage and cultural tourism are that it would help to promote 'quality tourism' and reduce the tourism industry's seasonality. And it might relieve pressure on congested resorts, provide income to defray some of the costs of restoring and maintaining the cultural sites, aid the regeneration of some older urban districts and promote an appreciation of heritage among the Maltese (Chapman & Cassar, 2004; Markwick, 1999). These are very convincing arguments. But Ashworth and Tunbridge (2005a,b) warn against an unthinking adoption of this specific product strategy in Malta. They note that the heritage sites are geographically scattered so that these tourists are likely to travel further, and this might lead to increased road congestion, more air pollution and a bigger tourist presence in inland communities. Already there have been problems for residents of the inland medieval walled town of Mdina because of the volume of tourists (Boissevain, 1996). It is also suggested that heritage tourists can be less loyal to a destination compared with other types of tourists. Consequently, Malta would need to reach those tourists using new channels, which will be difficult for the country as currently it is highly dependent on foreign tour operators. They argue that within this context, there would be a need for new organisations with adequate funding and expertise to manage the heritage sites and the shifts in tourist activities, and the islands have limited resources to achieve that.

Ashworth and Tunbridge (2005a) perhaps underestimated the need for Malta to develop higher-yield tourism in the context of intense global competition for low-cost tourism, Malta's rising living standards and wage levels, and the islands' very scarce resources. Moreover, Malta has very notable and underused resources for heritage tourism, including the capital city of Valletta and nearby 'Three Cities', which have many old buildings that currently are not used or are run-down and that are in a dramatic harbour setting. But it is the case that in practice there have been real problems in implementing policies for heritage and cultural tourism in Malta as it is difficult to gain short-term economic returns from restoring and upgrading heritage sites and this sector requires substantial public sector investment. Further, it may be that 'heritage tourism by its nature is more deeply embedded in other aspects of government policy than is the more spatially and functionally encapsulated, often enclave, resort tourism' (Ashworth & Tunbridge, 2005b: 31).

Consequently, the development of Malta's heritage tourism may well require effective co-ordination, leadership and investment from well funded government bodies, but as already mentioned, there is a shortage of funding for such activities in this small island state. These difficulties help to explain why Malta has been much less successful developing tourism based on heritage than it has in promoting large-scale, upmarket tourism projects. While the latter provide clear opportunities for developers and investors to make profits, the former may be much better suited to the country's circumstances.

Another complex issue relates to how an expansion of Malta's heritage and cultural tourist activities might relate to its existing, dominant beach tourism. This illustrates the importance of considering the mix of tourism types and their connections within growth strategies. In the case of Malta, Ashworth and Tunbridge (2005a) outline three possible options along a broad spectrum. One is to regard heritage tourism as an 'add-on' to Malta's more traditional tourism, with it being an extra reason for tourists to visit. Another is to develop heritage tourism as a separate type of holiday, which is separate but parallel to the development of beach tourism. And, finally, heritage tourism could be seen as a replacement or substitute for beach tourism. The last option might not promote sustainability in the short or medium term, as it could possibly write off much of the capital invested in tourist accommodation in the resorts. In this context, Briguglio and Briguglio (1996: 174) are inclined to the view 'that, at least in the Maltese Islands, alternative forms to mass tourism are attractive only if they supplement traditional tourism and if they enhance the potential of the island as a tourist resort'.

Managing Location

The complexity of tourism growth management is increased by the need to consider the diverse local contexts found at different spatial scales in destinations, and also the varied and dialectical connections and interactions between these locations and scales. The multiscalar implications of tourism growth management decisions need careful consideration. In the Maltese islands these multiscalar implications are affected by, for example, variations between the coastal resorts and the inland areas, and also between the main island (Malta) and its smaller sister island, Gozo (Fig. 5.1.).

In the case of the inland areas, quite substantial parts have been protected from intensive tourism development by Structure Plan zoning. Although large areas are not protected in this way, this zoning has tended to concentrate tourist facilities in the resorts. The concentration of tourism in resorts has the notable potential advantages of reducing impacts on the countryside, making efficient use of resort infrastructure and facilities, and providing tourists with the convenience of compact centres. At the same time it has been argued that within some resorts 'there is a threat of further concentration of activity in areas which may have reached or are close to reaching saturation' (Planning Authority, 2000: 38). In some resort areas, such as Sliema, St Julian's, Qawra and Buġibba, there are acute problems, such as traffic congestion, lack of parking, poor environmental quality and noise pollution. But Malta's Planning Authority (2000: 58) suggests that very occasionally small-scale accommodation development might be permitted in the rural interior if it would promote rural tourism 'whose main purpose is to experience the rural environment and its resources'. This was felt to be valuable as it could assist in rural development, including the reuse of farmhouses and hamlets that have been abandoned, although it was recognised that 'the size of the Islands may not allow an extensive development of various forms of rural tourism' (Planning Authority, 2000: 58; Malta Environment and Planning Authority, 2002b). Yet it should be recognised that this might well add new pressures in the countryside, such as from the tourist presence and rising property prices.

Tourism growth management must also consider the distinctive characteristics of the smaller island of Gozo, which is separated from Malta by 6 km of sea and is only roughly one-third its size. Compared to the main island, it is much less built-up and notably quieter and more rural. Its tourism industry is much smaller, much of the coast is undeveloped, and the resorts (of Marsalforn, Xlendi and Mgarr) are generally much smaller and fairly low-rise. Tourist nights on Gozo are approximately only 5% of nights in the whole Maltese islands, although Gozo attracts an estimated 850,000 day visitors annually from the main island (Gozo Tourism Association, 2000).

Many Gozitan residents want further tourism development in Gozo because the island's double insularity means it has far more limited employment opportunities compared to the main island. These residents often also consider they have been left behind and somewhat neglected in terms of economic development and political assistance compared to the main island. But opinions differ greatly about the forms in which Gozo's future development should take. Some have advocated the construction of a few large-scale, luxury tourism developments because that would attract higher-spending tourists. Among the more recent proposals has been a golf course, a yacht marina, a 250-bedroom hotel in an old fort and a holiday village combined with a marina. There has also been growing pressure to construct a runway for small aircraft to land so as to improve access to the island.

In contrast, others have strongly opposed large-scale, tourism-related projects on Gozo, even if they do help to attract higher-spending tourists. An election candidate for Alternattiva Demokratica, the Green Party, argued: 'large projects such as golf courses should be discarded since they do not address the needs of Gozitans ... These projects – which are irreversible – endanger the environment, the sea coast and the historical treasures of Gozo' (Anon, 2003). Many people consider that large-scale developments would spoil Gozo's relatively pristine environment. Indeed, many commentators have expressed similar sentiments to Schembri (1994: 50), who has asserted that Gozo's 'main attraction lies in its rural character, typical of the Maltese Islands before the advent of mass tourism'. Many Maltese, including many Gozitans, and also many tourists, consider Gozo's peaceful and relatively undeveloped nature to be among its most valuable features. As the Chairman of Alternattiva Demokratica claimed: 'There will be no mystique and no value added if Gozo is allowed to become a smaller, poorer and uglier clone of Malta' (Vassallo, 2003). Such sentiments have led many to call for further tourism development to be restricted to small-scale initiatives that draw on Gozo's distinctive features, especially through rural, heritage, religious, diving and agro-tourism. Such initiatives might attract higher-spending tourists while also allowing for more economic benefits to be retained by Gozitans.

Conclusion

It is often helpful to consider growth management of coastal resorts in their regional context due to the spatial spread of resort impacts. In the case of small islands, the implications of resort dynamics often extend island-wide, and for the Maltese islands there are implications for all the islands in this small nation state. Resort growth management must also be understood in relation to the interplay between local and global processes and trends.

This chapter has examined aspects of the complexity of tourism growth management and also of developing and applying relevant practical policies. It was argued that there is a need to appreciate the full relational complexity of society. Not only are there multiple elements in social and natural systems, but the interactions between them are dialectical and rich, they occur at different spatial scales, and they involve varied positive and negative feedback relationships. Related to these features, there are many complications for tourism growth management, and just a few of these were explored briefly for the specific case of Malta. It has been shown, for instance, how in Malta debates about growth management were influenced by issues of power and governance, and how they had implications across diverse social, economic, environmental and political domains. These elements were connected in complex, dialectical ways, and the connections were fluid and emerging. It was also shown how there were dynamic relations and tensions between differing types of tourism, between these tourism types and the overall volume of tourism, and between tourism development in different adjacent or nearby local contexts.

Unfortunately, work on tourism growth management can be rather reductionist, dissecting complex patterns into their component parts, which are then considered in isolation. Yet these elements cannot be understood as additive components that are isolated from their inter-relationships (Faulkner & Russell, 2001). There is a need for holistic and integrative perspectives that consider the reciprocal, dialectical relations between elements. These more holistic frameworks must also break out of tourism-centric thinking, and in particular this should include focusing on sustainable development as a whole rather than on maintaining tourism.

The case of Malta also illustrates how assessments of tourism's impacts and of tourism growth policies require a great deal of information across broad fields, such as economics, environment, society and politics. Such assessments involve combining concerns about material practices together with issues of environmental change and of equity and social justice. In that context, there is a need to take the duality of social and environmental change seriously, so that these are seen as relational categories rather than mutually exclusive processes (Bramwell & Lane, 2005; Harvey, 1996). Decisions about tourism growth involve making trade-offs that have varied political, sociocultural, economic and environmental implications. Our understanding of these trade-offs will be substantially improved by overcoming the academic division of labour that can seek to restrict tourism within a narrow disciplinary boundary (Johnston, 1983). We need to allow, for example, for a better understanding of the integration of natural and social systems (Farrell & Twining-Ward, 2004). We also require a better appreciation of the relations between entities and processes, such as between economic pressures, power relations, the processes of governance and the distributional outcomes. Thus, research in this field could benefit greatly from the use of critical perspectives, based on approaches such as political economy, together with empathetic consideration of the agency and viewpoints of individuals. Clearly the issues to be examined are wide ranging and entail incorporating many different disciplines simultaneously. Therefore there is a need for a more interdisciplinary approach and also more multidisciplinary working.

It was also argued that the diversity and nonlinearity of tourism's impacts often make it very difficult to predict the outcomes of tourism growth strategies. In addition, changes that affect tourism's impacts can originate from external and unexpected sources, such as from broad global pressures and trends. These are good reasons why the planning and management of growth should be seen as a continuous process of monitoring, learning, building collective awareness and capability, and of adaptation (Faulkner, 2002). And many would emphasise the importance of consultation and collaboration in these processes in order to widen participation and to incorporate a range of knowledge and views.

Chapter 6

Planning for Sustainable Development in Spanish Coastal Resorts

GERDA PRIESTLEY and JOAN CARLES LLURDÉS

Introduction

Spain has 8000 km of coastline, divided in two sections: the Northern stretch washed by the Bay of Biscay and Atlantic waters and the more extensive Eastern Mediterranean shores. To these must be added the two island archipelagoes: the Balearic and Canary Islands (Fig. 6.1). Over a period of some 50 years – coinciding approximately with the second half of the 20th century – these once deserted shores have become one of the most densely developed tourist destinations in the world. Although it is not the main objective of this chapter to trace the evolution of this development, the initial section of the chapter deals with this topic in order to establish a base for discussion. It explains how the coast was gradually built up, the limits of growth in terms of extension and capacity, and the source of demand that has been a significant determinant in the form of development in which second homes constitute a major component. For detailed analysis of the process, refer, for example, to Pearce and Priestley (1998), Barke *et al*. (1996) and, for statistics, to Ministerio de Economía (2004).

Most of the chapter, however, focuses on those aspects of coastal tourism development that are significant in assessing its present and future sustainability. Hence, attention is drawn first to the context in which tourism has developed in Spain, as this is fundamental to the understanding of tourism policy and planning. It will become evident that the emergence of measures that have contributed directly or indirectly to the improvement of the structural base of Spanish tourism and to the incorporation of sustainable practices came as late as the1990s. These include European, national, Autonomous Community and even municipal initiatives. Specific cases, embracing different territorial scales, are examined in detail, including the Andalusian coast, the Northern coastline and the municipalities of Calvià and Benidorm. The degree of success of legislative measures and planning mechanisms and

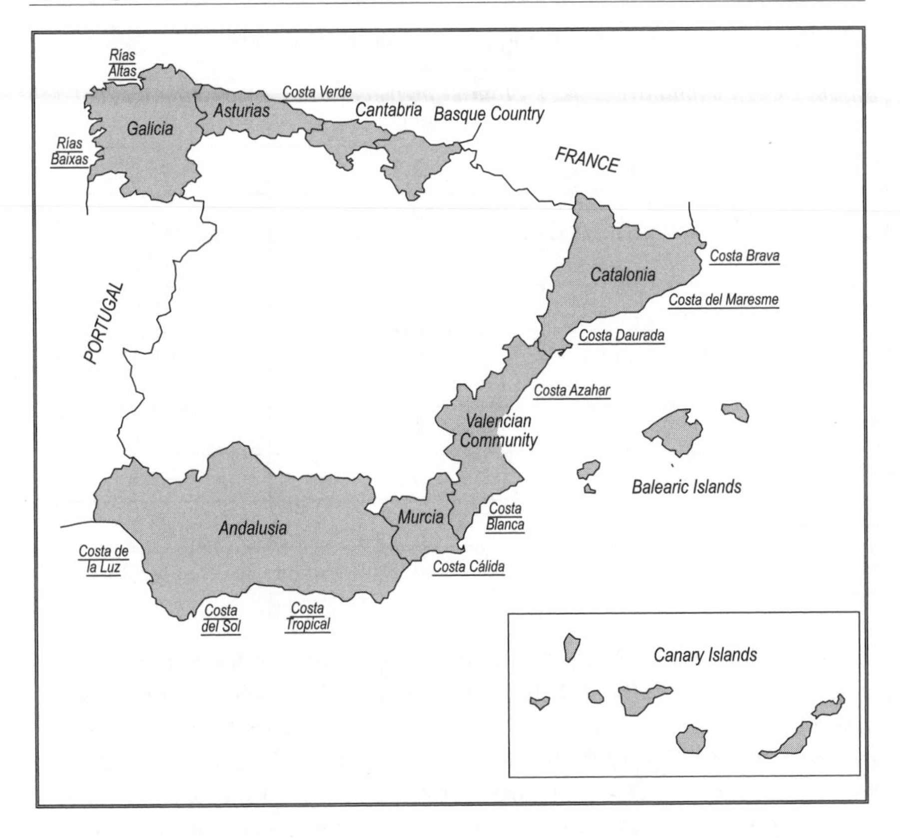

Figure 6.1 Coastal Autonomous Communities and main coasts in Spain

instruments is evaluated. The chapter concludes with the authors' assessment of the sustainability of Spanish coastal tourism in the future.

The Evolution of Spanish Coastal Tourism

Before the sun-lust era, holidaymakers preferred the cooler coasts and attractive landscapes of Northern Spain, staying mainly in cities such as San Sebastian and Santander. However, there is no doubt that the Spanish Mediterranean coast and island archipelagoes can be considered nowadays the paradigm of coastal mass tourism resort development, for over 85% of tourism demand is concentrated there (Table 6.1). Growth dates from the mid-1950s, but already, as early as 1980, Butler (1980) identified symptoms of overdevelopment in some regions and destinations. Certainly the trend has not changed since then, so that, by 2004, 34% of the first kilometre on the Mediterranean coastline had been built up, with densities rising to over 50% in some provinces, such as Málaga and Barcelona (Greenpeace, 2005).

Table 6.1 Tourist arrivals by Autonomous Community: 2002

Autonomous Community	*Tourist arrivals (%) 2002*	*Variation on 2001*
Catalonia	22.4	+ 15.2
Canary Islands	20.6	– 1.8
Balearic Islands	18.5	– 7.9
Andalusia	14.3	+ 2.8
Valencian Community and Murcia	10.4	+ 6.1
Cantabria	4.1	+ 18.1
Madrid	5.8	– 2.3
Other regions	3.9	+ 23.2

Source: Movimientos turísticos en fronteras (Frontur) (2004). Instituto de Estudios Turísticos (http://www.iet.tourspain.es/)

However, the type of development has by no means been uniform. It has varied both spatially and chronologically, as a result of the operation of various factors, of which local attitudes and municipal policy are key influences (Priestley, 1995a,b). In this respect, it is fundamental to understand the structure of urban planning and finance in Spain. Town planning has effectively been the responsibility of municipal authorities, through urban blue prints, *Plan de Ordenación General Urbana* (POGU), updated at rather irregular intervals. Government finance was awarded on the basis of permanent resident population (with no corrective coefficient to allow for seasonal influxes), so that, for revenues, municipalities depended, and still do, largely on construction (land sales and building permits) and housing (rates and property taxes). In the light of the operation of these factors, one can explain, for example, the existence of Benidorm, an exceptionally high-rise, high-density resort; and various ill-planned, sprawling, mass tourism resorts, such as Fuengirola, Torremolinos, Benalmádena, Salou, Lloret de Mar, Platja de Palma (encompassing the continuous sprawl of resorts East of the city of Palma from Can Pastilla to S'Arenal) and Calvià (Fig. 6.2). In all of these destinations, development occurred at an early stage of tourism growth, when a permissive attitude to construction initiatives was taken in many municipalities, so that, where investors were available, development took place on a large scale, more or less at random. No preconceived plan was designed, and no specific sites pinpointed for development. This is clearly illustrated by the differences in urban and tourism growth

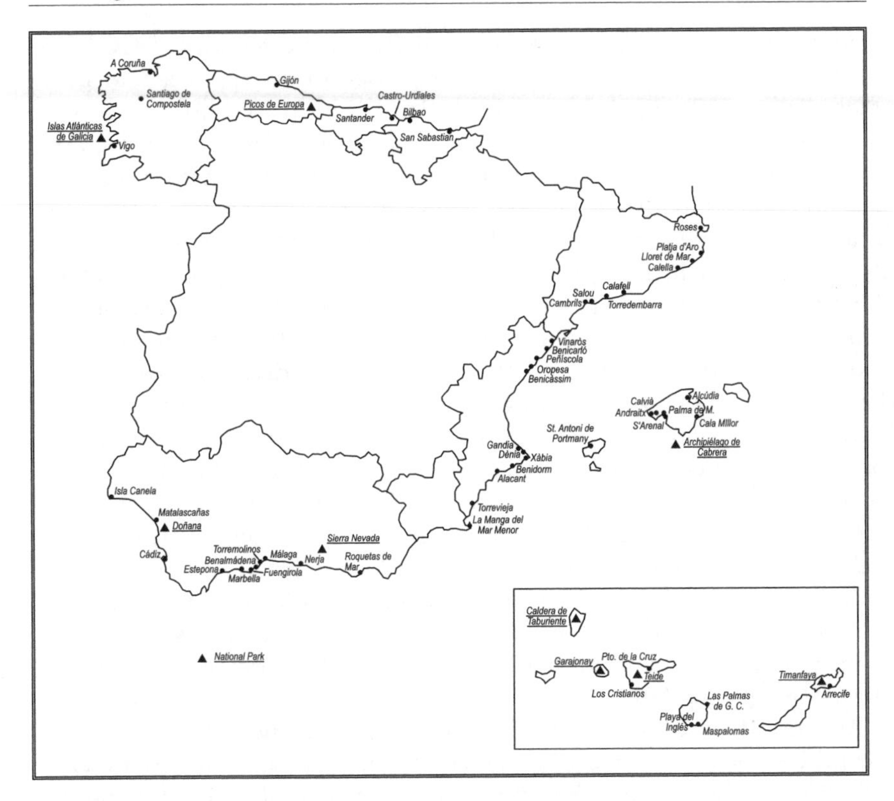

Figure 6.2 Coastal resorts and national parks near the coast

between Lloret de Mar and Tossa de Mar, on the Costa Brava, separated by only a few kilometres. Under the auspices of a local hotelier, in Lloret investment was encouraged and the town rapidly became the epitome of a mass tourism destination. In contrast, restrictive local policy safeguarded Tossa from the same fate in spite of being the first resort along this stretch of coastline to gain fame, from the filming of 'Pandora', starring Ava Gardner, in 1951 (Pearce, 1989: 61–62; Priestley, 1996; Priestley & Mundet, 1998).

Early development therefore catered for the foreign mass tourism market, based mainly on medium-sized and relatively low-quality hotels (one to three star categories) and small apartments for rent. Large, better-quality hotels were gradually added parallel to increases in prestige and demand within many major resorts, such as Lloret de Mar, Salou, Calvià, Benidorm, Benalmádena and Estepona. Even today, in regions that developed early, lower-quality hotels still dominate supply. This is particularly noteworthy on the Costa Brava where, in 2000, 41.6% of hotel beds were in the one and two star categories, 53.3% in the three star category and only 5.1% in the four and five star categories (DGCAC, 2005). Moreover, after 1970, increasing prosperity in Spain led to the emergence and flourishing of a domestic market for second homes. In some cases, this took the form of apartment blocks, either tagged onto existing resorts or in the form of ribbon development along virgin coastal sites. In others, low-density property developments, known as *urbanizaciones*, mushroomed on hillsides adjacent to the coast. The foreign market also participated in this phenomenon, attracted by the benign winter climate, sunny summers and favourable currency exchange rates. Initially, purchases were often also made for retirement homes – examples include the large number of British residents on the Costa del Sol and the Costa Blanca (King *et al.*, 1998). However, as air travel has become less expensive and supply more ubiquitous and frequent, foreigners have been able to make use of these homes as much as the local population. The Spanish Confederation of Hotels and Tourist Accommodation (CEHAT) calculated that 11.5 million tourists were lodged in unregistered accommodation in 2004 (CEHAT, 2005). In fact, with the help of ICT, many have made Spain their principal or only place of residence, while maintaining their jobs or economic interests in their country of origin. This is particularly so among the German community in Mallorca (Seguí, 2003a,b).

As a result, by 2001, 15.97% of the 3,233,127 residences in Spain were second homes, an average of 8.14/100 inhabitants (Serrano Fernández, 2003: 55). Of these, over 1.5 million were located in the Mediterranean coastal provinces, 269,000 in the Northern coastal provinces and 206,000 in the island provinces (Serrano Fernández, 2003: 67). In certain areas, the concentration of second homes is particularly high, where foreign and Spanish city-dwellers' demands coincide. For example, in 2002, the total number of residences on the Costa Brava was 197,902, of which 141,586 were classified for 'for tourist use' (DGCAC, 2005: 268–269). In 2001, these provided capacity for approximately 500,000 people, much more than the hotels, 78,451 people (DGCAC, 2005: 264), and campsites, 106,958 people (DGCAC, 2005: 262). On the Valencian Community coast, little undeveloped land remains, except for the protected areas. As a result, skyscrapers are being authorised in certain resorts, such as Cullera, providing 4500 residences in 33 blocks with a height of 25 storeys (Greenpeace, 2005: 50). In Murcia, the area around the Mar Menor lagoon, and especially the 500 m wide isthmus that separates the lagoon from the sea, accommodates 50.3% of the entire region's hotel capacity, 83.1% of registered apartment capacity and 64.5% of campsite capacity, a total of 19,500 beds (García Sánchez *et al.*, 2002). In both regions there are plans to continue constructing low-density housing inland in association with golf course development.

Trends in demand and supply

Over the half century of rapid tourism development, demand has grown incessantly, although economic benefits have not kept abreast of the number of arrivals, demonstrating that profitability has dropped over the decades (Table 6.2). Moreover, several crises of varying impact and consequence have occurred. The first of these, in the aftermath of the world petroleum crisis of 1973, led to the polarisation of mass sun, sand and sea package tourism for the foreign market, dominated by a relatively small number of tour operators, around a limited number of key resorts, which even now continue to attract the bulk of this market, notably Platja de Palma, Calvià, Lloret de Mar, Salou, Benidorm, Torremolinos, Benalmádena and Estepona. Over the following 20 years, most of these resorts gradually lost competitiveness in the international market, as evidenced by lower occupation rates, and the shortening of the season of high demand, which forced the closure of many small, poor, local hotels and encouraged huge price reductions in many others. A number of factors are responsible for this situation. In the first place, the initial crisis and, later, market concentration (sometimes approaching what was effectively a monopoly) made some hotels vulnerable to ruthless tour operators. As a result, profit margins dropped so much that renovation and refurbishing was not carried out. Hence, by the beginning of the 1990s, many resorts were suffering saturation and decline symptoms in the sun, sea and sand product and structural defects in the entire product had been detected (MCT, 1994). In fact, a second major crisis hit Spanish tourism at the end of the decade of the 80s, when visitor arrivals declined by almost 4%, the average length of stay fell by 10%, average expenditure per visitor dropped 15%, foreign bed-nights declined by 40% (Curtis, 1997: 82) and Spain lost 2.9% of the European sun, sea and sand market. It then became obvious that corrective measures were long overdue.

Meanwhile, tourist motivations had also changed, in line with postmodern trends, and the Spanish market was no exception. Cultural tourism, mainly in the form of short breaks to cities (notably Madrid and Barcelona), has increased significantly since 1990. Likewise, rural tourism has developed over the last 20 years, but to date represents only 1.9% of the total accommodation supply and 1.2% of demand, of which 84% is domestic (INE, 2005). Nevertheless, some form of the sun/coast product is still a key element of Spanish tourism, generating the bulk of demand. In fact, this sector generates 75% of the hotel business on the coast (Greenpeace, 2005: 9), albeit with the incorporation of diversifying elements, which have contributed to a reduction of seasonal imbalances. Of these the most important is undoubtedly golf, and the marked concentration of golf courses close to the Mediterranean coast and on the

Table 6.2 Number of visitors and tourists: 1994–2004

Year	*Visitors (millions)*	*Tourists (millions)*
1995	54.4	34.9
1996	57.3	36.7
1997	62.4	39.6
1998	67.8	43.4
1999	72.1	46.8
2000	74.5	47.9
2001	75.7	50.1
2002	80.0	52.4
2003	81.9	51.8
2004	85.7	53.6

Source: Movimientos turísticos en fronteras (Frontur) (2004). Instituto de Estudios Turísticos (http://www.iet.tourspain.es/)

island archipelagoes clearly demonstrates the relation of this product to coastal tourism (Fig. 6.3), although the concentration of courses on the Costa del Sol is greatest, capturing over half the total demand (Ortega Martínez, 2003: 19). The economic impact of golf tourism is considerable, generating just over half a million international visitors but as much as 3% of tourist income, as daily expenditure is four times that of an average sun, sea and sand tourist. To this must be added the multiplier effect and additional income generated as a result of property development, for a large proportion of foreign golfers own second homes in Spain (www.golfresidencial.com). Nevertheless, in many circles – ecological activists, local citizen associations, politicians in certain regions – the product is highly criticised on account of its water consumption and the property speculation it incites.

Other diversifying elements include nautical tourism, pinpointed in 1996 as a priority for support from the national government as a means to diversify the product base and reduce seasonality (TURESPAÑA, 1998). Certainly, there are a large number of marinas dotted mainly along the Mediterranean and Balearic Island coasts and the number of registered boats for leisure purposes rose from 92,538 in 1990 to 275,777 in 2003 (Ministerio de Economía, 2004). In 1998 (Ferradás Carrasco, 2001: 69) there were 266 marinas, providing direct employment to 3124 people and a further 23,409 induced jobs. The income generated amounted to €1225 million, of which boat charters contributed only €54 million (Ferradás

Figure 6.3 Golf courses in coastal Autonomous Communities

Carrasco, 2001). Hence, it is apparent that the use of boats is still highly concentrated in summer and closely related to the second home phenomenon. As a result, its contribution to achieving the objectives outlined is, to date, limited.

An additional diversifying element that has been introduced is the theme park concept (Esteve Secall, 2001). Two such parks have been constructed on the Spanish coast: Port Aventura at Salou, inaugurated in 1995, and Terra Mítica at Benidorm, which opened in 2001. The former has had some positive repercussions on demand and seasonality at Salou and other resorts nearby, for half of the 3 million annual visitors to the park stay overnight in the area (Esteve Secall, 2001), constituting about half of the total number of visitors (IDESCAT, 2005). The latter has been less successful and is, in fact, in financial difficulties, as it has registered a negative profit balance in recent years. Hence their role in rejuvenation of resorts should not be overestimated.

The contribution of tourism to the GNP rose to 10% for the first time in 1994, and had reached 12.1% by 2000 (http://www.iet.tourspain.es). However a crisis was identified in the tourism sector in 2001 when its contribution to the GNP began to fall (to 11.4% in 2003). The areas that suffered most were the mass tourism resorts, in particular the Canary Islands, the Valencian Community and in the Balearic Islands, where the number of visitor arrivals fell from 11 to 8 million (Govern de les Illes Balears, 2002–2005). Moreover, average tourist expenditure also dropped. Visitor numbers showed signs of recovery in 2004, recovering a 12.1% share of the GNP and providing 10% of all employment, although caution must be shown when interpreting statistics as income from tourism decreased by 2.8% in real terms in the same year (Díaz-Varela, 2004).

The upward trend continued in 2005, when tourist arrivals increased by 5.7% in the first six months (surpassing 24 million), mainly due to the recovery of the French and German markets (Díaz-Varela, 2004). Nevertheless, the net result is a current situation of oversupply and falling profit margins. The CEHAT calculated that 70% of the hotels suffered a drop of between 15% and 30% in profit margins between 2001 and 2004. Even so, new hotels have continued to open in recent years. The Valencian Tourist Office (*Agencia Valenciana de Turisme*) registered a 30.4% increase in hotel accommodation between 1997 and 2004. The unstoppable trend towards the acquisition of second homes by both Spaniards and foreigners also has had negative repercussions. In fact, 13% of foreign tourists own their own home in Spain. The proliferation of these private residences not only constitutes a negative impact on the environment but also jeopardises the economic benefits from tourism in the long-term. A clear indication of this is the fact that 62.35% of foreign tourists stayed in hotels in 2003, as compared with 70.53% in 1997, while 18.89% stayed in 'free' housing in 2003, a rise from the 1997 figure of 13.19% (Brunet Estarellas *et al*., 2005). In light of these trends, tourism demand has obviously been market driven, and supply provision by the private sector has tried to keep abreast of, or anticipate – sometimes intuitively – this demand. The introduction of significant top-down planning instruments has certainly been tardy. The following section examines the various tourism planning measures and their impact.

Tourism Planning in Spain

The context in which tourism has developed in Spain is fundamental to the understanding of tourism policy and planning (see Newton, 1996; Pearce, 1997 for details of public administration structure; Datzira-Masip, 1997 for details of tourism policy). In the aftermath of the devastation caused by the Civil War (1936–1939), Spain was politically ostracised and economically de-structured. Revenue was necessary for economic recovery based on rapid reindustrialisation and urban expansion. Land-use and town planning were therefore never a priority in the Franco era: an early law of 1956 (*Ley Régimen del Suelo y Ordenación Urbana*) was followed by another in 1963, which subordinated planning to tourism-related interests (*Ley de Centros o Zonas de Interés Turístico Nacional*). Hence there was little imposition of restrictions to development on a coastline which, until then, had mainly been home to the under-privileged fishing sector. Moreover, only rather rudimentary planning instruments existed. Urban planning was, and still remains, a municipal responsibility. Thus, much of the construction that took place in the early years was undertaken without valid permits, and successive revisions of municipal blueprints (POGU) tended to accept the status quo by legalising all existing buildings. In essence, a *laissez-faire* policy was adopted with regard to development. This situation was further aggravated by the fact that, by and large, for several decades revenues were not reinvested in infrastructure and service provision in the coastal resorts, where government subsidies were based on the permanent population, making no allowance for the needs of the huge influx of summer residents.

With the widespread acquisition of private homes on the coast by both domestic and foreign buyers, emphasis was placed on construction, to such an extent that at present, 9.5% of the GNP and 13.4% of employment is generated by this sector, as compared with 12.1% and 10% respectively by tourism (Ministerio de Economía, 2004). While not all construction has taken place on the coast and not all of it is tourism related, this sector indirectly adds considerably to Spain's economic dependence on tourism. By 1980, the Spanish tourism industry had become sensitive to competition from other destinations and to world and especially European economic trends. As a result, in the ensuing decades, the sector suffered successive fluctuations and crises. At the same time, or perhaps partly as a consequence, awareness of the concept of sustainability increased and numerous initiatives and measures were introduced in an attempt to stabilise the industry and achieve its long-term viability. Much has been written about the three pillars – economic, environmental and sociocultural – of sustainability, so no further discussion will be added here (consult, for example, Coccossis, 1996; Eidsvik, 1995; Hall, 2000; Hall & Lew, 1998; Stabler, 1997). In the case of Spain, however, it must be remembered that a network of resorts had already been laid down and that much of the coast had already been occupied prior to any attempt to apply the concept of sustainability to tourism development.

With regard to sociocultural sustainability, no significant conflicts arose at any time, as the local culture was essentially Western European.

In the early days, tourism was therefore seen as an opportunity to widen horizons and achieve integration in European society. The obvious benefits of employment opportunities and rising standards of living have been mitigated by inflation and rising property values, but few people consider the balance anything but positive. This is not the case with environmental aspects, where negative impacts on the coast make sustainability difficult. Two different categories of problems exist: (1) those arising in large, high-density resorts; and (2) those related to the ribbon development of lower-density private residences.

However, in the case of a mature destination, perhaps the most important issue is the economic sustainability of the sector, because, without economic viability, there is neither the money for, and interest in, investing in the environment, nor sociocultural acceptance and satisfaction. Nevertheless, nowadays both public administrations and the private sector are, by and large, aware of the need to apply sustainable criteria and good management practices, although this is not always supply driven, but rather is a response to tourist demands and the fear of losing competitive advantages. The trend to continue developing is well illustrated by the case of the Andalusian coast, where, in addition to several long-established mass tourism resorts, demand for private property is very high.

Case study: Construction on the Andalusian Coast

The situation on the Andalusian coast is paradigmatic. In all, 59% of the coastline is built up, reaching a maximum in Fuengirola, Torremolinos and Marbella, where 100%, of available land in the entire municipality is already occupied in the first two municipalities, and 95% in the last, including 20,000 residences without valid construction permits (Greenpeace, 2005: 20). As the coastal fringe is occupied, development has spread inland. The new POGU for Mijas, extending inland west and North of Fuengirola, plans for 23,000 new residences, and an extension further inland to Alhaurín de la Torre will result in the development of a town of 50,000 inhabitants and three golf courses. On the Costa del Sol, 29 hotels are currently being constructed, adding 2681 beds to the 90,000 that already exist, in spite of the fact that occupation rates fell to 69.39%, the lowest level since 2000. The Strategic Plan for a 92-km stretch on the western part of the Costa del Sol, published early in 2005, proposed the construction of new marinas providing 4000 new moorings, to increase the supply to an average of one marina every 13 km (Greenpeace, 2005: 20).

The Andalusian Atlantic shores are less developed, partly because of lower connectivity levels, and partly because the National Park of Doñana occupies a considerable area. However, this has not impeded the development of Matalascañas, a large, mainly second home resort on the edge of the park, which has been greatly criticised for possible contamination of the aquifer of the park's wetlands. The construction trend is fast encroaching upon other natural areas, such as the Playa de Isla Canela, a dune and lagoon area at the mouth of the River Guadiana on the Portuguese border. Construction commenced in 1991, at a distance of 20 m from high-water level, in spite of planning regulations that stipulate that habitable buildings must be least 100 m from the high-water mark, occupying and destroying natural dunes. Flooding in the winter of 1995–96 led to the construction of a protective wall with the subsequent erosion of the natural beach. Despite declaration of the illegality of the development in 1999, construction has continued and additional property developments are planned in the area (Greenpeace, 2005: 24).

This example is indicative of the influence that local government authorities have on land occupation for construction purposes. However, the national and 17 regional governments do have the power to influence – and in some respects to control – development. In fact, for many decades, some valuable landscapes have been protected from all encroachment by buildings. However, the most significant measures designed specifically for the tourism sector were not introduced until after 1990. These issues will be examined in the section that follows.

Initiatives Designed to Increase Sustainability

The 1990s saw the emergence of various measures that have contributed directly or indirectly to the improvement of the structural base of Spanish tourism and to the incorporation of sustainable practices. These include European, national, Autonomous Community and even municipal initiatives. However, some legislative measures were the forerunners of a variety of plans and instruments. For example, the National Park network was established in 1918 when two areas were designated as parks. There are now 13, of which 9 are on or near the coast (Fig. 6.2), but a network of other protected areas has also been established (Troitiño Vinuesa *et al.*, 2005). Current legislation, dating from 1989 (*Ley 4/89*), laid the foundation for the planning and management of natural resources (PORN) and classifies protected areas in four categories: (1) parks (national and nature parks); (2) nature reserves; (3) natural monuments; and (4) protected landscapes. The Autonomous Communities can also designate regional parks and other protected areas. Although some of these different types of parks are located on the coast, much more significant for the safeguarding of the coast was the Coastal Law of 1988 (*Ley 28/1988 de Costas*), which guaranteed the protection of unspoiled areas and fragile ecosystems.

It was not, however, until 1992, in the aftermath of the serious crisis in the tourism sector in 1988 and 1989 (González & Moral, 1996) that the Spanish Government produced a 'White Paper' on Tourism in 1990 (SGT, 1990), and subsequently introduced a comprehensive plan aiming to restructure and modernise the tourism sector, providing considerable financial support for far-reaching measures. This first *Plan Marco de Competitividad del Turismo Español*, also known as *Plan Futures*, covered the four-year period from 1992 to 1995 and was renewed with some modifications for a second period (Aranzadi, 1992; Brunet Estarellas *et al.*, 2005; Datzira-Masip, 1997; MCT, 1994; Pearce, 1997). Its main goal was to maximise societal well-being and, in line with the concept of sustainability, included social, economic and environmental goals. Its specific overall objective was to increase competitiveness, mainly through modernisation, professional training of human resources, the development of new products and quality improvement.

The instruments used at the local level were 'excellence' plans (*Plan de Excelencia Turística*, PET), applied mainly for improvement and balancing of mature coastal resorts and, 'dynamising' plans (*Plan de Dinamización Turística*, PDT) for diversification mainly in less developed heritage sites. Plans were funded jointly at national, regional, municipal levels and, in some cases, private sources. In 1992, Calvià was chosen as a pilot PET, and between 1993 and 1997, a total of 25 PET were initiated, including Gandía, La Manga, Torremolinos, Valle de la Orotava (Tenerife), Benalmádena, Peñíscola, Gran Canaria Sur and Roquetas de Mar, all major, mature destinations. (A further 28 were carried out between 1998 and 2002. See Brunet Estarellas *et al.*, 2005: 39–40 for a complete list, classified by type and location.) Nevertheless, in the first four-year period (1992–1995), of a total government investment of 95,582 million pesetas (approximately €573.5 million), most funding was targeted at promotion (62.5%), followed by modernisation (25%).

A new, but essentially similar, plan known as *Plan Integral de Calidad del Turismo Español* (PICTE) was designed to cover the 2000–2006 period (Brunet Estarellas *et al.*, 2005; Navarro de Vega, 1999). The main underlying goal was quality improvement, with ten specific objectives: quality in destinations, products, private enterprises and professional training, technological innovation, international co-operation, international expansion of enterprises, statistical information and economic analysis, promotion and support in commercialising. The principal instrument has been the establishment of quality regulations and their corresponding labels (such as the Spanish Integrated System of Tourism Quality in Destinations), to be applied on a voluntary basis, together with support for the acquisition of existing international certificates and European initiatives. Such instruments are compatible with ISO 9000 criteria, which guarantee the quality of products and services, by complying with predetermined standards. As a result, initiatives have been able to benefit from supplementary funding from EU sources. Overall, the programme marks another step forward in co-operation among the three levels of public administration: national, Autonomous Community and local, as all must agree on specific objectives, measures and their subsequent implementation. However, subsequent evaluation has cast doubts on the real tangible benefits of the initiatives (Brunet Estarellas *et al.*, 2005). Certainly, government support has made it possible for local councils to make improvements that they could not have financed otherwise, but, in many cases, the initiatives lack continuity. Moreover, it is certainly questionable whether or not the local scale can guarantee the achievement of the goals pursued.

At the same time, each Autonomous Community has been able to introduce its own initiatives, as responsibilities for tourism were transferred to them from central government after 1980 and new regional strategies were designed. The first 'White Papers' (*Libro Blanco*) on tourism were produced by the Catalan, Balearic and Valencian Governments in 1983, 1987 and 1990 respectively. The Balearic Community government has been particularly active in this respect, passing legislation on coastal protection, tourist accommodation provision, golf course development and natural parks, including the National Park of the Archipelago de Cabrera created in 1991 (*Ley 14/91 de 29 de abril*). Such measures have added up to the effective protection from development of over 60% of the entire coastline. In other cases, strategic development plans have been drawn up, such as the *Plan Insular de Ordenación del Territorio* (PIOT) for the Canary Islands, initiated in the late 1980s, the Andalusian regional plan – *Plan Integral del Turismo en Andalucía* (DIA) – in 1993, with its development strategy laid out in the *Plan Andaluz de Desarrollo Económico* (PADE) for the 1991–94 period. The first Autonomous Community to pass a Law of Tourism – to create tourism planning instruments – was the Basque Country in 1994 and all the Autonomous Communities have subsequently followed suit. The Balearic Community has been particularly active in legislating and regulating tourism development, which is understandable given the almost total dependence of the economy on the tourism sector. Early Decrees established, first, 30 m^2 (1984) and later 60 m^2 (1989) as the minimum area per new tourist bed created. Subsequently the 1995 Plan for the Organisation of the Balearic Tourism Supply – *Plan de Ordenación de la Oferta Turística* (POOT) – directly intervened in urban planning, by limiting the growth of supply, reducing building densities, improving infrastructures and services, and protecting natural areas. Further restrictions on building were introduced in 1999 by the *Directrices de Ordenación Territorial de las Islas Baleares*.

At municipal level, the Local Agenda 21 programme has been considered by the local governing authorities the most suitable in the application of sustainable development criteria and many resorts have used this instrument, usually in conjunction with a PET. Environmental management systems have also been introduced, using internationally recognised standards (especially ISO14001 and EMAS), often in conjunction with a Local Agenda 21 program (Fullana & Ayuso, 2002) as in Sitges (Campillo-Besses *et al.*, 2004). The Balearic Island administration has adapted EU regulations by decree and established its own system of environmental audits and management for tourist resorts, known as ECOTUR, and most of the major destinations have participated in the pilot study (Blázquez Salom, 2001: 44–45). The main instrument is a territorial audit, with a view to subsequently developing a Local Agenda 21 programme. Two examples will serve to illustrate the extent of success of some of the initiatives examined: Calvià, Mallorca and Benidorm, Costa Blanca.

Measures applied in mature destinations: The example of Calvià, Mallorca

The early development of the Balearic Islands, especially Mallorca, has led to the growth of a number of badly designed resorts. The most densely developed municipality is Calvià, an area of 145 km^2, with 56 km of coastline encompassing the resorts of Portals Nous, Palmanova, Magaluf, Santa Ponsa and Paguera. It has a population of approximately 50,000, 120,000 tourist beds and attracts 1.2 million visitors per year (Manchado, 1997). Early development was high-density and hotels were situated right on the waterfront and on rocky promontories, effectively privatising beaches and making access to the seafront difficult. In fact, 77% of tourist accommodation was built prior to 1980 (Manchado, 1997). In spite of the fact that 56% of tourist accommodation was on sites that provide less than 20 m^2 per bed, leading to obvious overcrowding, Calviá town council's new POGU elaborated in 1991 classified 16.5% of its land as urban and a further 11.9% as available for future development, including the entire seafront.

However, as already indicated, in 1992, Calvià became the scene of the first PET, with a total investment of over €9 million between 1993 and 1997. A certain degree of notoriety was achieved, as much publicity was given to the pioneer measure of 'sponging' (removing obsolete tourist accommodation to create open spaces) in Calvià. The process of environmental and urban renewal was enhanced through the implementation of a Local Agenda 21 programme, initiated in 1994, in conjunction with the PET. The plans focused on the four key aspects of urban development: (1) environmental quality; (2) spatial structure;

(3) social cohesion and quality of life; and (4) local economy (Blázquez Salom, 2001; Manchado, 1997; Prats, 1995, 1998, 1999). As a result, environmental criteria have been impregnated in all aspects of urban development and management, and a green corridor linking the coast with the inland hills has been designated. Subsequently, Calvià was awarded the European Environmental Prize in 1997. Certainly there have been benefits not only for the tourist sector – through image enhancement, increased demand and customer satisfaction – but also for the residents – economic renewal and quality of life – from the environmental improvements and much of the success of the initiatives is undoubtedly due to the combination of both programmes. Nevertheless, the proposals to curtail urban expansion have not altogether been satisfied in the new POGU drawn up in 1999.

The sustainability of large resorts: The example of Benidorm

The Valencian Community coast is densely developed for both hotel and private tourist accommodation. In 2005, 33% of the coastal fringe was occupied, rising to 49.3% on the Alicante Costa Blanca stretch (Greenpeace, 2005: 49). On this coast Benidorm is, without doubt, the paradigm of high-density mass tourism destinations. By the end of the 1980s it was a sprawling, untidy resort with notable deficits in urban planning, service provision and environmental conservation. It then had 33,000 hotel beds and about 130,000 apartment beds. It was highly dependent upon the UK tour operator market (67%) for its 3.5 million visitors and suffered badly in the 1988–90 crisis (Curtis, 1997). Nevertheless, by 1995 occupancy levels had recovered to 90% (from 70% in 1990) even though most hotels remain open all year. Key elements contributing to its success are: the upgrading of the 'tourist environment', including the beaches (EU Blue Flag), a well appointed seafront promenade on which vehicle traffic has been prohibited, urban landscaping and the provision of street furniture, a recovery of 'Spanish ambience' in the old town; refurbishing and upgrading of many hotels, most of which were built prior to 1980; diversification within the sun, sea and sand product, including beach activities and attractions, an ecologically sensitive wildlife attraction, a centrally located park affording pleasant walks and cultural events in its two open auditoria, a large range of entertainment events, including 20 local 'fiestas'; investment in infrastructures to provide good environmental management practices, which includes a desalination plant, benchmark waste disposal and treatment plants, and improvement of water supply; to this must be added a marketing strategy, drawn up in 1992. According to projections for 2012, total accommodation will rise to over 290,000 beds, including a 186-m-tall, 776-bedroom skyscraper already opened in

2000, and marketed as the tallest hotel in Europe. Various authors (Fuertes Eugenio *et al*., 1999; Rico Amorós, 1997) have drawn attention to the ensuing problems of water supply in the city, magnified by mass development on the entire Costa Blanca and the *Terra Mítica* theme park. However, higher-quality environmental practices and good management in pursuit of resort renewal and product development has enabled the destination to recover economic sustainability, at least in the medium term.

The Northern coastline: An integrated tourist product

As already noted, in spite of the early development on the Northern coasts, the Mediterranean and island coasts were preferred for mass development after 1950. As a result, hotel expansion was concentrated in the cities (principally provincial capitals), mainly to serve the business-related travel sector. Second home development has been much less intensive than on the Mediterranean coast: there are some concentrations on the Cantabrian coast, especially in Castro Urdiales, and on the Galician Rías Baixas, but elsewhere there is little development. In fact, only 5.4% of residences on the Basque coast are second homes (Greenpeace, 2005: 81).

However, in recent years, as tourist motivations and strategies have diversified, the traditional products of the region have expanded. These have been marketed as an integrated product, composed of attractive natural landscapes, which include both coastlines – such as the Cantabrian 'cornice', the Galician 'rías' – and mountains such as the Picos de Europa National Park. Visitors can also combine rural tourism with city stops, to visit sites such as the historical city of Santiago de Compostela or the Guggenheim museum in Bilbao. However, perhaps the most emblematic example of regional integration is the increasing popularity of the Camino de Santiago pilgrim route throughout the North, culminating in the Santiago de Compostela cathedral. In spite of administrative fragmentation – the Northern coastal area is made up of four different Autonomous Communities – the area is marketed as a single product known as Green Spain (Plate 6.1). In fact, Turespaña has played an important technical and co-ordinating role alongside the regions concerned (Pearce, 1997: 172).

From these examples it is clear that considerable progress in legislation, regulation and policy guidelines, both at national and the Autonomous Community level, has certainly been achieved. Hence, at least in theory, all valuable ecosystems and almost all undeveloped coasts are protected from encroachment. However, the execution of plans has not always kept abreast of their design. As Datzira-Masip (1997: 46) points out: 'The implementation of these (tourism policy) regulations is

Plate 6.1 TURESPAÑA 'Green Spain' marketing poster

one of the most important weaknesses of the country'. At the municipal scale, the PGOUs have not proved to be efficient instruments to regulate and control development, due to their late implementation, infrequent updating and incapacity to provide an overall strategy at a larger scale. In this respect, the municipal administrators are those mainly responsible for laxity in the face of infringements and, indeed, many have actively encouraged high-density construction and occupation of virtually all land available. In their defence, it must be recognised that this is understandable to a certain extent in the light of the structure of funding and revenue collection by local councils, which depends so heavily on building permits and property rates.

On the positive side of the balance, general awareness in both political and private enterprise circles of the problems and challenges facing Spanish tourism has existed for some time and social participation has grown, leading to the formulation of agreed plans. However, the initiative to introduce corrective measures has often been stimulated by situations of crisis. For example, the *Plan Futures* was designed in the aftermath of the 1989–90 crisis; similarly, clear signs of a loss of competitiveness anteceded the introduction of measures in, for example, Calvià and in Benidorm. Given the situation of high-density development in mass tourism destinations, strategies stress economic sustainability and good environmental and business practices as their main objectives. A certain degree of diversification of the basic sun, sand and sea product has been achieved, in which nautical activities and golf stand out as the most ubiquitous options. The former cannot, however, be considered necessarily a more sustainable option in environmental terms, in view of the impact of marinas on coastlines and beach formation.

In the case of golf, it is already a basic component of the tourism product on the Costa del Sol and some regions are promoting it as a key element in future development. These include Murcia and the Canary Islands. By contrast, in Catalonia there are many detractors, including environmental protection associations and socialist political parties, and the regional government has curtailed development in spite of having been the forerunners in Spain in the drawing up of an Environmental Plan for Golf Course Management in 2001. Opinions are obviously divided on the place of golf in sustainable tourism development (Ortega Martínez, 2003: 19; Priestley, 1995c).

Nevertheless, in spite of the density of tourism development, the level of satisfaction among tourists would appear to be high, as demonstrated by a survey carried out in 2002. Over 90% of foreign tourists considered the following aspects to be good or very good: quality of lodging, infrastructures, public, private and leisure services, cultural and sports activities, gastronomy, and leisure activities. Only prices were rated a little lower, giving satisfaction to 80% of the clients (Ortega Martínez & Loy Puddu, 2003: 257).

Conclusion: Future Sustainability

Bearing in mind the high-density development that exists on the Spanish Mediterranean and island coasts, it is certainly questionable to what extent sustainable measures can be applied to tourism in the future. As has been seen, virtually all the remaining unspoiled areas of coastline are officially protected, although some encroachment still occurs. In the summer of 2004, the Ministry of the Environment announced measures to enforce the protection of the first 100 m above the high-water mark, something already contemplated in the 1988 law! Nevertheless, by and large, in these areas conservation is the keynote in management. This has, however, had negative repercussions on adjacent areas, provoking the extension of tourism development on park fringes and inland in the areas already occupied.

In the context of global warming, the risk of desertification of a large part of Eastern Spain and the island archipelagoes constitutes a serious threat. Forest fires and water shortages are endemic to much of Spain. Recent outbreaks of fire have prompted the government to pass a decree prohibiting the reclassification of burnt woodland for housing development for 30 years after the fire, to discourage speculators from using this method to acquire building land. Likewise, recent proposals for piping water from some river basins (Tajo and Ebro) to a region with serious deficits (Murcia) have met with stiff opposition, as it is feared that this would simply enable further development of second home and intensive tourism development. Desalinisation plants would appear to be a less polemic option, in spite of the high cost and the amount of energy needed to produce potable water. In fact, they are already widely used in the island archipelagoes, providing, for example, 95% of water on Lanzarote, and 50% on Fuerteventura (Fuertes Eugenio *et al.*, 1999: 41).

The main needs of traditional sun, sand and sea tourism in order to achieve a sustainable product in the future have been identified in planning and policy statements as: quality, innovation and specialisation. The *Plan Futures* and subsequent initiatives were important in drawing attention to these problems, which affected many of the traditional resorts, as a stimulus to initiating improvements to increase competitiveness and in recovering image, perhaps more so than the actual measures introduced and resulting changes. The true value is that this is now an ongoing process. In the PICTE, environmental sustainability of the tourist destinations was pinpointed as a requisite for maintaining demand in the future. However, one must take a realistic attitude to this objective. In fact, in large resorts, strategies and policies are directed towards the development of 'sustainable cities', through good management practices applied to beaches, water provision, energy consumption and waste treatment, in an attempt to ensure a high-quality 'tourism environment'. The *Plan Futures*, together with the PICTE, also encouraged the private sector to participate in the innovation process and, partly as a result, many hotels and hotel chains are now introducing Environmental and Quality Management programmes.

It would, however, appear a much more difficult task to curtail ribbon development of low-density housing for three reasons: first, due to the continuous demand from both the national and European markets; second, because of the Spanish economy's reliance on the construction sector; and third, due to the temptations of local authorities, who are so dependent on much needed revenues from the sector. The system of municipal funding is neither transparent nor efficient and therefore requires reforming.

There has also been some achievement in the drive towards sustainability, as its paradigm has been incorporated in political discourse. The principles of this approach are best recognised in Local Agenda 21 plans, of which Calvià is an excellent example. It must be recognised, however, that political swings can also influence policy and vice versa. Nowhere is this clearer than in the Balearic Community, where the entire economy depends on tourism. For example, the right-wing government in the Balearic Islands in the late 1990s placed emphasis on environmental conservation and economic sustainability. They lost power in 2000 to a more left-wing nationalist coalition, who maintained environmental policies – attempting unsuccessfully to introduce an Ecotax – and adopted socially popular policies – such as limitations on construction and immigration. However, tourism demand fell during this period – from 11 million tourists in 2001 to 8 million in 2003 – and the economy suffered as a consequence. As a result, the right-wing party regained power in 2004, with promises to introduce measures aimed at economic recovery (Seguí, 2003a,b). This case demonstrates some of the difficulties involved in striking a balance.

It must be recognised that some form of sun, sea and sand tourism in the short and medium term is the only realistic base for tourism on the Mediterranean and island coasts. Indeed, this very point has been recognised, for example, in the Valencian Community Tourism Law (*Ley 3/1998 de 21 de mayo, de la Generalitat Valenciana*). Environmental quality is recognised as an important factor in market competitiveness (Ponce Sánchez, 2004). The measures introduced since 1992 have contributed to this goal, but, ideally, mature resorts should sacrifice volume and target higher-yield market sectors (Curtis, 1997). However, this is a difficult task, given the limited control that they have over distribution channels. Hence, given the current level of development and future plans, the principal objective must be to ensure the economic sustainability of the product, through improved management of the territory as a whole, of urban areas and of resorts; quality management and service in related businesses; and product renewal and differentiation. By contrast, the late development of the Northern coastal regions has safeguarded them from mass development, and the basis of a much more sustainable integrated product has been laid down there in recent years.

Chapter 7

A Tale of Two Islands: Sustainable Resort Development in Cyprus and Tenerife

RICHARD SHARPLEY

Introduction

For many coastal resorts, particularly in Southern Europe but also elsewhere, sustainable tourism development has become a dominant planning and policy objective (Bramwell, 2004a). Having experienced rapid and, frequently, unconstrained growth since the emergence of international mass tourism some 40 years ago, the initial euphoria over the economic potential of tourism development, manifested in the remarkable economic development of countries such as Spain, Greece, Malta and Cyprus, has been replaced by a number of anxieties and concerns over the future development of tourism. Inevitably, perhaps, such concerns focused initially on the environmental and sociocultural impacts of the transformation of coastal areas into mass tourism resorts (Coccossis & Nijkamp, 1998; Jenner & Smith, 1992; Priestley *et al.*, 1996). However, an increasingly competitive tourism market and transformations in tourists' demands and behaviour have served to focus attention more generally on the longer term 'economic vitality' of mass, resort-based tourism (Bramwell, 2004b: 2). That is, resorts that originally developed to meet the needs of 'traditional' sun-sea-sand mass tourism now suffer from environmental degradation, limited facilities, ageing infrastructure and, for tourists, poor value. As a result, they are less able to remain competitive in an expanding global tourism market and, as many Spanish resorts experienced in the late 1980s (Barke & Towner, 2004; Barke *et al.*, 1996), regeneration represents a significant challenge.

Whilst many tourist resorts in general face such a challenge, it is particularly acute within the specific context of island destinations. It has long been recognised that the virtually ubiquitous development of tourism in island micro-states is accompanied by a variety of potential negative consequences (Conlin & Baum, 1995; Harrison, 2001; Lockhart & Drakakis-Smith, 1997; Wrangham, 1999) and that the particular physical and socioeconomic characteristics of islands that render them so attractive to tourists also enhance their potential vulnerability to such consequences. More significantly, however, island tourism development is widely considered to be typified by the condition of dependency (Bastin, 1984; MacNaught, 1982; Milne, 1992, 1997); not only is the tourism sector frequently subject to the domination of, for example, overseas tour operators, airlines or hotel chains (Sastre & Benito, 2001), but also island economies are often dependent on a dominant tourism sector. Indeed, the top 25 nations ranked according to the contribution of tourism to GDP are all island destinations (Table 7.1). Consequently, the problems facing island tourism resorts may have significant economic, social and environmental implications for the island as a whole (Marín, 2000).

In response to these challenges, many islands have adopted tourism development policies that focus, in one form or another, upon sustainable resort development. Numerous examples of these are provided in the literature (for example, see Bramwell, 2004a; Briguglio *et al.*, 1996;

Table 7.1 The travel and tourism economy contribution to GDP (%), 2004

Rank	*Country*	*% of GDP*	*Rank*	*Country*	*% of GDP*
1	British Virgin Islands	95.2	14	St Vincent/ Grenadines	34.1
2	Antigua and Barbuda	82.1	15	Other Oceania	32.1
3	Maldives	74.1	16	Virgin Islands	31.9
4	Anguilla	71.9	17	Mauritius	31.0
5	Macau	61.3	18	St. Kitts and Nevis	30.0
6	Seychelles	56.7	19	Malta	28.5
7	Bahamas	56.0	20	Grenada	27.8
8	Aruba	54.5	21	Cyprus	27.6
9	Vanuatu	52.4	22	Kiribati	27.5
10	Barbados	52.2	23	Fiji	27.2
11	Saint Lucia	47.9	24	Guadeloupe	26.9
12	Cayman Islands	37.6	25	Dominican Republic	25.5
13	Jamaica	36.0			

Source: WTTC (2004: 64)

Ioannides *et al.*, 2001) although, typically, the longer-term sustainable development of island tourism in general, and island resorts in particular, is based upon policies that seek to both enhance the environmental quality of resorts and to diversify from the sun-sea-sand offering into alternative, more specialist, quality experiences in the hope of attracting higher-spending, 'quality' tourists. However, the degree of success in implementing these policies is variable (Ioannides & Holcomb, 2003), whilst even those destinations that have long sought to develop quality tourism have faced significant challenges. In Anguilla, for example, despite the successful development of upmarket tourism, a lack of land-use planning has led to uncontrolled expansion of the tourism sector, thereby threatening the future sustainability of the island's tourism industry (Wilkinson, 2001).

The purpose of this chapter, therefore, is to analyse and compare the efforts of two islands, Cyprus in the Eastern Mediterranean and Tenerife, the largest of the Canary Islands, to achieve sustainable resort development. In so doing, it will identify common challenges facing island tourism destinations as well as lessons that emerge from a comparison of the recent tourism development experiences of each island. Firstly, however, it is important to review briefly the need for and purpose of sustainable resort development in an island context.

Tourism and Sustainable Island Resort Development

Since it first emerged in the late 1980s, the concept of sustainable tourism development rapidly gained widespread acceptance and support. As Godfrey (1996: 60) noted, by the mid-1990s it had 'achieved virtual global endorsement as the new [tourism] industry paradigm' and nowadays it remains a principal tourism development objective. It has also, of course, attracted a significant degree of attention from practitioners and academics alike, spawning a plethora of policy documents, planning guidelines, statements of 'good practice', case studies, codes of conduct for tourists, academic books and research papers, and other publications.

However, despite the support for, and attention paid to, sustainable tourism development, it remains a highly contested concept, as does the broader, 'parental' paradigm of sustainable development itself (Dresner, 2002). Underpinning the debate is the inherent ambiguity and contradictory nature of sustainable development (Redclift, 1997), although it has been suggested that, paradoxically, therein lies its strength; it is 'palatable to everybody' (Skolimowski, 1995). In the tourism context, this has resulted in sustainable development being widely interpreted although, typically, it is manifested in what Hunter (1995) refers to as 'tourism-centric' definitions and development processes. That is, the focus tends to be on sustaining tourism itself and the environment upon which it depends as opposed to the potential contribution of tourism to the wider socioeconomic development of destination areas.

A full consideration of the well rehearsed sustainable tourism debate lies beyond the scope of this chapter (see for example, Sharpley, 2000a, 2002a). Nevertheless, the important point is that, despite the controversy surrounding the viability of the concept, few would disagree with the original objective or purpose of sustainable tourism development, namely, to be a 'recognised sustainable economic development option, considered equally with other economic activities when jurisdictions are making development decisions' (Cronin, 1990: 14). This is certainly a necessary objective in island micro-states where, as noted above, an intimate relationship exists between tourism and overall economic and social development. In other words, there are many examples where the rapid and expansive development of coastal tourism resorts on islands has resulted in rapid economic growth, yet such growth has been accompanied by significant social and environmental pressures and spatial concentration of development that has excluded the hinterland from the benefits of tourism. Thus, as mature island-based resorts face up to the challenge of remaining competitive, tourism policy has focused not only on the resorts themselves, but also on the sustainable development of islands as a whole.

Consequentially, island resort development typically embraces a combination of three inter-related policy dimensions: (1) land/infrastructure planning and management; (2) new product development; and (3) marketing. In practice, these are manifested in policies that, for example, restrict new accommodation proposals to higher rated developments, lead to environmental and infrastructural improvements, encourage the development of niche products such as golf or marina tourism, and support appropriate forms of tourism development away from the coast, such as agro-tourism or cultural tourism (see Getz, 1998). At the same time, marketing programmes target the 'quality' tourist, the overall aim being to reduce dependency on traditional sun-sea tourism markets whilst attracting higher-spending tourists and spreading the benefits of tourism more equitably. Of course, the widespread adoption of such policies suggests that resorts will not become more competitive but will simply vie for a share of the relatively limited 'quality' market, hence the argument that consolidation of the existing sun-sea-sand product may represent a more realistic alternative (Sharpley, 2003). Nevertheless, many resorts do follow the 'quality tourism' path although, as the following comparison of the experience of Cyprus and Tenerife now demonstrates, such a resort development policy may be problematic.

Cyprus and Tenerife: An Overview

The islands of Cyprus and Tenerife lie at opposite extremes of Southern Europe. Cyprus occupies a strategic position in the Eastern Mediterranean 75 km south of Turkey and 105 km east of Syria. Tenerife, conversely, is the largest of the seven islands that comprise the Canary Islands archipelago, situated in the Atlantic Ocean just 100 km off the coast of West Africa and some 1000 km south of the Iberian Peninsula (see Fig. 7.1). They also differ inasmuch as Cyprus[1] is an independent nation-state with its own system of national and local government whereas Tenerife, although benefiting from its own *Cabildo*, or island council, is part of the Canary Islands Autonomous Community, one of 17 such politically autonomous regions of Spain created by that country's 1978 Constitution (Pearce, 1997). Thus, Tenerife is governed by a regional parliament (although, as Bianchi (2004) notes, the degree of autonomy enjoyed by each autonomous region of Spain varies considerably). For this reason, neither Tenerife nor the Canary Islands as a whole appear in country-tourism league tables (such as Table 7.1 above) but are subsumed in data relating to Spain as a whole.

Cyprus and Tenerife also vary by geographical size. Tenerife's land area is approximately one third of that of the Republic of Cyprus, although their total populations are relatively similar (Tenerife's population of

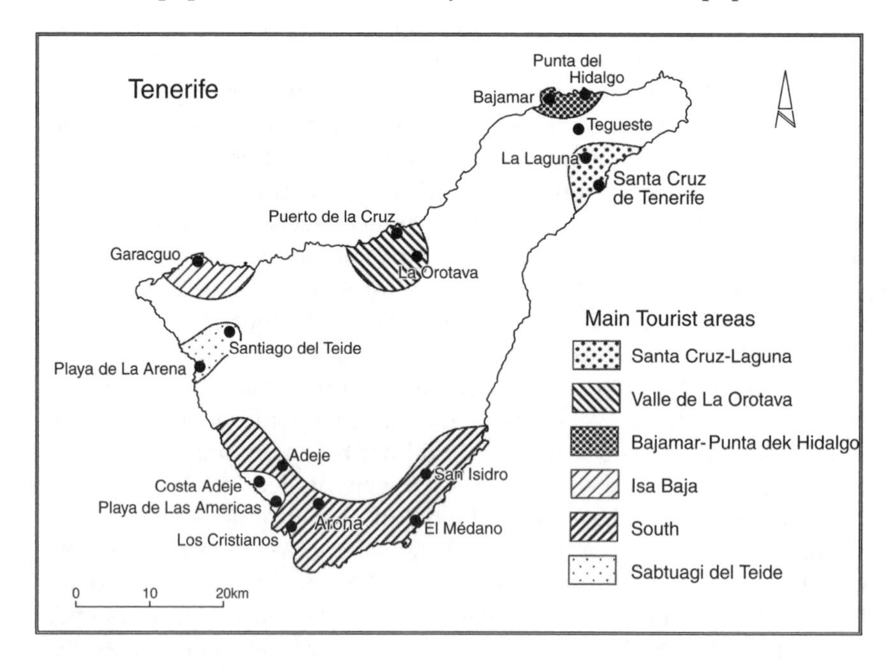

Figure 7.1 Tenerife

778,000 compares with around 680,000 in Cyprus). Both are also, of course, established tourism destinations although there are two important distinctions. Firstly, Tenerife's tourism industry and economy is significantly larger than that of Cyprus in both relative and absolute terms. In 2004, for example, Tenerife attracted almost 3.5 million international tourists (37% of all tourism to the Canaries), compared with 2.3 million arrivals in Cyprus – some 1.3 million 'domestic' tourists (i.e. from other Canary islands and the Spanish mainland) also visit Tenerife annually, contributing to a total of over 4.9 million arrivals in 2003 (Sonck, 2004). It is also estimated that the tourism economy contributes some 65% of Tenerife's GDP, compared to 27% in Cyprus. Secondly, tourist arrivals in Tenerife are relatively evenly spread throughout the year although, uniquely, the island is more popular as a winter sun destination; indeed, the Canary Islands are the only European coastal destination to attract more visitors during the winter than the summer months. Thus, 57% of all tourists to Tenerife visit between October and March, whilst the same six-month period accounts for 31% of annual arrivals in Cyprus (Table 7.2).

However, there are a number of similarities between the two islands. Not only are they roughly equidistant (four to five hours flying time)

Table 7.2 Monthly arrivals in Cyprus and Tenerife, 2004

Month	*Cyprus arrivals*	*Tenerife arrivals*[a]
January	56,504	336,267
February	75,705	345,100
March	111,945	334,585
April	191,251	308,673
May	261,646	206,790
June	264,799	202,271
July	305,978	263,138
August	305,926	255,840
September	303,506	231,846
October	278,976	334,121
November	114,048	316,012
December	78,723	322,427
Total	2,349,012	3,457,070

Source: Republic of Cyprus Statistical Service (2005); Instituto Canario de Estadística (2005)
[a]Excludes 'domestic' (i.e. Spanish) arrivals

from their main tourist markets, but they are also highly dependent on those markets. In 2004, for example, Britain accounted for over 56% of arrivals in Cyprus and 51% of arrivals in Tenerife; for both islands, Germany is the second most important market, accounting for 7% and 19% of arrivals respectively (Table 7.3). Both islands also experienced rapid expansion of their tourism industries from the 1960s up to the early 1990s in terms of both growth in arrivals and resort development. Equally, both islands have experienced a fall in tourist arrivals in recent years, although it has been more marked and over a longer period in Cyprus. Conversely, the development of accommodation has continued to increase and an oversupply of bed-spaces relative to demand is a now a recognised problem on both islands (Gil, 2003; McNutt & Oreja-Rodríguez, 1996; Oreja-Rodríguez *et al.*, 2004; Sharpley, 2000b, 2001a). Table 7.4 compares arrivals and accommodation supply data for both destinations. Of particular relevance to this chapter, the broad policy response of both Cyprus and Tenerife to the stagnation and potential decline of their tourist resorts (and the implications for their economies as a whole) has also been relatively similar. However, as the following analysis of each island now reveals, the manner in which this policy is being implemented has some significant variations.

Cyprus: Sustainable Resort Development

The development of tourism in Cyprus is notable in a number of respects. Firstly, there have been two distinct periods of tourism development on the island, preceding and following the Turkish invasion and subsequent occupation of the Northern third of the island in 1974. During the first phase, tourism development was centred on the burgeoning resorts of Kyrenia and Famagusta, signifying the birth of coastal mass tourism in Cyprus. Both resorts were, however, 'lost' as a result of the invasion, as was the international airport at Nicosia and, thus, the tourism industry had to be rebuilt again from scratch (Andronikou, 1987). Nevertheless, and as is well documented in the literature, the island's tourism industry was redeveloped rapidly and successfully during the latter phase (Ayers, 2000; Cope, 2000; Ioannides, 1992; Sharpley, 2003).

Secondly, both of these periods witnessed remarkable growth in arrivals and tourist expenditure, well in excess of average European and global growth rates. For example, between 1960 and 1973, arrivals and receipts in Cyprus grew by an annual average of 20% and 22% respectively (PIO, 1997) whilst, during the 1980s, tourist receipts grew by an annual average of 23% compared with 8.3% in Europe as a whole (CTO, 1990). Such growth was fuelled by an equally rapid expansion in the supply of accommodation, the great majority of which was located

Table 7.3 Principal tourist markets for Cyprus and Tenerife, 2004

Market	*Cyprus*		*Market*	*Tenerife*	
	No. of arrivals ('000)	***% of total arrivals***		***No. of arrivals***	***% of total arrivals***
UK	1332	56.7	UK	1764	51.0
Germany	161.6	6.9	Germany	671.9	19.4
Greece	133.4	5.7	Belgium	127.2	3.7
Sweden	83.9	3.6	Holland	119.8	3.5
Russia	83.8	3.6	Italy	95.6	2.8
Norway	50.7	2.2	Sweden	93.4	2.7
Switzerland	41.3	1.8	Finland	89.8	2.6

Source: Adapted from Republic of Cyprus Statistical Service (2005); Instituto Canario de Estadística (2005)

Table 7.4 Arrivals and accommodation supply in Cyprus and Tenerife

Year	*Cyprus: arrivals ('000)*	*Cyprus: bed-spaces*	*Tenerife: arrivals ('000)*[a]	*Tenerife: bed-spaces*
1975	47	5685	705	51,312
1980	349	12,830	805	64,472
1985	770	30,375	1300	68,906
1986	828	33,301	1506	75,400
1987	949	45,855	1812	87,455
1988	1112	48,518	2015	101,000
1989	1379	54,857	2018	116,326
1990	1561	59,574	1986	123,451
1991	1385	63,564	2275	128,017
1992	1991	69,759	2444	135,518
1993	1841	73,657	2554	138,404
1994	2069	76,117	2909	144,501
1995	2100	78,427	3012	147,576
1996	1950	78,427	2993	150,528
1997	2088	84,368	3157	154,588
1998	2222	86,151	3440	156,607
1999	2434	87,893	3591	160,848
2000	2686	88,423	3675	166,842
2001	2697	91,422	3811	170,137
2002	2418	94,466	3659	178,385
2003	2303	95,185	3582	177,738
2004	2349		3457	n/a

Source: Adapted from CTO Reports; Republic of Cyprus Statistical Service (2005); Instituto Canario de Estadística (2005); Cabildo de Tenerife (1995)
[a]Excludes 'domestic' (i.e. Spanish) arrivals

on the coast. By 2001, the island's total bed-spaces numbered 91,422, a sevenfold increase from 1980; over the same period, the number of bed-spaces in inland areas increased by just 11%, from 3902 to 4358. Not surprisingly, however, the growth and scale of tourism development along the coast, the subsequent pressures on natural and human resources (Apostolides, 1995) and the economic dependence on the tourism sector have long been considered unsustainable.

Thirdly, as noted above, in recent years arrivals in Cyprus have been more erratic. During the 1990s, arrivals demonstrated relatively little growth – between 1994 and 1998, total growth of just 7% was achieved, less than half the global rate. A significant increase was experienced between 1999 and 2001, primarily as a result of the short-lived popularity of Agia Napa as the clubbing centre of the Mediterranean. However, since 2001 arrivals have decreased alarmingly, as have receipts and, consequently, tourism's contribution to GDP. At the time of writing, the latest figures suggest a slight recovery in arrivals in 2004 (a 2% increase on 2003) although, most worryingly, tourist receipts continue to decline (3.2% down on 2003), indicating a decreasing average tourist expenditure. Average length of stay has also continued to decline, falling to 9.9 days in 2004 (Table 7.5).

The current problems facing the tourism sector in Cyprus can be explained, in part, by the characteristics of tourism to the island. Not only has Cyprus long been significantly dependent upon the British market, but tourism remains stubbornly seasonal with the peak summer season (July–September) accounting for almost 40% of annual arrivals. At the same time, previously restrictive air-travel policies, which encouraged the growth of inclusive tours, still influence tourists' mode of travel to Cyprus; indeed, although EU accession in 2004 will accelerate independent travel to the island, tour operators currently control some two-thirds of tourist arrivals. Combined with the spatial concentration of accommodation in the coastal resorts (which cover some 37% of the coastline) and the rapid development of the apartment/self-catering sector during the 1980s, this has underpinned the evolution of Cyprus into a mass, summer-sun destination, with 92% of all tourists staying in coastal resorts. Moreover, despite the more recent focus on the development of higher-grade hotels, attempts to attract higher-spending, quality tourists have largely failed, primarily as a result of the oversupply of accommodation and the power of tour operators to exert downward pressure on prices.

Given these problems, it is not surprising that, as discussed shortly, the most recent tourism policy for 2000–2010 (CTO, 2000) follows the contemporary and, arguably, generic 'quality' tourism path. However, the potential success of this policy is likely to be determined by the very factors that have, to an extent, fuelled the problems that it seeks to address. In other words, many of the challenges currently faced by the Cypriot tourism industry have been driven by the rapid and uncontrolled development of the island's coastal resorts, which, in turn, has resulted from the inability of the tourism authorities to effectively implement

Table 7.5 Cyprus: Arrivals, receipts and length of stay, 1999–2004

	1999	*+/–* *(%)*	***2000***	*+/–* *(%)*	***2001***	*+/–* *(%)*	***2002***	*+/–* *(%)*	***2003***	*+/–* *(%)*	***2004***	*+/–* *(%)*
Arrivals ('000)	2434	+ 9.5	2686	+ 10.3	2697	+ 0.4	2418	– 10.3	2303	– 4.8	2349	+ 2.0
Receipts (CY£mn)	1025	+ 16.7	1194	+ 16.5	1271	+ 6.5	1132	– 11.0	1015	– 10.4	982	– 3.2
Length of stay	10.3	–	10.4	–	9.8	–	10.3	–	10.0	–	9.9	–

Source: Adapted from Republic of Cyprus Statistical Service (2005)

national tourism policies (Sharpley, 2001b). For the purposes of this chapter, therefore, it is important to consider briefly the tourism planning process in Cyprus.

Cyprus: Tourism, government and planning

The political system in Cyprus is characterised by a presidential system of government, whereby the President exercises executive power through a Council of Ministers representing 11 ministries. Tourism falls under the remit of the Ministry of Commerce, Industry and Tourism although, as a symptom of conflicts and weaknesses in the planning process related to tourism development, land-use planning policy is the responsibility of the Ministry of the Interior, whilst environmental policy lies with the Ministry of Agriculture, Natural Resources and Environment (Loizidou, 2004). Legislative power is exercised by the 80-member House of Representatives. However, despite this centralised system, much of the day-to-day administration of Cyprus is undertaken at the local level. The island is divided into six administrative districts, each headed by a District Officer, whilst within each district local administration operates through a three-tier structure of independent Municipal Councils, Improvement Boards and Village Commissions.

Thus, for a relatively small nation, Cyprus has a complex, multilayered, democratic system of government, with a significant degree of authority delegated to the local level. There are, however, certain inherent weaknesses in the system:

- Formal structures for the implementation of policy at the national level do not exist. Instead, there is a reliance on informal contact and agreement between political and industry leaders as opposed to a formal consultation machinery; this, arguably, allows for political deals or favours that contradict or circumvent official policy whilst also permitting conflicts of interest.
- The multilayered governmental structure, requiring elections at some level virtually every year, encourages policies and decision-making based upon short-term political motives.
- This multilayered structure also places significant power in the hands of local municipal administrators, particularly mayors. With respect to tourism development, this gives the responsibility for land-use planning decisions, infrastructural development and other tourism-related activities to local politicians who, for electoral or other reasons, may not always make decisions in the wider regional or national interest.

As a result, tourism planning has suffered from a lack of formal implementation processes and the influence of local interests in decision-making. This, in turn, has allowed for excessive and, often, inappropriate developments along the coastal strip as well as insufficient infrastructural developments. More generally, however, the outcome of the complex system of government in Cyprus is that a land-use policy specifically for the intensively used coastal strip (that is, a coastal zone management plan) is nonexistent. As Loizidou (2004) observes, the number of involved authorities, the regular redefinition of coastal areas as tourism, as opposed to protected or agricultural, zones and, perhaps most significantly, the enormous financial interests involved in developing coastal areas for tourism, has resulted in a fragmented and erratic approach to coastal development. It is against this background that the Cyprus Tourism Organisation (CTO) has attempted to develop a sustainable resort development policy.

Cyprus's tourism policy

Given the importance of tourism to the Cypriot economy, it is not surprising that tourism has long been an integral element of national economic development policy whilst, in more recent years, specific policies have been introduced to guide the development of tourism. It is also interesting to note that, since the early 1980s, tourism policies have, in effect, attempted to encourage sustainable resort development. For example, during the 1980s, a variety of measures were introduced to limit coastal resort development, including financial incentives to encourage hotel and other tourism-related development in the hinterland and the controlled development of using luxury hotels in selected coastal areas, as well as a marketing policy refocused on attracting higher-spending, 'quality' tourists. Similarly, during the 1990s, tourism policy reflected the CTO's long term objectives of:

- reducing the rate of growth in tourism development;
- upgrading and diversifying the tourism product, utilising the island's environmental and cultural attractions;
- spreading the benefits of tourism around the island;
- attracting more diverse, quality markets;
- increasing off-season tourism; and
- increasing the level of spending per tourist.

Efforts were also made to limit the environmental impacts of excessive development. A moratorium on new hotel building was imposed in 1989 (though this proved ineffectual given the large number of applications approved prior to its imposition). Furthermore, in 1990, a Town and Country Planning Law was enforced, requiring all municipalities to submit local development plans for approval and, in particular, major hotel developments costing over CY£1 million to undergo an Environmental Impact Assessment.

The most recent tourism policy (2000–2010) continues to reflect the CTO's long-held objectives, albeit within the theme of developing quality tourism. The key elements of this policy are:

- a 'volume-value' strategy that seeks to optimise earnings from tourism by balancing limited growth in arrivals with an increase in visitor spending and length of stay;
- reducing seasonality;
- repositioning Cyprus as a tourism destination; in particular, less emphasis to be placed on sun-sea-sand tourism, whilst attention is to be focused on developing products, such as agro-tourism, that are based around the island's culture, natural environment and people;
- attracting 'quality' tourists through more effective targeting and segmentation; and
- marketing the island as 'a mosaic of nature and culture, a whole, magical world concentrated in a small, warm and hospitable island in the Mediterranean at the crossroads of three continents, between West and East, that offers a multidimensional qualitative [sic] tourist experience' (CTO, 2000: 33).

It is evident, however, that these objectives are unlikely to be met. Not only are relatively static arrivals figures being accompanied by falling revenues, indicating a declining spend per tourist, but hotel development along the coast continues apace. This is not to say that some success has not been achieved. Golf tourism has received a significant boost through the opening of two golf courses in the Paphos district, with three more under development, the construction of six potentially lucrative marinas has been approved and the development of agro-tourism has met with some limited success. Nevertheless, the island continues to attract a predominantly mass, summer-sun and lower-spending market dominated by arrivals from Britain, whilst declining receipts from tourism threaten the longer-term sustainability of the island's economy as a whole.

Undoubtedly, the lack of success in implementing tourism policies since the 1980s can be explained, in part, by the fact that the CTO is a relatively powerless body, whilst the governmental structures and processes discussed above have contributed to the continuing exploitation of the island's coastal areas. At the same time, however, there is little substance or direction inherent in the current policy; it adopts a 'blanket' approach that overlooks the different characteristics and strengths of different parts of the island as well as the potential needs of different markets. Nor is there any attempt to integrate the activities of key stakeholders in tourism on the island and, as a result, it would appear that there is little chance of sustainable resort development being achieved. In contrast, and as the following section argues, the approach adopted in Tenerife points to a much greater chance of success.

Tenerife: Sustainable Resort Development

Tourism in Tenerife remains relatively under-researched within the academic literature, although the development of tourism in the Canaries as a whole is considered by a number of commentators (for example, Bianchi, 2004; Gil, 2003; Marín, 2000). Equally, tourism data relating specifically to the island are also more limited. Nevertheless, the development of tourism in Tenerife has in a variety of ways been similar to that in Cyprus, albeit without the political turmoil that continues to afflict that island, and a number of important comparisons can be made.

The attraction of Tenerife as a tourist destination lies in both its location and natural features. Triangular in shape, it is not only the largest of the seven islands comprising the Canaries archipelago but also its highest point, Mount Teide (3718 m), is the highest mountain in Spain. As a result, the island has distinctive climatic regions, from the lush countryside, hilly coastline and more variable weather patterns of the North to the flat, arid and sunny Southern coastal region. It therefore offers a 'striking amalgam of landscapes' (Oreja-Rodríguez *et al.*, 2004) as well as a wealth of natural resources – some 47% of the island's land area is protected. Above all, however, it is the climate, with little seasonal variation throughout the year, that underpins Tenerife's tourism industry, particularly as Europe's principal winter-sun destination.

Early tourism to Tenerife can be traced back to the 19th century when Victorian travellers from Northern Europe began to visit the archipelago although, even by 1950, just 12,000 arrivals in the Canaries were recorded (Bianchi, 2004). From the late 1960s, however, the islands, in particular Gran Canaria and Tenerife, became the focus of mass tourism development. In Tenerife, such development occurred initially in the Northern coastal resort of Puerto de la Cruz, beneath the 19th-century hillside resort of La Oratava. However, significant overseas investment also fuelled the resort and urban development of the Southern coastline, where the resorts of Playa de las Americas and Los Cristianos came to epitomise the development (and resultant pressures) of mass tourism development on the island. Indeed, as Table 7.6 and 7.7 demonstrate, although Puerto de la Cruz was the dominant tourism region on the island up until the late 1970s, from the early 1980s the Southern resorts, located in the sunnier, desert zone of Tenerife became the main focus of mass tourism development.

Table 7.6 Number of bed-spaces in Tenerife, 1977–2003 (by tourism zone)

Year	*Zone 1 No.*	*Zone 1 (%)*	*Zone 2 No.*	*Zone 2 (%)*	*Zone 3 No.*	*Zone 3 (%)*	*Zone 4 No.*	*Zone 4 (%)*	*Tenerife total*
1977	3040	5.06	3269	5.54	32,032	53.37	21,618	36.12	60,022
1980	3043	4.72	3060	4.75	31,487	48.84	26,882	4.70	64,472
1982	2563	3.99	2507	3.90	29,238	45.49	29,962	46.62	64,270
1984	2369	3.45	2533	3.69	29,618	43.17	34,095	49.69	68,615
1986	2134	2.83	2041	2.71	29,173	38.69	42,052	55.77	75,400
1988	2000	1.98	2286	2.26	29,203	28.91	67,511	66.84	101,000
1990	2079	1.68	2539	2.06	29,789	24.13	89,044	72.13	123,451
1992	2363	1.74	2163	1.60	30,036	22.16	100,956	74.50	135,518
1994	2402	1.66	2315	1.60	29,991	20.75	109,793	75.98	144,501
1996	2175	1.45	2612	1.73	30,197	20.06	115,544	76.76	150,528
1998	2358	1.51	2718	1.73	30,997	19.79	120,534	76.96	156,607
2000	2365	1.42	2603	1.56	32,507	19.48	129,367	77.54	166,842
2002	2641	1.48	2640	1.48	33,199	18.61	139,905	78.43	178,385
2003	2634	1.48	2656	1.49	32,512	18.29	139,936	78.74	177,738

Source: Cabildo de Tenerife (1995); Oreja-Rodríguez *et al.* (2004)

Table 7.7 Tourist arrivals in Tenerife ('000), 1977–2003 (by tourism zone)[a]

Year	*Zone 1 No.*	*Zone 1 (%)*	*Zone 2 No.*	*Zone 2 (%)*	*Zone 3 No.*	*Zone 3 (%)*	*Zone 4 No.*	*Zone 4 (%)*	*Tenerife total*
1977	145.4	11.23	37.2	2.87	771.5	59.57	341.0	26.33	1295.1
1980	121.6	10.22	39.2	3.30	643.3	54.08	385.4	32.40	1189.5
1982	111.4	7.63	23.2	1.59	780.0	53.45	544.8	37.33	1459.4
1984	101.0	6.25	25.6	1.59	825.6	51.07	664.2	41.09	1616.4
1986	74.3	3.93	24.1	1.28	833.0	43.98	962.4	50.82	1893.8
1988	78.8	3.15	23.7	0.95	847.9	33.86	1553.3	62.04	2503.6
1990	102.5	3.78	30.7	1.12	798.1	29.41	1782.7	65.69	2713.7
1992	118.1	3.57	32.7	0.99	808.2	24.42	2350.0	71.02	3308.9
1994	132.7	3.4	42.2	1.08	876.5	22.43	2856.1	73.09	3907.4
1996	148.9	3.61	46.2	1.12	914.3	22.16	3016.1	73.11	4125.5
1998	152.2	3.49	49.0	1.12	943.2	21.60	3222.7	73.79	4367.2
2000	165.3	3.49	48.2	1.02	997.0	21.07	3520.0	74.41	4730.4
2002	163.5	3.39	50.8	1.05	987.4	20.44	3628.6	75.12	4830.3
2003	168.0	3.43	55.5	1.13	997.0	20.36	3677.5	75.08	4898.0

Source: Cabildo de Tenerife (1995); Oreja-Rodríguez *et al.* (2004)
[a]Figures include Spanish 'domestic' arrivals

Particularly striking is the transformation in the relative shares of both accommodation (bed-spaces) and tourist arrivals in Puerto de la Cruz (Zone 3) and Playa de las Americas-Los Cristianos (Zone 4) – Zones 1 and 2 refer to the smaller (in tourism terms) Santa Cruz and La Laguna regions around the Northeast tip of the island. In 1977, for example, Puerto de la Cruz accounted for 53% of total bed-spaces on the island and almost 60% of tourist arrivals; over the following 25 years there was virtually no growth in accommodation supply in Puerto de la Cruz, whereas the Southern coastal resorts' share of total bed-spaces grew to almost 79%. Not surprisingly, the latter resorts also accounted for 75% of tourist arrivals by 2003, compared with 20% in Puerto de la Cruz. It should be noted that the figures in Table 7.6 and 7.7 include Spanish domestic arrivals, which disguises the recent decline in international arrivals in Tenerife – since 2001, annual international arrivals have fallen by a total of almost 10%, representing one of the key challenges facing the sustainable development of tourism on the island.

There are, then, a number of key characteristics of tourism in Tenerife. Firstly, as noted earlier, it is more popular as a winter-sun destination, although the distinction between the winter and summer seasons in terms of tourist numbers is relatively small. Thus, the island's resorts do not suffer from the problems of seasonality that are common in other coastal resorts, including Cyprus. Secondly, Tenerife has experienced virtually unbroken growth in tourist arrivals since the early development of mass tourism on the island, with relatively high annual increases in arrivals being experienced during the mid-1980s and the first half of the 1990s. Since 2001, however, not only have international arrivals fallen, but also average length of stay and, hence, hotel occupancy levels have fallen – in 2003, for example, the average stay was 8.61 nights compared with 9.76 nights in 1990 (Sonck, 2004). Thirdly, the island has become increasingly dependent on the British market. In 1975, British tourists represented 29% of total international arrivals; by 1990 the figure had risen to almost 42% and, in 2004, it reached 51%. Finally, the development of tourism has been defined, as in Cyprus, by accommodation development. That is, the rapid growth of the Southern resorts, where some 60% of accommodation is self-catering/apartments, has determined both the location and character of tourism development although, again as in Cyprus, the major growth in accommodation supply in recent years has been in higher-grade hotels.

The main challenge facing Tenerife, therefore, is an excessive supply of accommodation compared with demand, although as McNutt and Oreja-Rodríguez (1996) and Marín (2000) note, the island suffers a number of environmental problems commonly associated with mass tourism development. As in Cyprus, however, it is the uncontrolled expansion of accommodation that lies at the root of the problems facing the island

and, again, this may be related to the system of governance and tourism policy.

A detailed consideration of the political-economy of tourism in Tenerife is beyond the scope of his chapter (see Bianchi, 2004) but, as with Cyprus, development of the accommodation sector in Tenerife has continued despite, rather than because of, tourism policy. That is, following the 1978 Constitution, the new regional governments began to address the consequences of tourism development and, in the case of the Canaries, a number of measures were introduced to control or restrict tourism development. These included the Law of Natural Spaces in 1994, which led to about 45% of the islands' total land area being protected from development, the Regulation of Tourism Law in 1995, which sought to establish more rigorous criteria for tourism development and the respective roles of local and regional planning authorities, and in 2001, a moratorium on new tourism developments. In Tenerife, this has been rigorously imposed, with previously granted planning permission being withdrawn if building has not been completed by 2006. However, not only are there a number of exceptions to the moratorium, such as the development of rural tourism, luxury accommodation developments or those with complementary offers, such as golf courses or marinas, but also, as Bianchi (2004) observes, powerful lobby groups and local political expediency have, as in Cyprus, served to diminish the impact of these tourism development policies. Nevertheless, it is certainly the case that regional legislation has had a positive impact on land-use and tourism planning in Tenerife.

Tenerife: Planning for Sustainable Tourism

In addition to a more rigorous legislative framework for tourism, sustainable resort development in Tenerife is being guided by a policy that seeks to promote quality tourism, the principal focus being upon the product (that is, the tourist experience) rather than the destination as a whole and, consequentially, specific plans in terms of both accommodation/facility development according to specific market needs and the potential of specific areas of the island. Significantly, it is also recognised that success will be dependent upon the co-operation of all stakeholders, including tour operators and other intermediaries (Sonck, 2004).

In developing and implementing this policy, two factors are of particular importance. Firstly, an organisation (the Tenerife Tourist Board, or *SPET*) with specific responsibility for tourism management in Tenerife was established in 1992, its membership drawn from both the public sector, such as the island *Cabildo*, and the private sector, the latter including major associations and tourism businesses. Secondly, the strategy itself is highly focused and integrated and is built around the complementary processes of specialisation by area and segmentation by product. In other words, the environmental/infrastructural development of specific areas of the island are linked to the characteristics/needs of those areas, whilst related segmented marketing and product development is also undertaken. In short, the strategy is based on the development of zones and brands.

Six brands have been developed:

Tenerife Select – aimed at quality, high spending tourists,
Tenerife Golf – developing specialist golf resorts,
Tenerife Natural – aimed at rural/nature-based tourism markets,
Tenerife and the Sea – the 'traditional' sun-sea-sand market,
Tenerife Convention Bureau – promoting the island as a conference destination, and
Tenerife Film Commission – developing the island's potential as a filming location.

In each case, the development of specific parts of the island is framed by the brand. Thus, for example, the development of the South coast resorts falls within the *Tenerife and the Sea* brand, the focus being on consolidating and improving the quality of the traditional resort experience. Conversely, the Santa Cruz/La Laguna (city) areas will be the focus of *Tenerife Select* up-market short breaks, taking advantage of new air services to the island, whereas the Valle de la Orotava and Isla Baja areas on the North coast will focus on the development of *Tenerife Natural* quality rural tourism facilities. At the same time, efforts are being made to integrate with tour operators; since 1992, some 22 operators, offering specialist holidays such golf, music or city breaks, have begun operations to Tenerife.

According to Sonck (2004), significant progress has been made. For example, eight new golf courses and 18 specialist golf hotels have been developed over the last decade, 14 upmarket spa complex projects have been established in five-star hotels and there has been a 20% annual increase in conference/incentive events. However, a number of significant challenges remain and it will be some years before the success of current policies can be evaluated.

Conclusion

The consideration of tourism planning policies in Cyprus and Tenerife in this chapter has been necessarily brief. Nevertheless, a number of conclusions can be drawn from the comparison of the experiences of the two destinations. In terms of challenges, both Cyprus and Tenerife face the challenge of a lack of competitiveness; they face declining numbers of mass-market, lower-spending tourists from traditional, main markets who are staying for shorter periods of time. Both destinations also have an oversupply of accommodation resulting from unplanned and unrestricted development and, despite the existence of planning laws and tourism policies, political-economic structures have limited their effectiveness, particularly in the case of Cyprus. In response, both islands have also adopted a 'quality tourism' development policy, although the manner in which this is being implemented suggests three important lessons.

Firstly, Cyprus continues to suffer from an inability to implement its tourism policies; it remains a mass, summer sun destination attracting lower-spending tourists. Conversely, some degree of success is evident in Tenerife although visitor numbers are also in decline. This implies that, as a prerequisite, appropriate laws/regulations must be introduced with the necessary structures to implement them. Thus, the organisation with responsibility for managing tourism policy should be endowed with either sufficient legal authority or, in the case of SPET, stakeholder commitment, to drive policy implementation.

Secondly, and related, an integrated approach is required. Whereas SPET is representative of the Tenerife tourism (public and private) sector and works with the international tourism industry, the CTO remains, in effect, a public sector marketing organisation dependent upon the co-operation and goodwill of the industry. Indeed, all too often the CTO and the major tourism associations and other relevant bodies, such as the trades unions, are at odds. Thus, the experience of Tenerife suggests that successful policy implementation depends upon the commitment and involvement of all stakeholders.

Finally, quality tourism policies must be based on a pragmatic assessment of the destination's potential in terms of physical, cultural and social resources and the markets it might attract. In particular, golf tourism is being developed in both Cyprus and Tenerife. However, this not only results in the adaptation of the natural environment but also places significant additional demands on the already limited water supplies on both islands. Therefore, the extent to which golf tourism contributes to sustainable island development, as opposed to simply attracting a niche, higher-spending market, must be questioned. More generally, and as some have observed, the intention of Cyprus to develop quality tourism bears little relationship to the island's resources or unique features relevant to its competitor destinations. As a result, its policy is largely generic and relates to neither specific areas of the island nor potential markets for the products it hopes to promote. Conversely, the approach of Tenerife has been to adopt a systematic appraisal of the needs and characteristics of its distinctive areas, to identify key brands and markets, and to develop its tourism products accordingly. Therefore, in conclusion, the likelihood of successful and sustainable resort development in Tenerife is much greater.

Note

1. This chapter focuses upon tourism development in the (Greek) Republic of Cyprus which, following the occupation by Turkish forces of the Northern third of the island in 1974, has experienced the more significant and rapid development of tourism. In contrast, the self-proclaimed Turkish Republic of Northern Cyprus (TRNC) remains relatively undeveloped and accounts for less than 3% of international tourist arrivals on the island as a whole (Warner, 1999), although the relaxation of border restrictions in 2004 should encourage growth in international tourism to the Turkish sector.

Part 3

The Pleasure Periphery and Managing the Postmodern Coastal Resort

Chapter 8

The Postmodern Resort and the Pleasure Periphery: The Case of Australia's Coastal Tourism Resorts

BRIAN KING

Introduction

As the world's largest island continent, with an extensive coastline of approximately 36,700 km, Australia has gained the reputation as a tourism destination that offers a wide range of attractive beaches and resorts. The diverse climatic zones, including tropical and subtropical areas, enhance the appeal of the coastline. In fact the lure of the country's tropical areas is a fairly recent phenomenon. During the 19th and early 20th centuries consumers preferred the cooler and more temperate climate characteristic of destinations such as Tasmania. Tropical areas were widely viewed as unappealing by those of European descent (Cilento, 1923). These changing consumer tastes impacted upon the evolution of the resort sector and those located in the more northerly and warmer parts of Australia have been developed almost exclusively during the post-war period. These developments now form a key element of Australia's pleasure periphery, offering Australian travellers a domestic alternative to overseas beach resort destinations in the South Pacific and Southeast Asia. They are also attractive to the maturing outbound markets of Europe and North America, where tourists have become increasingly attracted to long-haul travel and view Australia as appealing and attainable (Richardson, 1995). Australia's coastline is also readily accessible to the growing markets of Asia.

According to the Resource Assessment Commission (RAC) (1993), the coastal zone of Australia occupies about 1.3 million square kilometres, approximately 17% of the total land area. The zone contains the largest expanse of coral reef of any country, the third largest area of mangroves and has significant populations of endangered species. These features are indicative of the environmental values associated with the coastline, which have potential tourist appeal. The zone supports about 80% of Australia's total population and nearly half of the indigenous population, though the latter are largely clustered in the areas that are least developed for tourism. Of Australia's 9000 commercial tourism establishments, the non-metropolitan coastal zone accounts for nearly half, including 38% of all hotels and motels, 48% of caravan parks and 75% of 'holiday establishments' including self-contained flats, units and houses (RAC, 1993).

Following the first colonial settlement in Sydney in 1788 and into the Victorian period, population and development gathered pace along Australia's coastline. As the processes of urbanisation and industrialisation accelerated during the Victorian era, coastal resorts began to spring up, incorporating English-style promenades, piers and guest houses. In the state of Victoria around the city of Melbourne, investments made possible by wealth associated with the Gold Rush led to the creation of grand coastal resorts such as Sorrento, Cowes, Queenscliff and Lorne (Davidson & Spearritt, 2000; Hill, 2004).

Resort suburbs grew up close to the central urban areas of a number of the cities, emerging to form part of the wider urban area rather than self-contained seaside resorts. Manly and Bondi were developed close to Sydney, Glenelg to Adelaide and St. Kilda to Melbourne (see Plate 8.1). These beach-side suburbs are emblematic of Australia's urban beach culture and maintain their appeal as sought-after leisure precincts amongst city residents (Hanlan & Kelly, 2005). Though locals are the main audience for leisure-based activities, the various locales offer a range of tourist accommodation including properties managed by leading international chains. The provision of entertainment has always been a prominent feature of these resort suburbs. To help create an all-round resort experience, developers embraced the latest design

Plate 8.1 Bondi Beach Grand Resort and Spa

principles emanating from North America. The 'Luna Park' entertainment and theme park complex at St Kilda, which continues in operation, was built in 1912, and is one of seven across Australia that were modelled on the Coney Island theme park of the same name (built in 1903) (Holt, 2005). The fantasy and entertainment elements have had enduring appeal, indicative that Australian resorts have embraced a range of dimensions which extend beyond accommodation provision (Holt, 2005).

Because of the co-location of many Australian cities and resort settings, it is difficult to draw a clear distinction between resort development and urban development. All of Australia's eight state and territory capitals are coastal, with the exception of Canberra, the national capital. Brisbane, the capital of Queensland and a component of the extended conurbation of Southeast Queensland, is located close to the mouth of the Brisbane River and not directly on the coast. However the wider conurbation extends to the coastal resort setting of the Gold Coast. As Australia's third most populous urban area, the conurbation exemplifies the centrality of the coastline to all of Australia's largest settlements. Urban dwellers can take a short drive to the beach and take advantage of the available resort facilities.

The adjacent beach resorts have not however enjoyed an automatic monopoly of tourist-related appeal. With deindustrialisation and the growth of the services sector, Australia's cities have become increasingly attractive as leisure destinations in their own right – the artificial sandy beach adjacent to the Brisbane River is, for example, a major attraction of Brisbane's Southbank precinct. Such improved amenities have enabled cities to compete actively and effectively with resorts as tourist destinations. Whilst the coastal beaches retain their appeal, the lure of the cities with their diverse cultural, sporting and leisure options has forced the resort sector to diversify its appeal. A recent report undertaken by the Tourism Task Force (TTF) Australia, has however suggested that the pace of change is too slow and that many resorts are struggling to secure a distinct market positioning (TTF Australia, 2003).

Postmodern Perspectives

The various attempts to apply postmodern theory in the tourism literature have encountered widespread scepticism and occasional hostility, though advocates have highlighted its importance as a means of creating theoretical and applied links between tourism and the social and cultural domains (Dann, 1998). In Australia there has been a modest application of postmodernism to tourism (Davidson & Spearritt, 2000). Much of this analysis has however focussed on settlement and urbanism rather than on resorts, perhaps because of the wide range of leisure-based attractions offered by Australia's cities and the pace of real estate development in urban areas. One of the more obvious applications of postmodern principles to leisure settings has been to examine the contribution of architecture to the 'look and feel' of resorts. An examination of 'architectures of entertainment' in the case of Melbourne's Crown Casino complex was an interesting approach in an urban setting (Morris, 2001). The eclecticism of this construction is distinct from the prevailing resort styles of the 1980s and is symptomatic of the flamboyance of the various entertainment complexes located within Australia's largest cities. In terms of research applications, the most interesting cross-over has occurred where urban areas also function as resorts, such as in Queensland's Sunshine Coast and Gold Coast. In the case of the Gold Coast's Jupiter's Casino, a monorail provides a link with the nearby retail and hotel complex and is an earlier example of the emerging postmodern style.

A key postmodern principle readily applicable to resorts is dedifferentiation – the overlapping of previously autonomous domains such as high and popular culture, fashion, work, architecture, urban culture, tourism and education (Lash, 1991). Tourism has been described as increasingly dedifferentiated from these other domains (Brown, 1998). Within the wider discourse of postmodern tourism, examples of playfulness and fantasy are becoming increasingly visible (Urry, 1990). They are evident in a number of contemporary Australian resort developments. Whilst the modernist and Fordist concepts of economies of scale and functionalism are prominent in many of the motels and apartment blocks and in much of the urban architecture of 1960s and 1970s, to a considerable extent resorts constructed during the same period avoided this highly functionalist style. During the 1980s and 1990s, the play and fantasy elements were increasingly emphasised and a number of resorts progressively embraced pastiche and nostalgic forms, particularly in the Gold Coast, which may be regarded as Australia's dominant sun, sea and sand resort. One property that exemplifies this mode is the Hyatt Regency Sanctuary Cove, which forms part of an integrated resort and is a nostalgic interpretation of 1920s Queensland colonial architecture, as well as offering guests the reassurance of the latest comforts and technology.

In a section of his book *Creating Island Resorts*, which draws upon the work of Sack (1992), King (1997a) highlighted a number of parallels between resorts and shopping centres from the perspective of tourist consumption. He noted the postmodern trend evident in both settings towards the privatisation of space and consumption, with some Australian island resorts constituting a form of self-contained postmodern community. The author distinguished between the modernist component of Hamilton Island in the Whitsundays and other lower-key island resort developments (King, 1997b). As evidence of the juxtaposition of modern and postmodern forms, it was noted that Hamilton Island offers visitors a range of pleasure options and experiences ranging from 'Polynesian bures' to high-rise tower blocks and a replica early settler chapel, which is used extensively for Japanese weddings. He referred to the 'architecture of pleasure', which despite its long vintage in some resort settings is clearly embracing elements of postmodernism in its more recent manifestations (see Plate 8.2)

There has been a growing literature on Australian resorts, though authors have struggled with the definitional challenge. Many establishments persist in describing themselves as resorts, despite failing to satisfy some of the basic resort criteria (King & Whitelaw, 2003). Many of the earlier Australian resort studies were imprecise, given the absence of any widely accepted definition, though this situation has subsequently improved with the introduction of the Standard Classification of Visitor Accommodation (SCOVA) by the Australian Bureau of Statistics. Much of the early Australian writing consisted of historical accounts of the Victorian era resorts. More recently a number of historical accounts have also provided insights into the development of resorts located in the sun-belt and including the Gold Coast (Jones, 1986; Vader & Lang, 1980), the Sunshine Coast (Cato, 1989) and the Whitsunday Island resorts (Barr, 1990).

Though Australia is an island continent, its massive dimensions mitigate against any strong sense of 'islandness' for tourists or residents along much of the coastline. By way of exception, a number of islands are

Plate 8.2 Hamilton Island Reef View Hotel (Whitsunday Islands)

located off the coast and range from the least to the most highly developed. Islands offering resort-style accommodation include the World Heritage-listed Lord Howe Island (in New South Wales) and the former penal colony of Norfolk Island, where colonial heritage is a strong emphasis (Prideaux, 2004). Indicative of the diversity of island settings, the Cocos and Keeling Islands are found close to Indonesia and are quite distant from the Western Australia mainland (2800 km!). The population is predominantly Moslem and a major casino development was developed there though it has subsequently been closed (Alder *et al.*, 2000). A number of islands suited to resort development are located closer to the Australian mainland. These include Couran Cove Island Resort on South Stradbroke Island near the Gold Coast and Kingfisher Bay Resort on the World Heritage-listed Fraser Island, both of which emphasise their environmental credentials. The relationship between the coast of mainland Australia and the offshore islands has been a topic for research, with a particular emphasis on the emergence of regional identity and distinctive regional style (King, 1997a).

Some broader development theories have been applied to the resort sector in Australia by researchers. Prideaux (2000, 2004) for example examined Australian resorts in the context of the development spectrum. When investigating the planning and development of integrated resorts, some authors have questioned whether the benefits accruing to local communities as claimed by the developers are real (Stanton & Aislabie, 1992). The role of local governments and communities in such development has also been a focus of study (Richins & Pearce, 2000). Some attention has been given to the Gold and Sunshine Coasts as part of the wider process of coastal urbanisation (Mullins, 1990). The population of the Brisbane and Moreton regions is expected to reach 2.8 million by 2011 – close to the current population of Melbourne (Parliament of Queensland, 1987). One of the more promising academic approaches to resort development and management was Faulkner's examination of the process of 'revisioning' the Gold Coast as a destination using an interdisciplinary approach incorporating a variety of innovative techniques (Faulkner, 2002).

Domestic and International Markets

There was minimal international visitation to Australia prior to 1975, other than for purposes of visiting friends and relatives and for business travel. As these markets were not seeking resort-style experiences, the resorts of this period were focussed predominantly around the needs and demands of the domestic market. The pace and scale of development in Australia's coastal resort sector has however been increasingly influenced by the volume of international tourist visitation, despite the fact that a relatively small proportion of international visitor nights are spent in resorts. This small share of visitation to resorts also applies in the case of the domestic market, though the large overall volume means that most resorts continue to target domestic visitors often in addition to international visitors.

For Australian travellers, self-contained accommodation has long been the preferred choice for main summer holidays, whether in the form of apartments (which have dominated the supply of accommodation on the Gold Coast) or holiday homes (in less concentrated and densely populated destinations) (Tomljenovic & Faulkner, 2000). Such preferences were generally not conducive to the development of self-contained resorts. Southeast Queensland provides an instructive example of this dynamic. Despite their appeal as domestic destinations, coastal resorts on the Sunshine Coast such as Maroochydore and Alexandra Headland were until recently virtually hotel-free zones, with apartments dominating the supply of accommodation. Resort-style accommodation reached Maroochydore as recently as 1992 when the Twin Waters resort was opened. This property is now managed by Accor Asia Pacific under its Novotel brand.

Changing lifestyles and consumption patterns have helped to shape the coastline in the post-war period. With growing affluence, the ownership of 'beach shacks' or holiday homes proliferated, resulting in considerable residential ribbon development and sprawl along the coastal fringe. In its earlier manifestations, such developments were informal in style and catered for second-home owners, retirees and low-key relaxation for visitors and residents rather than for structured entertainment. Relentless growth has however propelled the Gold Coast and the Sunshine Coast into the top 12 urban concentrations in Australia and the accelerating provision of more sophisticated leisure activities is evident. These urban areas have developed into highly decentralised and sprawling residential expanses with 'post-suburbanisation' now characterising much of the coastline to the North and South of Brisbane (Essex & Brown, 1997). Though not as pronounced as is the case in equivalent communities in California and Florida, these resort-style settlements with their ethos of pleasure, lifestyle and entertainment exhibit a range of postmodern features. In the USA, postmodern beachside lifestyles have been popularised by television 'sitcoms' such as *Baywatch*, *Miami Vice* and the *OC*. In Australia the long-running *Home and Away* and the shorter-lived *Sylvania Waters* have played a similar role. The Australian version of the reality TV show *Big Brother* is filmed on location at the Dreamworld theme park on the Gold Coast, providing further evidence of the cross-over and postmodern dedifferentiation between popular media and tourism. Of Australia's various resort settings, it may be argued that the Gold Coast exhibits the features of postmodernism most conspicuously. Some authors have speculated about whether tourist regions elsewhere will emulate the style and processes evident on the Gold Coast, such as Sanders' (2000) examination of the Leeuwin–Naturaliste region of Western Australia. Despite the investigation of potential parallels in such studies, the Gold Coast experience does appear to be exceptional.

Though resorts were slow to develop along the mainland of Northern Australia, a number of island resorts had been developed somewhat earlier. Examples from the Whitsundays group in Queensland include Hayman Island (dating from 1927 and remodelled in the post-war period), Dunk Island (1956), Great Keppel Island (1967) and South Molle Island (1970). These are archetypal island resort destinations, which attracted visitors from the Southern states, especially during the winter months and formed an important component of Australia's earlier pleasure periphery. Apart from such notable exceptions, most of Australia's more remote coastline was and remains undeveloped. For a number of reasons, such underdevelopment is most extreme in the remoter coastal zones of Western Australia and the Northern Territory. With domestic aviation strictly regulated until the early 1990s, airfares were high. Australia's population centres of Melbourne and Sydney are 3–4 hours flying time from Cairns in Far North Queensland and further to the rest of the tropical North. Overseas destinations were generally viewed as more fashionable than their domestic counterparts. Despite this pattern, there are examples of resort development in remote coastal locations. These include the Cable Beach development at Broome in the Northern (and remote) section of Western Australia and the Seven Spirit Bay Resort in the Northern Territory's Arnhem Land. Voyages Hotels and Resorts is currently developing an eco-lodge at Wildman River, in Arnhem Land and is scheduled to open in 2007. Such isolated resort locations are commercially marginal, though with the growing popularity internationally of boutique-style resorts, they are likely to form an increasingly important component of Australia's resort product range.

The dispersal of resorts across Queensland is indicated in Fig. 8.1, indicative of the fashion shift from the cooler parts of the country to the subtropical zone, particularly along the more populated easterly coastline.

Though coastal resort development in Australia has been limited in scale relative to the vast size of the continent, it has always been considerably more extensive than any tourism developments occurring inland. 'Outback' images have long enjoyed iconic status, but the provision of 'outback' accommodation has been minimal, apart from motels located along the various highways. Whilst international visitors do seek out commercial accommodation adjacent to major inland attractions such as Ayers Rock (Uluru) and Kakadu, most of the tourist

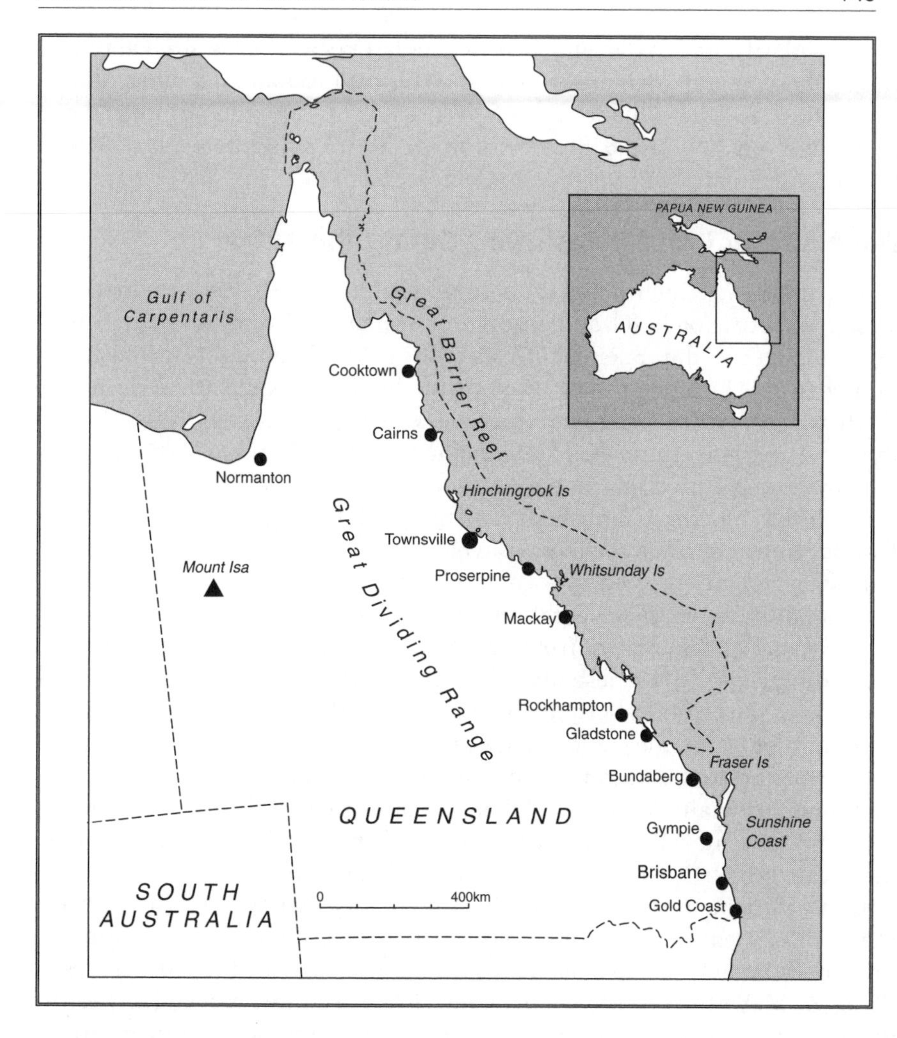

Figure 8.1 Map of Queensland and Australia

activity and associated development is associated with the coastline. The major exception is the Alpine ski regions of Victoria and NSW, where substantial resort investments have occurred. Investment in these resorts has continued unabated, though the acceleration of global warming has made winter sports increasingly marginal in Australia. This medium- to long-term prognosis is likely to confirm the dominance of the coast as the major focus for resort development. Though tanning and sunbathing are less popular than was previously the case because of the growing awareness of the risks associated with skin cancer, the diversity of climatic conditions across Australia means that any aggregate decline in the popularity of coastal and beach-oriented recreation is unlikely. In cases where inland areas are attracting significant visitation, a substantial proportion is often made up of resort visitors travelling into the hinterland on day trips, thus reinforcing the leading role of coastal resorts as generators of visitation (Getz, 1999).

Development and Investment during the 1980s

The increasing international share of visitor arrivals has provided a strong impetus for hotel and resort investment and development. The introduction of the Boeing 747 aircraft in 1975 brought increasing numbers of European and American holidaymakers to Australia (Richardson, 1996). Long-haul travellers and particularly those from the USA (where there was less incidence of VFR-induced travel to Australia) demanded international standard accommodation of the type exemplified by the established transnational lodging chains such as Holiday Inn, Hilton and Hyatt. Developers responded to this demand with energy and engaged in a construction boom in the lead up to the Australian Bicentennial celebrations in 1988. A substantial proportion of this investment emanated from Japan, where outbound tourism was expanding rapidly. Japanese investment was focussed on both the major cities and on resort-style developments, with the latter occurring predominantly on the Gold Coast and around Cairns. The Sunshine Coast (around Noosa) and the Whitsunday Islands also attracted sizeable investments. Examples of the 'glamour and glitz' style resorts of the 1980s include the Mirage Gold Coast and Port Douglas properties and the Hyatt properties at Sanctuary Cove and Coolum.

Characteristic of the boom and bust mentality that appears to govern the development of accommodation in Australia, the growth of supply proved ultimately unsustainable and a bust ensued in the early 1990s (King & McVey, 2006; McVey & King, 2003). The lull reached a peak during the period 1994–1996 when there were no major resorts developments of any kind occurring in Australia (TTF Australia, 2003). Westpac, one of the nation's major banking groups, became by default one of the leading owners of hotels in Australia. A number of the Westpac-owned properties were subsequently acquired by Australian-based investment funds, often at a substantial discount on the original development cost. Such losses cast a shadow over attitudes towards resorts within the investment community.

A number of the 1980s and 1990s developments within Australia occurred in pristine locations and entailed the construction of substantial infrastructure. The five-star Sheraton Mirage Resort at Port Douglas was the first of many luxury developments in the Far North Queensland area. This region is closer to Asian source markets such as Japan, Korea and

Singapore and allows tourists to leave their home country immediately after work and to arrive in Australia on the following morning. Consumers have the prospect of shorter and more price-competitive beach holidays and the wide range of visitor source markets give Far North Queensland a distinctly cosmopolitan feel. Domestic holiday travel to this area has, on the other hand, been limited because of its relative isolation from Australia's major population centres. Airline deregulation has recently stimulated domestic visitation, thereby enhancing the viability of resort investments and producing a better balance between international and domestic visitation.

In marked contrast to its pioneering Port Douglas counterpart, the Sheraton Mirage Gold Coast was established in an already successful domestic destination (i.e. the Gold Coast), albeit one which at that time lacked any provision of five-star hotel accommodation. The property was targeted at free-spending leisure visitors with many expected to come from Japan and the USA. Although the site location of the property (Southport) was relatively undeveloped, the investment was essentially a redevelopment and expansion rather than a greenfield development. The adjacent site has subsequently attracted retail developments and the Palazzo Versace hotel, which describes itself as 'the evolution of the Versace lifestyle, a place of Renaissance splendour and ease' (Palazzo Versace, 2005). Indicative of the postmodern melange of styles, Palazzo Versace is now located adjacent to a MacDonald's family restaurant (see Plate 8.3).

Resort Planning and Development

Australian governments have progressively attempted to adopt a more strategic and holistic approach to coastal management. The Coastal Zone Strategy was initiated by the Commonwealth Government in the early 1990s and examined tourism in the context of Australia's other main coastal activities – fishing and aquaculture, residential development, and resource exploitation and exports (RAC, 1993). In practice, achieving coherent coastal management (including resorts) has been challenging because of the sometimes competing powers and interests of Commonwealth, State and Local Governments. Most of the management and planning functions have been undertaken at state level, with very different practices in evidence. State governments have generally exhibited a degree of enthusiasm towards resort development that has not been matched at the local authority level.

During the 1980s the Queensland Government played a strong advocacy and facilitation role in support of expansionist holiday-related property development. Whilst developments on the Gold Coast had occurred in a largely unplanned and sporadic manner, the Government

Plate 8.3 Palazzo Versace (Main Beach, Gold Coast)
Palazzo Versace combines the design features from the opulent palaces of Europe and the classical architecture of Roman times, coupled with the highest level of decor and ambience created by Europe's eminent Grand Couturier – Versace. The grand design of this 205-room five-star hotel befits its location on the Gold Coast's Broadwater. Palazzo Versace has a choice of three restaurants, Lobby Lounge Bar and a pool bar for light snack.

sought to regularise the process of development and management for the largest resort properties. In providing legislation to support the largest integrated complexes, Queensland's Integrated Resort Development Act (Parliament of Queensland, 1987) transferred responsibility for a range of activities traditionally associated with local councils (e.g. roads and utilities) to the developers. Resort developments covered by the legislation included Sanctuary Cove (near the Gold Coast), Hamilton Island (in the Whitsunday islands) and Laguna Quays Resort (on the Whitsundays mainland).

In part because of its location close to the Gold Coast, Sanctuary Cove is an instructive example of a large-scale integrated resort. It was a precursor to a number of other equivalent developments and was accompanied by the passage of dedicated legislation – The Sanctuary Cove Resort Act (Parliament of Queensland, 1985). The resort exhibits common characteristics with many US-style 'gated communities' in the sun-belt states and combines a range of elements including residential development, second homes, hotels, retail development and a marina. Commercial viability was enhanced by the proximity of the growing Southeast Queensland conurbation, as well as by its climatic appeal for visitors from the Southern states. Indicative of the postmodern crossover between popular culture, events and resorts, the resort opening involved the staging of an activity billed as the 'Great Event' – a greatly hyped double-billing of Frank Sinatra and Whitney Houston. The mix of musical genres was unmistakably postmodern.

In contrast to the experience of Queensland during the 1980s, when resort developments generally proceeded rapidly and with few impediments, proposals along the more sensitive sections of the coastline south of the Queensland/New South Wales border encountered considerable community resistance. A proposal to site a Club Med Resort at Byron Bay on the coast of Northern New South Wales was ultimately abandoned after a sustained campaign of opposition by local residents and environmentalists. Resistance galvanised around the view that an integrated resort would be dominated by 'outsiders'. Objectors sought to retain the existing low-key and informal style of the area (Essex & Brown, 1997). Whilst the growth of the resident and holiday populations has continued unabated over the period since the development was abandoned, the defeat is indicative that integrated resorts may struggle in any contest with more established and ostensibly less formal coastal provision that is viewed as servicing domestic needs adequately.

In Queensland the previously gung-ho attitude towards resort development became more muted in the 1990s with the election of a Labour Government. During the earlier period, the developers had tended to get their way whenever objections had been raised. This occurred in the case of the Iwasaki resort development at Yeppoon near

Rockhampton in Central Queensland. Local residents demonstrated against the proposal because they feared that it would produce an 'enclave' of Japanese retirees. Despite the opposition, the development did proceed, though what emerged was a mainstream resort with substantial domestic visitation and no single overseas nationality occupying a dominant position. By contrast, a late 1990s proposal by Keith Williams, the original developer of Hamilton Island, for a resort on Queensland's Hinchinbrook Passage did not proceed. The increasing strength of the environmental lobby and the emphasis of the state government on sustainability resulted in the abandonment of the proposal at a relatively early stage of development (albeit after the process of land clearing was well underway).

Given the concentration of population along Australia's coastal fringe, it is not surprising that the current and future development of coastal resorts is closely associated with opportunities for residential development. Coastal land-use has been under particular pressure in areas close to the major conurbations such as North and South of Brisbane (the Gold Coast and the Sunshine Coast) and Sydney (though the various national park areas along the New South Wales coast constrain this sprawl). Even in Victoria, with its more temperate climate, coastal sprawl is evident along the Mornington Peninsula (Southeast of Melbourne) and in the Surf Coast Shire (South and West of the city of Geelong). This sprawl has involved a combination of city commuters and new residents attracted from the city by the prospect of a 'Sea Change' (Beeton, 2001). As is common in many established resort destinations, the population of these localities increases markedly during the main holiday periods. Seasonality is most noticeable in the cooler Southern state of Victoria, South Australia and Tasmania, where self-contained resorts are relatively rare, despite the enduring appeal of the beach amongst intrastate travellers. These states offer a range of spectacular coastal settings, which would lend themselves to smaller-scale resort development, but a combination of opposition from environmentalists and markedly seasonal demand has impeded development.

A number of postmodern features have been prominent in the various resort developments that have occurred since the 1990s property crash. Whilst the 1980s developments on the Gold Coast were largely modernist with fairly standardised high-rise constructions, the foundations were already taking shape for the emergence of the Gold Coast as a pleasure- and fantasy-oriented playground. The 1980s witnessed a diversification of the Gold Coast tourism product range with the introduction or redevelopment of theme parks (Movieworld, Wet'n Wild, Seaworld and Dreamworld), entertainment facilities (Jupiter's Casino), marinas (Fishermen's Wharf) and retail development. The Gold Coast has been described as 'a greater concentration of theme parks, resort worlds and tourist-oriented shopping centres than anywhere else in Australia' (Holmes, 2001). This combination of factors reinvigorated the appeal of the destination for domestic visitors and made it internationally competitive. With the emergence of gambling and themed experiences, the Gold Coast is assuming some of the characteristics of a coastal Las Vegas. The architecture has become more whimsical and eclectic and less blatantly modernist. Recent themed hotel developments have included the Phoenician (the ancient world of the Mediterranean – 'a mecca for the worried, weary and overworked'), the Moroccan ('a tropical oasis in the heart of exciting Surfers Paradise') and Palazzo Versace (classical European and an association with the Versace international fashion brand) (see Plate 8.3).

From a development and ownership perspective, the generally poor record of profitability amongst resorts Australia-wide relative to city hotels has been a major challenge. Room yields and occupancies have been lower and there has been a greater dependence on the more volatile leisure markets (as opposed to corporate travellers). The various resort properties started during periods of great optimism, but which subsequently fell victim to oversupply are symptomatic of the high risks associated with resort development. Located on Queensland's Whitsunday coast, Laguna Quays opened in 1992 at a cost of AU$270m and was sold in 1999 for AU$13m. Another example is Daydream Island located off the Whitsunday Coast, which was developed at a cost of AU$100m in 1989 and sold for AU$12.5m in 1999. The boom and bust mentality is a continuing challenge to the sustainable development of the sector.

Conclusion: Into the Future

The future of coastal resort development will continue to be focussed on the main population centres in Southeast Australia, with the less readily accessible areas of Western Australia and the Northern Territory remaining constrained by the tiny size of the local market. Over time however, relatively isolated resort clusters such as Cable Beach in Broome, Western Australia will continue to expand, albeit dependent on the provision of direct flights from key overseas markets in Southeast Asia. The expansion of low-cost carriers out of source markets such as Singapore will assist further development along the Far North Queensland coast with a smaller spin-off in more remote areas. Further south and closer to the population centres of Southeast Queensland, growth will be underpinned by domestic demand both local and interstate, albeit reinforced by further inbound growth from markets such as China, India and the Middle East. The process of post-suburbanisation along the coastline will continue, with tourist activity remaining clustered on the Gold Coast.

The popularity of the various smaller retreats or special interest style developments that were developed during the second half of the 1990s is likely to continue into the future. Though facing their own development challenges, these smaller properties are an effective response to the market shift towards multiple short-break holidays. They also offer the prospect of receiving development approval on sites adjacent to major iconic natural attractions, where larger-scale developments are liable to attract opposition. A modest expansion of smaller lodge-style resorts may occur in the Southern part of the continent in areas such as Margaret River, Western Australia and Tasmania, following a pattern of success already evident in New Zealand. Prospective special interest developments may include golf and wine resorts, eco-tourism resorts, spa resorts and safari resorts.

The prospective longevity of another late 1990s trend – a wave of serviced apartment resort properties – is harder to anticipate. Outside the Gold Coast it is probably unlikely that this style of development will catch on in Australia. Whilst many new resort developments will continue to espouse a philosophy of multiownership, partly with a view to facilitating cash-flow during the initial development phase, the future of multistorey apartment blocks is less clear. The new 80-storey Q1 resort tower on the Gold Coast is the first of its magnitude in Australia and the developers claim that it will be the tallest structure of its kind in the world on completion. Features include a rainforest to be located on levels 67–70! Q1 may be a precursor of more to come, or more likely will follow the tower blocks of Hamilton Island as the last to be developed for many years, as the trend shifts back to lower-rise and less obtrusive development (over the past 30 years the emphasis on island resorts has been on low-rise development). Given the parallels mentioned previously between the Gold Coast and Las Vegas, the rise of Dubai as a coastal resort city in the Middle East is noteworthy. Dubai is now challenging Las Vegas as the world's biggest concentration of hotel and resort construction and the ostentatious style of the various hotel and resort developments invites comparison with QI and Palazzo Versace on the Gold Coast. Dubai's tallest hotel will feature branding by the international fashion label Georgio Armani, symptomatic of the accelerating cross-over between fashion, tourism and architecture. Only the Gold Coast could be viewed as paralleling this postmodern extreme – in many ways it remains an exception to the rule in Australia.

Following a similar trend already evident overseas, spa and health resorts have emerged as a prominent component of the Australian resort sector. The trend towards health resorts was pioneered by the Hyatt Regency Coolum on Queensland's Sunshine Coast, which opened in 1988. Located close to the beach, this resort is adjacent to a golf course and introduced an innovative range of physical, spiritual and artistic therapies for guests. Since the opening of the property, health resorts have proliferated across Australia with some offering more of a medical focus and others a more mainstream emphasis on relaxation (Bennett *et al.*, 2004). As with other resorts, health resorts and spas face competition from equivalent city-based leisure provision. Many city hotels even feature spas and the growth of interest in healthy activities has led to a revival of some longer-established forms (e.g. the reopening of the Sea Baths complex at St. Kilda in Victoria after many years of closure).

Coastal resorts are likely to continue to play an important role in Australia's appeal as a destination into the future. They will however need to diversify at an accelerating rate in view of the growing competitiveness of sun, sea and sand style tourism internationally. Given the strength of Australia's natural attractions, beach resorts may need to look inland to supplement their appeal. In the case of the Gold Coast this may involve the hosting of cultural and sporting events as well as gambling and linking more closely with the hinterland rainforests and waterfalls (Hudson, 2003). With the onslaught of post-suburbanisation along significant stretches of the coastline, Australian resorts will undoubtedly be exemplars of postmodern trends into the future, with the Gold Coast remaining the most prominent exponent.

Chapter 9

Malaysia's Pleasure Periphery: Coastal Resort Development and its Consequences

JOAN HENDERSON

Introduction

Tourism in Malaysia has grown in a distinctive manner, which reflects wider economic, political and sociocultural conditions in the country. Its coastal resorts are an outcome of the interplay of these numerous forces and this chapter examines the dynamics and consequences of the development process and the emergence of a variety of types of resort. These share certain problems experienced by destinations elsewhere, but the defining characteristics of the country and especially the place occupied by the Islamic religion add another layer of complexity to the dilemmas and their management.

The chapter opens with a brief review of general circumstances in Malaysia, followed by an account of its tourism overall. Coastal destinations in Peninsular Malaysia and their evolution are then discussed and attention moves to the physical and sociocultural impacts of resort development. Particular tensions related to religious matters and political responses are outlined in the final section. Such topics have not been extensively researched or publicised, but merit attention. It is hoped that the analysis will contribute to an improved understanding of coastal tourism in a rapidly modernising society where many adhere to a conservative faith which can appear tied to the past.

An Era of Change in Malaysia

The history of tourism in Malaysia and its current state can be best appreciated against the background of more general economic and social change since the federation was founded in 1963. The country has undergone industrialisation and economic transformation (Harper, 1998) under a government dominated by the Barisan Nasional coalition, led by UNMO (United Malays National Organisation). Agriculture and minerals have been superseded by manufacturing and services, which together account for about 80% of GDP (EIU, 2004). Economic progress has been directed by a series of five-year plans and Vision 2020 was launched in 1991, the objective being that Malaysia will be a fully developed nation by that year (Shamsul, 1996). It is deemed to have reached the rank of medium human development by the United Nations Human Development Programme and the GDP per capita in 2002 was US$9120 (UNDP, 2004). There are, however, regional disparities and Western states are more urbanised and prosperous than those in the North and East, which remain predominantly rural, with corresponding contrasts in standards of living. The new Malaysia has an urban middle class of affluent consumers and is symbolised by the capital of Kuala Lumpur's skyline of towering buildings.

Malay Muslims comprise about 60% of the population, which numbered an estimated 26.5 million in 2004 (EIU, 2004). The religion of Islam is integral to concepts of Malay-ness and central to Malaysian life (Kessler, 1992) and bumiputera (literally translated as sons of the soil and a term used to describe ethnic Malays and indigenous peoples such as the aboriginal tribes of Borneo) have been the subject of affirmative action programmes. This has resulted in a tendency towards the cultural and political marginalisation of other groups (Milne & Mauzy, 1998; Worden, 2001), including Chinese and Indians, who represent 24% and 7% of inhabitants respectively (Department of Statistics Malaysia, 2001). Nevertheless, and despite racial violence in the late 1960s, an uneasy pluralism exists (Crouch, 2001).

The Malay Muslim community itself has been divided by Islamic revivalism and greater religious orthodoxy, which more liberal elements argue is undermining civil liberties and alienating non-Muslims (Nagata, 1987). Another complication is deciding what constitutes proper Islamic belief and conduct with scope for interpretation of the relevant scriptures (Esposito, 1999). At the same time, modernisation and associated consumerism are increasingly powerful influences. Many of the younger generation seem pulled between Middle East style Islamic extremism and Westernisation, although some commentators maintain that the latter is blunting the appeal of the former (BBC, 2005). The outcome can be a curious hybrid culture in which tradition and modernity are juxtaposed. Such a predicament faces other races within Malaysian society and raises questions about the meaning of national and cultural identities there in the 21st century.

Tourism reflects these shifting parameters, which are a source of both opportunities and constraints for the industry and its customers. Economic progress has stimulated demand for domestic and outbound travel, while permitting public expenditure on development and marketing, which has facilitated inbound flows. An uninterrupted governing regime has also been in a position to devise and implement long-term pro-tourism policies. Nevertheless, tourism is an arena in which sociocultural and political disputes find expression and require resolution if enterprises are to function successfully and tourists to be satisfied. Aspects of coastal resort tourism illustrate the complexities of the relationship between tourism and the external environment in a manner that is explained in later sections.

Tourism in Malaysia

International and domestic tourism have seen significant growth in Malaysia in recent years and the industry has featured prominently in physical and economic strategic planning (Khalifah & Tahir, 1997; Musa, 1999; Sadi & Bartels, 1997). Considerable emphasis has been given in these plans to investment in coastal centres and their promotion as primary and secondary locations (Basiron, 1995; *TTG Daily News*, 2005; Wong, 1990). The current high priority allocated to tourism is indicative of its actual and possible contribution to income, employment and foreign exchange earnings (de Sausmarez, 2003; McVey, 2001), which was first acknowledged in the 1970s. It is now the most lucrative service sector and hailed as a key driver of growth and a means of diversifying the economy (EIU, 2004).

In addition to anticipated financial rewards, government is interested in tourism because of its role in articulating and reinforcing a unifying sense of national identity, of especial relevance for a young nation of mixed races that have not always enjoyed harmonious relations (Henderson, 2003a; Wood, 1984). Tourism is the responsibility of the Ministry of Culture, Arts and Tourism, which funds Tourism Malaysia, the National Tourism Organisation. It had a budget of RM30 million (US$7.9 million) in 2005 when it was expecting over 16 million tourists (Bernama News, 2005).

Inbound arrivals exceeded 7 million by 1990, but the 1990s were marked by a series of damaging events like the Gulf War and 1997 Asian financial crisis, which impeded activity, as shown in Table 9.1. Recovery was interrupted by the outbreak of the Severe Acute Respiratory Syndrome (SARS) virus in 2003, followed by a record 15.7 million arrivals and receipts of over RM30 billion (US$7.9 billion) in 2004 (Tourism Malaysia, 2005). Most overseas tourists are intraregional and the leading markets for 2004 are listed in Table 9.2, headed by Singapore, which is connected to the Malaysian Peninsula by causeway and bridge. Outside of the Asian region, North America and Europe generate large amounts of visitors and there has been a boom in Arab tourists from the Middle East (*Saudi Arabian News Digest*, 2004).

Domestic tourism has been encouraged for several decades, sometimes accompanied by curbs on spending abroad to try to reduce economic leakages due to mounting outbound travel (Ministry of

Table 9.1 International tourist arrivals in Malaysia, 1994–2004

Year	*Arrivals (millions)*
1994	7.19
1995	7.46
1996	7.13
1997	6.21
1998	5.55
1999	7.93
2000	10.22
2001	12.78
2002	13.29
2003	10.58
2004	15.70

Source: Tourism Malaysia (2005)

Culture, Arts & Tourism, 1992; Richter, 1993). According to official statistics, domestic trips rose from 8.32 million in 1997 to 15.8 in 1999, and overnight stays by nationals equal those of overseas visitors (McVey, 2001). Domestic and regional tourism are set to benefit from the burgeoning of low-cost airlines in Asia, not least Air Asia, which has its headquarters in Malaysia and is executing an aggressive expansion programme. Details of the geographical spread of both domestic and overseas hotel guests are contained in Table 9.3, which indicates the pre-eminence of West coast destinations and the Klang Valley where the capital is located. The Malaysian climate is a tropical one of high temperatures and humidity throughout the year, but there is a slight seasonal effect because of the monsoon which deters visits to Eastern shores from November to March. Core attractions for tourists are natural and cultural heritage, although purpose-built amenities, events and shopping are now heavily promoted.

Malaysia's Coastal Resorts and Development Models

Malaysia occupies an area of 330,113 square kilometres and comprises 11 states on the Malaysian Peninsula and two (Sabah and Sarawak) on the island of Borneo. It has an extensive coastline and over 1000 offshore islands, representing a valuable tourism resource that is constantly highlighted in marketing material. The coast and islands have always

Table 9.2 Origin of Malaysia's international tourists, 2004

Country	*Arrivals (thousands)*
Singapore	9520
Thailand	1518
Indonesia	790
Brunei	454
China	550
Japan	301
Taiwan	190
Hong Kong	80
India	173
USA	145
Australia	204
UK	204
Saudi Arabia	39
United Arab Emirates	21

Source: Tourism Malaysia (2005)

Table 9.3 Malaysia's domestic and international hotel guests by region, 2003 (% share)

Locality	*Domestic*	*International*	*Total*
Klang Valley	22.9	43.8	31.6
Penang	7.8	15.3	10.9
West Coast (excluding Penang)	27.2	14.9	22
East Coast	13	4.3	9.4
Highland resorts	6.8	6.6	6.7
Island resorts	8.9	7.5	8.3
Sabah	6.1	4.3	5.4
Sarawak	6.5	2.8	4.9

Source: Tourism Malaysia (2005)

been important assets and the basis of marine tourism, which encompasses conventional beach holidays and specialised products like diving, made possible by the rich marine life and coral reef ecosystems (Basiron, 1995). Beach destinations of varying size and type have evolved over time along the coast and on certain islands (Hofmann, 1979; Wong, 1986) and principal centres are depicted in Fig. 9.1. There are, however, comparatively few major resorts of a traditional character and much development has taken the form of individual hotels or combinations of accommodation properties that are self-contained and all-inclusive. These sites are frequently termed resorts or hotel resorts and advertised as such, but there is insufficient data to allow their distribution to be mapped. The better known and more accessible places serve domestic and international markets, while others are visited mainly by Malaysians and some Singaporeans.

Popular mainland resorts include Port Dickson and Cherating, the former said to have the best beaches on the West coast which extend for 15 km and are backed by casuarina trees. A range of accommodation from budget to luxury is available in the town and on coastal roads. Many visitors to the beaches are excursionists, often family groups, who travel to the coast in order to enjoy picnics and bathing (Basiron, 1997). Cherating, once a village, is associated with the Club Mediterranee tour operator and was one of its first Asian properties. The area is largely rural and home to several other hotel resorts.

Tourism on Malaysian islands has been determined by geographical factors and Wong (1993) classifies them according to extent, resources and access. Penang is an example of a sizeable island that is capable of supporting comparatively large-scale tourism. It covers 285 square kilometres and has good air, road and ferry links. Over half a million live on the island where over 60% of residents are Chinese, a legacy of its history, and it has a diversified economy. There are 35 officially registered hotels, five of which are five star, as well as apartments, motels and hostels. Resort hotels are clustered on the Northern beaches, particularly the 2.5-km strip of Batu Ferringgi (Tourism Penang, 2005). The main island of Langkawi (an archipelago of 104 islands, three of which are inhabited) comprises 478 square kilometres and rivals Penang in popularity. It has 25 hotels and hotel resorts, from the luxurious in secluded grounds to the more modest by the jetty in the town. The population numbers approximately 62,000 and tourism is a key industry (Journey Malaysia, 2005).

Another category is that of smaller islands that are suitable for less intensive tourism such as Tioman, Pangkor and Redang. Tioman is 39 km long and 12 km wide and is the most developed of the volcanic islands that make up Tioman National Park. It is reached by water and has an airstrip, but there are asphalt roads only around the main entry point.

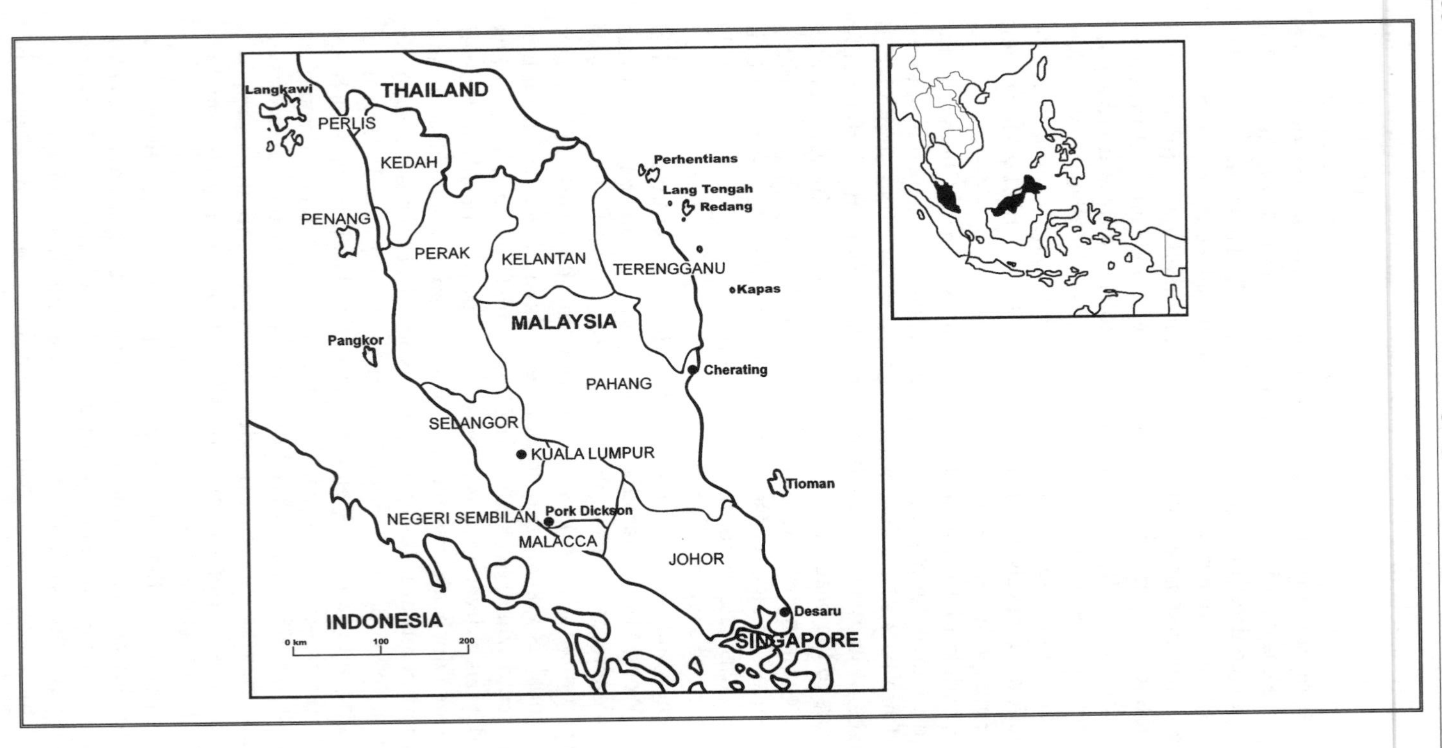

Figure 9.1 Malaysian states and coastal and island resorts

The island is sparsely populated and about 2700 live in six villages or kampungs. Visitors can choose to stay in beach huts and chalets, some of which have air conditioning, or in a beach, golf and spa hotel resort. Pangkor has a 7-km coastline, but 15 hotels and hotel resorts, three of which claim to be luxury class. These are centred on four beaches on the Western shore with scattered fishing settlements in the East. It is accessible by air and ferry (Malaysia Hotels, 2005). The main island in the Redang group has a total of 16 resorts, three of international standard and one with a golf course, and a campsite. Ferries serve the island and an airstrip recently opened. A village community of almost 250 rely on fishing and tourism (Redang, 2005).

Finally, there are the smallest and more remote islands, with restricted amenities, which are drawing more tourists (Din, 1997). These are illustrated by Pulau Kapas, Pulau Lang Tengah and the Perhentians in the northerly and less developed Terengganu state. Simple dive facilities and cabin-style accommodation are offered alongside clear waters, white beaches, coral reefs and tropical forests (Tourism Malaysia, 2004). Numerous other islands receive visitors, or have the capacity to do so, and seclusion and an absence of development is an attraction for the more adventurous.

Coastal resorts in Malaysia thus exhibit great diversity (see Chapter 11 for more in-depth discussion of this issue) and the phrase is applied to primitive campsites near villages on isolated islands, concentrations of high-rise blocks characteristic of parts of the Mediterranean and individual hotel resorts of assorted standard, size and design. In certain instances, development has been essentially unplanned and uncontrolled. Traditional settlements, once inhabited by a few residents who depended on fishing and rice farming, have undergone dramatic changes together with the immediate physical landscapes. Such a case is Batu Ferringgi, originally a fishing village, which grew from a site with only two small hotels and several second homes in the 1960s to a busy conglomeration of multi-storey hotels by the 1990s (ADB, 1996; Smith, 1992a).

An alternative to ad hoc development is integrated beach resorts, which are common throughout Southeast Asia and are 'planned environments with a number of hotels which share infrastructure, recreational features and other facilities' (Smith, 1992b: 211). Their characteristics of centralised and co-ordinated design and management permit economies of scale and control and consistency in operations. Projects are usually completed over a five to ten year period and can assist in averting the environmental deterioration that accompanies some resort expansion (Smith, 1992c).

Desaru in Malaysia originated at about the same time as Nusa Dua on the Indonesian island of Bali, often quoted as one of the more successful integrated resorts in the region. The 1973 master plan envisaging ten hotels was never fully implemented, however, and the resort's performance has been disappointing (*The New Straits Times*, 2004). Although Singaporeans still visit, improved communications have brought more distant Malaysian locations within their reach and the Desaru Development Corporation is seeking to revive its fortunes (*The Straits Times*, 2005a). Desaru's experience is not unusual and the grandiose schemes of resort developers can be frustrated by unexpected occurrences, failure to secure government backing and financial setbacks.

Langkawi does not correspond to either the ad hoc or integrated model and has been developed as a result of federal and local government initiatives. Its designation as a Duty Free Port in 1987 acted as a catalyst and subsequent progress has been guided by the Langkawi Development Plan (1990–2005). About RM300 million (US$79 million) of public funding was invested in infrastructure and the commercial sector spent approximately RM4 billion (US$1.1 billion) on accommodation during the 1990s. Arrivals rose from 200,000 in 1986 to almost 2 million in 1997 and a new master plan prepared by the Langkawi Development Authority anticipates further growth (Kayat, 2002). Much of the accommodation stock is resort hotels and these are typical of the trend previously noted whereby hotel companies are developing their own complexes. These can be fairly isolated, with limited public access, and frequently incorporate spas and occasionally private villas.

Physical impacts of resort development

Smith (1992c) describes how many beach resorts in Southeast Asia have environmental and social problems, aggravated by inadequate planning, which detract from their appeal. These conclusions are of relevance in parts of Malaysia where the environment has been neglected in the rush to secure short-term economic returns from tourism. Overdevelopment and pollution have occurred with damage to beaches, coral reefs and marine life (Hall, 1997). Construction of facilities and the clearing of coastal vegetation and mangrove swamps have destroyed ecosystems and exacerbated coastal and soil erosion due to natural forces. Abdullah (1992) estimates that many beaches have almost disappeared so that the proportion of the coastline usable for leisure is less than 5%.

Heavy demands on water from residents and tourists can mean a fall in the groundwater table and saline intrusion. Waste water is discharged into the sea and garbage disposal facilities to deal with the heavy littering are unsatisfactory. A poor regulatory framework for diving operations, conflicts over the use of coastal resources and lack of development control have been additional weaknesses (ADB, 1996). Such have been the impacts on land and sea of Batu Ferringi's transformation to an urban resort that the sustainability of tourism there has been undermined and there are doubts about its long-term future (Bui, 2000). Overcrowding is also evident in Port Dickson (Basiron, 1997) and even marine parks are suffering, despite formal protection.

There are over 35 marine parks and islands such as Tioman, Payar and Redang have become a focus for nature-based tourism. The parks where these islands are found received 213,172, 133,775 and 63,825 visitors respectively in 2002 (Ainul, 2003). Clearance at some sites has led to sedimentation harmful to coral, which is also affected by pollution from sea vessels. Many islands have no solid waste disposal systems or sewage treatment plants. Coral reefs are further disturbed by careless snorkellers and boat anchors, and souvenir hunters are an added threat to biodiversity. There are 20 marinas and yacht clubs in Malaysia, with plans for another 22 (Basiron, 2004), and proposals for a marina on Tioman are being resisted because of fears for the environmental quality of the island and its waters. Local indifference and a degree of official corruption have been cited as barriers to surmount if islands like Tioman are to be conserved (Wikipedia, 2005).

Tourism development may involve some resettlement and questions of local access to the coast are examined by Ainul (2003). She explains that beaches in Malaysia are formally gazetted for public enjoyment, but the National Land Code allows state authorities to take over any land within their borders. Foreshores of good beaches can therefore be allocated for the building of resorts aimed at foreign visitors, excluding locals who are confined to degraded public beaches. Although not yet a widespread practice, there have been incidents in Penang, Langkawi and Port Dickson of hotels barring locals from the beaches in front of their premises. As well as fuelling resentment, pressures on remaining public areas are augmented as overseas visitors, domestic tourists and excursionists all compete for space.

While environmental protection legislation and regulations do exist, these may be deficient and Environmental Impact Assessments (EIAs) are not compulsory for accommodation units of less than 80 rooms. EIA procedures can also ignore the progressive effects of a series of projects, and divergences between federal and provincial laws may discourage effective conservation and planning. Integrated beach resorts might be seen as one answer to tourism's difficult relationship with the environment, but such centres too have negative environmental outcomes. Even if resorts themselves are well maintained and responsibly managed, spontaneous and unsightly development can happen immediately outside the boundaries and impinge on their appearance and ambience.

Sociocultural concerns

With regard to sociocultural concerns, research is not extensive within a Malaysian context and King (1993) cautions about exaggerating tourism's power to precipitate harmful change. Nevertheless, Hong (1985) reports on the ways in which tourism disturbs resident lifestyles in Penang and Din (1997) comments on a sense of anxiety about declining moral standards in both Penang and Langkawi. In a study of the latter, Bird (1989) concludes that locals are usually ignored in decisions about tourism development and may be resentful. Other researchers have uncovered popular support for tourism there and believe that opinions about its merits are determined by individual values, personal dependence on the industry and willingness to adapt (Kayat, 2002).

Integrated beach resorts and hotel resorts have specific sociocultural and socioeconomic disadvantages that can offset their advantages. Socially, there may be little meaningful contact between tourists and residents, as evidenced by the Club Mediterranee resort at Cherating (King, 1993). Discord can be engendered by exclusive and expensive properties that alienate residents and provoke xenophobia, especially where the economic gap between them and tourists is manifestly wide. Opponents in general have criticised the nature of the work provided and the employment of expatriates and non-locals in senior and management positions. Opportunities for entrepreneurship and informal hawking are restricted by the character of all inclusive resorts, limiting the monetary gains accruing to local inhabitants (Freitag, 1994).

There are particular religious concerns in Malaysia and these have assumed greater prominence in the past decade, linked to the Islamic movement made reference to in the introduction. Religion is a potential cause of tension between residents and visitors and amongst the latter who include Muslim and non-Muslim Malays, overseas Muslims and international tourists of other religions or no faith. For its more orthodox followers, Islam demands submission to rigorous rules of conduct, dress and diet. Close proximity of unmarried men and women and physical displays of affection, alcoholic consumption, revealing clothes, nude or nearly nude sunbathing, gambling and prostitution are all contrary to Islamic practice. However, these often accompany tourism and are commonplace in beach resorts around the world. Muslims are also expected to conform to a timetable of prayers and should only eat and deal with food declared halal, requirements which tourism employers may be unaware of or choose to ignore (Hong, 1985). Exposure to international Western-style tourism, whether direct or indirect, could further lead to a questioning of religious doctrine and observances and possible deviations from these.

Overt clashes between residents and tourists of the same religion on theological grounds appear unlikely and, indeed, promotional material stresses the sociocultural affinity between Muslim guests and their Malaysian hosts. This does not necessarily mean that such tourists are assimilated into society and one journalist thought it newsworthy to recount how 'white robed Arab men and their wives and daughters, modestly covered in dark veils' can be seen on the streets of Kuala Lumpur in the tourist season (*The New Sunday Times*, 2004). There is, however, perhaps greater scope for friction when visitors are non-Muslims and accustomed to a hedonistic Western lifestyle. Din (1989: 551–552) writes of the 'permissiveness, lavishness, servitude and foreign-ness' of mass tourism, which he contrasts with Islamic piety and its 'ascetic abstinence and humility'. Although not all Malay Muslims match this ideal, tourist attitudes and behaviour may offend them and contradict religious strictures. Issues of difference between the two groups have political implications and can lead to government intervention, as outlined in the final section.

The Politics of Tourism

Race and religion are defining features of Malaysian politics as well as society. The government, led by a Malay party headed by Dr Mahatir for 22 years until his retirement in 2003, has energetically pursued modernisation and full development whilst seeking to retain and demonstrate a dedication to Islam. A degree of secularisation has been acceptable, and inevitable in view of Malaysia's racial mix, and the authorities have presented the country as a model of moderate Islam (Nagata, 1994, 1997). The position has been attacked by the chief opposition party, Parti Islam SeMalaysia (PAS), which claims to be the defender of the Islamic faith and talks of turning Malaysia into a theocracy. PAS has modified its agenda in order to help establish partnerships (EIU, 2005) and only governs the state of Kelantan, but does have a following throughout the country.

The leadership in the post-Mahatir era thus faces the task of dealing with the threat posed by PAS and creating a '21st century Muslim democracy in a multi-ethnic society' (Hardy, 2005). The parties have been vying for the role of the guardian of Islam, a struggle that has prompted an 'Islamicisation' of politics and decision making. The new prime minister has reacted by promulgating a progressive vision of Islam that seems to have met a sympathetic response from the electorate (EIU, 2004), yet hostility from some quarters. The stance adopted has significance for tourism because it affects internal conditions and stability and relations with the outside world, shaping Malaysia's image

as both a tourist destination and recipient of foreign investment in the industry.

Approaches to international tourism by governments of Islamic countries vary and Din (1989) proposes alternatives of accommodation, rejection and isolation. In Malaysia, there were official reservations in the 1960s about young independent travellers because of their moral decadence (Din, 1997). High-spending foreign vacationers, confined in exclusive resorts, and business tourists were initially preferred in a bid to protect locals from the subversive influences of the 'hippie' culture (Richter, 1993). There has been a reappraisal in the intervening years, as revealed earlier, and the policy now goes beyond accommodation to enthusiastic engagement. While appreciative of religious sensibilities and sensitivities, there is a willingness to try to meet the demands of overseas visitors for familiar leisure environments where religion does not intrude. A pragmatism therefore prevails, which is derived from economic imperatives and observable in broader economic goals to secure investment and accelerate industrialisation (Nagata, 1997).

A strategy of support for tourism is shared by most provincial authorities, but it became a topic of contention in 2002 in Terengganu. The PAS government, which was later defeated in the 2004 elections, was committed to the 'Islamicisation' of the state, which extended to the tourism sector. Measures such as the banning of bikinis, separate swimming pools for men and women, and more rigid regulations on entertainment licensing and alcohol sales were mooted. The plan led to disagreement with central government, was strongly opposed by the tourism industry and generated worldwide publicity (Henderson, 2003b).

The controversial steps were never completely implemented, but the debate that took place continues to resonate. It was echoed in discussions in 2005 about the work of the Federal Territory Religious Department, whose officers are charged with the enforcement of Islamic law (*The Straits Times*, 2005b). There was speculation that intensified religious policing could be sanctioned at state, if not federal, level with suggestions that the Chief Minister of Malacca had set up vice squads to enforce morality there (EIU, 2005). Such a move would have repercussions for both domestic and international tourists, especially Muslims, and the operation of the industry.

These events illustrate the dilemmas for destination authorities, residents, the tourism industry and tourists which can arise in tourist destinations where many locals are bound by a strict religious code. It also indicates some of the difficulties facing less conservative Malay Muslims and other ethnic groups wishing to participate in domestic tourism. Possibilities of discord are heightened in the relaxed atmosphere of a beach resort setting where visitors may assume that they can dress (or undress) and behave in a self-indulgent manner which seems licentious to some observers. Managing the encounters between tourists and locals and averting conflict in these situations poses challenges that all stakeholders have a part to play in overcoming. Visitors are already advised about ways of avoiding giving offence and continued efforts to promote mutual understanding would seem critical.

It must be acknowledged that there have been few reports of serious trouble between tourists and residents at coastal resorts in Malaysia arising from religion. Nevertheless, there is a likelihood that incidents do occur and the consequences of resort development for local communities and their concerns is an important area for further study. Such research could include an evaluation of the contribution of the hotel resort and whether it reduces the chances of confrontation. The significance of visitor nationality is another avenue to explore and tensions in Malaysia may be muted because Western tourists, arguably the most disruptive in the sociocultural sphere, account for a comparatively small percentage of the total. Those from neighbouring countries, many of which are also multiethnic with Muslim populations, may have greater knowledge of the religious customs of others and act accordingly.

Studies of sociocultural matters and tourism impacts as a whole are urgently needed as Malaysia endeavours to meet its ambitious official target of 24.6 million international arrivals by 2010 (*The Business Times*, 2005). Projections may be overoptimistic, but do raise questions about the management and sustainability of development at such a pace. These are especially acute for more vulnerable coastal sites.

Conclusion

The dynamics of coastal resort development and outcomes discussed in the chapter are not confined to Malaysia and can be observed in many countries that are anxious to expand their tourism industries. However, the evolution of its resorts and their current status reflect the unique history of the country as an independent nation and prevailing economic, political and social conditions in the 21st century.

As Malaysia has advanced economically, there has been public and private investment in infrastructure and facilities, which now attract international tourists from the Southeast Asian region and the rest of the world. Increasing prosperity has created a new middle class of consumers who are desirous of escaping the stresses of urban life to relax on the coast. Accommodation options range from five-star hotels to more modest self-catering chalets and basic campsites. At the same time, Malaysia is still a developing country and certain resorts and leisure pursuits are beyond the means of many nationals. The less affluent are drawn to the beaches, but select accommodation and activities suited to their budget and are often day trippers. Financial constraints and lack of resources and expertise in the public domain, as well as the absence of political will, may also impede effective planning and contribute to coastal environmental degradation.

In addition, tourism emerges as an economic and political tool which has been used by government to strengthen the economy and reinforce its own position. Success as an international destination casts a favourable light on rulers and enhances the country's stature as a member of the global community, helping to cement alliances in other fields. Coastal resorts have benefited from this official interest, but have sometimes been negatively affected by the speed of development, lack of controls and wrangling between federal and state authorities.

Finally, coastal resorts are not immune to the trends that are reshaping Malaysian society and culture. While modernisation appears to favour a consumer culture that affords commercial opportunities for the tourism industry, Islamic revivalism and radicalism could influence, and perhaps undermine, aspects of leisure demand at home and abroad. The nature of the dominant Islamic religion imposes certain obligations on the tourist industry and non-Muslim tourists which must be respected to minimise the risk of conflict. Visitors to many resorts comprise a mixture of races, religions and nationalities whose needs will have to be reconciled and satisfied if this key form of tourism is to realise its full potential in Malaysia.

Chapter 10

Natural Heritage as Place Identity: Tofino, Canada, a Coastal Resort on the Periphery

ALISON GILL and ERIN WELK

Introduction

Although Canada possesses the world's longest coastline and is bordered by three oceans, it is not renown for its coastal resorts, of which there are few. The short cool summers of both the East (Atlantic) and West (Pacific) coasts are a contributing factor, as is the concentration of over 80% of Canada's population in the heartland of Southern Ontario and Southern Quebec, centred on the metropolitan areas of Toronto and Montreal – far distant from the coastal peripheries. The summer holiday tradition in this heartland of the nation is to spend time in 'cottage country' north of the cities on the lake-strewn Canadian Shield (Halseth, 1998). There is some tourism development along the East and West coasts, but it serves a local or regional market. However, within the last two decades significant changes have occurred in the revaluing and reimaging of Canada's coasts with respect to tourism. On both East and West coasts, traditional resource extractive industries – fishing and logging – have suffered decline in the face of global economic restructuring. In an effort to diversify, coastal communities have often looked to tourism as their economic salvation. Further, there has been recent escalating demand for accessible coastal property as amenity migrants (largely second-home owners) seeking lifestyle opportunities are drawn to an increasingly scarce commodity. Tourism has even had some impact on the remote Arctic coast as tourists seek exotic cultural and natural heritage experiences. Such trends are reflective of the demands of postmodern tourism.

In this chapter we focus our discussion on the West coast of Canada, a deeply fjorded coastline that, except in its southern reaches, is largely inaccessible by road. Vancouver, Canada's third largest metropolis, with a population of over 2 million, boasts many beaches within its city boundaries. On Vancouver Island, sandy beaches along the East coast bordering the Strait of Georgia have long attracted families from Vancouver, the Lower Mainland and Victoria to traditional family beach resorts. Children's summer camps and more exclusive fishing lodges only accessible by boat or float-plane still remain as vestiges of an earlier tourism era – and in the latter case as examples of the continued elitism of inaccessibility.

The coastal resort of Tofino, a small community of 1700 people on the tip of Estowista peninsula on Vancouver Island's West coast, serves as an example of how a coastal village once dependent on fishing, and to some extent coastal logging, has transformed into a resort community reflective of postmodern societal values. We trace the evolution of tourism in the resort from its origins around 1970, through various developmental phases. In many ways this echoes the resort cycle stages of Butler's (1980) model – Tofino's tourism identity has evolved from a remote counterculture/surfer village to an internationally marketed year-round resort with a diverse set of attractions predominantly based on its natural heritage resources. Tofino now attracts around 1 million visitors a year (Personal Communication, Tofino Chamber of Commerce, 20 July 2005) and in recent years the resort has attracted external capital in the development of upmarket hotels and residential real estate.

To establish a context for the case study, we first present a Canadian perspective on how post-Fordist restructuring has affected tourism and place identity. In the subsequent discussion section, we focus on the commodification of natural heritage resources and the consequent management of conflicting values. In this we draw upon the findings of recent (2005) empirical research in the community that employed field observations, key informant interviews and document analysis to examine transitional aspects of tourism development.

Post-Fordist Restructuring, Tourism and Place Identity: A Canadian Perspective

In *Consuming Places*, Urry (1995: 173) observes that 'there are some striking changes taking place in how the environment is being 'read', how it is appropriated, and how it is exploited, ... these changes increasingly depend upon the economic, social and geographical organization of contemporary tourism'. In a Canadian context, tourism is playing a significant role in transforming the way in which many coastal communities are seeking to reinvent themselves as a means of survival in a post-Fordist economy (Gill *et al.*, 2003). The nature of these transformations is a function of revaluing coastal environments for their consumptive uses. In the case study presented, these values include a heightened awareness of, and appreciation for, natural heritage. Institutionally this awareness is reflected in the introduction of Canada's *Oceans Act* (1997), which extends concern for oceans and coastal management beyond traditional fishing and transportation uses to include responsibility for and regulation of coastal activities such as tourism and recreation and the establishment of Marine Protected Areas (Gill *et al.*, 2003).

Post-Fordism, neoliberalism and globalisation have had a profound effect on hinterland regions of British Columbia, resulting in widespread economic restructuring and resultant job loss (Howlett & Brownsey, 2001). In coastal regions of British Columbia, the emerging post-productive landscape is not one of transformation from an agricultural economy – such as that extensively documented in the case of rural Britain (Wilson, 2001) – but one of transformation from a staples resource production system (Innes, 1930) – notably fish and timber – to a more diversified landscape in which tourism and recreational resources have become valued (Hayter, 2000; Ommer & Newell, 1999). While some places are still dependent on traditional productive activities, in other places evidence of a new consumptive economy characterises the landscape. Aguiar *et al*. (2005: 137) observe in the context of Kelowna, British Columbia (a town in interior British Columbia) that 'post-Fordism gives priority to the space of consumption over production, an important interest in place-making and the selling of these ideas becomes paramount'. Invariably conflicts result from the influx of new residents and/or tourists drawn by the new economies. Contestations over consumptive versus productive land uses relating to issues such as local governance, power relations and increasing housing costs define the nature of debate over the nature of place and place identity (Aguiar *et al.*, 2005; Gill & Reed, 1997, 1999; Reed, 1997).

In response to the demands of the postmodern tourist, the creation of place identity differs from that of earlier eras. In coastal settings, traditional family beach activities still exist in some places but the products of the postmodern resort are more diversified and customised to more individualised forms of production (Agarwal, 1999). The values reflected in postmodern tourist activity relate to tradition, heritage, subjective well-being, environmental protection and other quality-of-life concerns (Jenkins, 2000). This new cultural awareness calls for a renewed search for authenticity and encounters that are different from those attainable from mass tourism (Oakes & Minca, 2004). As expressed in the nature of the tourist gaze (Urry, 1990), tourists seek to observe places as a series of symbols and signs that they experience and interpret according to their own set of meanings. As part of the commodification of place, natural resources and symbolic landscapes (such as unspoilt landscapes) can be transformed into a marketable product through the creation of linked production systems (Jenkins, 2000). As Garrod *et al*. (2006) conclude in a UK context, the reconceptualisation of rural resources as 'countryside capital' provides a more holistic and integrated understanding of the rural tourism production system, which includes essential components that may either be tangible or perceptual.

With an emphasis on quality-of-life values, the blurring of boundaries between tourism/leisure and other aspects of individuals' lives is also a marker of postmodernism. Thus, in resort communities the distinction between residents and tourists is confounded by the role of second-home owners who themselves range from those who own a single family residence to those who have varying degrees of fractional ownership in a condominium development or time-share property (Hall & Muller, 2004; Kuentzel & Ramaswamy, 2005; Venturoni *et al.*, 2005). From a community perspective, perhaps the real distinction is between those who work in the community versus those who, for lifestyle reasons, live in the community (both permanently or part-time) but do not work there (Best, 2005). Changes to the social structure of communities are inevitable. As Kneafsey (2001: 778) observes in a discussion of changing rural cultural economy in Brittany, France, '[n]ewer social relations are layered over and mediated through, the sedimented social relations already established within places'.

In response to the values embodied in postmodern society, heritage tourism has grown rapidly. However, as Nuryanti (1996) argues, the relationships between tourism and heritage are complex. This argument is reinforced by Poria *et al*. (2003), who contest heritage tourism is a phenomenon based on tourists' motivations and perceptions as opposed to specific site attributes. While the term 'heritage tourism' is most commonly associated with cultural heritage, it also includes natural heritage that encompasses not only designated parks but also valued landscapes and wilderness areas. In the USA the construct of 'wilderness' is deeply embedded into the cultural identity of the American West and underlies the early formation of National Parks (Nash, 1967). While there is much debate over the definition of 'wilderness' (Nash, 1967), National Park designation represents a social construction of wilderness that has reinforced the signifiers that have attracted tourists (Shaw & Williams, 2002). Although the *US Wilderness Act* (1964) defines wilderness as a road-less area essentially un-impacted by human activity, Tuan (1974) refers to wilderness as a 'state of mind' and Hendee *et al*. (1978) identify three fundamental values associated with wilderness – experiential, mental and moral restoration, and scientific.

In Canada, where there are extensive areas of uninhabited territory, 'wilderness tourism' has become a commodified product that is seen to encompass a range of adventure tourism and eco-tourism activities that attract an international market, especially from Europe and the USA. Although marketed as wilderness, many coastal B.C. landscapes, while apparently uninhabited, represent the resources of an industrialised forest economy as well as the traditional lands of First Nations people

(Willems-Braun, 1997). White (1999) has examined the process by which tourism landscapes in the Clayoquot Sound area of Vancouver Island (including Tofino) have been 'authored'. He suggests a process whereby landscapes are first identified – a stage of recognition and exploration; then signified through the creation of selected images. The third stage involves evaluation when a hierarchy of values for landscape resources is negotiated with stakeholders and government, and a fourth stage of designation that installs and empowers a land and resource use regime. The transformation of a landscape from one of resource production to one of tourist consumption is a contested one that involves various changing stakeholder alliances over time, with the media playing a significant role in effecting change in the broader public arena (White, 1999).

Tofino, British Columbia: A Coastal Community in Transition

Tofino and its neighbouring community of Ucluelet, located on the West coast of Vancouver Island, are the only coastal settlements that provide direct access to the open coastal waters of the Pacific Ocean. As the result of international attention drawn to the conflict over logging in the area, Tofino has become associated with the entire Clayoquot Sound region, an area of 349,947 hectares that is now designated as an international biosphere reserve that contains some of the world's largest untouched tracts of old-growth temperate rainforest (Carruthers *et al*., 1997). The physical attributes of the region have played a significant role in the evolution of the community as a tourism destination. Tofino has experienced several definable phases of growth during the past 40 years, and the landscape has evolved from one of production to one of consumption (Table 10.1). This transition has at times resulted in divisive

Table 10.1 Key stages in the tourism development of Tofino

Date	*Key stages*
Pre-1970	Counterculture migrants (hippies and surfers)
1970s	Park development
1980s and 1990s	Environmentalists
Late 1980s	Eco-feminists
1990s	Resort development
2000–present	Amenity migrants

community relationships as emergent post-productive values have challenged established traditions.

Aboriginal settlement in the area predates the arrival of European (British and Spanish) explorers and settlers in the 1700s. Many of the names of the coastal landscape surrounding Tofino are demonstrative of the mythic past of local tribes such as the Nuu-chah-nulth, Opitsaht, Ahousaht and Hesquiat (White, 1999). Ongoing First Nations land claims negotiations are reminders of the contestation that still exists over ownership and use of the land. Early white settlers, who accessed this area by water, were well established by the end of the 19th century, first on islands in Clayoquot Sound and later at the present site of Tofino, where the sheltered East side of the narrow Estowista peninsula offered a safe harbour from the exposed Pacific Ocean and served the needs of fishermen and loggers. The first road access was constructed in 1959, when a road to Port Alberni, 126 km to the east, connected Tofino to an existing road system. In the early 1960s, this resulted in the influx of the first counterculture ('hippie') migrants into this remote coastal fishing community. Some of these early migrants were avid surfers drawn to the huge waves of the outer coast.

In 1971, the area immediately south of the Tofino municipal boundary was designated by the Federal Government as one of three components of the Pacific Rim National Park Reserve. The park consists of dramatic seascapes along the exposed Pacific Ocean coast with many islands, inlets and beaches against a backdrop of mountains cloaked in temperate rainforest. With park designation and the paving of the road in 1972, Tofino, by default, became a service centre providing accommodation, food, gas and groceries to park visitors. The controversy that began in 1988 over logging within the Clayoquot Sound area epitomises the era of environmentalism. Over 800 protesters gathered in Tofino to support the Nuu-chah-nulth First Nations in preventing the logging of Meares Island located across the inner harbour from Tofino. In total, over 900 environmental protesters were arrested during the 'war in the woods' in what was Canada's largest act of civil disobedience (Langer, 2003). With the assistance of international environmental organisations such as Greenpeace, the protest and subsequent negotiations with the provincial government forced concessions over logging and resource extraction in Clayoquot Sound. By 1993, the Clayoquot Land Use Decision identified tourism landscape values and designated scenic corridors in a land use plan (White, 1999), thus signifying the transformation of the landscape to one of consumption rather than production. In 2000 the entire Clayoquot Sound area, including the town of Tofino, was designated by UNESCO as an international biosphere reserve.

The international media exposure resulting from the environmental conflict led to a significant growth in tourism to Tofino and the surrounding area during the 1990s. Eco-adventure tour operators set up operations to meet growing demand. Whale watching along with the viewing of other marine mammal and birds (e.g. porpoises, seals, sea lions, and bald eagles) was especially important (Personal interview, Tourism operator, 22 July 2005). Killer whales (orcas) and grey and humpback whales migrate up and down the coast providing seasonal opportunities for viewing. This activity was based at the inner harbour, the site of the original fishing village, where there is sheltered moorage. Other tourism operations, such as sightseeing (both from boat or float plane), fishing charters and kayaking were also based in the harbour. Thus, with the exception of beach combing and surfing, earlier tourism activities centred on the village and the sheltered inner harbour area. Local beaches remained primarily the recreational, and to a limited degree residential, domain of local inhabitants with surfing aficionados being the primary users. Tourists seeking beach experiences were drawn to Long Beach within the park.

While initially catering to a range of visitors, by the mid-1990s development became increasingly targeted at higher-end, international travellers and new development focused on the spectacular beaches of the outer coast. Although there are some locally owned establishments, including some bed and breakfast operations, these new hotels often represented the first significant flow of external capital and operators to the resort. Additional resort attractions such as spa facilities and fine dining restaurants were developed to cater to the luxury market. However, the real turning point in positioning Tofino in the international market came with the introduction of winter storm-watching as a commodified product. The Wickaninnish Inn, one of the new luxury resort hotels, was the first to highlight storm watching as a November through February attraction, Designed to attract visitors during the previously quiet winter months, storm-watching has become a major draw of visitors to the entire community (Wickaninnish Inn, 2005b).

During the past five years, Tofino's development has been characterised by three emerging trends: the growth of amenity migration; the development of surfing as a tourism attraction; and a nascent First Nations cultural tourism product. The influx of wealthy tourists, attracted by luxury hotels and unique experiences, has triggered tourism-related amenity migration to the area. This has contributed to land and property speculation, particularly on land immediately adjacent to beaches and the coastline and led to rapid increases in property values throughout the municipality of Tofino. Indeed, local residents have coined Chesterman Beach, one of the main beach areas with access to open Pacific water, as 'millionaires' beach' (Personal interview, local resident, 5 August 2005). Amenity migrants include both permanent and second-home owners. Permanent amenity migrants include retirees, 'foot loose' professional, and local small business owners. Rising property values have forced some local residents to leave the community due to increasing property taxes and living costs (Personal Communication, local resident, 4 November 2005).

While surfing has been a part of Tofino's identity since the early counterculture days, it was not commodified to any degree until recently. The explosion of surfing on the beaches of Tofino and Pacific Rim National Park is in part a reaction to the global popularity of the sport, and in part due to the repositioning of Tofino from a small picturesque fishing village with counterculture overtones to an international resort destination. From one surf shop and surf school in 1999, the surfing establishments had grown by 2005 to five surf schools and four other surfing retail and rental outlets.

The third emerging trend relates to the involvement of First Nations people in the tourism industry. Although this region is rich in First Nations culture, it has been natural not cultural heritage that has contributed to place identity in Tofino. One First Nations business owner in Tofino cites tribal politics and disagreements as one significant reason for the lack of First Nations involvement in the tourism industry (Personal interview, 24 October 2005). Although there have been two native art galleries operating in Tofino for some time, there has been little heritage interpretation. A First Nations band owns a franchise for a chain hotel (Best Western) but management is predominantly non-native. There are some signs that this is changing. Recently, a First Nations cultural interpretive and eco-adventure kayaking business has commenced operation. The First Nations business owner predicts that the finalisation of the treaty process with the provincial and federal governments, which he claims set his people back because they did not recognise what they owned, will slowly allow First Nations tourism to develop (Personal interview, 24 October 2005). Visitor demand for cultural tourism products has been further stimulated through enhanced interpretive efforts of the Pacific Rim National Park and the Clayoquot Biosphere Reserve office in Tofino.

Discussion

Each settlement phase in Tofino has brought residents and tourists who have introduced new values and ideologies. Each new era is layered upon the last, and this diversity results in contested values relating to wilderness, heritage and the future direction of tourism development.

Peripherality, wilderness and natural heritage

Peripherality and inaccessibility have been defining factors in Tofino's development as a tourist destination. Identity (indeed 'status') as 'the end of the road' – the furthest point West that one could drive in Canada – has in itself been an attraction. However, as Darling (1991: 4) observes, '[the] harbinger of land use conflict in Clayoquot Sound was probably the road from Port Alberni to the West Coast'. By providing access to the previously isolated area, the notion of wilderness was threatened. Road access allowed logging access to areas of the Clayoquot Sound as well as access by settlers who no longer needed to access Tofino by boat. For the counterculture migrants of the 1960s and early 1970s, some of whom were US draft dodgers avoiding the Vietnam conflict (CBC Radio, 1970), this remoteness was an element of the desired amenity. While today a paved... road and float plane make the community more accessible, the experience of getting to Tofino enhances the sense of reaching the edge of the continent.

The significance of remoteness is grounded in the concept of 'frontierism' and the related notion of 'wilderness'. While the frontier thesis as propounded in the USA by Frederick Jackson Turner in the late 19th century saw American culture and identity as a product of encounter with the Western environment (Turner, 1962), many Canadian historians have also adopted the idea of the frontier as a distinctive force in Canadian history (Careless, 1954). This environmentally deterministic view, linked to ideas of carving civilisation out of the wilderness, has been a powerful force in environmentalist thinking in both the USA and Canada, although the frontier in the USA was an agricultural one as opposed to a resource frontier in Canada (Careless, 1954). In Tofino, the 'end of the road phenomenon', combined with the 'last settler syndrome' (Nielson *et al.*, 1977), whereby new residents resent further development or settlement, has contributed to conflict over defending the sense of 'wilderness' versus tourism and residential growth. One statement by a business owner in Tofino summarises this conflict:

> the town got popular for a number of reasons. It is beautiful, and it's an escape town, and it's always been an escape town for those people who moved here in the 60s and 70s. So they move here from outside the community, and the people that move here bring their world view with them, and they see the town changing, however they don't like that change. And then they are angry about it. So tourism almost created the anger. (Personal Interview, 25 October 2005)

Tourism attention was first drawn to the natural heritage of the Tofino area with the designation of the Pacific Rim National Park Reserve in 1971. The Park promoted an image of a preserved pristine coastal wilderness of rich coastal temperate rainforest, tidal shore ecosystems and marine wildlife (White, 1999). The designation of the area south of Tofino as a National Park and the social construction of the area as 'wilderness' not only displaced residents (and a garage and bakery) from Long Beach but also was antithetical to the ideas of wilderness held by some residents in Tofino who considered that park designation and the resulting influx of visitors would lead to destruction of the area (Personal communication, long-term resident, 22 July 2005). Tuan's (1974) idea of wilderness as a 'state of mind' – one seemingly espoused by many 'counterculture' residents of Tofino at the time – conflicted with the notion of 'park wilderness', especially where a fee was charged in order to experience the wilderness.

However, for the tourist, the contrast between the 'wilderness' park environment and the surrounding forest landscape was heightened as access to the park brought visitors through a highly productive forest region that in the latter part of the 1970s and early 1980s was harvested using a progressive clear-cut logging technique, that left few trees. The resulting landscape was one of destruction that was not only aesthetically unappealing but also alarming in its apparent ecological destruction (White, 1999).

While the National Park designation attracted the first wave of tourists to the area, it was the ensuing battle between environmentalists and the forest industry in the early 1990s over the logging of old-growth timber in the Clayoquot Sound area that really established the importance of accessible wilderness in people's image of Tofino. The angry debate and mass acts of civil disobedience were played out on a global stage and drew intense media interest. Throughout the dispute Tofino's place identity was shaped in a global arena in part by aerial photographs that depicted Tofino as flanked on one side by large tracts of untouched and pristine wilderness, and on the other by a spectacular wild coast and pristine beaches. Further, as Willems-Braun (1997) highlights, the region, as portrayed in a popular coffee table book, *Clayoquot: On the Wild Side* (Dorst & Young, 1990), was depicted as virtually void of human habitation. The title of a section of his article on the discussion of the politics of nature in British Columbia – 'Saving "Wilderness": Nature as the Absence of (Modern) Culture' – aptly captures what he refers to as 'environmental racism', whereby the voices of First Nations are excluded in discourses on natural resources (Willems-Braun, 1997: 18).

While the debate over forestry and the coastal location was quite incidental, the visual images of stunningly beautiful coastal landscapes and seascapes triggered a significant increase in tourist numbers, including visitors from Europe. German visitors were especially attracted to the area as they had a strong national environmentalist movement and had thus been exposed to extensive media coverage of the conflict (Hayter & Soyez, 1996). Whether they were drawn to see the site of the environmental debate and old growth forest or to experience the beauty of the coastal environment and engage in its eco-tourism opportunities is unknown. In the mid-1990s, the need for investors to enhance returns on high-end hotel development on the outer coast by attracting a viable year-round market seems to underlie the drive to add value for visitors by offering a diversity of attractions and activities (Sutherland, 1999). The seasonal repositioning of Tofino as a place where one can experience the rawness of nature was an inspired innovation. As one British Columbia tourism website proclaims 'Take a break from your winter skiing trip to experience the raw power of the mighty Pacific Ocean, as ferocious waves roll in from Japan and pound the shores of the rugged west coast – nature in all its fierce majesty!' (Vancouver Island, 2005).

The packaging and marketing of bad weather as a commodity reflects the power of the 'tourist gaze' – once the experience is signified the tourist seeks to gain that experience. Now, as one promotional web site observes, international visitors are 'defying logic' by flocking to Tofino to go storm watching (Vancouver Island, 2005). The combination of 'raw nature' and luxury accommodations, spa facilities and fine dining has been highly successful. As the Wickaninnish Inn website states, 'The storm-watching experience can be enjoyed in luxury and at close range from this location, with every room featuring an ocean view, soaker bathtub and fireplace for optimum viewing and ambiance' (Wickaninnish Inn, 2005a). The prime positioning of the viewer and the scene hints at the era of the picturesque and romantic perspectives on landscape, and the associated social distinction of tourists that occurred in the late 18th and early 19th century in both Europe and North America (Towner, 1996). The commodification of nature and wilderness on Tofino's outer coast also carries echoes of an earlier era of tourism to Canada's national parks when in the late 1800s the railway companies constructed grand hotels in the Rocky Mountains such as Banff Springs Hotel where the wilderness was juxtaposed with civilisation and could be experienced at a safe distance. In Tofino, it is primarily the elite tourists and amenity migrants that have captured the prime vantage points along the coast. Although the beaches are public domain, access points for visitors are restricted.

Community conflict: Growth or no growth

The transition from a fishing- and forestry-dependent community to a tourism destination has been evolving in Tofino for the past 40 years. While the environmentalist debates surrounding logging define the most painful era of community contestation, especially pitting Tofino residents, many of whom were environmentalists, against their neighbours in Ucluelet, who were predominantly forestry workers, recent contestation has surrounded tourism-community related issues (Ungerleider, 1995). The values and actions of the second major wave of residents, who arrived in the late 1980s and 1990s, have at times conflicted with those 'old guard' members of the original counterculture community – some of whom acquired sizeable tracts of land during the 1960s and early 1970s. Pressure for development is intense as the availability of land in the municipality is limited because of the peninsular location and the boundary of the park to the south, but some residents have resisted selling their land to developers. Long-term residents are concerned about loss of control to outside interests (both commercial and residential), especially those developing along the outer coast where they also resent loss of access to local beaches. Local residents worry about affordable housing and the overall effects on 'community' caused by the influx of amenity migrants. As one member of the Tofino Housing Authority stated, 'sustainable housing is . . . something that is sorely needed in this town to keep people living and working here. You know, instead of commuting from Ucluelet, and one after another people are moving out of here' (Personal interview, 14 July 2005).

In current debates, the environmentalists and more conservative old guard community members have been divided into two factions and represented by two major community institutions: the Tofino Chamber of Commerce (TCC) and the Tofino Business Association (TBA) respectively. Efforts to manage tourism development have caused considerable controversy over the past 10 years. Relations of power in the community of Tofino continue to be acted out through different management decisions and contestations, where prior alliances or adversarial relationships confuse and complicate management processes. Management strategies have been introduced to constrain development, preserve residential areas, and to control the capacity on beaches and associated amenities of parking and trail networks. The influx of new surfers and associated businesses and surf schools is precipitating additional clashes over appropriate use and capacity on the area's beaches, while part-time residents and second-home owners that are allowing their properties to be used as vacation rental units are changing the make-up of established residential areas (Personal Interview, Municipal Councillor, 5 August 2005).

Initiatives to stop further tourism development have been championed by environmentally inclined members of the community, and have sometimes had support from members of the old guard of long-term residents. One environmentalist and business owner reflects on attempts to reduce the rate of tourism development: 'I think particularly the green sector of the community has tried to slow down willy nilly development. In a sense they have been effective, as we have had a moratorium on development in the last couple of years' (Personal communication, 10 August 2005). However, simply stopping tourism development without a clear plan for future management of growth creates pressure on the city's planning department as increasing numbers of applications are stalled. The same resident elucidated the problems with this type of management tactic: 'rather than deal with things, this is just sort of delaying it, and an unintended consequence of doing that is that you get bad development when finally that dam breaks' (Personal communication, 10 August 2005). Local municipal councils have oscillated between development and nondevelopment ideologies. This inconsistency has limited the ability of the community and the tourism industry to thrive in harmony.

In 2004, the municipal council attempted to regulate and control vacation rental properties. The ensuing conflict pitted vacation rental owners, many of whom are part-time residents and second-home owners, against local residents, bed and breakfast owners and those residents in favour of less tourism activity. Once again, the battle lines were drawn between the TCC, whose members generally supported regulation of vacation rental properties, and members of the TBA, who supported vacation rental owners. Although as one manager of a large resort observed, 'the TBA seems to have, I wouldn't say control, but a little more influence ... because they keep themselves cohesive and they have clear direction on what their issues are' (Personal communication, 14 July 2005). Nevertheless, the municipal council eventually passed a bylaw that requires the owner of the vacation property to reside in any house being used for vacation rental purposes – however enforcement of this law has proven difficult.

Conclusion

The events and circumstances that have contributed to Tofino's place identity are unique – as is true of any place. However, the evolution of Tofino as a tourist destination draws attention to several key factors of how natural heritage is utilised and commodified in the process of creating place identity. The case study also highlights the contestation that occurs as tourism destinations evolve and change. This is especially evident in the case of Tofino, where tourism represents the transformation of the landscape from one of production to one of consumption.

A central theme that runs through Tofino's place identity is its isolated location at the end of the road on the edge of the continent. Coasts have long been represented as the end of a journey, whether for early pioneers in their westward journey across the USA or adventure-seeking travellers seeking the periphery. In the Americas, it has been the Western Pacific coast that for both historical and geographical reasons has been represented as the periphery. 'End of the road' signifiers can be found in promotional materials in coastal places ranging from Patagonia to Alaska. The importance of isolation in defining insiders from outsiders is also observed by Larsen (2004) in his study of an isolated community in interior Northern British Columbia. Some of the tensions in Tofino have their roots in the resistance of longer-term local residents to further tourism and residential development.

The image of isolation is linked to the commodification of natural heritage as 'wilderness', which has become a defining feature of place identity for Tofino. The notion of wilderness has become layered in a complex manner as it has evolved along with development and change in the community of Tofino. It was first constructed for tourist consumption within the confines of the Pacific Rim National Park Reserve. Subsequent conflict over land use in the Clayoquot Sound region portrayed wilderness as untouched and complete tracts of old-growth forest. With tourism growth, portrayal of 'the wild' shifted to the ocean as a wilderness environment. Although the old-growth forests on the mountain slopes serve as a scenic backdrop to the ocean, tourists' attention is drawn to the ocean either as active participants in adventure and eco-tourism activities such as marine wildlife watching, fishing, kayaking, surfing or beach combing or more passive activities, as their gaze is drawn to the ocean, especially during winter storms.

As Hall and Page (1999: 222) observe, 'the value of wilderness is not static. The value of a resource alters over time in accordance with changes in the needs and attitudes of society'. While viewing a winter storm from the window of a luxury hotel or boating with a dozen fellow passengers on a whale-watching trip would hardly class as a true 'wilderness' experience, the experiential and 'mental and moral restorational values' of wilderness outlined by Hendee *et al.* (1978) are embodied in the wilderness product that defines Tofino as a destination. What is perhaps surprising in the creation of Tofino's place identity as a tourist destination is that it has been constructed around natural heritage to the virtual exclusion of cultural heritage. However, there has been a history of resistance by First Nations in the Clayoquot Sound area to engage with the 'colonial' economy (Willems-Braun, 1997). Nevertheless, the richness of First Nations culture in the coastal Pacific Northwest of North America is internationally renown – especially the highly developed artistic representations of culture expressed in the creation of carved totem poles, elaborately carved jewellery, masks and other artefacts, and this offers considerable opportunity for the engagement of First Nations in developing a cultural tourism product.

Perhaps the essence of Tofino's place identity is epitomised in the *Common Loaf* organic bakery and café. Begun by a female entrepreneur during the counterculture era, it served as an informal community centre, and even today continues as a local's hangout. The notice board is full of information on ride sharing, requests relating to affordable accommodation or the offering of informal services. In many ways it encapsulates what attracts visitors and new residents alike to Tofino – the small, friendly, picturesque fishing village in a spectacular setting. It also embodies the community's true cultural heritage, that of its environmentalist roots – for Tofino has never been a First Nations community. However, like so many small communities that become successful tourism destinations, success itself maybe led to its destruction as a community. The following statement taken from a real estate website suggests local planning and management control may have already been left too late.

> Tofino, population 1500 (sic), is now the resort town for a mix of Hollywood celebrities, Calgarian oil money, Vancouver retirees and hip young surfers. Some are already calling it the next Whistler and, if housing demand is any indication, it's already in the big league. (Coast Realty Group, 2007)

Part 4

Coastal Resort Structures: Variation Versus Standardisation

Chapter 11

The Development of South Africa's Coastal Tourism Resorts

ROBERT PRESTON-WHYTE and CATHERINE OELOFSE

Introduction

Contemporary tourism resort development along South Africa's 3751-km coastline (Earthtrends, 2005) is largely the product of forces that have driven political, economic and social change over the last decade. The peaceful transformation to a black majority government in 1994, and favourable neoliberal macroeconomic policies, have had the effect of boosting levels of disposable income for certain groups within South Africa (Euromonitor, 2005; Irwin, 2004), with much of it spent on domestic consumption, such as property investment in the coastal zone. As Langeni (2005: 100) comments, 'low interest rates have, in the past three years, driven the property market as the affordability of homes has increased across income groups'. In addition, international interest in South Africa, with growth in arrivals averaging 10.3% (South African Airways, 2005a), has increased, and this has led to higher levels of investment, particularly in the coastal zone. The result is increasing demand for holidays in coastal towns and cities, the ongoing construction of holiday homes in coastal resorts, new 'eco-node' developments in previously underdeveloped areas, and the accelerated provision of state-managed and community-driven eco-tourism experiences in wildlife conservation areas.

The attraction of the coastline owes much to the diversity of spaces that reflect the changing forces of nature. Biophysical variety is made possible by the latitudinal extent of the country through almost 15°, which means that weather-producing systems from tropical, subtropical and temperate features of the general circulation exert controls over different parts of the coastline. This, in turn, shapes biophysical characteristics by influencing the weather-producing systems (Tyson & Preston-Whyte, 2000), the distribution of species (Van Teylingen *et al.*, 1993), the movement and direction of warm and cold ocean currents (Niiler, 1992) and the nature of upwelling that brings deep nutrient-rich water to the surface (Bang, 1971).

The recent history of coastal resort development has been one of intense property speculation and investment in reviving new and previously 'undiscovered' areas, as well as progress in conservation environments geared towards community involvement. These developments are discussed here in terms of the drivers responsible for the creation of waterfronts, the search for new lifestyles, the rejuvenation of stagnating resort towns, the conservation of pristine wilderness shorelines, the shaping of community-based tourism ventures in tribal areas, and the quest for the undiscovered location. Coastal tourism resorts are then shown to have a variety of faces that reflect global trends, meet different needs, respond in new ways to political visions, adjust to the transformation of society and accommodate increasing levels of expendable income.

The drivers identified here have emerged from research conducted by the authors in a range of projects within the coastal zone in South Africa, as well as from a review of media publications on coastal developments. This has permitted the development of a typology of tourism development regions and a spatial classification of the coastline into tourism development regions (Amar & Associates, 2005; Garland & Oelofse, 2005; Oelofse, 2005; Preston-Whyte, 2001; Scott & Oelofse, 2005). This research is supported and informed by case study reviews on tourism development pressures and opportunities in the coastal zone (City of Cape Town, 2003; Hauck & Sowman, 2003; Scott, 2006).

In the context of South Africa's turbulent political history, it is important to note that tourism resort development occurs within and for the middle-to-high income sector in the country. Resort developments often take place in close proximity to social conditions of extreme poverty and underdevelopment. The large gap between the rich and poor in South Africa, and the development challenges facing the majority of South Africans, who are still in need of basic shelter and services (United Nations Development Programme, 2003), must be acknowledged if resort development is to be sustainable. While the nature of these poverty-stricken areas and their problems is not discussed here, reference is made to politically driven attempts to address the challenge of underdevelopment through community-driven tourism resort projects.

Drivers Underpinning Tourism Development

From the time of the earliest colonial settlement until the first democratic elections in 1994, the location and occupancy of coastal resorts along virtually the entire coastline was informed and controlled by white political and economic domination over coastal resources that ranged from secluded wilderness coastlines to the beaches of coastal towns. In general, development was patchy, being restricted to seaside activities at coastal towns and fishing cottages along accessible stretches of the coastline.

All of this has changed over the last decade, with domestic and international demand for the consumption of coastal resources accelerating in step with drivers that inform the spatial classification of coastal resort development types shown in Fig. 11.1. The nature of the drivers reflects changing wealth and expenditure patterns (Euromonitor, 2005; Irwin, 2004), reacts to government intervention through policy formation and implementation (South Africa, 2000) and responds to social and cultural yearnings for a simpler lifestyle perceived to be embedded in past landscapes (Hilton-Barber, 2005). Given their importance in shaping coastal development, they deserve greater elaboration, and this is provided by identifying and discussing (a) improved linkages to the global economy, (b) increasing levels of expendable income with concomitant shifts in quality-of-life expectations, (c) government insistence on policies of environmental management, (d) government's economic and social reforms relating to resource redistribution and empowerment constructed around the notion of 'responsible tourism' and (e) the search for undiscovered destinations that convey images of 'authentic' coastal landscapes untrammelled by the perceived ravages of modernity.

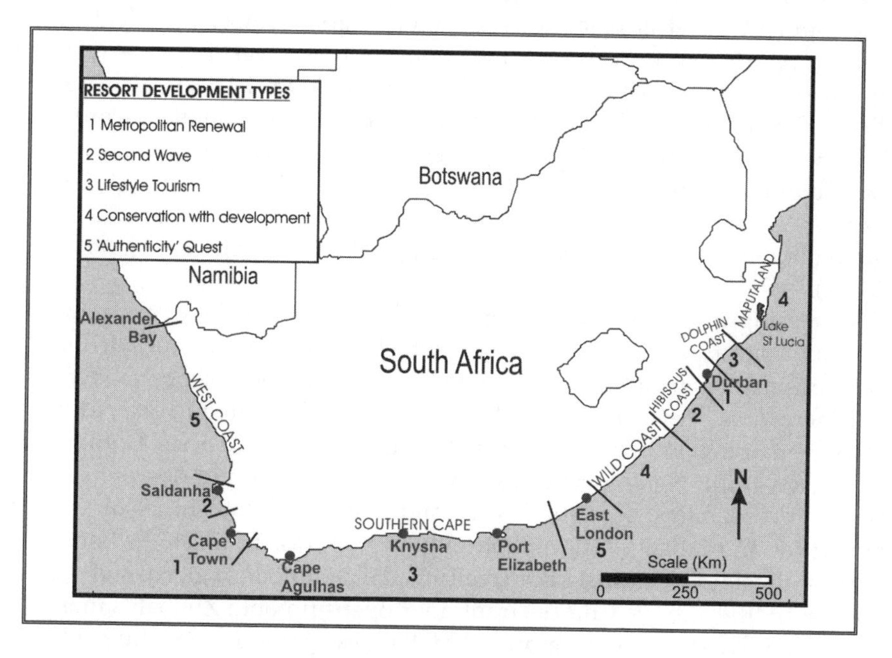

Figure 11.1 Resort development types

With the demise of the apartheid regime and its associated isolationist policies, South Africa soon began to feel the effect of *linking into the global economy*. Three main factors have aided and hastened this process. First, the government's neoliberal macroeconomic policy has boosted investor confidence through success in its Growth, Equity and Redistribution Programme (GEAR) strategy, which focused on attracting global investment (Irwin, 2004). Secondly, the government's sound monetary policy has succeeded in bringing inflation under control and this has further boosted investor confidence (Langeni, 2005). Thirdly, the dramatic weakening of the Rand between 2000 and 2002 made South Africa an affordable place for international buyers in search of second homes in an exotic setting. This market, which is now well established, continues to flourish, even with the recovery of the Rand over the last three years. As Langeni (2005: 99) comments: 'The South African economy continues to enjoy a fantastic run, driven by key domestic factors like rising consumer demand, a strong Rand, economic growth and a low inflation and interest rate environment'.

The impact of international as well as local coastal resort development initiatives is rapidly becoming visible along the coastline. Pezula, an eco-estate located on the dramatic cliffs of the Knysna Heads along the Garden Route of the Western Cape, reflects international standards in tourism resorts in a developing country (Plate 11.1). This luxurious development consists of a five-star hotel, a golf course, the Field of Dreams Sports Centre, as well as the opportunity to invest in property in an exclusive, gated eco-estate (Manthorp, 2005; South African Airways, 2005c). The resort has won numerous national and international awards: Best South African Development, The Most Environmentally Aware Development in the World, The Only Hotel in South Africa on both UK and USA Condé Nast Traveller Hot Lists 2005 and the Diner's Club International Award of Excellence (Pezula, 2006; South African Airways, 2005b).

Increasingly, global development trends play a role in shaping the type and nature of the developments which, despite a gloss of African symbolism, remain grounded in global representations of postmodern coastal resorts. The exclusive Zimbali coastal resort situated in one of the three remaining indigenous coastal forests on South Africa's Dolphin Coast, KwaZulu-Natal, prides itself on its African flair and design with first-world facilities, security, luxury and comfort (Pilotfish, 2006). An advert for an exclusive R12 million property (almost 12 times the South African President's annual salary) reflects the postmodern global style of the resort: 'the antique Chinese front door opens up onto Zimbali's most spectacular rim-flow pool, embraced by Balinese pavilions on either side with the warm Indian Ocean beyond' (*Sunday Tribune*, 2005a: 58).

Plate 11.1 Lifestyle coastal tourism, Pezula resort, Knysna

The attraction of these developments is boosted if nearby beaches acquire the sought-after international 'Blue Flag' award. This award, which has only recently been applied in South Africa, is made annually based on standards of environmental management, beach cleanliness, safety, water quality and available amenities. In 2005, 20 beaches along the South African coast were awarded the Blue Flag eco-label. Of these, ten are along the KwaZulu-Natal coastline, five along the Eastern Cape coast and five in the Western Cape. The number of awards in 2005 represents a major leap relative to 2004, but the most important feature, usually noted in the marketing of these beaches, is the international recognition of beach quality (Booth, 2005). South Africa is the first country outside Europe to receive such recognition (Southern Explorer Association, 2005).

Lifestyle tourism emerges as another growing driver of coastal resort development as the increase in expendable income by a growing number of high earners (Euromonitor, 2005; Irwin, 2004; Langeni, 2005) is directed towards indulging in tourism-related activities perceived to enhance their *quality of life*. Evidence of this trend is the development of a range of tourism products that reflect this demand. An example of these products are eco-estates, which offer leisure activities such as golf, spa and wellness centres, secluded beaches and sport centres (South African Airways, 2004a).

Lagoon Bay at Hoogkraal in the Western Cape is one such resort, described as, 'A truly unique lifestyle estate which offers two Retief Goosen Signature Championship Golf Courses; salt water lagoon; several secluded beaches; five star international hotel; Boutique Shopping Centre; Spa and Wellness Centre' (South African Airways, 2004a: 125). Simbithi Eco-Estate at Ballito on the KwaZulu-Natal coast is another example, described as '. . . a golf lovers paradise, breathless views, reconnect with nature, eco-friendly architecture, pristine coastline' (South African Airways, 2004c: 150).

The houses in these resorts tend to be exclusive and postmodern in design, using themes, designs and behaviour codes to ensure uniformity. They are laid out making intelligent use of the ecological resources of the area in order to convey images of wilderness to the inhabitant, while residents live in the comfort of their designed and controlled gated community. Thesens Islands and Pezula in Knysna, are examples of developments where the global style of postmodern resort estates is reflected by unified architecture (in the case of Thesens the style is colonial maritime) and a strong link to the environmental character of the site (Holm & Holm, 2003).

An interesting form of lifestyle tourism, directed towards beautifying and sculpturing the body through plastic surgery, has also emerged. This 'product' caters mainly for international tourists and offers specialised treatments at affordable prices by first-world standards, with the chance to recuperate in a beautiful coastal environment. The combination of environmental charm and proximity to a modern metropolis makes the Southern Cape coast an ideal location for such activities, an example of which can be found in a private hospital at Knysna (Life Healthcare, 2005).

Retirement also signals a lifestyle change and the flow of mainly white retirees have impacted on the nature of many small coastal towns such as Knysna and Plettenberg Bay in the Western Cape. Developments to cater for special needs of this group, such as frail care, have been constructed in association with resort developments. These older residents are attracted by the increasing number of services offered in smaller coastal towns as a result of the growth of tourism and leisure activities. The demand for these retirement developments along the coast is increasing as retired people continue to move to the coastal zone (Statistics South Africa, 2001).

The impact of rapid, unplanned growth of coastal tourism resorts became a growing concern in the late 1980s, and triggered *policy development* for coastal zone management by the Council for the Environment (1989; 1991). In 1998, a Green Paper on Coastal Management Policy was released (South Africa, 1998a), followed in 2000 by a White Paper on Sustainable Coastal Development (South Africa, 2000). These developments took place against parallel policy debates that led to the White Paper on the Development and Promotion of Tourism (South Africa, 1996), and the Tourism in GEAR Strategy Document (South Africa, 1998b). Through the concept of 'responsible tourism', government and business are expected to co-operate in the development, management and marketing of the tourism industry with a high priority placed on the incorporation of local communities, particularly in areas with high levels of poverty. These sentiments are echoed by advocates of the 'pro-poor' tourism strategy (Ashley & Roe, 2002) and those who believe that tourism can be managed in a manner that promotes community development without compromising sustainability (Sharpley, 2002b; Wahab & Pigram, 1997).

The White Paper on Sustainable Coastal Development (South Africa, 2000) promotes sustainable economic development to protect and sustain South Africa's sensitive coastline, while at the same time ensuring that coastal development plays a key role in alleviating poverty in South Africa. The Environmental Conservation Act (South Africa, 1989) and the National Environmental Management Act (South Africa, 1998c) play a role in regulating development along the coastline through the application of the Environmental Impact Assessment procedure. However, the success of this mainstream procedure in managing and controlling development is questioned (Oelofse *et al.*, 2006). New approaches that adopt a more strategic view are now being considered, such as the moratorium on and resultant strategic assessment of proposed golf and polo estates in the Western Cape coast, which was commissioned by the Western Cape Provincial Government in 2004 to assess the impact of these developments on the environment. There are currently 83 existing and 33 proposed golf estates along this sensitive coastline (Department of Environmental Affairs and Development Planning, 2004).

The development of private estates, which theoretically support high standards of environmental planning as part of the requirements of the environmental assessments they have to undertake, and as part of their own marketing strategies, is seen as a way of using private–public partnerships to protect coastal resources. Many of these developments promote economic spin-offs in their planning and environmental applications (Oelofse, 2005; Scott, 2006).

Sadly, the goals of broader economic development are not always achieved. Along the Southern cape coast there are numerous examples of developers that have co-opted local communities with promises of employment or other benefits to support their development in the Environmental Impact Assessment, only to find that the promises do not materialise (SABC TV, 2004). Perhaps the most vivid example of this type of exploitation is a development undertaken by an international developer in Plettenberg Bay who promised the local community a clinic in return for their support for his development. The building was built but it stands empty, with no resources for doctors, nurses or medicines (SABC TV, 2004).

The guiding principles of *responsible tourism* emphasise private sector involvement with an emphasis on community participation and empowerment and the need for close co-operation between stakeholders. There is a commitment to sustainable environmental practices and an undertaking by government to provide an enabling framework for the industry to flourish (Rogerson & Visser, 2004). While the notion of responsible tourism extends to all facets of tourism, it has particular relevance to high levels of underdevelopment and poverty that occur in tribal authority areas such as Maputaland and the Wild Coast. The means of achieving responsible tourism goals are packaged in a number of different ways, but they all fall under the umbrella of conservation *with* development. Ironically, apartheid policy led to the location of black homelands in many of the most beautiful, remote and wild spaces along the coastline. As a result of this legacy they remain underdeveloped, although this is now changing. It is in these areas, where communities live subsistence lifestyles under tribal authority, that community-driven tourism projects have emerged (Greater St Lucia Wetland Park Authority, 2004; Hauck & Sowman, 2003).

The conservation with development concept is also used to legitimise high-income exclusive private resorts, such as Umngazi River Bungalows on the Wild Coast in the Eastern Cape, which are being developed in nodes along sections of the coastline that contain impoverished communities. Lodges and private game reserves that have developed within the Greater St Lucia Wetland Park also reflect this approach, with high-income tourism being used to drive empowerment imperatives (Greater St Lucia Wetland Park Authority, 2004; 2005).

The final driver that we believe to be important in shaping coastal resort development is the *quest for authenticity*. Resort developments often begin with the discovery of small coastal towns that echo images of the past and where traditional lifestyles are retained. Such places provided the need for the 'authenticity' sought by many tourists who wish to escape the homogeneity of modern urban landscapes. Small towns along the West coast of South Africa, such as Paternoster, Lamberts Bay and Vredenburg, reflect this trend, as do those in the Eastern Cape, such as Chintsa and Queensbury Bay (Golding, 2005; Raramuridesign, 2006; West Coast Tourism, 2006). Tourists are able to enjoy the timelessness of these towns and admire their history and culture in the vernacular of the architecture, the simplicity of lifestyles

Plate 11.2 West coast authenticity, Paternoster
Source: Ina Loubsher, Paternoster Properties (2006)

and the resistance to globalising changes. Many such towns have primary activities such as fishing or mining that creates a sense of place and a special mystique. The attraction of small fishing harbours, where community fishers launch their boats, or estuaries where local fishers trail nets for their daily catch, are places of endless spectacle and satisfaction (Plate 11.2).

Resort Development Regions

The five drivers described above can be found to apply along much of the coastline. However, certain drivers predominate in shaping the nature and form of coastal resort development in particular regions. A typology of these developments, constructed around what we believe to be the dominant regional drivers, is set out in Fig. 11.1. The nature and impact of the dominant drivers for each coastal resort development deserve special attention and these are discussed for each region.

Metropolitan seaside renewal

Over the last decade, seaside renewal in the Cape Town metropolitan area and the booming property market have been driven by lifestyle quests and the national government's successful policies in creating investor confidence. The natural environment is a key asset with its rocky shoreline (Dardis & Grindley, 1988; Tinley, 1985), hot, dry summers supporting a thriving wine industry, and iconic Table Mountain. These appropriately frame the vibrant cultural life with protected colonial buildings housing trendy upmarket restaurants and coffee shops, art museums and music venues.

With these attributes, Condé Nast readers ranked the city as 15th in their ordering of the most desirable city destinations in the world (Condé Nast, 2004). Global attention is visible in high property prices for second-home purchases, driven by international buyers. The city has become the playground of the world's rich, with many local residents unable to enter the property market. The Cape Town waterfront, which was developed in the early 1990s, has been a key focus of tourism development. It now attracts more international visitors than the Kruger National Park (McCarthy *et al.*, 2000). Tourism has capitalised on both cultural and natural assets, such as Robben Island and Table Mountain, and the resources from surrounding vineyards. A recent advert for the V&A Waterfront draws attention to '... Table Mountain, the Atlantic Ocean, Robben Island, a hundred fishing boats. And that's just the view from the parking lot' (American Express, 2005: 6–7). Tourists that visit this city are predominantly middle- to high-income earners who can afford to pay the high prices for accommodation, leisure and cultural activities (Webb, 2005).

Durban is the second South African city that boasts a desirable seaside playground, underscored, in 2005, by the award of Blue Flag status to five of the city's beaches (Booth, 2005). The city's popularity owes much to nature's bounty, which provides fine weather throughout the year as well as a 7-km sandy beach washed by the warm Agulhas Current. Although the beachfront hotels and apartments have gone through a number of phases of gentrification (Preston-Whyte, 2001), they generally fail to attract tourists with a taste for luxury. Instead, the seaside is visited mainly by lower- to middle-income tourists (Preston-Whyte, 2001).

The failure to compete with Cape Town as a destination for high-income tourists is a matter of concern for Durban's tourism authorities. School holidays, national holidays and weekends now attract large crowds of low- and middle-income black tourists to the swimming beaches, with Robinson (1999: 1) reporting that, 'two hundred thousand flock to Durban's beaches in peaceful start to 1999'. The beachfront is geared for mass tourism as the modern architectural style proclaims (see Plate 11.3).

Competition with Cape Town, and recognition of Durban's waning attraction for more wealthy tourists, spurred the construction of an international conference centre, the symbolically named Suncoast Casino overlooking the ocean, and most recently, the Point Waterfront Development. This new and extensive inner city renewal project located on derelict land on the edge of the harbour mouth includes a world class aquarium, a waterworld, high-income postmodern property and office space developments, and a proposed waterfront development (Scott &

Plate 11.3 Metropolitan renewal: Durban's modern seascape

Oelofse, 2005). It is optimistically anticipated that this improvement will kick-start urban renewal and lead to the gentrification of the inner city areas adjacent to the sea (Scott, 2006; Scott & Oelofse, 2005).

Second-wave tourism renewal

Lifestyle preferences and economic renewal have played a significant role in driving a second wave of tourism renewal of coastal resorts that were initially developed in the 1930s along the coastline south of Durban. The popularity of the region, with mainly white middle-class tourists from the Transvaal (now Gauteng) and Orange Free State (now Free State) provinces, increased after WWII, and led to ribbon development of resort towns such as Scottburgh, Uvongo, Southbroom and Hibberdene, and an economy linked to the tourism sector (Southern Explorer Association, 2005). The preference for this coastline lies mainly in the safe swimming beaches, year-round warm climate and proximity to Johannesburg (Southern Explorer Association, 2005).

In the 1980s, the East coast resort towns began to stagnate as many tourists transferred their attention to the newly discovered, less seedy and more exciting resorts along the southern Cape coast and Cape Peninsula. However, in line with Butler's (1980) resort cycle model, rejuvenation is one possible outcome of the cycle, and this is taking place. Land prices, which are lower than elsewhere, have attracted property developers. For example, the new Ekubo Coastal Estate at Leisure Bay on the south coast of KwaZulu-Natal, which like Zimbali offers the opportunity to build 'your Bali inspired dream home in paradise ... land from R375 000 with beautiful wetlands and coastal forests' (*Sunday Tribune*, 2005b: 16), is far more affordable than its Dolphin Coast counterpart. Beach management is recognised to be part of the new vision, with five beaches graded as Blue Flag in 2005 (Booth, 2005). The result is high-density cluster housing for the second-home and retirement market in and adjacent to the older resort towns. With faith in symbolism, the region markets itself as the 'Hibiscus Coast'. The coastline north of Cape Town is beginning to show similar trends, with buyers and developers beginning to express an interest in the remote underdeveloped villages and settlements along the seashore beyond Saldanha (West Coast Tourism, 2006).

Lifestyle tourism

This form of tourism has emerged in the past 10 years, and is shaping the nature of tourism in the Southern Cape coast and Dolphin Coast of KwaZulu-Natal. In the Southern Cape, this is partly a result of the rapid growth of international tourism in Cape Town, as well as the presence of beautiful and underdeveloped southern Cape coastal towns such as Knysna, Plettenberg Bay and Cape St Francis (Holm & Holm, 2003).

A number of waterfront developments and marinas have been developed in line with postmodern trends in cities elsewhere in the world (Amar & Associates, 2005; Holm & Holm, 2003). The Pezula Hotel reflects the quality and style of these resort developments (Plate 11.1). In addition, exclusive gated communities have been and are being developed on large tracts of land that previously were used for industry, agriculture or covered by fynbos vegetation. Pezula, marketed as Africa's first luxury resort estate (South African Airways, 2004b), prides itself on rehabilitating a large piece of coastal land that previously was under plantation forestry, and returning the area to its natural fynbos vegetation (Oelofse, 2005). Notwithstanding the marketing capital earned through these conservation efforts, the ecological costs of 'greenfield developments' need to be measured in terms of the impacts of golf courses, sports centres, wellness centres and eco-estates (Department of Environmental Affairs and Development Planning, 2004; Oelofse, 2005).

The transformation of the so-called 'Dolphin Coast' began with white flight from Durban beaches that became deracialised in 1989, and from Durban's central business district as a commercial centre after 1994 (Preston-Whyte, 1999; 2001). Umhlanga Rocks, located 20 km north of Durban, was the first coastal resort to be 'discovered'. From a cluster of fishing cottages nestling in thick dune forest and one hotel in the1960s, Umhlanga Rocks is now lined with exclusive high-rise apartments, timeshare properties and hotels. Soaring property values ensure that only the very rich can gain access. The new proposed Pearls Development along the beachfront of Umhlanga is advertised as follows: 'Do you speak the language of luxury? Do you understand the quintessential desirables of life . . . such as panoramic views, exquisite design and exclusive style? Pearl Dawn is the answer to great comfort and extravagant living. Priced from R2 million' (South African Airways, 2005b: 152).

Creeping affluent coastal development northward from Durban has turned into a flood. The region is firmly on the radar screen of developers who recognise, in their marketing strategy, the demand for a secure lifestyle, breathless views, the need to reconnect with nature, eco-friendly architecture, access to pristine coastlines and golfing facilities combined with a natural setting (South African Airways, 2004c; *Sunday Tribune*, 2005c). These high-income 'eco-node' developments are sensitively carved out of indigenous coastal forests in order to preserve environmental authenticity, and usually are accompanied by a golf course. Zimbali is an example of a development that draws on international investment money, expecting to compete with Cape Town in the globalisation stakes for high-income residents, while complying with coastal zone management prescriptions. In both the Southern Cape and Dolphin Coast, land scarcity coupled with demand has driven prices beyond the means of all but the rich (*Cape Times*, 2005; *Sunday Tribune*, 2005c). The development boom has also attracted large numbers of the poor and unemployed in search of the opportunities these developments may offer (Oelofse, 2005). This leads to a highly polarised social context with the very rich and the very poor living in close proximity, with little space for middle-income residents (Oelofse, 2005).

Conservation with development

The notion of 'responsible tourism' in the coastal regions of Maputaland and the Wild Coast is closely allied to the need for economic development and community empowerment. These were the conditions under which the Greater St Lucia Wetland Park was granted World Heritage Site status in 1999. The government responded with the World Heritage Convention Act of 1999, which led to the creation of the Greater St Lucia Wetland Park Authority to manage the park in line with conservation priorities and community needs.

Conservation with development is a weighty responsibility given the pressures on the still pristine sector of the Maputaland coastline, made up of marine reserves extending southwards from Kosi Bay to include the Maputaland Marine Reserve, Sodwana Bay National Park and St Lucia Marine Reserve. On land, the Tembe Elephant Reserve, Ndumo Reserve and Mkuzi Reserve in the north provide a feast for the consumption of wildlife experiences, while the 36,000 hectare Lake St Lucia offers similar encounters in an estuarine setting. It is generally recognised, however, that sustainability of these wilderness areas cannot be guaranteed without local economic development to provide wealth creation along with social and political empowerment of local communities (O'Riordan *et al*., 2000).

The Greater St. Lucia Wetland Park Authority is tasked with development responsibility within the broader development objectives of the Lebombo Spatial Development Initiative. The intention is to attract investment in lodges and hotels and thereby generate jobs and stimulate local economic growth. However, there are obstacles to be overcome. The notion of Western-style democracy is often resisted in traditional communities, which means that political-inspired violence simmers beneath the surface. HIV/AIDS threatens the fabric of local communities, while crime and corruption remain a problem (Allen & Brennan, 2004).

The so-called Wild Coast differs from Maputaland in the rocky nature of this isolated and pristine coastline. The region is not for the faint hearted, the unfit, or those afraid to take their vehicles on testing roads. As a former homeland of the apartheid regime, it remains a highly underdeveloped area that is populated by dispersed rural communities that live largely subsistence lifestyles. Despite its potential, coastal tourism is not yet well developed and consists of a few older hotels constructed during the 1950s and 1960s and still operating as homely places for middle- to upper-income visitors. Typically, these family-owned hotels are located on a spectacular estuary with accommodation in small seaside cottages. Local community members are employed to service the hotels, and as a result, these resorts tend to have a strong relationship with the surrounding community.

Umngazi River Bungalows is an example, located on the Wild Coast amongst subsistence rural communities. As part of its contribution to 'responsible tourism', the hotel employs local people. A local entrepreneur operates a fishing service where he rents rods and his knowledge to eager tourists (see Plate 11.4). In community-driven projects such as the Amadiba Adventures Horse and Hiking Trail, which is owned and run by an indigenous community, 'you encounter the warm Pondo people, cleanse your soul beneath crystal waterfalls, canoe untouched rivers and hike among wild animals in a nature reserve' (Amadiba Adventures, 2005).

Authenticity quests

Spaces of *authenticity* exist where fishing and mining takes place in remote coastal villages. Both of these activities occur along the West coast of South Africa, where time seems to have stood still and communities appear relatively untouched by the modern world. The coastal towns of Paternoster, Vredenburg and Lamberts Bay, to name a few, continue to

Plate 11.4 Fishers and community involvement: Umngazi, Wild Coast

reflect their original function, which is subsistence and commercial fishing. This landscape of timelessness and authenticity is reflected in Plate 11.2. Despite their harsh arid environment and remote locations, these towns have succeeded in retaining their traditional resident population (Raramuridesign, 2006). Hotels are old-fashioned family establishments that hold 'sokkies' (traditional Afrikaans dances) on Saturday nights. It is cultural events such as these that tourists seek to experience. However, trendy tourism resort development is starting to appear in some of these recently 'discovered' towns.

Mining towns on the West coast have their own special mystique. In Douglas Bay for example, tourists are able to gaze on the homes of diamond divers. These people are employed by the mining industry and live in converted double-deck buses and small beach cottages. Tourists also come to gaze on the wild flowers that herald the first spring rains and cover the semi-desert landscape in a blaze of colour. Each year, this phenomenon is eagerly awaited and leads to an annual pilgrimage to the West coast. The coastal towns benefit from these natural events but somehow manage to retain their timeless quality and, thereby, their attraction (Raramuridesign, 2006; West Coast Tourism, 2006).

Quaint, remote settlements can also be found on the Eastern Cape coast constructed around vintage resort infrastructures. Small resort towns such as Chintsa, Queensbury Bay and Kei Mouth are notable for the exceptional natural beauty of their surroundings and low levels of development. These towns are made up of collections of private holiday homes, as well as self-catering and bed-and-breakfast accommodation constructed on the edges of the beaches and estuaries. They are surrounded by vistas of open space which create a sense of wilderness, timelessness and existential authenticity. The towns are small-scale, the shops are local and intimate, and the atmosphere proclaims an antique lifestyle. Roads are often un-tarred and visitors boast about lack of mobile phone reception. However, these qualities are unlikely to remain for long, measured in terms of rising property prices (Hilton-Barber, 2005). Chintsa, in the Eastern Cape, represents a small coastal village undergoing such change. 'Prices in Chintsa are up six-fold over the past two years. Although there has been substantial overseas interest the vast majority of buyers are South African.' These include upbeat investors, enthusiastic golfers, families with young children, and those wishing to scale down – seeking quality of life in a world class secure estate' (Golding, 2005: 75).

Conclusion

This chapter provides a spatial typology and interpretation of coastal resort development along the South African coastline based on the influence of five drivers described as metropolitan renewal, second-wave renewal, lifestyle tourism, conservation with development and the quest for authenticity. Although these drivers occur in various degrees of importance throughout the length of the coastline, the dominance of particular drivers in specific regions permits a broad spatial classification. The typology is not cast in stone and may change over time as new drivers arise, or existing drivers gain or lose importance.

The drivers shaping coastal resort development are a product of the political and economic progress that has taken place since the country's first democratic elections in 1994. The government's macroeconomic GEAR strategy that has encouraged international investments signalled a return to the community of democratic nations. At the same time, its monetary policy has reduced inflation and provided a sound foundation for wealth creation. In addition, government policy initiatives have combined sustainable coastal management objectives with private–public partnerships directed towards satisfying both the tourist and the plight of the poor and unemployed. This is manifested through a policy of 'responsible tourism', which shapes tourism delivery in underdeveloped rural areas under the banner of conservation with development in Maputaland and the Wild Coast.

The growth in certain sectors of the South African economy, as well as a sustained period of lower interest rates, has provided expendable wealth available for tourism consumption. This has been invested in various ways. In some regions, such as the Hibiscus Coast, second homes and timeshare arrangements have led to the rejuvenation of coastal resort towns; in others such as the Southern Cape coast and Dolphin Coast, lifestyle quests by the wealthy have shaped development around notions informed by security, exclusive accommodation and high levels of environmental quality. Regions such as the West coast and Eastern Cape are in the process of early discovery by tourists fascinated by the timelessness of coastal villages.

Resort developments face serious challenges in the fluid and changing landscape of tourist preferences. The investment in coastal property must be measured against the fickle nature of tourism and its sensitivity to changes in global markets, overdevelopment, political unrest and perceptions of crime. Given the unequal distribution of wealth, resorts that cater for the rich while ignoring the surrounding sea of relative poverty, are unlikely to be sustainable in the long term. South Africa is in a privileged position given that many areas of the coastline remain underdeveloped. Concepts of natural and social integrity need to become an integral part of coastal zone management if the coastline is to avoid the irreversible sacrifice of natural areas to development expediency. The 'development is progress' lobby is currently powerful, and indeed, it is the image of exclusivity, wealth and quality lifestyles that create the dream, and hence the demand, that drives coastal development. The challenge is to avoid development of the sort that prompted Paul Theroux (1983: 17), on his hike along the British coastline, to comment that, 'a country tended to seep to its coast; it was concentrated there, deposited against its beaches like the tide-wrack from the sea'.

Chapter 12

Resort Structure and 'Plantation' Dynamics in Antigua and Coastal South Carolina

DAVID B. WEAVER

Introduction

The purpose of this chapter is to comparatively examine the structure of resorts in Antigua and coastal South Carolina (and the Sea Islands in particular) from the perspective of the Dependency paradigm, which, it is argued, still provides a useful framework for contextualising the evolution of tourism and resorts in these locations, as well as in other parts of the pleasure periphery, even though it has largely fallen out of academic favour. The first section briefly outlines Dependency Theory and its relationship to the concept of the pleasure periphery, which at least in the Caribbean and the Southern USA is expressed in the idea of a persistent 'plantation system'. The second section describes in general terms how coastal South Carolina and Antigua were incorporated into the pleasure periphery, and this is followed by a more detailed analysis and discussion of resort structure in the two case studies.

Dependency Theory and the Pleasure Periphery

The three chapters in the third section of this book reflect the extent to which the concept of the pleasure periphery has been widely adopted as a framework for contextualising the aggressive global expansion of 3S (sea, sand, sun) and allied forms of tourism, particularly since the mid-20th century. For many academics, the term is used simply because it captures in a concise and clever way the basic geographical (i.e. 'periphery') and sectoral (i.e. 'pleasure' tourism) contours of this process. When analysing the resorts and other spatial structures that have accompanied the formation of the pleasure periphery, however, it is crucial to recall the highly political and politicised origins of the term as it was conceived by Turner and Ash (1975) during the era of the so-called cautionary platform (Jafari, 2001). Specifically, it is imbued with the neo-Marxist ideology of Dependency Theory, which was articulated in the 1960s and 1970s to describe the existence of economically, politically and culturally dominant capitalist 'core' regions such as Great Britain and Spain that allegedly obtained and maintained a period of ascendancy through the formal or informal acquisition of subordinate 'periphery' regions that provided natural resources and markets to the latter on a coerced preferential basis. According to Buchanan (1968: 83), 'capitalist development simultaneously generated development and under-development, not as separate processes but as related facets of one single process', and it is therefore appropriate to describe how Asia, Africa and South America were 'underdeveloped' or 'peripheralised' by the great capitalist powers of Western Europe (Amin, 1976; Beckford, 1972; Frank, 1967; Rodney, 1972).

Interpreted from a Dependency context, the Caribbean islands and Southern USA were among the first non-European spaces to be peripheralised, with sugar and cotton respectively symbolising the exportable wealth that enriched the core. Integral to the effective functioning of this core–periphery relationship was the articulation of a large-scale plantation-based economy consisting of a network of extensive agricultural estates and an attendant class of wealthy planters supported by specialised systems of transportation, captive labour, service centres, finance, defence, etc. So entrenched did this structure become following the eradication of the indigenous cultures in the 1600s that Mintz (1971) refers to the existence of a pervasive 'plantation system' that permeated all aspects of the periphery economy, culture and society, even after the decline of the agricultural products that gave rise to this system.

Parallels between 3S tourism and the plantation economy

This contention is crucial to understanding the implications of the emergence of the pleasure periphery and the types of resorts that developed within that region. Essentially, 3S tourism emerged in the post-WWII period, at least in suitable areas of the Caribbean and Southern American littoral, as a viable and increasingly lucrative successor to an export agricultural economy that had been declining for many decades due to factors such as the Confederate defeat in the US Civil War, the emancipation of the slaves (in the 1830s in the Caribbean and the 1860s in the Southern USA), competition from new production spaces in Africa and Asia, and environmental degradation (Watts, 1987). According to researchers in the tourism field who were influenced by Dependency Theory, the new 3S tourism sector was readily accommodated within the plantation system, so that radical sectoral change was accompanied by only partial systemic adjustment. Parallels between the plantation economy and the tourism economy include a typical hotel occupational hierarchy with whites in high-status ownership and managerial positions, mixed race persons in mid-level managerial and supervisory positions, and persons of unmixed African descent accounting for most menial employment. Further perpetuating a state of underdevelopment in the contemporary 3S tourism industry is a pattern of expatriate or local elite dominance of investment and capital accumulation, a tendency toward large and relatively self-contained resort enclaves, reliance upon a small number of markets, a tendency toward sectoral 'monoculture' as tourism becomes increasingly dominant within the local economy and a high level of seasonality (Hills & Lundgren, 1977). Finney and Watson (1975), accordingly, refer to the latter as a 'new kind of sugar', while Harrigan (1974) and Erisman (1983) regard it as a new form of slavery predicated on an ethos of black servility.

Weaver (1988, 2005) more generally proposes a 'plantation' variant of Butler's (1980) destination life cycle which commences with the peripheralisation process (that is, when an infrastructure to accommodate visitors from the core is initiated) and entails an incipient tourism sector accommodated within the plantation economy and encouraged in part to attract potential white settlers. Urban guesthouses mainly operated by mixed race persons indicate a further link to the plantation system, as does the numeric dominance of the tourist flow from the core market. The transition to a tourism-based economy is facilitated by the ease with which suitably situated plantation owners, consisting of expatriates as well as local elites, can opportunistically convert their properties (both the land and the manor houses) into 3S resorts. A prominent spatial characteristic, subsequently, is the development of tourism-dominated resort/real estate strips along the coast, and their juxtaposition with an area of local settlements in the interior that provides a convenient reservoir of cheap labour. Paradoxically, these interior spaces lack any direct tourism presence (or any significant commercial farming for that matter) but form an integral component of the functional tourism landscape because of their critical labour provision role. Paraphrasing the Dependency theorists, it can be argued that the coastal strip (or 'tourism core' within the broader pleasure periphery) becomes developed by maintaining the interior (or the 'tourism periphery') in an underdeveloped state. In part this is because the reliance and emphasis on tourism precludes meaningful investment in farming or other activities that would benefit the interior.

The reference to the plantation and the plantation system, while clearly intended as more than mere analogy, should not be taken too literally. Aside from the fact that a hotel is not a plantation and a tourist consuming the sun and sea *in situ* is not sugar or cotton being produced for *ex situ* consumption, the contemporary plantation system is not maintained by a structure of institutionalised slavery, and at least in the

Caribbean, most of the tourism-dependent islands are formal colonies no longer. Adding to the scepticism toward the plantation/tourism linkage is the fact that the mother paradigm of Dependency has itself been largely supplanted since the 1980s by purportedly more sophisticated and less essentialist models such as World Systems Theory (Wallerstein, 1979) and, more recently, by the discourse on globalisation and the neoliberal 'Washington Consensus' (Williamson, 1990). The collapse of the 'socialist alternative' during the early 1990s and the concomitant rapid economic development of the East Asian periphery have been cited as further evidence of the paradigm's irrelevancy. Nevertheless, Surin (1998) calls for the reanimation of Dependency Theory, citing the increasing polarisation of wealth between and within states as a direct result of the unfettered asymmetrical capitalism unleashed by the forces of globalisation and American hegemony. In the following sections, evidence from Antigua and South Carolina is presented to evaluate the extent to which Dependency Theory and the plantation framework usefully define the structure of resorts in the contemporary 3S pleasure periphery of North America.

Incorporation of Antigua and South Carolina into the Pleasure Periphery

The Caribbean island of Antigua, where the plantation variant of the destination life cycle was first identified (Weaver, 1988), has experienced three stages of tourism development so far. The first, between the mid-1600s and mid-1900s, was characterised by informal, small-scale tourism activity accommodated mainly within the dominant agricultural plantation economy. During the brief second stage from about 1950 to 1970, an economic reversal occurred wherein tourism assumed the dominant position formerly occupied by agriculture (accounting for about 60% of GNP). This was due more to the collapse of commercial agriculture than the growth of the tourism industry, though as mentioned above, this collapse both encouraged the pursuit of tourism and was accelerated by this pursuit. The rapid absolute growth of tourism in the post-agricultural era, and its emergence as a major industry dominating much of the Antiguan littoral, characterises the post-1970 third stage of tourism development, even though the contribution of tourism to the GNP increased only slightly above 1970 levels. Overnight tourist visitors (the indicator most relevant to the resort sector) increased from 10,000 in 1955 to 49,000 in 1965, 63,000 in 1975 and 140,000 in 1985 (Weaver, 1992). Since the early 1990s, the figure has fluctuated in the range of 200,000–240,000, with 234,000 overnight visitors recorded in 2003 (World Tourism Organization, 2004). This stability, which is also reflected in the number of available hotel rooms, indicates a 'mature' destination (Baldwin, 2005;

Lazare *et al.*, 2001). The intensity of tourism relative to the local population is reflected in the ratio of visitor-days to the latter. Assuming an average length of stay of seven nights (McElroy, 2004), there were 1,638,000 stayover-days in 2003. When added to the approximately 350,000 cruise ship excursionists, a ratio of 30 visitor-days per resident per year results.

Tourism-related data for the South Carolina pleasure periphery is more difficult to obtain as the focus area of recreational tourism development is not a discrete geopolitical entity like Antigua but rather a mainly biophysical region (i.e. coastal) within a state within a country. This problem is overcome partially by adopting the criterion of the South Carolina Coastal Conservation Council (SCCCC), which designates eight counties as the state's coastal zone. Prior to the mid-20th century, tourism activity in this area was extremely limited, in large part because of the isolation of the so-called Sea Islands that dominate the coastline. Resort and residential development commenced in some areas during the 1950s, but even by the mid-1960s high-density outdoor recreation land use and activity was restricted to Myrtle Beach, while low-density activity was becoming significant in selected locales such as Hilton Head Island and several islands near Charleston (Fussell, 1965). Facilitating factors such as the completion of the Interstate expressway network have since allowed coastal South Carolina to emerge as one of the country's premier 3S tourism/recreation regions. The most tourism-intensive area is the Grand Strand, an almost continuous 100 km long zone of resort and residential development along the North coast anchored by the high-rise strip of Myrtle Beach. The remaining area is a complex zone of barrier islands and estuaries where exclusive low-density resorts and residential estates are rapidly coming to occupy the coastal areas that are not already occupied by a variety of high- and low-order protected areas. During the early 2000s, the eight coastal counties accommodated about 65 million visitor-days per year, 95% within just the three nodes of Myrtle Beach (i.e. high-density resort strip), Charleston (urban) and Hilton Head (low-density resort and residential) (Department of Parks, Recreation and Tourism, 2005). Given the residential population of approximately one million, this yields a ratio of 65 visitor-days per resident per year.

Aside from this higher ratio and the large absolute number of visitor-days, basic departures from the Antiguan experience include the overwhelming dominance of the domestic market (with about 97% of all visitors being residents of the USA), and the fact that the great majority of day-only visitors arrive by land-based transport rather than cruise ship. Also notable is the extent to which conventional tourism activity (i.e. day-only and short-term stayovers) in coastal South Carolina coexists and blurs with residential tourism, seasonal residents and permanent residents both retired and active in the work force. Some indication of the recent rapid growth of tourism in the South Carolina pleasure periphery is provided by Hilton Head Island, which increased its total visitor intake from 250,000 in 1975 to 1.5 million in 1995 (Town of Hilton Head Island, 2005).

Structure of Resorts

Resorts are characterised by their increased size and diversity both in Antigua and South Carolina. In the former, the 28 establishments identified as resorts in 1987 averaged 45 units. In 1997 the average number of units increased to 97 units while the number of establishments actually decreased slightly to 27 (Baldwin, 2005). Epitomising the 'new wave' in integrated Antiguan mega-resorts is the twin-resort complex of Jolly Harbour Villas and Jolly Beach Resort, which cover several hundred hectares on the Western coast of the island. Among the facilities found here that are increasingly recognised as requisite to complexes of this scale are a large multi-storey hotel, villas (rental and/or owner-occupied), golf course, marina, shopping mall, casino, restaurants, private beach and marina. A diverse array of in-house activities (e.g. helicopter tours, sailing, deep sea fishing) lends further weight to the operation's contention (reported on its website) that it constitutes a 'self-sustaining community'. Similar integrated resorts in coastal South Carolina include the Wild Dunes Resort on the Isle of Palms near Charleston (two 18-hole golf courses, 17-court tennis centre, conference centre, 365 villas and homes, etc.) and the Hilton Head Marriott Beach and Golf Resort (512-room hotel, three 18-hole golf courses, 25-court tennis centre, marina).

Increasing size and diversity both support a Dependency/plantation perspective, in that large size equates with power and with the concentration of this power in the hands of a relatively small number of large operations. Diversity of accommodation and activity options attests to the status of Antiguan and South Carolinian resorts as relatively self-contained enclaves in which client expenditures are mostly internalised, to the detriment of local, small-scale businesses and suppliers not affiliated with the resort. With regard to ownership, a major difference between the two case studies is the geography of ownership, with Baldwin (2005) noting that 88.4% of Antigua's 2630 beachside rooms are foreign-owned. In South Carolina the resort corporations are overwhelmingly based in the USA, though not necessarily within the state. With regard to employment, the occupational hierarchy described above is still apparent in the contemporary Antiguan tourism industry to the extent that managerial positions continue to be filled mainly by expatriates and menial positions by local Afro-Caribbeans and migrant workers (legal and illegal) from other Caribbean islands. Menial positions in coastal South Carolina resorts have similarly been long dominated by local African-Americans (Harris, 1988; Thomas, 1980).

Spatial context and dynamics

Some of the most compelling evidence for the continuing relevance of the Dependency/plantation model derives from an investigation into the broader structural relationships between the resorts and nearby communities. In both Antigua and South Carolina, resorts occupy coastal property that has appreciated dramatically in value since the mid-20th century because of its proximity to the sea and sand. The establishment of 3S tourism resorts requires that this property first be acquired, and then maintained for the privileged use of the tourist and resident clientele. In the Sea Islands of South Carolina, some resorts were established on defunct plantations acquired more or less intact by developers from their often absentee landowners. Others were established on assembled smaller properties purchased from African-American owners descended from local slaves who obtained this land from the government after the Civil War.

The latter mode of land acquisition for resort development has proven highly controversial in locations such as Hilton Head Island amidst claims and perceptions that some owners were tricked into selling their property on unfavourable terms (Thomas, 1977), or were compelled to sell due to an inability to pay property taxes that were continuously escalating due to inflation induced by the nearby development of resorts (Harris, 1988). The incorporation of Hilton Head Island as a 'limited service' municipality in 1983 further alienated local African-Americans by failing to provide basic municipal services such as water or sewerage to areas outside the residential resorts (where they were privately provided) while simultaneously imposing strict zoning regulations that were incompatible with the largely subsistence-based rural lifestyle of many of the African-American residents (Danielson, 1995; Faulkenberry *et al*., 2000). Incorporation, notably, was possible because of the influx of supportive white residents into the residential resorts, which inverted the traditional racial balance of the island and effectively disempowered the traditionally self-sufficient descendants of the slaves. In 1950, the latter accounted for more than 95% of Hilton Head Island's population of 1125 (Danielson, 1995), but by 2000, this had been reduced to about 8% of the almost 34,000 residents, according to the US Census Bureau.

Similar displacements have occurred on other major Sea Islands, and while these have not always been as dramatic as the Hilton Head example, it is still valid to assert the transformation of the Sea Islands in the span of just 50 years from an isolated semi-subsistence African-American culture area to a suburban variant of the pleasure periphery populated by wealthy and mainly white residents and tourists. Increasingly common are 'mega-resort agglomerations' such as Hilton Head Island where five or six such operations are found side-by-side.

Though largely displaced as residents, the local and regional African-American underclass, as noted above, still serves as a critical source of cheap manual labour for the coastal resorts of South Carolina. In many cases these individuals have relocated to more affordable locations away from the coast, yet join other workers in those locations in long commutes to the coastal resorts for low-wage employment that precludes purchasing housing nearby (Faulkenberry *et al.*, 2000). Harris (1988) contends that about one-half of the African-American workers on Hilton Head Island were bused in daily from as far as 140 km away during the late 1980s. Yet, despite the indispensability of this labour, there has also persisted the widespread perception among African-Americans that they are not welcome in the resorts or on the Sea Islands more generally beyond this labour role (Danielson, 1995; Harris, 1988; Thomas, 1977). Animating such perceptions is the enclave and private nature of most resorts, which usually entails gatehouses, fencing, security patrols and other means of controlling access. Harris (1988) further describes a pass system of labour access in some resorts that he compares to the race-control policies employed at that time by the apartheid government of South Africa. Perhaps the most blatant and symbolic example of insensitivity for many African-Americans has been the overt use of the term 'plantation' in the actual name of some resorts, and as an informal term to describe the Sea Island residential estates, a usage that is often accompanied in brochures by images of an idyllic antebellum lifestyle. Another complaint is the loss of access to land traditionally used for hunting, fishing and gathering, and to burial grounds now situated on the residential plantations.

Such considerations compel Faulkenberry *et al.* (2000) to accuse 3S tourism in coastal South Carolina of spawning a pervasive 'culture of servitude', as per the rhetoric of Dependency Theory. Even more disturbing, however, are the words they quote from an African-American Sea Island resident deploring this culture: 'I think it's a feeling of almost going back into slavery. Like they're saying you can't come to the big house tonight' (Faulkenberry *et al.*, 2000: 92). Similar sentiments are frequently expressed in present-day Antigua, despite a number of notable differences relative to South Carolina. As with the latter, tourist-oriented and residential resorts are occupying an ever-increasing share of the coastline of the small (281 km^2) island. Unlike South Carolina, this expansion has not included the physical displacement of islander residences, most of which are located in small villages situated away from the coastline. Instead, the pattern of establishing resorts on abandoned coastal plantations (called 'estates' here), as in some parts of the Sea Islands, has been almost universal. A further departure from South Carolina is the fact that the Afro-Caribbean population of Antigua has retained its overwhelming numeric dominance due to more limited out-migration options and the lack of emphasis on residential resorts occupied by permanent residents from outside of Antigua.

While residential displacement due to tourism has been minimal or even nonexistent in Antigua, perceived curtailment of access to coastal resources has been an ongoing concern of major proportions. Baldwin (2000) describes how developers' attempts to construct stereotypical landscapes and seascapes of powder-white beaches and swaying coconut palms have resulted in the widespread destruction of ecologically vital but 'unsightly' mangroves, salt ponds and salt marshes (or 'flashes') that traditionally were an important source of food, fuel and craft material for Antiguans as well as an incubator for marine and bird life harvested elsewhere – especially in so far as 300 years of predatory plantation agriculture had severely depleted the productive capacity of the massively degraded interior (Lorah, 1995). In other cases, retained salt ponds have been seriously disturbed by the discharge of raw sewerage from resorts or the blocking of tidal inlets by resort construction. Beaches, while designated as public space, have often become effectively inaccessible to local residents because of the establishment of resorts and associated boundary fences in access areas. The property associated with the Jolly Harbour Resort (see above) provides a well documented example of tourism-related environmental degradation and efforts by local residents, including petitions and protests, to resist this degradation (de Albuquerque, 1991). A focal point for resistance as well was an ill-fated attempt to develop the 4.6-km^2 Asian Village themed resort on Antigua's relatively isolated Atlantic coastline, a project that was to have involved the permanent immigration of 2000 Malaysian workers (Baldwin, 2005).

To a greater extent than in South Carolina, local villages in Antigua are often located adjacent to tourist and residential resorts (e.g. the village of Bolans with Jolly Harbour, Five Islands with Galley Bay, Old Road with Curtain Bluff, and Freetown with the ultraexclusive Mill Reef residential resort), creating a stark juxtaposition between the Third World-like village tourism periphery and the First World-like resort tourism core. As with South Carolina, the relationship is symbiotic to the degree that the resorts depend on the labour provided by these villages while villagers derive much of their employment from the resorts. Yet, similarly, the local Afro-Caribbean population often feels alienated from the resorts, which are also comparable to South Carolina in their use of the historical term 'estate' and in sometimes adopting the names of former plantations (e.g. Mill Creek and Yepton).

Discussion and Conclusion

The current structural situation with respect to resorts in both coastal South Carolina and Antigua, despite several major differences, seems to corroborate many of the basic systemic contentions about core/periphery relationships put forward by the advocates of Dependency Theory, indicating that the latter still provides a useful context within which to situate the evolution of the contemporary pleasure periphery. Without doubt, the structure has increased exponentially in size since the Dependency hey-days of the 1970s, and it may well be that the disequilibrium between the tourism core (i.e. the coastal resorts) and the tourism periphery (i.e. nearby communities providing labour) has actually increased, given the dominance of free market policies during the late 20th century and the accompanying dynamics of capitalist globalisation. It is therefore surprising that resistance to this process appears to have been negligible, apparently being largely confined to anecdotal citations of disgruntlement among local residents, occasional protests, 'attitude problems' among menial labourers and, among some academics and social activists, plaintive and mostly ineffective calls for 'fair trade' in tourism (e.g. Cleverdon, 2001).

This lack of active resistance on the part of the people most negatively affected may owe to several factors, including the out-migration of the disaffected, resort to passive modes of resistance (as in the slavery era), effective adaptation to changing circumstances, and resignation in the face of the overwhelming power of the government and corporate forces (and perhaps the trade unions in the case of Antigua) that have aided and abetted the process and stand to gain the most from its outcomes. In the face of the latter, local African-American and Afro-Caribbean communities have lacked effective support from counteracting organisations. In South Carolina, there is evidence that the National Association for the Advancement of Coloured People (NAACP) assisted Hilton Head residents in their efforts to retain their property and livelihoods, while many ad hoc community and environmental organisations have been formed in Antigua to protect the coastal environment and the people's access to its resources (Baldwin, 2005).

Clearly, however, these have not halted or reversed the peripheralisation process or its intensification. It may also be, as per the claims of the advocacy platform (Jafari, 2001) and supporters of capitalism and globalisation more generally, that many or most residents actually *support* this process because of the resulting benefits that they have gained. These include employment suitable for an unskilled labour force, access to better schools and services, and opportunities to obtain a financial windfall through the sale of land. Supporters of resort tourism can point out that Antigua, a symbol of the plantation model of tourism development, is ranked 34th among 200 or so countries in terms of per capita GNP (US$8770), while Dominica, often cited as an example of 'alternative' tourism based on local control and small-scale eco-tourism, ranks 60th (US$3190) (Weaver & Lawton, 2006) (allowing that this does not take into account the *distribution* of wealth within the population). It is also no doubt the case that a small but increasing proportion of tourists, resort residents and managers are themselves of African descent, thereby diluting the racial underpinnings of the Dependency argument.

Beyond the issue of resistance, there are at least four emerging issues within contemporary resort structure that have not been discussed above but may have an important influence on future pleasure periphery dynamics and stakeholder relationships. One may be described as 'interiorisation', because it entails the penetration of the pleasure periphery resort landscape into the interior as available coastal property becomes too scarce and expensive. In South Carolina, this is manifested in the growing popularity of retiree-dominated residential resorts on reservoirs, and by the proliferation of golf courses and equestrian facilities. This again raises the question as to whether a similar process of displacement and alienation is likely to occur in relation to the much larger African-American population in these areas.

A second issue is the effect of globalisation, one outcome being the further erosion of the 'poor black–rich white' dichotomy as the stakeholders of both the tourism core and periphery become more internationalised. On Hilton Head Island, for example, Hispanics (11% of the population) currently outnumber African-Americans, while Eastern Europeans account for a growing proportion of the labour force in a variety of positions. In Antigua, the fact that the government initially approved a scheme (Asian Village) that would have involved the immigration of 2000 Malaysian nationals is another illustration. Among the many implications is the possibility of conflict among competing factions within the low-wage labour cohorts.

A third issue is the blending of the tourism and non-tourism elements within the pleasure periphery, as illustrated by the importance of residential resorts, particularly in South Carolina. Conventional short-stay tourists increasingly share resort space with permanent and seasonal residents, many of them retirees. Near Charleston, a substantial proportion of resort inhabitants in the Sea Islands are commuters. The clearest implication here, as best illustrated on Hilton Head Island, is the attainment of political power over traditional populations by wealthy newcomers who will not hesitate to bring into effect policies that further their own perceived self-interest. Finally, the role of protected areas merits further consideration. According to Akama (1996), many of the great game preserves in East Africa were established by the colonial powers to alienate local tribes from their traditional lands. Such blatant motives may not have been the case in South Carolina, but protected areas nonetheless prohibit, like private resorts, much of the resource extraction that local residents traditionally relied upon, and preclude any possibility of reclaiming traditional residences. As in Kenya, they also mainly serve the recreational and aesthetic needs of white beachgoers and eco-tourists. Interpreted in this way, the expanding resorts and protected areas along the Sea Islands of coastal South Carolina together constitute, from the perspective of the displaced local African-American, an ever-tightening 'zone of exclusion' where the interests of the core are always paramount.

Chapter 13

Re-engineering Coastal Resorts in Mexico: Some Management Issues

SHEELA AGARWAL and GARETH SHAW

Introduction

Tourism has long been a major source of national, regional and local economic activity in Mexico. In 1997 for example, tourism accounted for 3.5% of Mexico's Gross Domestic Product (GDP) and directly or indirectly supported one out of 10 jobs (Anpudia, 1997). Currently, tourism is the third most important economic activity in Mexico, representing 8.3% of the nation's GDP. Furthermore, the country currently ranks 8th in the world in terms of the number of international visitors it receives, and 10th in the world with regard to the generation of international tourism revenues (World Tourism Organization, 2005). Much of Mexico's tourism development has been focused along the coastline, and has traditionally involved the creation of mega-resort structures which are based primarily on sun, sea and sand tourism. More recently however, the development of eco-tourism is influencing the construction of Mexico's coastal resorts (Healy, 1997; Kersten, 1997), thereby reflecting shifting modes of consumption and the demand for new forms of tourism (Poon, 1993; Urry, 1990). Consequently, vast stretches of Mexico's Californian, Pacific and Caribbean coasts host a dichotomy of resort structures, with mass tourism and an alternative form of tourism at polar extremes.

This chapter explores coastal resort development in Mexico and argues that although resort structures appear to vary, there is in fact very little difference in management issues that arise from each type of development. Indeed, in this context, it is argued that eco-tourism is a camouflaged form of mass tourism development that is strongly engineered and standardised. Thus, in the first part of this chapter, coastal resort development in Mexico is explored, focusing in particular on the birth of the mega-resort. This is followed by an examination of some more recent and allegedly environmentally friendly resort developments. In the second part of this chapter, some of the management issues that have arisen from resort developments in Mexico, including the impacts of intensive tourism development and the continuing pressure of tourism development along Mexico's coast, are discussed.

Mexico's Coastal Resorts: Variability or Standardisation?

Following the Second World War, the Mexican government identified marine and coastal areas as an important part of its long-term national development strategy, and targeted tourism as a key component (Neto, 2002). Coastal resort development initially focused on a few key geographical areas in Mexico, and throughout the 1950s and 1960s, development was overwhelmingly concentrated in Acapulco, Zihuatenjo, Mazatlán and Puerto Vallarta, situated on Mexico's Southwest coast, and on Cozumel, an island situated just off the Southeast coast (Fig. 13.1). These resorts benefited from improvements to public infrastructure and they boomed following construction of road and rail links to Mexico City (Clancy, 2001; Healy, 1997).

From the 1970s onwards, the Mexican government emphasised tourism's potential as a major source of foreign exchange and employment. This was evidenced in 1974 by the creation of the agency, the *Fondo do Promoción de Ifraestructura Turística* (National Trust Fund for Tourist Infrastructure [INFRATUR]), which later became known as the *Fondo Nacional de Fomento al Turismo de México* (National Fund for the Promotion of Tourism in Mexico or a National Fund for Tourism Development) or FONATUR. This agency was tasked with the administration and provision of financial support and incentives for the construction of hotels, tourist condominiums, restaurants and other tourism-related infrastructure. Thus, at the beginning of the 1970s, as well as promoting existing tourist destinations (Acapulco, Mazatlán, Puerto Vallarta, Zihuatanejo and Cozumel), FONATUR initiated the development of a handful of mega-resorts. These were entirely new planned beach resorts that were to be located along the Pacific, Californian and Caribbean coasts (Clancy, 1995, 1998, and in particular 2001 for a fuller discussion of the complex economies of the large developments).

The birth of the 'mega-resort' in Mexico

According to Gladstone (2006), after an exhaustive computer-aided analysis of potential sites that took climate, topography and flight times from major US cities into consideration, three states – Baja California Sur, Oaxaca and Quintana Roo – were targeted by FONATUR for the development of four beach orientated mega-resorts, these being Los Cabos, Loreta, Ixtapa and Cancún (Fig. 13.1). A fifth site, Bahías de Huatulco, was added in the mid-1980s. These locations are geographically dispersed throughout the country, had previously been subject to

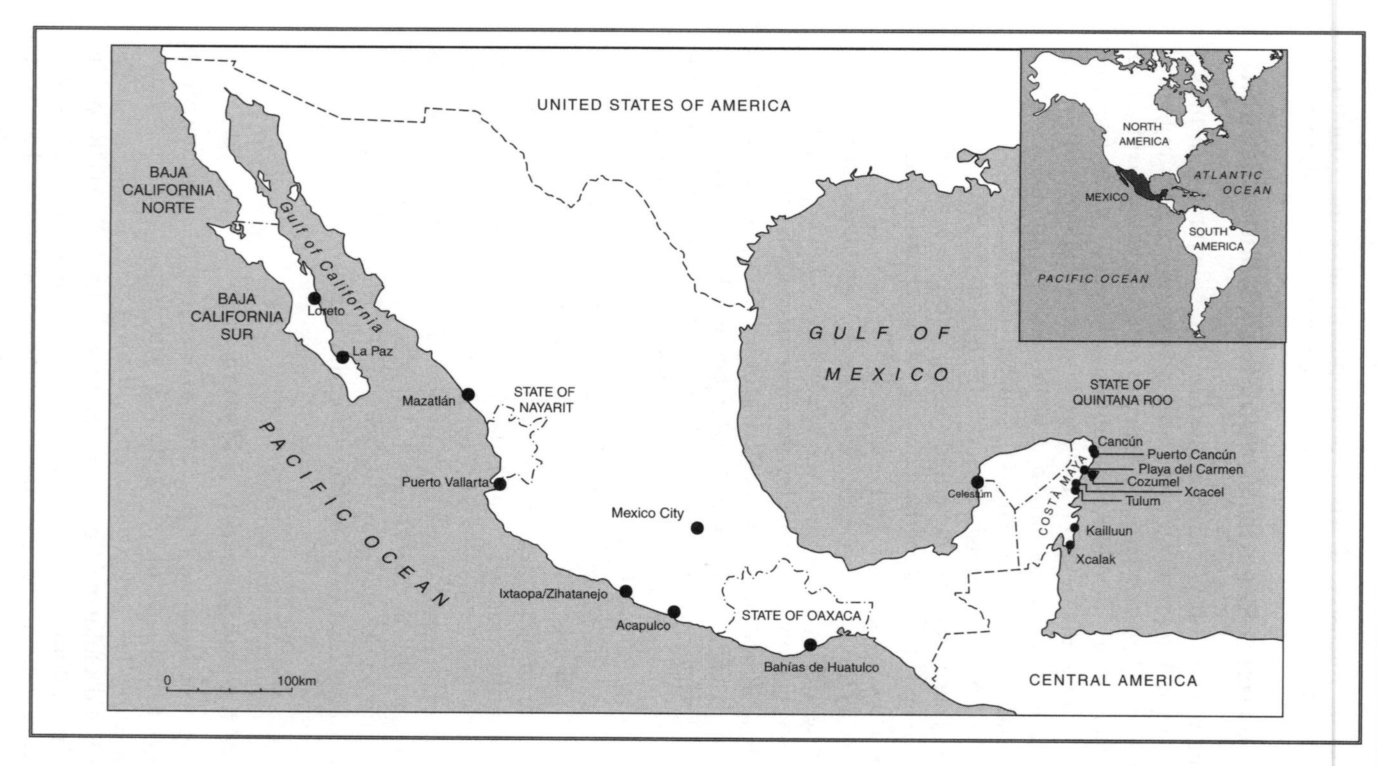

Figure 13.1 Map of Mexico and location of places named

scant tourism development, and were developed in phases: Cancún and Ixtapa were developed first, followed by Los Cabos, Loreto and Bahías de Huatulco (Clancy, 1998).

Cancún is arguably the most famous of all of Mexico's mega-resorts. Despite certain disadvantages such as distance from the region's major cities (for example, approximately 1820 km from Mexico City, 380 km from Chetumal and 321 km from Merida), a deficient highway infrastructure, lack of available trained manpower and nonexistent local capital, there were important reasons for the selection of Cancún as the site of a mega-resort. As well as the natural beauty of the area and its proximity to some of the world's most famous Mayan sites, the need to successfully compete with tourist destinations in the Caribbean Basin provided one of the main driving forces behind the creation of Cancún (Cancún Convention and Visitor Bureau, 2005). A master plan was drawn up in the early 1970s which made provision for three key features:

(1) a tourism zone without permanent residential areas, but with hotels, shopping centres, golf courses and marinas;
(2) a residential zone for permanent residents, with residential and commercial areas, roads, public buildings, schools, hospitals and markets; and
(3) an international airport (see Shaw & Williams, 2004 for a site map of Cancún).

The first hotels in Cancún opened in 1974, these being Playa Blanca, Bojorquez and the Cancún Caribe. By 1976, the resort hosted 18,000 inhabitants, it benefited from stable migratory patterns, it had created more than 5000 jobs and 1500 hotel rooms and it attracted approximately 100,000 visitors in the winter season of 1976–77 (Cancún Convention and Visitor Bureau, 2005). Between 1983 and 1988, Cancún experienced explosive growth with more than 12,000 hotel rooms being built and another 1100 being projected or under construction, and it accommodated more than 200,000 inhabitants. From 1989 onwards, Cancún was Mexico's most dynamic city despite the occurrence of seemingly insurmountable problems that have dogged its development. These include a lack of regular flights, the 1982 devaluation, natural disasters and, more recently, the collapse of North American tourism due to the terrorist attacks of 11 September 2001 (Cancún Convention and Visitor Bureau, 2005). The resort still contributes a large percentage of Mexico's tourism-related revenue and accounts for much of Quintana Roo's GDP (Hiernaux-Nicolas, 1999). It currently houses more than 500,000 inhabitants, has become the country's largest tourism resort, and is the most prosperous city in the Yucatán Peninsula. It is also the Caribbean's premier destination, surpassing even the Bahamas and Puerto Rico (SECTUR, 2003).

Ixtapa meanwhile, in the South central state of Guerrero (near Acapulco), was built on a FONATUR-expropriated large coconut tree plantation near the established coastal resort of Zihuatanejo. The first hotel was built in 1971, and the town was subsequently renamed Ixtapa-Zihuatenejo. By 1975, Ixtapa had 11 hotels with 491 rooms and currently hosts half a dozen world-class international resort franchise hotels (from Club Med to Radisson) and half a dozen more renowned Mexican brand hotels (Presidente Intercontinental and Las Brisas). Other developments in Ixtapa include a marina, which transformed a great mangrove lagoon and offers slips for more than 600 boats, two golf courses, and a yacht and golf club house which boasts a swimming pool, spa, fitness club and restaurant. Luxury condominiums and private villas surround the marina and golf course (www.villaixtapa.com/ixtapa_zihuatanejo.htm).

For the last 10 years, Ixtapa has generated between $120 and 150 million US annually, with 308,000 tourists arriving by air in its lowest year, and 415,000 in its busiest year, with foreign tourists accounting for up to 43% of the total number of arrivals. Hotel occupancy rates have been reported at 84%, giving Ixtapa-Zihuatenajo the best hotel occupancy rate in the state of Guerrero, outperforming Acapulco, and consistently having among the highest rates in Mexico (www.villaixtapa.com/ixtapa_zihuatanejo.htm). In 2005, a new toll road connecting Ixtapa/Zihuatanejo to Morelia, Michoacan (pop. 577,570) was completed, reducing the drive time between Zihuatanejo and Michoacan's capital from 8 hours to less than 4 hours, and it has already dramatically increased the flow of domestic tourism to this resort. This highway places Ixtapa-Zihuatanejo within the same driving distance from Guadalajara (Mexico's 2nd largest city) as Puerto Vallarta. A rise in local investment and construction projects is mirroring the optimism that this added accessibility brings. Indeed, four large Mexican developments from corporations well established in other Mexican resorts have already started construction on first-class hotels, spas, exclusive suites and condominiums in Ixtapa, and two international companies, one of which is Intrawest Corporation of Canada, has recently opened a new resort in Zihuatanejo on La Ropa Beach (www.villaixtapa.com/ixtapa_zihuatanejo.htm).

Los Cabos and Loreto, two of the five mega-resorts that were developed in the early 1980s, are both situated in the Western state of Baja California Sur. Los Cabos comprises two existing fishing towns, Cabo San Lucas and San José del Cabo, separated by a 29-km stretch of beach. Following investment by FONATUR in an airport, opened in 1984, development has occurred along the stretch of beach separating Cabo San Lucas and San José del Cabo. In particular, it has included the opening of seven new championship golf courses and has led to the promotion of Los Cabos as the golf capital of Latin America.

Additionally, this resort now possesses more than 40 hotels, numerous timeshare apartments and tourist condominiums, and there are at least 3000 new private homes and 60 major restaurants. As historical and cultural sightseeing is limited, outdoor recreation is the resort's main activity. The area is renowned for its deep-sea sport fishing, scuba diving, snorkelling, surfing and windsurfing. More recently, the resort's accessibility has been further improved by the introduction of a non-stop air service from Houston via Continental Airlines and Dallas via American Airlines, while Alaska Airlines serving the West coast and America West's flights out of Phoenix are bringing in Midwest visitors (Cabo San Lucas Villas, 2006).

In contrast, Loreto is sited on a stretch of sand expropriated by FONATUR, south of Nopoló, a small fishing town, and is being developed in nine stages, targeted at US and Canadian tourists. Following an initial surge of development and promotion, the resort struggled due to the lack of air service and investment (Bajaquest, 2006). However, its fortunes changed in 1989, when the La Paz based company Aero California began operating non-stop flights from Los Angeles International Airport. Currently 5000 villas, 980 condominiums, 6 boutique hotels with 1500 rooms, a golf course, a shopping centre, spa and a medical clinic are being planned for construction (Brooke, 2005).

The last of the five mega-resorts to be initiated, Bahías de Huatulco, is comprised of nine bays, located in the Southern state of Oaxaca. Determined to create a resort that offers some of the finest natural beauty of Mexico, along with all the modern conveniences of Mexico's mega-resorts, FONATUR began developing Huatulco in 1983 in accordance with a carefully designed master plan. The plan is being undertaken in two phases: the first is focused on two of Huatulco's bays – Santa Cruz and Tangolunda – and was completed in 1988. The bay of Santa Cruz and the city of Santa Cruz were the area's principal settlement when development began in the early 1980s, however, Tangolunda is the most developed of the nine bays, hosting six ultramodern resorts, including the largest Club Med in the Western hemisphere, an 18-hole golf course, a shopping area and several restaurants. A total of 1300 rooms have been created and in its first year alone, Huatulco received some 60,000 tourists (Clancy, 2001). Phase two began in 1988 and by its end-point, scheduled for 2018, FONATUR expects Huatulco to surpass Cancún in size, offering some 30,000 hotel rooms and hosting more than 2 million guests per annum (Brooke, 2005). Development is currently focusing on Chahue, a third bay next to Tangolunda, and the resort's largest. A marina is under construction that will soon receive cruise ships. There are currently no hotels open on this beach; however, about a mile inland is the city of Crucecita (population

7000), with several tourist-class restaurants, a disco, a good municipal market, a four-star hotel and an attractive main square.

In all five of these mega-resorts, various state agencies were granted powers over site planning, infrastructure provision, real estate development and marketing (Clancy, 1998, 2001). Since 1974, FONATUR has financed approximately 85% of the hotel rooms built in Mexico (TED, 1998) and FONATUR (1994) estimated that these five mega-resorts now account for 40% of Mexico's foreign tourism revenue. Moreover, in addition to control over the development process, the state also owns and operates many hotel properties; Gladstone (2006) states that in both Cancún and Bahías de Huatulco, either FONATUR itself or other government hotel chains such as Hotel Nacionalera own a large share of the rooms. But tourism development in these five resorts also involved foreign investment as multilateral lending agencies such as the IDB and the World Bank lent the Mexican government over US$20million in the early 1970s for the development of Cancún and Ixtapa (Clancy, 1998, 2001; Hiernaux-Nicolas, 1999).

Although the government's primary motivation for developing these mega-resorts was to generate foreign exchange, Gladstone (2006) notes that Mexico's state planners also recognised that they were all located in historically underdeveloped regions, and would therefore bring economic and social benefits to the areas in which the resorts were situated. Thus, in conjunction with the development of tourism, policies of directed migration were also initiated in an attempt to encourage large numbers of landless people from the North and central parts of Mexico to the sparsely populated Yucatán and Baja California Peninsulas (Gladstone, 2006). The state of Quintana Roo, for example, experienced annual average migration rates of 9% between 1970 and 1990, and 7.4% between 1990 and 1995, with Cancún acting as a magnet attracting people from all over Mexico to work in the construction and service industry supporting tourism. In just 25 years, over 300,000 Mexicans have migrated to Cancún to take advantage of employment opportunities offered by this development (Robadue *et al.*, 1997). Indeed, based on Hiernaux-Nicolas and Rodriguez Woog's (1990) study of the Mexican tourism industry, Gladstone (2006) estimates that out of those resorts that specialise in international tourism, Cancún accounts for more than half the total number of workers, closely followed by Puerto Vallarta, Ixtapa, Los Cabos, Cozumel and Loreto. Moreover, he states that employment in Mexico's international tourism resorts 'represents a sizable percentage of the country's employment in tourism production, and about one third of the total employment in Mexico's major tourist centres' (Gladstone, 2006: 84).

However, the Mexican government has not just been concentrating its efforts on developing mass tourism. During the past decade, efforts have been made to diversify the market (Euromonitor, 2006), with attempts to utilise the vast array of attractions, other than the sun and sand, that Mexico has to offer (Healy, 1997; Kersten, 1997). Thus, pre-Columbian archaeological sites, colonial architecture, indigenous people and cultures, nature parks and virgin rainforest, wildlife, fishing and hunting, and photographic panoramas are all attributes that are currently being promoted and marketed. Given the nature of these resources, it is not surprising therefore that they are forming the basis of the development of alternative forms of tourism, in particular eco-tourism (Van den Berghe, 1994).

Eco-tourism and Mexico's coastal resorts

In addition to Mexico's mega-resorts, there are a number of recently developed small eco-tourism coastal resort developments primarily along the Mayan Riviera, the 120-km corridor from Cancún to Tulum, and the Costa Maya – the remote southernmost portion of the Yucatán coast to the border of Belize (Fig. 13.1). This is an area of high biodiversity and rich coastal ecosystems, and is bordered by the Sian Ka'an Biosphere Reserve, Belize's Hol Chan Marine Reserve and the Meso-American reef system. For example, Kailuum, located on the Costa Maya and approximately four hours drive time from Cancún airport, is a small, exclusive resort operated by the Turquoise Reef Group, a company that specialises in small and alternative beach resort facilities. It markets itself as an eco-tourism destination as it is set behind a freshwater mangrove lagoon, it consists of 17 low-rise units and it strives to limit the negative impacts of tourism upon the natural environment (www.eco-tropicalresorts.com).

Other examples include Eco Paraiso XiXim, nestled on a three-mile virgin beach at Celestún, Costa de Cocos, located at Xcalak, the Hotel Las Palapas, situated in Playa del Carmen and Papaya Playa, located near Tulum (www.eco-tropicalresorts.com). All of these eco-tourism resorts appear to conform to Honey's (1999: 22–24) seven key characteristics of 'real' eco-tourism, as shown in Table 13.1. This is partly because they are all self-contained, low-rise, low-density developments that are built out of local natural materials.

Moreover, all profess to be ecological in the sense that they recycle water and waste and by developing only a fraction of total land available, they encourage biodiversity and conservation. For example, in the case of the Eco Paraiso XiXim, only 1.2% of owned land has been developed (Hotel Eco Paraiso, 2006). Furthermore, all promote low-impact activities such as bird watching and engage in some form of visitor education either through the provision of interpretive trails, forest and reef interpretive guided tours and/or heritage centres (www.eco-tropicalresorts.com).

Table 13.1 Honey's seven key characteristics of 'real' ecotourism

Key characteristics of 'real' ecotourism	
(i)	Involves travel to natural destinations
(ii)	Minimises impact
(iii)	Builds environmental awareness
(iv)	Provides direct financial benefits for conservation
(v)	Provides financial benefits and empowerment for local people
(vi)	Respects local culture
(vii)	Supports human rights and democratic movements

Source: Collated from Honey (1999: 22–24)

In this respect, eco-tourism serves its two intended goals: it is not only a means of conservation, but also a way of providing employment for local people. The extent to which these coastal resort developments may be considered to be eco-tourism is further reinforced by the fact that they are marketed through an eco-tourism directory of tropical resorts and lodges. This stipulates that such resorts must do their best to help the ecosystem where they are located and adhere to eco-tourism tenets that help promote sustainable tourism (Eco Tropical Resorts, 2006).

The development of eco-tourism along Mexico's Caribbean coast has been aided, in part, by the initiation of an extensive regulatory system of legal instruments for resource management, which is aimed at limiting inappropriate development. In 1994, the first ecological zoning strategy in Mexico was adopted in Quintana Roo (Fig. 13.1), which involved the establishment of 45 zones along the Cancún corridor with density restrictions of 5–25 rooms per acre; some conservation zones in the area of Tulum were also set aside (Robadue *et al*., 1997). A number of biospheres such as Sian Ka'an and Yum Bolom were also created in an attempt to stop the gradual encroachment of tourism development. According to Creel *et al*. (1998), the intent of biosphere reserves is to protect ecosystems that have not been altered significantly by human activity. In Mexico, protected areas are conceptualised as multiple-use zones, consisting of core and buffer zones. The former are off-limits to human activity, except scientific research, while the latter allow some economic activities by local people. Through this combination of conservation and sustainable use, biosphere reserves offer a challenge and a great deal of potential for people to reach a dynamic equilibrium with nature (Rosado-May, 1994).

In addition, the state of Quintana Roo is also promoting low-impact development that both protects the long-term sustainability of tourism investment and preserves the coastal environment. This is an entirely voluntary initiative based upon a practitioner's manual of guidelines for low-impact tourism development practices. Rubinoff and Tobey (2006) state that these guidelines address issues concerning the management of beaches, dunes, wetlands, vegetation, wastewater, solid waste, and the use of energy and water resources. They are based on a comprehensive assessment of the coastal resource base and ecosystem dynamics, incorporating design and management techniques that have proven effective in other regions around the world. One of the key messages is the benefit to both industry and society of mitigating damage from natural hazards through low-cost and straightforward preconstruction practices. These include the use of construction setbacks, incorporating vegetated dunes with native vegetation and taking into account previous hurricane and erosion history in development planning. However, these are not the only efforts to encourage mass coastal tourism resorts to be more sustainable, as attempts are also being made to encourage existing mega-resorts to become more environmentally friendly.

'Eco-ising' Mexico's coastal resorts

Efforts at 'eco-ising' Mexico's existing mega coastal resorts are also becoming evident. By and large this is being achieved through linking beach attractions with broader cultural and historical themes. One such example is Huatulco, located on the Southwest coast of Mexico, marketed as the hemisphere's first 'eco-tourism' resort (Si Mexico, 2006). Although two of its nine bays were developed during the 1980s in the first phase of its development, plans for phase two have earmarked the majority of the resort's 52,000 acres as ecological reserves and implemented strict building codes which dictate hotel architectural styles and limit buildings to six storeys in height. Another illustration of the 'eco-isation' of existing mega-resorts is whereby, amid the urban sprawl of high-rise tourist accommodation, hotels such as the Hotel El Rey Del Caribe located in the centre of Cancún promote their use of solar hot water heaters and dryers, recycling and composting, and promote themselves as eco-tourist destinations (Hotel Rey Caribe, 2006).

Healy (1997) also cites several other examples of the eco-isation of mass tourism resorts, particularly in the state of Quintana Roo. For example, about an hour's drive south of Cancún there is an elaborate new development called Xcaret. Admission is about US$30 and the area has many of the elements of a recreational theme park. Although Xcaret features beautifully landscaped natural areas, some of its attractions such as snorkelling through Mayan caves were created with a great deal of earthmoving and even dynamiting. According to Healy (1997: 6), 'Elsewhere along the coast between Cancún and Tulum, the 880 acre

Playcar Resort at Playa del Carmen advertises itself as a unique and paradisiacal eco-development. Its attractions include 10 five-star hotels and a golf course described as the only one in the world adorned with Maya ruins'. The principal ecological attraction is the Xaman-Ha aviary, with 65 species of tropical birds, located on 3.7 acres of preserved forest. Other examples of eco-marketing are Xel-h, the world's largest aquarium, and X'caret, an eco-archaeological park (Lead International, 2004). Both these commercially oriented parks located on the Mayan Riviera make some effort to promote ecological sensitivity, but X'caret in particular has been criticised as just an amusement park with painted green wash (Mader, 1996).

Whilst eco-tourism and more sustainable forms of mass coastal tourism resort development are clearly being pursued in Mexico, as they are associated with more benefits than costs at local, regional and national levels, it is apparent that in some instances the sustainability of these developments is clearly questionable. This contention of course is not new, as a multitude of academics, notably Cater and Lowman (1994), Fennell (2003), Mowforth and Munt (2003), Swarbrooke (1999) and Wheeller (1994) have debated the issue of whether eco-tourism is eco-friendly or is a marketing gimmick that involves the camouflaging, repackaging and relabelling of mass tourism into what is seemingly a more environmentally acceptable form of tourism. In particular, these authors highlight the fact that many eco-tourists are not primarily motivated by a desire to protect the eco-system but rather by a desire to see the native eco-system. Indeed Wheeller (1994) states that eco-tourism is synonymous with ego-tourism as it allows tourists to behave as they have always behaved but with a clear conscience. Instead, he claims that it is a micro solution to the macro problem of tourism. Moreover, Swarbrooke (1999: 43) argues that eco-tourism is not inherently small-scale as it is likely to evolve like other forms of tourism have evolved, prompting the author to state 'today's ecotourism, tomorrow's mass tourism'.

According to Burford (1997), eco-tourism in Mexico tends to involve groups visiting Mayan ruins, nature reserves and hot springs and taking raft trips, and is merely a marketing ploy disguising mass tourism. Bowermaster (1994: 134) in particular notes examples of eco-tourism's negative side and states that 'in the Yucatán, Mayan ruins are crumbling under the feet of too many tourists', and the fragile coral reefs around St. John are endangered by hordes of divers. The scale and impacts of related developments are indistinguishable from mass tourism resorts. However, the development of eco-tourism need not revolve around scale (Thomlinson & Getz, 1996), as sustainable tourism might actually be furthered by large-scale eco-tourism if benefits are high and negative impacts are kept low through sound management. In a major review of eco-tourism in Australia, Blamey (1995) concluded that three dimensions of eco-tourism should be recognised: it is nature-based; embodies education (concerned with both natural attractions and sustainability issues); and is sustainably managed. Hawkins (1994: 261) believes that general agreement exists that eco-tourism involves 'minimum density, low impact activities'. The term 'low impact' is ambiguous, but certainly involves consideration of the capacity of eco-tourism resources. However, when capacity is exceeded (or management of the resource is inadequate), eco-tourism causes problems. Since the early 1990s Wheeller (1994) has in fact argued that far from being a solution, eco-tourism has represented a possibly damaging state of affairs. It has opened up new locations to the tourist gaze and the resultant destination life-cycle replicates the very problem that it was supposed to solve. This is clearly evident in some of the tourism management issues that Mexico is currently facing.

Management Issues

A complex picture currently exists within Mexico in terms of its coastal resorts, with their development continuing to present a number of key management issues, including the impacts of intensive tourism development and the continuing pressure for development.

In a span of less than 30 years, many of Mexico's coastal resorts have undergone a major transformation. Intensive development and an influx of people have converged on an extremely fragile and unique coastal ecosystem creating rapid and in some cases irreversible negative environmental impacts (Lead International, 2004). For example, before its development Cancún was a barrier and an important nesting site for seabirds and sea turtles. In one of the first steps in Cancún's development, the government joined both ends of the island to the mainland with a causeway. As a result, the flow of freshwater to the lagoon was restricted and the coastal landscape was permanently changed. Sections of the lagoon were subsequently filled and 148,200 acres of nearby mangrove and rainforest were destroyed for development (Wiese, 2000). Imported exotic species replaced the indigenous plants crucial to preventing erosion and maintaining the coastal equilibrium.

The reef along the coast of the Yucatán forms part of the Meso-American reef, the second longest barrier reef in the world, which extends from the northern tip of the peninsula southward along the coasts of Belize, Guatemala and Honduras. The Yucatán Peninsula's coral reefs are a major biological and economic resource for both tourism and fisheries (AAAS Atlas, 2000), but they are delicately balanced ecosystems and extremely vulnerable to the effects of coastal development, such as over-fishing, land-use change and pollution. Thus, offshore, the effects of tourism development and harvesting for tourist consumption have depleted substantial numbers of fish and shellfish. Extensive sections of the coral reef are dead or damaged from the impact of tourists' snorkelling and scuba diving in the water. Disturbance to marine life has also been caused by the intensive use of recreation craft, such as jet skis, and the damaging consequences of frequent boat tours and boat anchors (Neto, 2002). The influx of large numbers of tourists, combined with the high rates of consumption associated with international tourists, also created a serious waste management problem. One ecologist stated:

> Any time you gather 300,000 permanent residents and the occupants of 20,000 hotel rooms in one area, there are going to be accumulations of mountains of garbage and Cancún was no exception. (Wiese, 2000: 4)

The region's freshwater resources are also increasingly vulnerable due to high rates of population growth and a practically nonexistent urban sewage system (Robadue *et al.*, 1997). The development of coastal resources has created complex social as well as environmental pressures.

Many negative social impacts were also created, particularly in Cancún. Tourism development has contributed to increasing social polarisation. Although it is an important source of employment, most workers in the tourism sector tend to earn less than workers in socially comparable occupations. Rapid tourism development also puts pressure on the availability and prices of resources consumed by local residents, such as food, energy and raw materials, and intensifies competition for land resources, leading to land speculation, rising land prices and increased pressure to build on agricultural land (Neto, 2002). Although the tourist infrastructure was planned in Cancún, there was no corresponding plan for accommodation for the workers in the tourism industry. As a result, many illegal or irregular settlements sprung up along the resort's outskirts. These settlements lack services such as potable water and sewerage. Furthermore, because of the peninsula's fragile limestone hydrology, the water supply is easily contaminated and disease is a constant problem in these settlements (Lead International, 2004).

Perhaps one of the greatest social impacts of tourism is the pressure it places on local culture. The Yucatán Peninsula is frequently marketed as a land of the Maya to tourists who come not only to soak up the beautiful white sand beaches, tropical climate and deep blue Caribbean waters, but to experience the culture and achievements of the Mayan civilisation. The culture that they have struggled to maintain is now juxtaposed uneasily with the wealth and glitter of the mega-resorts (Lead International, 2004). Today, the Maya people are some of the most economically and socially marginalised people in Mexico. Thus, levels of poverty on the peninsula are generally higher than the national average, and they are much higher in the traditional Mayan areas than in other areas of the peninsula. Extreme poverty was estimated to be 41% for the entire peninsula in 1990 (Lead International, 2004), and is a problem that is highly likely to be exacerbated with continued pressure for coastal tourism development.

Despite the fact that the Mexican government has advocated the development of more sustainable forms of tourism, efforts to develop tourism are increasing in intensity and are focusing on mainstream (resort) tourism. As the first major tourism development on the Yucatán Peninsula, Cancún has influenced subsequent development along this coastline (Lead International, 2004). The Riviera Maya and the Costa Maya (see Fig. 13.1) are now the fastest-growing resort areas in Mexico (The Unofficial Guide, 2005), with developments including: large, inclusive resorts interspersed with small boutique accommodation, budget hostelries, marinas, cruise ship piers and golf courses. Playa del Carmen, a backpacker village turned trendy resort with restaurants and folk art shops has been constructed. More recently, Puerto Cancún, a huge, deluxe marina with low-impact hotels, is projected for development as well as a major resort development within the Cancún-Tulum corridor (The Unofficial Guide, 2005). The pressure for tourism development is revealed by FONATUR's plans to utilise and replicate a golf and marina formula to develop several locations in and around Cancún, along the Mayan Coast, on the island of Cozumel, as well as in Los Cabos and the coast of Nayarit (Table 13.2). Of the six locations pinpointed for development, four are on the coast and involve the construction of mega-resorts that are able to cater for a significant number of tourists.

Within the coastal protected areas and biospheres, there is also huge pressure for development, a point that is evident by the initiation of a zoning process along the Cancún corridor to reduce the density of development. Although it halved the amount allowed in Cancún, it nevertheless authorised over 200,000 additional rooms for the Cancún tourist corridor (Creel *et al.*, 1998). Balancing economic development with conservation is not helped by the fact that protection and conservation is not guaranteed. The biosphere reserves and protected areas of the Yucatán Peninsula, for example, continue to face serious threats from two main sources. The first is the negative impacts of intensive tourism development, and its encroachment on still pristine coastal areas. The second pressure is the vulnerable economic situation of the very poor, subsistence-based local communities living in or adjacent to the reserve and protected areas whose livelihood depends on utilising coastal resources. With continued tourism development and increased population growth, both of these threats are escalating inexorably,

Table 13.2 Selected coastal tourism resort projects planned by FONATUR

Location	*Proposed development*
Loreta Bay	5000 villas, 980 condominiums, 6 boutique hotels with 1500 rooms, a golf course, a shopping centre, spa and medical clinic, catering for primarily US and Canadian tourists.
Escalera Nautica	A series of new, existing and improved marinas approximately 120 nautical miles apart along the Pacific and Sea of Cortes Coasts, followed by the same along the Sea of Cortes coasts of the states of Sinora and Sinalo.
Los Cabos	Golf and marina development catering for 150–600 boats, and including an 18-hole golf course, residential villas and two low-rise hotels.
Nayarit	Golf and marina development catering for 150–600 boats, and including an 18-hole golf course, residential villas and two low-rise hotels. New integrally planned resort, comprising of three separate areas: (1) Litibú, (2) El Capomo and (3) La Pênita. It will comprise a total area of 2175 acres and by 2025 it will have tourist and residential lodgings for 14,500 rooms, three golf courses, beach clubs, a marine theme park, a marina with 150 slips, an airdrome and shopping and recreation centres. It will cater for over one million tourists per year, generate US$866 million, create 17,400 new jobs and attract US$1,800 million in private tourism investment.
Island of Cozumel	Golf and marina development catering for 150–600 boats, and including an 18-hole golf course, residential villas and two low-rise hotels.
Costa Maya (between Majahual and Pulticub)	New integrally planned low-density resort consisting of hotels and Mayan village type cabins, golf courses and a theme park, completely integrated with nature, surrounded by five protected nature reserves, which meets rigorous environmental standards. Comprising 31,344 acres and offering 6000 hotel rooms, it is targeted at those attracted to eco-tourism and adventure travel, diving, fishing and golf. Expected to create an estimated US$730 million in earnings from foreign tourism.

Source: Brooke (2005)

jeopardising the ecological integrity and future sustainability of coastal resources (Lead International, 2004).

The tenuous nature of protection and conservation in Mexico is illustrated by a number of continuing struggles against large-scale developments along the coast of Quintana Roo. X'cacel is one such example of this struggle outlined by Cantú (2001); it is a stretch of beach 115 km south of Cancún and the most important nesting site for endangered green and loggerhead turtles. The beach and the surrounding area were a federal reserve until 1992, when control passed to the state authority. In 1997, despite the government of Quintana Roo's commitment to keep the site as a protected area, formalised in the 1994 management plan of the Tourist Corridor, the state Governor, Mario Villanueva, sold the property to the Spanish corporation Sol Media. Sol Media's plan to develop a large 450-room all-inclusive resort on the beach was delayed due to the illegal and suspicious conditions of the sale – the low price of $2.2 million, suggesting possible kickbacks and corruption (Cantú, 2001). Allegations of corruption were confirmed when Villanueva disappeared in 1998, just as his term ended. He was pursued by Interpol and listed as an international fugitive by a *Wall Street Journal* article in 1999. More than three years of campaigning by local and international NGOs, as well as many scientists, sea turtle biologists and members of local communities in Quintana Roo, led to an important victory for coastal conservation – the suspension of the hotel project by Mexico's ministry, SEMARNAP, in April 2001 (Lead International, 2004).

Another recent conservation success is the purchase of the Pez-Maya property to the north of the Sian Ka'an Biosphere Reserve in January 2002 (Lead International, 2004). The local NGO 'Amigos de Sian Ka'an' and US-based group 'The Nature Conservancy' worked together to raise US$2.7 million to pay for the acquisition and protection of Pez Maya. Previously, several developers had tried to acquire the property, and with zoning designations as small as 50 m, Pez Maya's shoreline was in danger of being subdivided into as many as 60 parcels (The Nature Conservancy, 2002). The property is only 62 acres, but it is ecologically important as a breeding ground for terns, sprety, American crocodile, manatee, and loggerhead and green sea turtles, and its waters contain one of the world's most pristine coral formations. Pez Maya is also critical as the gateway to Sian Ka'an Biosphere reserve. The acquisition of Pez Maya represents an important step to slow development along this coastline, and to act as a buffer to protect Sian Ka'an from the impacts of hotel development that is relentlessly encroaching southward (Lead International, 2004). Clearly Mexico faces a number of challenges in the future.

Conclusion

While Mexico has excelled in attracting visitors to its coastal resorts, it has – despite its biodiversity – done little to effectively promote eco-tourism. Although emphasis is placed on low-density developments set amongst protected areas and biospheres, which promote activities associated with the environment and culture for the most part, these developments are similar to the mega-resorts that were built during the 1970s and 1980s. They are relatively large-scale, they aim to attract substantial numbers of tourists to large tracts of pristine and fragile coastline, and they are standardised in their approach, combining golf with marina developments. Due to the government's focus on mass tourism, it is not surprising therefore that most alternative tourism projects in Mexico have been initiated by nongovernmental organisations, such as the Nature Conservancy, Conservation International, Na Bolom and many other smaller regional groups (Kersten, 1997).

However, Mader (1996) states that despite the negative impacts associated with mass coastal resorts along with false and potentially destructive eco-tourism, there are persuasive arguments for the location of developments that more closely meet eco-tourism criteria within the market area of mass coastal resorts. This is because tourists drawn to Mexico primarily by sun and sand attractions can receive environmental education through a day trip to a genuine natural area and the revenue generated can then be used to support the area's protection. Perhaps though, the greatest problem is harmonising the tourist images of the mega-resorts with the idea of eco-tourism (Mader, 1996). Mass tourism destinations such as Cancún, Bahías de Huatulco and Puerto Vallarta are ideal jumping-off points for day or overnight trips to nearby protected areas. This type of activity has been termed as add-on eco-tourism. It could educate the mass tourist, allow careful control of tourist behaviour (by allowing only guided trips), and above all, generate funds for the protected area and its adjoining population. Add-on eco-tourism could also help ensure the economic survival of small nature tourism firms, which often have difficulty putting together enough visitors for weekend-long trips. However, it is imperative that this type of tourism is planned and managed carefully in order to avoid the occurrence of further negative impacts.

Part 5

State Intervention and the Planning and Development of Coastal Resorts

Chapter 14

The Role of the State and the Rise of the Red Sea Resorts in Egypt and Israel

NOAM SHOVAL and KOBI COHEN-HATTAB

Introduction

To date, most investigations of seaside resorts have focused on North American, European and, especially, British seaside resorts, the latter forming the basis of most research in the field (Agarwal, 2002; Barett, 1958; Corbin, 1992; Durie, 1994; Fisher, 1997; Gilbert, 1939, 1949; Lencek & Bosker, 1998; Shaw & Williams 1997a; Towner, 1996; Walton, 2000). By contrast, only a minority of seaside resorts in the Eastern Mediterranean basin and Middle East have been subjected to comparable, systematic scrutiny. As a result, very little has been published on the subject (Apostolopoulos *et al.*, 2001; Cohen-Hattab & Shoval, 2004a,b; Gonen, 1981; Ioannides, 1992). Interestingly, however, studies generally conclude that the Eastern Mediterranean and Middle Eastern seaside resorts both emerged and flourished at the expense of their more established counterparts, including and above all Britain's traditional seaside resorts (Agarwal, 2002).

For centuries, it was the Eastern Mediterranean basin's many religious as well as historical and cultural sites that drew visitors to the region, a trend that did not change with the advent of modern tourism in the mid-19th century. The new-style tourists, who flocked to the region courtesy of Thomas Cook & Son or American Express, did so for much the same reasons as their predecessors. They too congregated around Egypt's pyramids and temples and swarmed Palestine's holy and historical sites; all of which were and have remained the area's chief attraction well into the 20th century. Past decades, however, saw a new type of tourism penetrate the region: seaside resort tourism. Its effect on the Eastern Mediterranean's tourist industry was nothing short of prodigious, leading to, among other things, a massive increase in the various tourist services – including, and above all, accommodation services – offered by the region's ever-mounting number of seaside resorts. Such was its impact that, as will be seen, seaside resort tourism soon came to occupy a lion's share of the area's entire tourist industry.

The following chapter discusses the development of seaside resort tourism in Egypt and Israel, both of which have stood at the forefront of the coastal resort tourism revolution in the Middle East. The two countries have, over the past two decades, diversified their tourist industry in much the same way, encouraging and developing seaside resort tourism in their more remote coastal areas: specifically the Red Sea, which lies at some distance from both their principal, traditional tourist sites (see Fig. 14.1). But there are other similarities too, as the emergence of seaside resort tourism in Egypt and Israel was, as shall be seen, closely and perhaps primarily allied to the 1979 peace agreement. This agreement led to the demilitarisation of the Sinai Peninsula and, no less importantly, created a positive political climate, both of which proved crucial to the development of tourism in the area. Since then, Israeli tourists have flooded to the Sinai Peninsula's seaside resorts, which of course provide another vital connection between the two areas. Furthermore, this chapter details and analyses the development of coastal resort tourism in Egypt and Israel's Red Sea holiday retreats. It focuses on the processes, characteristics and circumstances common to seaside resort tourism in both countries, while at the same time emphasising those elements unique to each. The question of the development of seaside resort tourism will be tackled primarily by probing the changes that took place in the area's accommodation services over time; accommodation services being commonly considered as representative of tourist activity in general (Shaw & Williams, 2002). Given that Israel's Red Sea coastline is a mere 12 km long, as compared to Egypt's several hundred kilometres long coastline, the comparison between the two countries' resorts will be subject based rather than geographically oriented.

Political Stability and Tourism Development

Political factors have always played a part in tourism development and are an integral part of tourism studies. Many societies and nations tend to shape their tourist industry – i.e. formulate rules and regulations – in accordance with elected political and ideological factors (Hall, 1994; Matthews & Richter, 1991). This trend is particularly marked in totalitarian regimes, in which the private sector is effectively nonexistent and the state exercises a virtual monopoly over the country's tourist industry. In these states, tourism is fundamentally a political issue, totally subservient to the regime's interests (Richter, 1980; Sönmez, 1998).

Yet even in democratic, free-market societies, the tourist industry is subject to, albeit more abstruse, political and ideological influences. In many cases, the tourist industry, anxious 'to sell' its country to tourists, often fashions 'mythic' cultures, which in turn redefines the country's

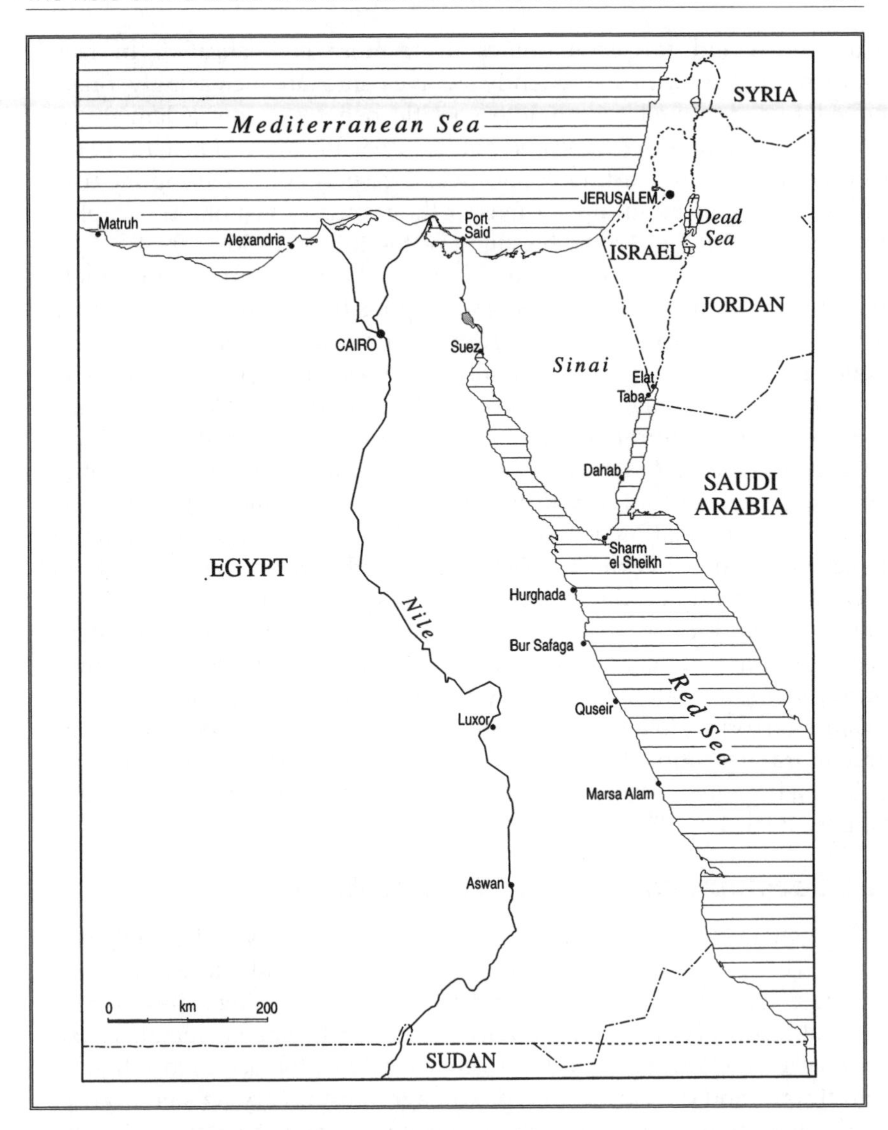

Figure 14.1 Israel and Egypt's principal seaside resort areas and towns

political, social and cultural reality (Hall, 1994). The complex relationship between political stability and tourism is amplified in times of conflict and war. Contrary to conventional wisdom, tourism does not grind to a halt in periods of political, even military instability. A review of tourism in conflict zones reveals that belligerent situations will not always lead to a dwindling of tourist activity. More than that, it indicates that in conflict situations, tourism's political and ideological roles gain an added significance and its use becomes even more sophisticated. In fact, tourism in these cases frequently evolves into an increasingly finely honed tool designed to promote specific belief systems (Clements & Giorgio, 1998; Ionised & Apostolopoulos, 1999; Pizam & Mansfeld, 1996). German tourism in wartime France was a case in point. During the war, the Nazis organised groups of tens of thousands of visitors to occupied France, with Paris often the highlight of the tour (Gordon, 1998).

But it is not always the powers that be who use tourism to promote political goals. In frictional situations, opposition parties and minority groups may also use tourism in order to gain influence or make a point, although in these cases it generally assumes the form of a negative strategy, which seeks to undermine tourism and thus weaken the regime (Sönmez, 1998). Terrorists too use tourism to further their political objectives. True, terrorists often attack tourists simply because they offer an easy target. But an attack on tourists also guarantees the terrorists instant international media coverage, while at the same time helping to wreck the country's economy (Richter & Waugh, 1986). In addition, it can and has been argued that tourism prompts terrorism, as in the case of Egypt, where tourists, seen by some as the representatives of Western civilisation and its corrupt consumer culture, are regarded as a direct threat to local Islamic society (Aziz, 1995). Hence, tourism can both 'inspire terrorist violence by fuelling political, religious, socio-economic or cultural resentment and be used as a cost-effective instrument to deliver a broader message of ideological/political opposition' (Sönmez & Graefe, 1998: 426–427).

The Development of Israeli Seaside Resorts

For generations, most visitors to Palestine were motivated by religious ideals. Thus, the city of Jerusalem, sacred to the world's three principal monotheistic religions and boasting a great many heritage sites of both cultural and historical importance, was, and indeed remains, the country's chief attraction. In time, other localities too acquired religious significance and developed into pilgrimage sites of varying significance. In the mid-19th century Palestine opened its gates to the West, thus playing an important part in the development of modern tourism (Cohen-Hattab & Katz, 2001).

Under the British mandate (1917–1948), specifically during the 1930s, resort tourism along Palestine's Mediterranean coastline surged (Cohen-Hattab & Shoval, 2004a). British officials, as well as the many soldiers based in the country during the late 1930s and the Second World War, generated a growing demand for more and more varied tourist services (Cohen-Hattab, 2001; Cohen-Hattab & Katz, 2001; Cohen-Hattab & Shoval, 2004b). The establishment of the state of Israel in 1948 saw the beginning of a fairly long period of economic austerity, which stifled the development of the country's coastal resort towns. In the 1960s however, a boom in global tourism, the result of cheaper air flights and the introduction of large aircrafts, prompted the Israeli government to start viewing its seaside resorts as an important source of foreign currency revenue. The emphasis, largely by default, was on Israel's Mediterranean resorts, as, at that time, most of the country's Jewish and Christian religious sites, including East Jerusalem, Hebron, Jericho and Bethlehem, were under Jordanian rule. All this would change following the Six Day War, which marked the beginning of several far-reaching geopolitical changes in the region.

Having brought all of the city of Jerusalem under Israeli jurisdiction, as well as providing better access to the Dead Sea, the Six Day War (1967) was to encourage, albeit indirectly, the decline of Israel's traditional Mediterranean resort towns. The appeal to tourists of both the Dead Sea, with its unique healing properties and spectacular desert scenery, and the Southern port town of Eilat, with its temperate winter climate, unspoilt beaches and stunning coral reef, was obvious, as were the two resorts' advantages over their more traditional Mediterranean counterparts (Azaryahu, 2005; Mansfeld, 2001). Moreover, thanks to the introduction of air conditioning in the 1960s, it was now possible to build viable resorts in areas of extreme climate, such as the Dead Sea, throughout the year, and Eilat in the sweltering summer months. Not surprisingly, the Israeli government was quick to restructure its tourism development budget, funnelling most of the money available into the construction of tourist resorts in these areas.

Growth trends in Israeli tourism, since 1948, reveal that tourism to Israel fluctuates tremendously, mostly as a result of the Middle East's volatile security situation. Thus, while flourishing in times of relative tranquillity, tourism to the country will promptly decline with the first signs of violence and war; a trend that, incidentally, is a characteristic of Middle Eastern states as a whole, including Egypt (Mansfeld, 1996). 1978 saw one million tourists entering the country for the first time. In 1994, Israel crossed the 2 million mark. This upward trend received a further boost following the signing of the Oslo accords in 1993 and the start of intensive peace negotiations between Israel and the Palestinian Liberation Organization. In 2000, some 2.7 million tourists arrived in Israel, more than had ever visited the country to date. The outbreak of the Second, or Al-Aksa, Intifada, in September 2002, however, triggered a drastic fall in the number of inbound tourists, with only 861,000 tourists entering the country that year – the lowest figure for some time. Since then, tourism to Israel has recovered somewhat with approximately 1.5 million tourists visiting the country in the 2004 (State of Israel Central Bureau of Statistics, 2003–2005).

The development of Eilat

Following its War of Independence (1948), Israel began, almost immediately, to extend its hold on the border town of Eilat. Situated in the country's southernmost tip, Eilat was, and remains still, of huge strategic and economic importance. In close proximity to the point at which Israel borders its then enemies, Jordan, Egypt and Saudi Arabia, Eilat was of supreme military significance. It was of no less value economically – the port of Eilat afforded Israel with a direct link to the Indian Ocean, and so access to the markets of Asia and East Africa. Other than these port-related military and civil pursuits, Eilat's economy was based on, mainly heavy, industry. Of these industrial enterprises, located both within and outside the town, the most noteworthy were the Timna copper mines, some several dozen kilometres North of Eilat. A fall in copper prices, in the 1960s, however, led to a swift cut back in production and by the mid-1970s the mines, which had opened with great fanfare in 1958, shut down completely (Amiran *et al.*, 1995). Oddly, in view of what was to come, tourism did not figure at all in the town's make-up during the 1950s and 1960s, with neither the Israeli government nor town planners allotting it a key role in Eilat's economy. All this was to change in the 1970s, as Eilat metamorphosed into one of Israel's primary tourist destinations.

As noted, the Six Day War marked a turning point in Eilat's development. No longer was it Israel's southernmost outpost, the town was now a transit point on the way to the newly conquered Sinai Peninsula. The commencement in 1975 of charter flights to the local airport meant that thousands of foreign tourists could now fly directly to Eilat, thus precipitating a new period of intensive development apropos the town's burgeoning tourist industry (State of Israel Central Bureau of Statistics and the Ministry of Tourism, 1980). The 1979 peace agreement with Egypt drove this process even further: partially thanks to the geopolitical stability it engendered, but also because, with the return of the Sinai Peninsula to Egypt, Israeli entrepreneurs, hoping to sink money into the region's booming tourism business, had little choice but to fall back on Eilat (Azaryahu, 2005). As a result, from the end of the 1970s tourism emerged as Eilat's principal industry in terms of numbers employed and scale of investment (State of Israel Central Bureau of Statistics and the Ministry of Tourism, 1980).

The rate at which the number of hotel rooms rises (or declines) is commonly used as a measure indicating the growth (or lack thereof) of tourism in a given area. Between 1975 and 1988, the number of hotel rooms in Eilat rose from 1863 to 4447, two and a half times more than the average national growth rate (Amiran *et al.*, 1995). This trend continued, even increased, between 1989 and 2002, with Eilat's share in the number of hotel rooms in Israel, as whole, rising progressively. In 1989, Eilat accounted for a mere 16% of Israel's overall number of hotel rooms; by 1997, with the town now boasting 8020 hotel rooms, Eilat's share rose to an impressive 26% (State of Israel Central Bureau of Statistics and the Ministry of Tourism, 1999). In 2005, the town contained close to 11,000 hotel rooms, or 28.6% of the total number of hotel rooms available in Israel (see Fig. 14.2).

The First Intifada (1987–1993) had more or less passed Eilat's tourist industry by. In 1989, the number of tourists flying into the town on charter flights was roughly same as in 1987. Such was not the case with the First Gulf War (1991), which, as an event of global significance, struck at the heart of Eilat's tourist industry, the town's person-night occupancy rate falling from 84%, in February 1990, to a new all-time low of 33%, in February 1991 (Amiran *et al.*, 1995). Yet, the Gulf War notwithstanding, Eilat, from 1980 onwards, was soon to outstrip all other Israeli seaside resorts in terms of person-night occupancy rates. In 1990, for example, Eilat accounted for 18% of all person-night occupancies in Israeli coastal resorts; in 2004, its share in the country's room night occupancy doubled to an impressive 36% (State of Israel Central Bureau of Statistics and the Ministry of Tourism, 2005).

Eilat's emergence as Israel's principal seaside resort can be understood only if a clear distinction is made between the country's inbound and domestic tourists. The signing of the Oslo accords injected new life into the region, precipitating, among other things, a marked rise in inbound tourism to Eilat. Inbound tourism to the town peaked in 1995 to a rate of

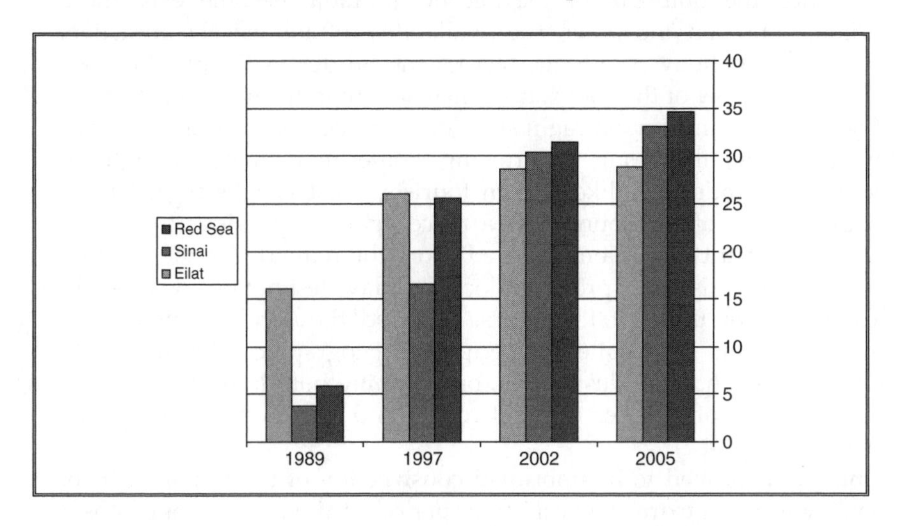

Figure 14.2 Hotel development (number of hotel rooms) in Israel's principal tourist areas

1,700,000 person-nights (State of Israel Central Bureau of Statistics and the Ministry of Tourism, 1996). Conversely, the deadlock and eventual failure of the political process signalled, among other things, by the assassination the Israeli Prime Minister Yitzchak Rabin at the end of 1995 and the onset of a horrific series of suicide bombings in Israel at the beginning of 1996, affected a decline in inbound tourism to Eilat. As a result, its share in the country's tourist industry as compared to domestic tourism began to fall steadily.

But security considerations were not the only reason why the 1990s saw the number of Eilat's inbound tourists eclipsed by that of Israelis visiting the town. Thanks to the globalisation of Israel's economy – itself partially a result of the Oslo process – the 1990s witnessed a rapid rise in local living standards, which allowed more and more Israelis to travel to Eilat for weekend or longer breaks. The construction of seaside resorts in Egypt (to be discussed later), with their almost irresistible combination of low prices, stunning scenery and unspoilt beaches, also played a part in this process, capturing much of Eilat's European market. The failure of the Arafat–Barak Camp David summit in the summer of 2000, followed by the outbreak of the Second Intifada in September of that year, saw inbound tourism to Eilat plummet to new depths, the number of international charter flights into Eilat dwindling from 920 in 1998 to 108 in 2003 (State of Israel Central Bureau of Statistics and the Ministry of Tourism, 1999, 2004).

The decline of inbound tourism to Eilat over the past few years was the result of, on the one hand, Israel's fraught security situation, which has, since the outbreak of the Second Intifada, become ever more perilous, and, on the other, the availability of immensely attractive, inexpensive holiday resorts just across the border in Egypt's Red Sea province. In view of the above, the conclusion that the mounting number of hotel rooms and person-night stays in Eilat over that past decade was, by and large, the result of growing domestic demand is nigh on inescapable. Indeed, unlike foreign tourists, most Israelis regard Eilat, on the fringes of the country, as a place apart, impervious to Israel's explosive security situation. 'Isolated' from the reminder of the country, it became most Israelis' preferred local holiday destination. As a result, Eilat has, over the past few years, acquired thousands of new hotel rooms, turning it, despite its peripheral geographical location, into Israel's largest holiday destination, outstripping both Jerusalem and Tel Aviv in terms of number of hotel rooms and person-night occupancy rates (see Fig. 14.2).

But what proved to be unbridled construction of thousands of hotel rooms within an extraordinarily brief period of time turned out to be a mixed blessing; boosting Eilat's economy in the short term, it also had an adverse affect on the town's two principal tourist attractions: its pristine coastline and breathtaking desert scenery. Over the past several years, Eilat's coastline has mutated into little more than a jam-packed, highly concentrated cluster of hotels, fronting tiny strips of crowded beaches. Such intensive, unrestrained development has wrought havoc on Eilat's natural habitat. The recent rapid decomposition of the town's coral reef is merely one, highly visible, sign of the environmental destruction brought about by rampant overdevelopment (Even-Zur & Yovel, 2004; Zakai & Chadwick-Furman, 2002). Should matters continue, Eilat's chances of regenerating its diminishing inbound tourist market are not good. Indeed, the falling numbers of inbound tourists not only underpins the argument that Eilat has long passed its optimal carrying capacity, but are also indicative of the fact that its life-cycle as a seaside resort is probably, as Mansfeld correctly foresaw, reaching its end (Mansfeld, 2001).

The Development of Egypt's Red Sea and the Sinai Peninsula Coastal Resorts

For centuries, Egypt's antiquity-based tourism centred at one end on Cairo and its immediate environs, and at the other on the Upper Nile Valley, encompassing the Valley of the Kings, neighbouring Luxor, Aswan and the Abu Simbel Temple. The Second World War saw tourism to Egypt reach a nadir, which continued following the outbreak of the 1948 war against Israel. The Suez Crisis produced a further decline in numbers, with a mere 50,000 tourists entering the country as compared to 100,000 the year before. In 1966, Egypt, having enjoyed 10 years of relative peace, boasted a record 579,000 visitors. It was, however, another eight years before the country's tourist industry was able to present similar figures, Egypt having in the meantime fought two more bloody wars: The Six Day War in 1967 and The October War in 1973 (Meyer, 1996).

The 1979 peace agreement with Israel and the opening up of Egypt to the West in the early 1980s combined to produce a steady rise in inbound tourism. For the past 10 years, only Saudi Arabia, among the Middle Eastern countries, could claim more inbound tourists than Egypt, and this mostly thanks to the millions of Muslim pilgrims that crowd its holy sites each year. In 1995, the number of inbound tourists to Egypt was 2,872,000. By 2003, this figure had doubled, reaching a monumental 5,746,000 (WTO, 2004). In the years 1989–1998, inbound tourism to Egypt rose, on average, by 7.7% a year, way above the global annual average growth of such tourism. Inbound tourism's contribution to Egypt's economy also mounted to the point where it made up a quarter of all of the country's foreign income (Swinscoe, 1999). In terms of dollar revenue earned from inbound tourism, Egypt outstripped all neighbouring countries: its income from inbound tourism in 2003, for example, being

$3.76 billion, some 30% of all dollar revenues from tourism in the Middle East as a whole. These striking figures can be explained, in part, by the fact that almost 80% of Egypt's tourists come from outside the Middle East, mainly Europe (Kester & Carvao, 2004).

Over the past 20 years, tourist accommodation services throughout Egypt, but particularly in the Red Sea and Sinai Peninsula, have mushroomed; evidence of the massive increase in the number of tourists visiting the country (WTO, 2004). Seaside resort tourism in both the Red Sea and Sinai Peninsula had, from the very beginning, deliberately targeted the European market. There were several reasons why it was thought, and rightly so, that European holidaymakers would be drawn to these particular areas. For one thing, they boast a temperate climate, as opposed to the harsh desert climate of the Upper Nile Valley; a climate, which, moreover, was at its best during Europe's winter holiday season. Then there were the Red Sea's stunning white beaches, where tourists could, throughout the year, either bask in the sun or immerse themselves in pleasantly warm seawaters. Improvements in air and land transportation meant that it was now possible to ferry tourists from the centre of Egypt to its geographical periphery with relative ease, while other various technological advances effected a substantial improvement in the level of the tourist services on offer in these more distant coastal areas. All this proved doubly important in light of the growing number of terrorist attacks on tourists in the years 1992–1994. Following these attacks, all of which took place in the Upper Egypt region, the number of European tourists to Luxor, for example, fell by 83%, while in Aswan the person-night occupancy rate plunged to a mere 20% (Swinscoe, 1999). At the same time, the number of visitors to Egypt's Sinai Peninsula and Red Sea coastal resorts, far removed from the terrorist maelstrom, rose considerably (Swinscoe, 1999).

Egypt was no stranger to terrorist attacks. The difference in 1992 was that it was the country's tourists who had now become the terrorists' principal target. Opening up Egypt to the West, and to Western cultural, social and economic influences, had turned Egypt's tourists into natural and easy prey for the country's militant Islamic groups. With tourism widely regarded as an invaluable way of strengthening ties between countries, East and West, and, in the case of Israel and Egypt, cementing the peace between these two erstwhile enemies, it was hardly surprising that those adamantly opposed to Egypt normalising its relations with both the West and Israel began increasingly to target hotels, tourist sites and tourists. The fact that the Egyptian government's survival was, is, largely dependent on tourist revenues also persuaded various subversive elements to target tourists. Striking at the country's tourist industry, they hoped to destabilise and eventually destroy the government. Thus, for most of Egypt's extremist political and religious zealots, the country's tourists not only encapsulated all that they hate, but offered a perverse means to achieve their myriad goals.

Between 1992 and 1997, Egypt suffered 10 major terrorist attacks, all targeting tourists. Not surprisingly, 1992 saw inbound tourism to Egypt fall by 22% as compared to 1991, with person-night occupancy rates falling by 30% (Swinscoe, 1999). In November 1997, Egypt sustained its biggest terrorist attack against tourists to date, as armed gunmen opened fire on a tourist bus, killing 58 tourists and 4 Egyptians. The November killings dealt a heavy blow to Egypt's tourist industry, which lasted for well over two years (Swinscoe, 1999). Consequently, the Egyptian government soon concluded that it had no choice but to invest more time, money and effort to increase its security, as well as to reassure and restore the confidence of prospective tourists. In 1994, it launched a six-year plan specifically designed to tackle the problem. The plan, which now moved into high gear, called, on the one hand, for vigorous action against the country's terrorist organisations, and, on the other, for an extensive promotion campaign to revitalise tourism to Egypt. Both aims would, the plan posited, be achieved, among other things, by means of numerous additional police patrols in various tourist hotspots plus constant police protection for all tourist buses (Aziz, 1995; Swinscoe, 2000; Wahab, 1996).

As part of its plans, the government began to encourage the development of tourist resorts in the Red Sea and Sinai Peninsula, an area that, while remote from Egypt's traditional tourist centres, was equally remote from the pernicious influence of Egypt's militant Islamic organisations. Thus, the past several years have seen a massive increase in the number of hotels, guesthouses and hostels in the area. In the years 1989–2005, the number of hotel rooms in Egypt's Red Sea resorts multiplied by 21, rising from 1890 to 39,033 (Egyptian Hotel Association, 2005). The figures for the Sinai Peninsula were even more impressive, with the number of hotel rooms multiplying by 26, rising from 1444 rooms to 37,951 (see Fig. 14.3). This compared to Cairo, which until the mid-1990s had led Egypt in terms of number of hotel rooms (Swinscoe, 2000). In 1989, Cairo contained 17,829 hotel rooms, in 2005, the number was 23,446 rooms, a modest rise of a mere 5617 (see Fig. 14.3). Projected growth trends for hotel rooms in Egypt revealed that at the end of the 1980s, hotel rooms in the Red Sea and Sinai Peninsula comprised a trifling 9.5% of all hotel rooms in Egypt (Swinscoe, 2000). In the early 1990s, the Sinai Peninsula and Red Sea resorts' share in the total number of hotel rooms in the country rose dramatically, reaching 42% by 1997 (Swinscoe, 1999). This upward trend continued well into the 21st century, with the majority of Egypt's hotel rooms now concentrated in the area. In 2002, Egypt's Red Sea and Sinai Peninsula resorts accounted for 61.7% of all the hotel rooms in Egypt, a figure that rose to 67.5% in 2005 (Egyptian

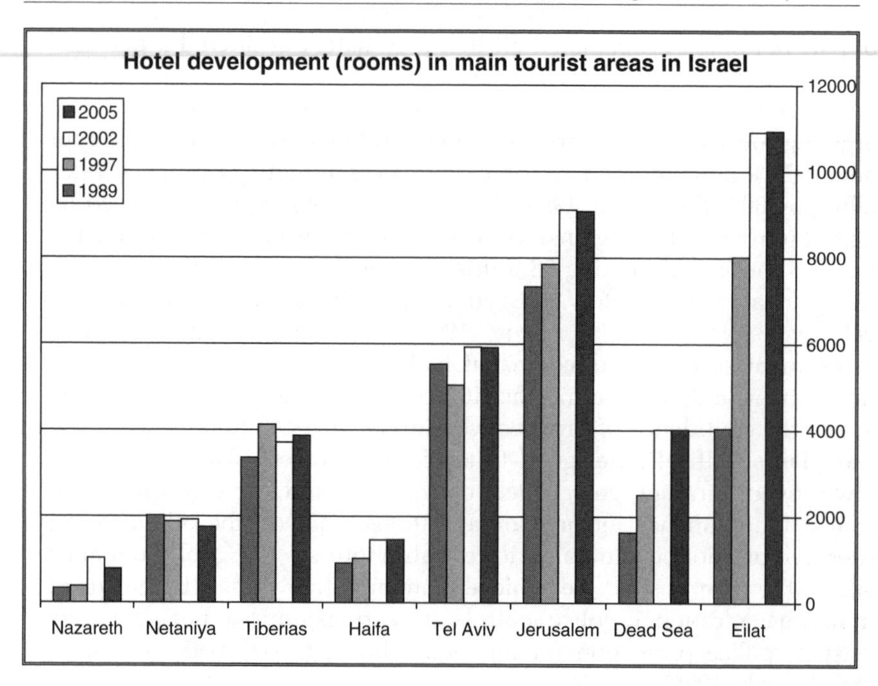

Figure 14.3 The relative share of hotel rooms in the Sinai Peninsula, Red Sea and Eilat within the total number of hotel rooms in Egypt and Israel's principal hotel areas

Hotel Association, 2005). It was in the Sinai Peninsula, however, where the most significant increase in the number of hotel rooms took place, doubling from an already noteworthy 16,486, in 1997, to 33,064, in 2005 (see Fig. 14.3). Unfortunately those rapid developments in Sinai also attracted terrorist attacks, which previously did not occur in those resort areas: first the terrorist attacks on the Hilton Taba and two additional resorts in October 2004 and recently the terrorist attacks in Sharm el-Sheikh in July 2005.

In terms of domestic tourism following Israel's withdrawal in 1982, tourism in the Sinai Peninsula rocketed, becoming one of, if not the most striking development in the area. Interestingly, it was a process fuelled in no small measure by Israeli tourists who thronged to the region, particularly during the holiday seasons. By the second half of the 1990s, some several hundred thousand Israelis had crossed the border into Egypt, the vast majority heading for the Sinai Peninsula. In 1997, 287,000 Israelis visited Egypt, the largest number of inbound tourists from a Middle East country that year. 1999 proved a peak year for Egypt-bound Israeli tourism, with some 387,000 Israelis entering the country. The outbreak of the Second Intifada saw a substantial fall in the number of Israelis visiting Egypt, with figures plummeting, in 2001, to a shoddy 117,000. This downward turn soon reversed itself, and in 2002 Egypt welcomed 150,000 Israeli tourists to the country, a figure that doubled itself in 2003, reaching 320,000: 33,000 more than had visited the country in 1997. The upward swing continued in 2004 with some 397,000 Israelis entering the country, more than had ever visited Egypt before (see Fig. 14.4). The figures for 2004 could have been higher still, but for the devastating terrorist attack on Taba's Hilton hotel in October of that year, which together with other several terrorist incidents in various seaside resorts south of Taba resulted in an abrupt fall in the number of Israeli tourists entering Egypt. Regarding the year 2005, it's still hard to estimate what will be the impact of the terrorist attacks in Sharm el-Sheikh on the 23rd of July.

The development of accommodation services along the Sinai Peninsula's coastline during this period far outstripped that of other areas in Egypt, with Taba, Dahab, Nuyaiba and Sharm el-Sheikh soon boasting first-class tourist infrastructures. As a result, each year dozens of flights from Europe landed in Sharm el-Sheikh's airport, bringing with them hundreds of thousands of European tourists all anxious to spend their holidays in the region's splendid new beach resorts (Meyer, 1996; Swinscoe, 1999). Accelerated development also tempted many Egyptians to the area in search of work. Abandoning the big cities of Cairo and Alexandria, they flocked to the Sinai Peninsula, changing, in the process, its demographic make-up.

But if it was the locals who provided the industry's work force, it was largely foreign rather than Egyptian capital that financed it (Swinscoe,

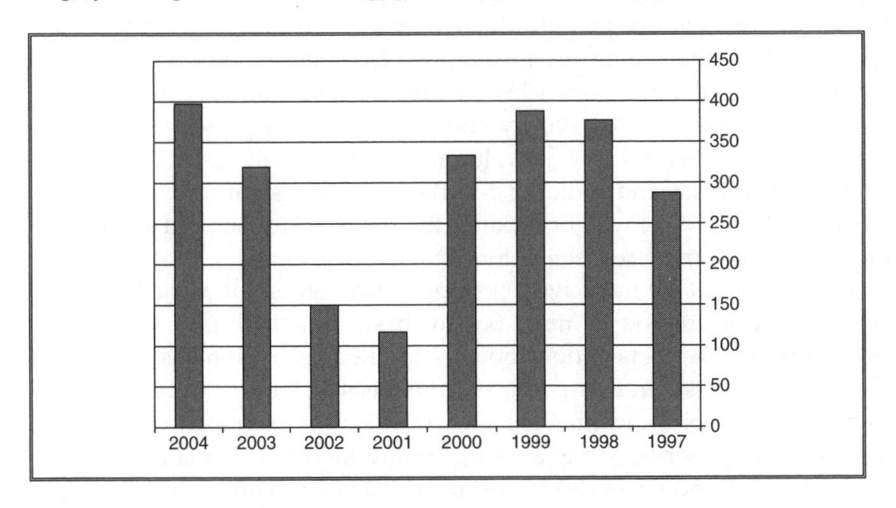

Figure 14.4 The number of departures of Israelis to the Sinai Peninsula ('000s)

1999). This, combined with the absence of any kind of central planning, plus insufficient government guidelines or supervision, resulted in rampant overdevelopment. Ecological questions, for instance, were almost totally ignored and to dire effect. To date, other than preserving the region's national parks, notably the coral reef of Ras al-Mohammad, environmental considerations have played virtually no part in the development of the region's tourist infrastructures. Thus, Dahab's main waste disposal dump was built bang in the middle of Wadi Dahab, swamping the area with refuse each time the Wadi's waters rise above a certain level (Shaalan, 2005; Shackley, 1999).

Conclusion

In the past 20 years tourism to Egypt and Israel underwent a similar transformation, with seaside resort tourism largely replacing these countries' hitherto religious and heritage-based tourism. That this was indeed the case is attested to by, among other things, the massive growth in tourist services and especially accommodation services on offer in Israel's seaside resort town of Eilat, and – which is hardly surprising given that the region's coastline falls mostly under Egypt's jurisdiction – to an even greater extent, in Egypt's various old and new beach resorts in the Sinai Peninsula and Red Sea. The reasons behind the boom in resort tourism in Eilat, on the one hand, and Egypt's Red Sea provinces, on the other, were much the same. Boasting exquisite, virginal topographies, a balmy, temperate climate, and far removed from the two countries' often volatile, geographical, political and demographic centres, both offered tourists a quiet, sunny, peaceful haven. Hoping to escape, if only for a few days, from their countries' miserably cold winter months, Europeans were understandably tempted by the area's exotic, sun-kissed beaches. Yet, in both cases it was security considerations that proved to be the main impetus behind the development of coastal resort tourism. Promoting tourism and building resorts in these distant and relatively calm regions was one way of tackling the havoc terrorism had wrought on the two countries' respective tourist industries.

The result was the intensive development of tourist infrastructures in an all too brief period of time. So much so that there is a very real possibility that in terms of development the Red Sea region has reached, if not exceeded, saturation point. On the basis of current development trends – the rapid and massive growth of tourist services, especially accommodation services, the absence of any kind of adequate government planning and supervision, and the consequent damage inflicted on the environment – it would not be unreasonable to predict that, like seaside resort tourism elsewhere, most notably in Britain and the

Mediterranean, it will not be long before resort tourism in the Red Sea stagnates and declines.

It is an unhappy prognosis given that economically the majority of the area's resorts depend almost exclusively on tourism for their livelihood and in its absence would collapse entirely. This, in turn, would have grave effect on both countries', but especially Egypt's, economy, the latter being to a large extent reliant on tourist revenues. The Sinai Peninsula's economy hinges entirely on resort tourism, and, above all, on Israeli tourists. Should the latter decide to shun its resorts, it would have a damaging effect on the area's economy. When, at the beginning of the 'Second Intifada', the numbers of Israeli tourists plummeted – as they did following the 2004 terrorist attack on Taba as well – economic activity in the Sinai Peninsula ground to a virtual halt. In order to prevent this and other unwelcome developments it is clear that the authorities, in both countries, local and central, must assume, and quickly, a key role in planning and supervising the Red Sea's resort industry. Should the present anarchic situation continue, the medium- and long-term damage to the environment and so region's economy will prove incalculable.

Acknowledgements

The authors would like to extend their thanks to the Jewish National Fund's 'Land Use Research Institute' for its financial support and to Mrs Tamar Sofer, chief cartographer of the Department of Geography at the Hebrew University of Jerusalem, for drawing the map used in this chapter.

Chapter 15

Clientelist Relationships: Implications for Tourism Development in the Declining Coastal Resort of Kusadasi, Turkey

FISUN YÜKSEL and ATILA YÜKSEL

Introduction

Planning is necessary to co-ordinate and synchronise the development of tourism, to balance competing and sometimes conflicting claims on the same limited resource base, to maximise the positive impacts of tourism development and to minimise its adverse effects (Pearce, 1981). While planning is taken as a requisite to minimise the negative effects of tourism development, its formulation and implementation are complex processes that are fraught with difficulties. In particular, within Less Developed Countries the resources may be scarcer (Morah, 1996), and the planning process may lack pluralism, democracy and the involvement of key local community institutions (Burns, 1999). Moreover, public participation may be viewed as unnecessary, unwieldy, time-consuming and an idealistic dream (Haywood, 1988). Also, planning for tourism development may not be backed by appropriate tourism-related legislation and regulations (WTO, 1993), and the implementing bodies may be weak, have limited authority or lack experience (Morah, 1996). In addition, in the context of less developed nations, uncertainties existing in the political and socioeconomic environment may be high (Morah, 1996; Tosun, 2000), and powerful bureaucracies may dominate the legislative and operational processes (Tosun, 2000). There may be a high staff turnover due to political interference, which may in turn undermine organisational morale, and the central administrative tutelage may curb the capabilities and willingness of local government (Tosun, 2000). Furthermore, organised and powerful business interests may become power centres that serve their own interests at the expense of indigenous people (Tosun, 2000; Yüksel, 2002).

However, plan formulation and implementation, and thus tourism development, may also be affected adversely by the existence or absence of a number of other factors. These include a lack of incentives to co-operate and the existence of various obstacles that inhibit collective action. Characteristics of a centralised approach to tourism management, which might include coercive decision-making, ambiguous balances between responsibility and authority, a distant bureaucracy, limited participation in decision-making, and uneven power relations, may also inhibit planning efforts (Syrett, 1997). Moreover, misuse of resources, a lack of accountability, non-transparency in decision-making, excessive rules and regulations, priorities set that are inconsistent with appropriate development, a high degree of concentration of political power, and an incompetent administration may constitute barriers to effective planning and development. Last but not least, the nature and the extent of clientelist/patronage relationships can stifle investment, inhibit the provision of public services and increase inequality and inappropriate tourism development (Dreher *et al.*, 2004). For example, in a high-intensity clientelist administrative culture, tourism development projects may be approved for investment without careful attention to sustainable development criteria. There are examples demonstrating the negative impacts of clientelism on tourism planning and development. Intensity of corruption, clientelism and nepotism have dominated the Antiguan political scene, and were reported as major stumbling blocks for the Caribbean island's tourism development (Conway, 1997). In a recent report on sustainable tourism development, the European Union Commission warned that clientelism can really harm people's respect for local authority (EcoClub, 2003). The non-cooperation of locals in formal plan preparation, their non-compliance with regulations and implementation, and consequently, their reliance on informal social networks in Crete were reported to have resulted from the dominance of individualism and political clientelism, and the consequent mistrust of government (Briassoulis, 2003).

Although clientelism, which involves the disbursement of financial, employment or other forms of patronage in exchange for political support, is regarded (Günes-Ayata, 1994a; Lambsdorff, 2004) as a common phenomena in many continents (for example, Latin American, South European, Middle East and North African), its extent, dynamics and implications have been unexplored, particularly in relation to tourism development. More specifically, due to methodological and conceptual challenges, the concept of clientelism has not been adequately integrated into the planning, tourism development and destination management literature. Focusing on Kusadasi, a resort located on the Southwest coast of Turkey (see Fig. 15.1), this exploratory research examines the relationships between perceived levels of patron–client relationships in local government and the community's evaluation of satisfaction with the present stage of tourism development, and their attitudes toward future tourism. It further explores the least/most valid

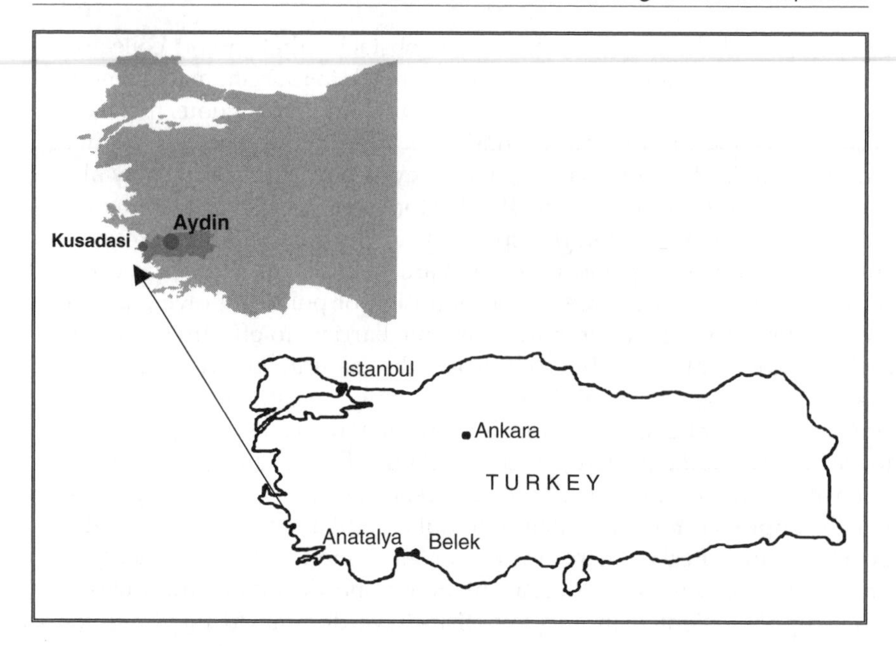

Figure 15.1 Map of Kusadasi, Turkey

means of getting tourism-related things done in local public institutions from the point of view of community members, and in doing so, ascertains Kusadasi's community propensity to clientelist relationships. To this end, first the potential role of clientelism as a barrier to appropriate tourism development is discussed through a review of conditions giving rise to the growth of such relationships. Following this, the political culture of Turkey is detailed to provide the reader with an understanding of its peculiarities and of whether it contains any of the conditions conducive to the flourishing of clientelist relationships. The research methodology is outlined, followed by a discussion of the findings.

Clientelism

Clientelism, or relations of patronage, involves direct and indirect support of 'one's own people', including family, friends and ethnic group (Henry & Nassis, 1999: 44). Political clientelism 'represents the distribution of resources (or promise of) by political office holders or political candidates in exchange for political support, primarily – although not exclusively – in the form of the vote' (Auyero, 1999: 2). More precisely, the patronage system consists of 'parties of patronage, a patron state, and a client society dependent for its welfare on patronage parties which (use) the resource of the state to keep "clients" happy' (Sunar, 1999: 32). It has traditionally been seen as a feature of *gemeinshaft*-type societies, where relations of reciprocity bind individuals and groups, and social and material benefits are exchanged for commitment and support (Henry & Nassis, 1999). Clientelist relations are seen as hierarchical arrangements, as bonds of dependence and control are based on power differences, and on inequality. They are characterised by the simultaneous exchange of instrumental (economic and political) and 'sociational' or expressive (for example, promises of loyalty and solidarity) resources and services (Auyero, 1999). In the clientelist culture, individuals are protagonists who are in opposition to organised corporate groups. Clientelist relations are said to be neither fully contractual nor legal – in fact, they are often illegal – but are based on more informal, though tightly bound relationships, and on understandings (Henry & Nassis, 1999). Clientelist relationships represent a realm of submission, a cluster of bonds of domination in opposition to a realm of mutual recognition of equality and co-operation (Auyero, 1999). In this relationship, patrons are compelled to rely on their clients to solidify their position (Roniger, 1994). Clients are expected to provide their patron with specific resources; they must accept the patron's control over their access to markets and public goods. In return, clients are protected from social or material insecurity and are provided with goods, services and social advancements (Roniger, 1994).

A generally negative image of clientelism permeates scholarly analyses (Henry & Nassis, 1999). The majority of researchers' (for example, Henry & Nassis, 1999; Roniger, 1994) view is that clientelism undermines development; politicians target the poor for clientelist payoffs, taking advantage of their need for immediate benefits and of their limited information and autonomy. Clientelism discourages the provision of public goods; it deters the entry of challengers and hence it is associated with local political monopolies and pockets of authoritarianism in transitional democracies. It keeps voters' incomes below what they would be if politics were competitive, and because it feeds on poverty, clientelism creates an interest among politicians in economic stagnation. It is the politics of the self-enclosed village, controlled by patrons and notables. Central and/or local governments misuse the mandate of welfare improvement that have been entrusted to them, while creating funds and/or allocating resources over which they have control, in order to favour third parties with whom they have political interest networks (Carkoglu, 2000). According to Adaman and Carkoglu (2001: 2) 'In the absence of a coherent political ideology to motivate and mobilise the electorate on non-patronage based politics, it becomes rational for voters to vote for those which they perceive to be providing them special favours'. Patronage relations prosper when loyalty and support, instead of efficiency, become the benchmark of economic decisions. In terms of resource allocation, clientelism defines the criteria for inclusion and exclusion (Günes-Ayata, 1994a).

Clientelism is seen as defying the modern notion of representation and legal order through appropriation and manipulation of resources by placing 'friends' in the strategic positions of power and mechanisms of control (Roniger, 1994). Patrons and clients are not interested in the generality of equality and legal rules. Rather, they are interested in resources, and they are on the lookout for situations that are to their advantage (Roniger, 1994). Such networks are used to divert public resources to consolidate power and private gains. They can constrain the enactment of universalistic policies and discourage the development of community participation and support that is required for general policy implementation (Günes-Ayata, 1994a). Needless to say, the existence of patron–client networks in the public sphere is usually conducive to widespread bribery and corruption. There might be cases where government agents sell 'government property for personal gain' (Shleifer & Vishny, 1993: 599). Government officials may engage in malfeasant behaviour, such as giving illegal passage through customs, provided of course they have discretion over the provision of government property (as in the case of controlling the customs), whenever the agent's 'superiors are either privy to the deal themselves or else cannot monitor the agent's behaviour adequately' (Rose-Ackerman, 1987: 287). Although an ideal officer should make decisions on the basis of objective, meritocratic criteria, under bribery a willingness-to-pay procedure will dominate the public sphere, creating losses of welfare (Adaman & Carkoglu, 2001).

While some authors (Adaman & Carkoglu, 2001) use corruption and clientelism interchangeably, the literature points out significant differences between clientelism and corruption in terms of resources employed (votes versus money), actors involved (voters–patron/broker versus civil servants), presence of power (asymmetry versus equality), legality versus illegality and public versus secret. Although the resources employed are different (votes for favours in clientelism versus money for favours in corruption), there are two factors providing continuity between clientelism and corruption: (1) both are based on the direct exchange of material benefits; and (2) both are built around domination networks (Máiz Suárez & Requejo, 2002; Pizzorno, 1992). Often, the presence of one signals the presence of the other.

The conditions under which political clientelism is expected to flourish are defined in the literature as follows: (1) the existence of a strong state controlling a considerable proportion of the economy; (2) a lack of consensus concerning the operationalisation of objective measures of social justice; and (3) a lack of public confidence in the objectivity of measures and processes employed in resource allocation, such as political intervention on more partial grounds, is accepted as legitimate and/or inevitable (Henry & Nassis, 1999). Corruption, bribery and patron–client relationships may be related to the deficiencies of the political system (Dreher *et al*., 2004). Social and cultural factors (e.g. religion) may shape social attitudes towards social hierarchy and family values and thus may determine the acceptability, or otherwise, of corrupt practices. Economic factors (degree of openness) may restrict trade and impose controls on capital flows. This creates rents and hence enhances the incentives to engage in corrupt activities. The significant role of the public sector in the economy affords public officials some degree of discretion in the allocation of goods and services provided, and this increases the likelihood of corruption (Dreher *et al*., 2004). Corruption, bribery and patron–client relations may offer greater gain to officials who exercise control over the distribution of the rights to exploit natural resources. Some of these conditions are deemed to hold true for the Turkish political context as a whole.

Political Culture: Turkey

Turkey has regularly held free and competitive elections since 1946. The number and the influence of political parties has changed during this time (Tessler & Altinoglu, 2004). The country has experienced a two-party political system at times and a multiparty system at others. Electoral politics has been frequently dominated by highly ideological rival parties. In addition to party competition and electoral politics, Turkish politics has also been characterised by a number of military interventions (Tessler & Altinoglu, 2004). Turkey does not appear to be a consolidated democracy despite the history of competitive elections. As it possesses some but not all of the characteristics of democratic political systems, it should probably be described as an 'unconsolidated', 'incomplete', 'electoral' or 'delegative' democracy (Tessler & Altinoglu, 2004). Turkey's governance is strongly centralised, with considerable power vested in the President's office, the Council of Ministers and Ministries (Mahalli İdareler, 2003). The State Planning Department's five-year national development plans exemplify the centralised policy-making process (State Planning Department, 1997). That process is also evident in the tourism sector, which after the 1980 coup became a high-priority development sector (Goymen, 2000; Korzay, 1994; Toledo, 1985; Tosun & Timothy 2001; TYD 1992; Yüksel *et al*., 1999).

In general, the administrative structure of Turkey is characterised by a strong central government whose territorial administration is governed by a system of provinces that function according to the principle of deconcentration (Destan, 1998; Kocdemir, 1998). Municipalities, Special Provincial Administrations (SPAs) and Village Administrations are the three main public administrative entities established to meet local needs.

The Law relating to local administration (the Municipal Law 1580) regulates the formation, duties and powers of these entities. At the provincial level, the governor is the representative of the State, of the government and of each of the ministries separately; he is also their executive agent (OECD, 1993). The tasks entrusted to SPAs come under the following headings: public works, training and education, health and social assistance. The tasks entrusted by law for municipalities may be grouped under the following headings: urban infrastructure work, organisation and control of commercial activities, preventive and curative health measures, social security and assistance, control of a municipal police force, of the services provided by companies and individuals, and organisation of cultural and sports services (OECD, 1993).

For both the provinces and municipalities there are councils with members elected every five years. The functional framework for the municipalities was established under the Municipalities Act of 1930 and, along with many other Acts, they assign a wide range of responsibilities. These include urban planning and implementation, surveys and mapping, the regulation of construction and construction permits, land development and the opening of new settlement areas, the construction and maintenance of parks and urban roads, the provision of water, sewage and gas services, the collection and disposal of garbage, and the cleaning of public spaces (Unal, 1992; Yeter, 1993). According to article 127 of the 1982 Constitution, the central administration has the power of administrative control over local government in the framework of principles and procedures enshrined in law. The administrative control over local authorities is exercised over their activities, decisions, actions and personnel (Donmez, 1999). This supervision can take the form of the approval, postponement and even cancellation of some decisions. This is usually done through judicial control of the administrative acts of local authorities (Yalcindag, 1997).

Despite the favourable atmosphere of the liberal policy framework of the 1980s, it is hard to claim that significant devolution of power to local authorities has taken place. The political importance of municipal administration had continued to increase over the last two decades. Even though municipalities in Turkey have become more powerful in terms of the magnitude of resources they have control over, the centralised government still plays an important role in resource creation and resource allocation (Adaman & Carkoglu, 2001). A heavily centralised administrative system, characterising Turkish administrative culture thus has implications for tourism development, particularly when the municipality is run by the party other than the ruling party of the centre. Thus, central government is likely to tighten their tutelage over the municipalities under the control of their rival. Eventually, the reactions of the municipalities will grow and demands for a populist devolution of power will take place (Adaman & Carkoglu, 2001). Turkey's highly centralised public administration has been criticised as not being adequately responsive to user and local needs and for cost-inefficiencies (OECD, 2004). The centralist and bureaucratic tradition of Turkish administration causes many problems, including an increase in the formalism of administration, an unnecessary increase in the number of personnel, delays in the realisation of local projects and plans, and difficulties of co-ordination. Additionally, the lack of an active, sensitive and responsive citizenship in relation to local affairs and authorities constitutes another serious problem for the Turkish local government system (Yalcindag, 1997). Consequently, the overly centralised system of control by the Ministry of Culture and Tourism causes some serious delays. All projects across the country have to be evaluated, inspected and approved by the relevant authorities in Ankara, while the local offices of Ministry of Tourism play only an administrative role. This not only causes delays to inspections and approvals, but also makes the maintenance of effective control difficult. Overlapping responsibilities and functions between the Ministry of Culture and Tourism and other relevant ministries also slows down project approval and operational stages in investments. The process of developing tourism zones and allocating state land to investors through long-term leases has been seriously hurt by corruption scandals (Taclan, 2004). Because of this, both investors and the government have become extremely cautious in recent years, and this has slowed down the development of new tourism projects (Taclan, 2004).

A number of theoretical studies have repeatedly asserted that both central and local governments in Turkey are infested with patron–client networks (Adaman & Carkoglu, 2001; Carkoglu, 2000). The public administrative system is claimed to be working not on the basis of economic efficiency, or responding to constituency needs and promoting merit, but rather it is motivated primarily on the basis of corrupt patron–client allegiances (Adaman & Carkoglu, 2001; Carkoglu, 2000). Public expenditures and government employment in Turkey are areas traditionally suffering from suspicions of favouritism (OECD, 2004). The business environment in Turkey was in the past, and is to some extent still, characterised by high administrative burdens and uneven application and enforcement of requirements across firms (OECD, 2004). Corruption, favouritism and influence peddling is rife, even several parliamentary enquiries are under way involving prominent politicians suspected of embezzlement (European Union, 1998). A major judicial investigation began in August 1997 and involved dozens of former members of the administration, mayors and politicians accused of committing irregularities in open tendering procedures (European

Union, 1998). Turkey ranks as the 77th country in the Transparency International (TI) Corruption Perceptions Index (CPI). This index assesses 146 countries in terms of the degree to which corruption is perceived to exist among public officials and politicians. In a recent study, examining the extent to which patronage is widespread, it was found that patronage (favouritism, nepotism, populism, discrimination and inequality) was highly observable at both local and central levels (Adaman & Carkoglu, 2001). Günes-Ayata (1994b) notes that there has been a proliferation of clientelism since 1980 and the carrying out of personal favours for the constituents is still seen as a primary job of elected local and central officials. Members of Parliament spend every morning responding to the demands of voters. Most of them keep files for each client, registering all favours rendered so that they can claim favours in return (Kara & Koksal, 1988 cited in Günes-Ayata, 1994a).

Kusadasi: Past and Present

Kusadasi was one of the first holiday resorts in Turkey to be developed, situated on its Southwest coast. Coupled with Turkey's growing emphasis on tourism during the 1980s, Kusadasi has been transformed from a resort town visited mainly by domestic visitors into a destination that draws international tourists in high volumes (Yüksel & Yüksel, 2005). As of 2002, Kusadasi alone accounted for nearly 5% of overall tourism revenues generated in Turkey (Ergul *et al.*, 2002). Thus, in addition to high numbers of domestic visitors, it receives approximately 500,000 international visits annually, the majority of which originate from Western Europe (Ergul *et al.*, 2002). Services, trading, construction, transportation, fishing and agriculture are the main sources of income, with the hospitality industry being the town's leading sector (Tunc, 2005). Available statistics for 2004 suggest that the resort's total bed-space capacity of tourism-licensed hotels including holiday villages and camp sites reached 45,000. The industry is, however, very fragmented, dominated by small-scale and often out-dated hotels ($N = 346$ of 497 licensed hotels), with small bed capacities (Tunc, 2005). Capacity constraints on room supply create difficulties in matching hotel products to variations in demand, a problem that is exacerbated by the fact that the tourism season is concentrated within a few summer months only. The majority of hotels remain closed between mid-October to April, and this is one of the reasons for the resort's low annual occupancy rates (Yüksel & Yüksel, 2005). Moreover, the rate of exit from the industry is high and many hotels sell for under their true real estate value (Ergul *et al.*, 2002).

These are not the only problems that Kusadasi is experiencing however, as the development of the tourism industry has started to degrade some of the natural resources in the region (Yüksel & Yüksel, 2005). Largely unregulated tourism development has resulted in distorted urbanisation and weak local infrastructure, and this has damaged the natural environment resulting in particular in water, marine and soil pollution. In this respect, before the tourism season of 2001, some major tour operators decided to omit Kusadasi from their sale list because of such problems as overconstruction, an underdeveloped sewage system and water pollution (Ergul *et al.*, 2002). There is inadequate quantifiable information as to where the town stands in terms of its life-cycle, however, according to Ergul *et al.* (2002), many tour operators declared that the image of the town has deteriorated significantly due to a lack of planned development. Recently, the town's visitor profile has changed as more visitors are being received from East European countries, and a noticeable decline in tourism revenue continues (Yüksel & Yüksel, 2005). Furthermore, a recent study found that residents of Kusadasi had negative perceptions of tourism's impacts on the quality of the environment, exhibited a negative community attitude, and perceived tourism to be responsible for crowding and congestion (Tatoglu *et al*., 2002). Present tourism development in Kusadasi exhibits many, if not all of the characteristics of stagnation (e.g. unfashionable image, high property turnover rates, lack of new investment and surplus bed capacity) (Tatoglu *et al*., 2002; Yüksel & Yüksel, 2005). The resort's authorities are aware that the decline will accelerate unless corrective and preventive measures are initiated (Yüksel & Yüksel, 2005). While it is not simple, decline may be offset if countermeasures are adopted, such as the reorientation of tourist attractions, environmental quality enhancement or the repositioning of the destination within an overall market (Agarwal, 2002).

The effectiveness of such measures and the appropriateness of tourism development however, heavily depends upon the removal of an inherent clientelist culture that is embedded within the present Turkish public administrative system. Such a culture encompasses inequality arising from favouritism, nepotism and discrimination. The existence of patron–client networks in the public sphere is usually conducive to widespread bribery, corruptive behaviours, service inefficiency, the sacrifice of public interests to individual interests, a waste of resources and chaotic tourism development. To put it simply, if satisfying one's own people or supporters at the expense of objective criteria becomes the departing point of decisions, and rules and regulations are generally evaded through personal connections, appropriate tourism development sounds like an unrealistic dream. For example, 'the lack of sectoral planning, ineffective control, the lack of participation by local people, the abuse of political power, the get-rich-quick mentality coupled with dubious practices, inconsistencies in the planning criteria and procedures, and the general lack of tourism culture (is likely to result) in missed opportunities and inadequate and inappropriate tourism development (in Turkey)' (Sezer & Harrison, 1994: 82).

Research Methodology

Investigating clientelist relations in operation clearly presents potential difficulties, as client–patron relationships may imply illegal activity (Henry & Nassis, 1999). A survey method was chosen to elicit frank responses on this topic. A self-reply questionnaire was thus developed to examine five interconnected issues: (1) the adequacy of local government in fulfilling its principal and ancillary services relating to the development of tourism; (2) the extent of existing corruptive behaviours regarding the utilisation/distribution of resources for the development of tourism and their influence on important dependent variables (e.g. economy, private life, business life and tourism development); (3) the extent of patronage relations indicated by the absence/presence of equal treatment rendered to each individual/firm pursuing tourism-related enquiries/applications in public institutions; (4) opinions as to the most frequent, valid and effective means employed in the pursuit of such applications/enquiries (e.g. acquiring tourism investment/operation licence from public institutions); and (5) participants' overall evaluations as to the adequacy of the present form of tourism development. Questions were partly developed from exploratory interviews and largely from the relevant literature and previously used scales (Adaman & Carkoglu, 2001).

More specifically, the first section of the questionnaire aimed to gather evaluations of participants on the adequacy of local government (i.e. municipalities) in delivering core infrastructural services, and promotional activities, together with inspection services necessary to observe appropriate development and operation of the tourism industry. The second section of the questionnaire instructed the participants to evaluate the perceived intensity of corruption, political favouritism, fellow townsmanship, partisan behaviours, populism and bribery that exist at present in relation to the distribution of public tourism resources (land, funds and technical support). The next section focused upon the degree of equality in the treatment by public institutions of those applying/enquiring for tourism investment/operation licences. The next section dealt with most valid and invalid means employed by individuals in obtaining the required service(s) from the local government.

A pre-test preceded the field research and accordingly a few modifications were made to the wording of the statements. Kusadasi, which represents a typical coastal resort in Turkey, was chosen for the field research. The pre-test was run with university students and academics who had been residing in Kusadasi for more than two years. Graduate students were then trained for the administration of the questionnaires. The town was divided into six zones, and the household interviewing method was employed. Forty households were targeted from each zone. Following the introduction of the survey objectives, consent of the households to take part in the survey was sought. Due to the length of the questionnaire and sensitivity of some of the questions, only half of the 240 forms were returned complete. This produced 125 usable forms. The average completion time was 25 minutes. Due to the objectives of the research, descriptive statistics (means and standard deviations) and bivariate correlation analyses were conducted.

Before proceeding with the results of the study, it is important to note its limitations. The sample size is rather small, thus future studies should have a larger sample size. Personality and demographic characteristics of the sample may have impacted on the perceived intensity of patronage relations and corruption. The reader is thus cautioned when interpreting the findings of this exploratory research.

Results and Discussion

Fifty-three percent of the participants were male. The ages of the respondents range between 20 and 67, with the mean being 32.8. The majority of participants (54%) hold a university degree, and of all the participants 87% reside in Kusadasi and the rest in the nearby boroughs and villages. Fifty-five percent of the respondents have been living in Kusadasi for more than five years, and 40% of them for less than five years. The majority of respondents were employees (45%), followed by employers, students, housewives, retirees, unemployed and others. The reported income ranges between 250 and 3000 New Turkish Liras (€150–€1400). The majority of the participants (51%) earn their income from tourism, with the hospitality industry being the main generator of jobs (38%), followed by travel agencies (20%). Only 60% of the respondents provided an answer to the question of 'which party do you support?' The respondents are mainly supporters of the ruling party (15%), followed by the Republican Party (12%), the Nationalist Party (5%), the Motherland Party (3.2%) and others. This almost reflects the present distribution in the parliament. Cronbach α scores provide evidence for the reliability of the scales (0.82 for corruption-bribery scale, 0.94 for patronage relations scale and 0.81 for most-least valid means scale). These scores suggest that each scale is internally consistent and capable of measuring the construct that it is supposed to measure.

Corruption and bribery index

An analysis of statements developed to measure perceptions of respondents on the intensity of corruptive behaviours revealed some interesting findings (Table 15.1). According to the results of the study, corruptive behaviour was perceived to occur frequently in the public sphere which controls the distribution of tourism resources. This is followed by seeking partisan interests, discrimination, fellow townsmanship, political favouritism and populism.

Table 15.1 Corruption and Bribery Index

	Mean	*Std. deviation*
Bribery	4.3505	0.98996
Partisan	4.2946	1.01020
Discrimination	4.2545	1.12059
Fellow townsmanship	4.2545	1.06173
Corruption	4.2130	1.82430
Political favouritism	4.1892	1.10793
Populism	4.0769	1.09449

Based on a 1–5 scale (1, least to 5, most frequently)
Source: Author's survey

Patronage relations index

An analysis of the responses to the patron/client relationship statements suggest that local public institutions were perceived to be unequally treating individuals who were obtaining their services (Table 15.2). The mean scores suggest that representatives of public institutions are perceived to seek economic and/or political gains when it comes to equally exercising institutional polices and procedures to everyone (3.75, $sd = 1.28$). This means the same procedures are not followed in every case and measures for policy implementation vary according to the businessman/organisation concerned. The respondents believed that local public institutions are not impartial in terms of equal distribution of institutional resources (e.g. information, know-how, technical support and funds) to all applicants seeking such support (3.75, $sd = 1.29$). Thus it appears that distribution of such resources is not based on the fulfilment of basic qualifications but on favouritism. Local public institutions were perceived to be highly unequal in the allocation of regional resources (land, etc.) for tourism purposes (4.05, $sd = 1.13$). Again, this implies that the appraisal of applications is based on judgements biased by personal

Table 15.2 Patronage Relations Index

Impartiality in	*Mean*	*Std. deviation*
Distribution of institutional resources	3.7253	1.28293
Policy/procedure implementation	3.7500	1.28922
Processing of business enquiries and files	3.8652	1.15001
Inspection of services	3.9222	1.09368
Sanctions	3.9647	1.22908
Subcontracting	4.0455	1.01607
Distribution of national resources	4.0543	1.13258
Construction planning	4.0556	1.15497
Delivery of infrastructural services	4.0674	1.16578

Based on a 1–5 scale (1, strongly agree; 5, strongly disagree)
Source: Author's survey

connections/influences. They were also perceived to be highly unequal in the processing of business files of people pursuing their business-related enquiries (3.86, *sd* = 1.15). This indicates that final decisions are shaped not by the merit of the application but rather who the applicant knows and whether s/he is within the circle of personal connections. The statement eliciting the degree of agreement amongst the respondents with regards to the equal treatment of all businesses while controlled by public institutions for prices and/or hygienic conditions showed strong disagreement (3.92, *sd* = 1.15). Scores show that local public institutions favour some people over others when it comes to implementing/inspecting their construction plans (4.05, *sd* = 1.15). It appears that local public institutions treat some individuals who are violating the rules and/or evading taxation entirely differently (3.96, *sd* = 1.22). They are perceived to favour some companies/individuals when subcontracting for some major tourism-related projects (e.g. pavement construction) (4.04, *sd* = 1.01). Local public institutions were perceived to seek economic and/or political gains in the delivery of compulsory infrastructural services to tourism entrepreneurs and establishments. Overall, high scores mean that the delivery of public services, the distribution of resources and the control of tasks are run on the basis of favouritism and patron–client relationships. So local public institutions do not seem to distribute collective benefits to an entire population, but instead focus these benefits on individuals or specific groups via exchange circuits and networks.

Getting things done

An examination of answers to the most and least valid means perceived to be employed by individuals in the pursuit of enquiries and obtaining the required service(s) from the local government indicates that trying to establish parochial ties with the person in charge or to find a relative or a kin at the relevant department is perceived as the most valid means (2.52, *sd* = 1.30) (Table 15.3). Submission of all necessary documents/files to the department responsible was rated as the second most valid means likely to work in acquiring the services, information and files (2.53, *sd* = 1.33). Using external means such as putting pressure by using media or television, and to put pressure by organising a mass demonstration or protest was perceived as the least valid ways of getting things done in local public institutions (3.12, *sd* = 1.36 and 3.59, *sd* = 1.42 respectively). This shows the exploitation other than legal ways to get around the rules and regulations by the public.

Table 15.3 Most valid means for getting things done in local public institutions

Means	*Mean*	*Std. deviation*
Parochial ties	2.5222	1.30881
Submit files and wait for a reply	2.5376	1.33969
Telephone from a higher authority	2.6044	1.44437
Present business cards of acquaintances/influential	2.6842	1.45327
Gifts and favour promises	2.7667	1.28998
Media	3.1264	1.36232
Mass protest	3.5926	1.42107

Based on a 1–5 scale (1, most valid; 5, least valid)
Source: Author's survey

Attitudes toward present and future tourism development

Six questions were used to obtain the respondents' overall assessment of the appropriateness and the adequacy of tourism development in the town (Table 15.4 and Table 15.5). The first question, designed to gauge the respondent's satisfaction with regard to the current stage reached in tourism development, reveals that respondents were very discontent with the present situation in town. The mean score for their satisfaction was 4.12, with a standard deviation of 1.18 (higher scores indicate stronger disagreement with the statement). The second question revealed that the present form and stage of tourism development has put

Table 15.4 Attitudes toward present and future tourism development

	Mean	*Std. deviation*
Tourism industry will not improve in the near future	3.3158	1.24852
Present tourism development puts the town ahead of its competitors	4.1739	1.10552
Kusadasi tourism will be better than today in the near future	3.6477	1.19424
Restructuring in Kusadasi tourism is a necessity	1.9490	1.42418
Restructuring will be successfully realised	2.6277	1.44419
Satisfaction with the present stage of tourism development	4.1250	1.08821

Based on a 1–5 scale (1, strongly agree; 5, strongly disagree)
Source: Author's survey

Kusadasi behind its main competitors (4.17, *sd* = 1.10). The analysis revealed that respondents were somewhat pessimistic in that they did not believe the situation would improve in the future (3.31, *sd* = 1.24) and would not be any different from today in the years to come (3.64, *sd* = 1.19). The respondents showed a high level of agreement with the question eliciting the need to restructure tourism development (1.94, *sd* = 1.42). The mean score suggests that the town may succeed in its attempt at restructuring (2.62, *sd* = 1.37). The respondents further reported that the present level of patronage-based bribery and corruption

Table 15.5 Effect of patronage relations, bribery and corruption on economy, family life, business life and tourism development

	Mean	*Std. deviation*
Patronage relations, bribery-corruption affect national economy	1.6598	1.19797
Patronage relations, bribery-corruption affect local tourism development	1.6939	1.24692
Patronage relations, bribery-corruption affect business life	1.7263	1.08610
Patronage relations, bribery-corruption affect my personal life	2.3939	1.38371

Based on a 1–5 scale (1, strongly agree; 5, strongly disagree)
Source: Author's survey

affected the national economy, tourism development, business and family life (Table 15.5).

Composite scores for both the bribery-corruption scale and the patronage scale were formed and subject to a correlation analysis. The results suggest that there are strong direct associations between bribery-corruption and client/patron relations (Table 15.6). The correlation coefficient (0.60) suggests that an increase in the clientelist relations is likely to result in an increase in bribery and corruption (or vice versa). Inverse relationships between bribery-corruption and satisfaction with development (-0.284) and between clientelist relations and satisfaction with tourism development (-0.429) were observed. This indicates that a unit increase in the perceived level of clientelist relations would decrease contentment with the appropriateness and/or adequacy of tourism development in the town. The same holds true for the association between perceived level of clientelist relations and the town's current position in contrast to other competing tourist destinations

Table 15.6 Associations between patronage, bribery-corruption and attitudes toward town's current and future tourism development (TD)

	Intensity of client/ patron relations	*Intensity of bribery-corruption*
Bribery-corruption	0.599**	
Satisfaction with the present stage of TD	– 0.284*	– 0.429**
Negative attitude (tourism industry will not improve in the future)	0.085	0.269*
Negative attitude (stage of present TD puts the town behind its competitors)	0.374**	0.375**
Positive attitude (Kusadasi tourism will be better than today in the near future)	– 0.240	– 0.343*
Restructuring in the tourism is a necessity	0.020	– 0.041
Restructuring will be successfully realised	– 0.055	0.141

**Correlation is significant at the 0.01 level (2-tailed). *Correlation is significant at the 0.05 level (2-tailed).
Source: Author's survey

nearby (– 0.374 and – 0.375 respectively). This provides indirect evidence of community confidence in the public institutions' attempt to improve the town's tourism industry in the future. These associations are of great importance, and may provide some explanation as to why community participation remains low in tourism-related projects (Yüksel & Yüksel, 2005) (i.e. community inertia/apathy to calls for meetings relating to new tourism projects, etc.). Community support is necessary for tourism development. These results suggest that local and national rules and regulations concerning tourism are weak and that individuals are able to circumvent legal constraints through power peddling and bribery. Clientelist relations may thus foster the uneven concentration and distribution of resources.

Conclusion

The reviewed literature suggests that there are numerous factors that have the potential to exert either positive or negative effects on tourism development. The proposition of this study is that clientelism, but particularly social networks, may play an important role in tourism development, as resource allocation decisions are prone to manipulation by local/central patrons or clients and such relations are likely to put off participatory/collaborative tourism development. Clientelist relations may influence the competition for power, patterns of control, distribution and redistribution of resources, the formulation and implementation of policies, and access to public services, contracts and economic ventures (Roniger, 1994). In other words, considering other factors remain the same, the nature and intensity of patronage relations and corruption will be likely to determine the efficiency of local government services. This in turn will have implications for tourism development through the erosion of community trust in public institutions, which is likely to result in the local community isolating itself from the tourism development process.

The results of the study provide some evidence for the above proposition. It seems that rules and regulations can be flexed according to personal connections (Table 15.2 and Table 15.3). This implies that anything is possible with a proper recommendation in the allocation of tourism resources and provision of services (Günes-Ayata, 1994a) in Kusadasi. Compulsory qualifications may be ignored in the utilisation/distribution of local/national resources for Kusadasi at the expense of such incentives as votes, support, favour, social visibility, honour and perceived power. Widespread non-compliance with regulations, a consequence of clientelism, in Kusadasi is likely to prevent appropriate tourism development. Public funds needed for sustainable tourism development could be misused, causing resource constraints, and this is likely to inhibit the provision of effective public services. Perceived inequality may trigger Kusadasi public mistrust in local governments, which in turn may increase the level of public reluctance in participating in tourism-development decisions. Abstention from meetings is a precarious element in collaborative decision-making. The initial spirit and impetus in public meetings is an important ingredient for the effectiveness of subsequent stages. Tourism development requires effective co-ordination of activities of both public and private institutions and individuals. Tourism development projects may be stalled without co-ordination (Timothy, 1998) and any lack of co-ordination is likely to frustrate the potential opportunities for community to involve itself in tourism development (Tosun, 2002). This would be a missed opportunity (Yüksel, 2002).

The presence of a high degree of corruption and clientelist relations, exacerbated by the present administrative culture in Kusadasi suggests that by-passing universalistic rules and regulations is possible. To curb the obnoxious influence of vested interests of power-holders at local levels and to confront the clientelism of local areas in an environment rife with rent-seeking opportunities, a strong and effective mechanism for accountability and transparency must exist (Hart, 2002). It is therefore suggested that researchers and authorities identify the intensity of clientelism and develop appropriate mechanisms to remove its negative effects. Unless clientelism is recognised and treated, the resources allocated for the preparation and realisation of the projects both in Kusadasi and other similar destinations in Turkey are likely to be wasted. In order to provide potential solutions to these challenges, local administrations should take into consideration citizens' expectations, their level of satisfaction with municipal services, and their views of equal treatment and democratic participation. Another warning to the Kusadasi authorities is the high level of peoples' susceptibility to corrupt behaviour, as evidenced by their scores to the most and least valid means of getting things done (Table 15.3). This suggests that combating clientelism would be difficult. In fact, variations in the density of corruption often depend more on people's willingness to be corrupt, that is, on the moral cost of the corruption, than on the structure of incentives at a given time.

It must be noted that clientelism is not limited to a specific type of culture (Günes-Ayata, 1994a). In contrast to modernisation theorists' assumptions whereby patronage based on familial patterns is replaced by the rational allocation of resources on the basis of universal (rather than personal) rights, the survival of clientelist relations embedded in social relations reflects its persistence (Günes-Ayata, 1994a). This may be attributed to the fact that communities are not bounded, homogeneous entities, but are 'socially differentiated, diverse and often aspatial' (Günes-Ayata, 1994a: 21). Aspects of social identity such as gender, class, income, age, ability and origins divide and cross-cut so-called community boundaries. Social life may be pervaded by diverse and often conflicting values and resource priorities, rather than by shared beliefs and interests. Struggle and bargaining may characterise such conflicts (Leach *et al.*, 1997). Future tourism development research should therefore integrate clientelism as an important independent variable. Finally, the removal of clientelism requires an examination of the nature and the intensity of existing, if any, corrupt behaviours and patronage relations, and their likely implications for services provided by local governments that influence the development of tourism in an area. Bottom-up processes are unlikely to emerge and succeed without local or regional populations and administrations being prepared to face their situation (Von Meyer *et al.*, 1999). If a clientelist approach to tourism development is to be eliminated, it must first be exposed. Identifying the intensity of patronage relations and corruption is thus important, as corruption is a daunting obstacle to sustainable tourism development, and results in a major loss of public funds needed for appropriate development, both in developed and developing countries (Lambsdorff, 2004).

Acknowledgements

We would like to give our special thanks to Ali Erkut Yuksel and Aleyna Berra Yuksel for their help with the present research.

Chapter 16

Conclusion: Future Implications for the Development and Management of Coastal Resorts

SHEELA AGARWAL and GARETH SHAW

Introduction

This book has considered the global phenomena of mass tourism in coastal resorts and draws attention to the diversity of such environments, in terms of the variety of planning and management issues being experienced, alongside some of the conceptual complexities that surround their study. Its origins are derived from the recognition that coastal resorts have been a relatively neglected area of study, as outlined in Chapter 1 (Shaw & Agarwal). Moreover, the majority of existing research has been undertaken within Northern and Southern Europe, largely at the expense of wider global considerations. This book has addressed this knowledge deficit by examining coastal resorts through a series of worldwide case studies. It therefore provides a flavour of the issues being experienced by such resorts globally, many of which are at varying stages of development and subject to different modes of state intervention, in a range of environmental settings.

This final chapter reviews the key themes of the book's subsequent contributions and attempts to place these in a wider management context. It begins by summarising the main issues and their management implications, which have emerged from the five thematic sections: (1) coastal resorts in transition; (2) the diversification and sustainable development of coastal resorts; (3) the pleasure periphery and managing the postmodern coastal resort; (4) coastal resort structures: variation versus standardisation; and (5) state intervention and the planning and development of coastal resorts. This is followed by discussion of the potential impact such key issues have for the future planning, development and management of coastal resorts. In particular, the focus of this discussion is directed towards three key aspects of coastal resort management, innovation, knowledge transfer and management, conflict resolution, and post-disciplinary perspectives, which have been identified from all of the book's contributions as having an important overarching influence on the future of coastal resorts.

Mass Tourism Coastal Resorts: Key Themes and Management Implications

Examining coastal resorts in transition, or in other words, those resorts which Butler (1980: 11) termed as having 'passed steadily through all of the postulated states [of the Tourist Area Life Cycle]', provided the first over-arching theme within which to frame their examination. In this context, Chapter 2 (Gale) examined the causes and consequences of broad structural economic and cultural forces for the post-mature coastal resorts of Northern Europe, whilst Chapter 3 (Shaw & Coles) analysed the current state of British resorts along with potential strategies for survival. Chapter 4 (Agarwal) developed discussion of responses to decline further, through an assessment of the capacity of Southwest England's coastal resorts to respond to global forces.

An emerging issue from these three chapters is the social, economic and environmental problems that many mass tourism coastal resorts across Northern Europe are experiencing. This is perhaps a reflection of the fact that 'resorts are extremely dynamic tourist spaces, which have often changed form a number of times' (Shaw & Williams, 2004: 237) due to the impact of a complex array of factors. Such factors include changes in consumer tastes, the quality of the tourism product, and the level of competition and the globalisation of the resort, as discussed in Chapters 1–3. However, it is premature to talk generally of the failure or decline of all mass tourism coastal resorts in Northern Europe, as they vary considerably in terms of the nature and scope of the difficulties experienced. Clearly, those with most severe problems may be found within Britain, whilst countries such as Sweden and Denmark appear to be experiencing relatively few problems. Although such variations may in part be explained by the fact that British resorts developed much earlier than those elsewhere in Northern Europe, the effectiveness or otherwise of restructuring strategies to address decline may also account for the varying fortunes of Europe's mass coastal resorts.

In this context, resort restructuring is another emergent issue, which is discussed in Chapters 1–4, along with its relative success. In contrast to the rather belated and reactive responses that characterised British resort regeneration throughout the 1970s until the early 1990s (Cooper, 1997), detailed in Chapters 2 and 3, it is clear from Chapter 2 that lessons have been learnt from the British experience and a more proactive approach is being adopted within resorts elsewhere in Northern Europe. Resort restructuring is being used to address widely differing situations and in light of this, is perhaps more appropriately conceptualised as an adaptive paradigm which 'acknowledges that resorts may follow several different local development paths determined according to context and local circumstances' (Agarwal, 2005: 366).

But, despite the fact that British resorts have attracted increased policy attention, as outlined in Chapter 3, it remains the case that many are essentially failing tourism destinations, and that there has been a failure to put into place workable policies (Shaw & Williams, 2004). This point is also raised and developed further in Chapter 4 by Agarwal, who questions the extent to which the institutional landscape is helping or hindering resort restructuring within Britain. Nevertheless, although British resort restructuring may represent a 'policy failure' and 'policy limitation' (Shaw & Williams, 2004: 241), in light of the variable economic performance of coastal resorts across Northern Europe, the issue of failure and decline of coastal resorts in this context has been grossly exaggerated. Clearly, some are performing well, whilst others are struggling, thereby highlighting the importance of understanding local settings in the context of global socioeconomic processes, as there are many factors that may affect the deployment of local action.

However, reasons for the differential economic performance of Northern European coastal resorts are unclear and have been linked generally to the ability of some to provide flexible tourism products to cater for changing, and more specialised, niche market demands (Agarwal, 2002; Shaw & Williams, 2004). This point is highlighted in Chapter 3, but as Shaw and Coles demonstrate, there is no evidence to suggest a declining interest in the mass sun, sea and sand package holiday and thus there must be other factors that influence the success or otherwise of the resort economy. Such a point is raised by Agarwal (2005), who emphasises the high dependency of resort change on context (for example, global, international, national, regional and local processes) and on the place-characteristics of resorts (including scale, location, morphology and/or past patterns of development).

Consequently, alongside the urgent need for studies that examine the effectiveness of local action and the key factors that are essential to its success, more research is required of the functioning of coastal resorts. On the one hand, this may involve analyses of the determinants of economic performance, similar to those that have been undertaken in rural environments (Agarwal *et al.*, 2006; Courtney *et al.*, 2004). On the other hand, such research may entail more detailed examinations of the problems that Northern European coastal resorts are experiencing and consideration of the extent to which their problems are a by-product of a declining national tourism industry. A greater understanding of both aspects may help to aid the management and sustainability of these resorts in the future.

The diversification and sustainable development of coastal resorts was the second key theme examined in this book. Its inclusion reflects the recognition of the benefits and particularly the costs of coastal tourism in Southern Europe, which has promoted diversification away from 'sun, sea and sand' traditionally associated with its resorts, into alternative forms of tourism that are characterised by higher spending patterns and lower volumes of visitors and niche markets (Bramwell, 2004c). Drawing on a case study of Malta, the complexity of studying tourism growth management issues and of developing and applying relevant practical policies is discussed in Chapter 5 (Bramwell). This theme is then further explored in Chapter 6 by Priestley and Llurdés, who assess the current and future sustainability of Spain's mass tourism resorts, together with an evaluation of success of legislative measures, and planning mechanisms. In addition, Chapter 7 (Sharpley) focuses on sustainability and resort redevelopment in Cyprus and Tenerife. More specifically, Sharpley identifies common challenges facing island tourism destinations as well as the lessons that emerge from a comparison of recent tourism development experiences of each island.

The difficulty of managing growth is an issue that recurs in all three chapters. Bramwell (Chapter 5) argues that any attempt to manage a destination's tourism growth needs to recognise the full complexity of the relationships and issues involved. In particular, he demonstrates that there are dynamic synergies and tensions between different types of tourism, between these tourism types and the overall volume of tourism, and between tourism development in adjacent or nearby local contexts. Such a contention is reinforced by Priestley and Llurdés, in Chapter 6, who state that although the immediate Spanish coastline has been protected, this has had negative repercussions on adjacent areas, resulting in the extension of tourism development on park fringes and inland. Sharpley, in Chapter 7, discusses this issue further and identifies three obstacles to managing growth in Cyprus and Tenerife. These include: (1) an inability to implement tourism policies; (2) the lack of an integrated approach and stakeholder collaboration; and (3) a mismatch between the development of quality tourism products, potential markets and the destinations' potential in terms of its physical, cultural and social resources.

The difficulty of developing and managing coastal resorts in a more sustainable manner inevitably raises questions concerning their future sustainability. This is because, even though sustainable tourism initiatives and policies may be implemented, according to Bramwell (Chapter 5) their outcome is hard to predict due to the diversity and nonlinearity of tourism's impacts. In addition, as Priestley and Llurdés (Chapter 6) note, given the high-density development that characterises many coastal resorts in the Mediterranean, the extent to which sustainable measures can be applied to resorts in the future is debatable. Sharpley (Chapter 7) is also sceptical about the future economic sustainability of resorts on Cyprus and Tenerife in light of their lack of competitiveness as evidenced by declining numbers of mass market tourists, their dependence on lower-spending tourists from traditional markets and an oversupply of accommodation. Clearly the future sustainability of these environments is far from certain, and is not helped by the lack of clarity surrounding the meaning of sustainable tourism. In the absence of a widely accepted definition, combined with the fact that its achievement is often limited by partial consensus and the need for compromise and trade-offs (Bramwell & Sharman, 1999; Mowforth & Munt, 2003), it is hardly surprising that sustainable development remains such a challenge to coastal tourism destinations. Moreover, its measurement is beset by complex issues such as scale (i.e. macro or micro), the length of monitoring period (i.e. short, medium or long term), and by the difficulty of establishing performance indicators (Hunter & Shaw, 2007; Li, 2004; Miller, 2001; Twining-Ward & Butler, 2002). Despite the fact that some headway has been made recently (English Tourism Council, 2001b; Hunter & Shaw, 2007; Twining-Ward & Butler, 2002), research of this nature is still in its infancy and with the exception of Hunter and Shaw (2007), it tends to be extremely parochial, focusing on the localised monitoring of destination-based impacts and resource demands at the expense of greater consideration of the global consequences of tourism. Given this lacuna, further research is therefore required into how best to monitor and evaluate sustainable tourism in coastal resorts, including the development of a robust set of indicators.

The third theme dealt with in this book concerns the pleasure periphery and the management of the postmodern coastal resort. This draws on the ideas of global competition and the development of postmodern structures, and discusses the influence and consequences of deep underlying structural socioeconomic changes for selected coastal resorts. King's Chapter 8 emphasises the growing development pressure on coastal areas in Australia, alongside the need for management strategies that can sustain both global demands and domestic pressures. Chapter 9 (Henderson) examines the dynamics and consequences of the development process for Malaysia's coastal resorts, and compares the problems of unplanned and uncontrolled growth with those associated with planned, integrated resorts. Finally, Chapter 10 (Gill & Welk) focuses on the West coast of Canada, highlighting how engagement with the tourism industry and the drive to create a new tourist space has led to commodification of the natural heritage.

Featured within each of these three chapters is the occurrence of tourism-related social and religious tension. King (Chapter 8) details instances of community resistance to a number of integrated coastal resort developments along the South coast of Queensland and New South Wales. Furthermore, Henderson (Chapter 9) discusses the growing tension between Islam and tourism in Malaysia, played out within the policy-making arena, and notes that increased Islamic Revivalism and radicalism may undermine the demand for domestic and international tourism. In Chapter 10 Gill and Welk highlight social contestation to tourism development in Tofino, Canada as its economy evolves from being primarily production-oriented to one of consumption. The occurrence of tension and conflict is of course not an uncommon consequence of tourism, having been captured in many models of destination evolution, perhaps the most well known being Butler's Tourist Area Life-Cycle (1980) and Doxey's Irridex (1975). Social and religious conflict within tourist destinations is not a new phenomenon but is a problem especially associated with the pleasure periphery (Shaw & Williams, 2004), as tourism development often occurs in countries that are culturally dissimilar to those of international tourists. Much has also been written within the tourism literature on the most effective ways in which to manage tourism's negative impacts (e.g. Mason, 2003; Wall & Mathieson, 2006), and of the benefits of stakeholder assessment, community involvement, participation and collaboration in the tourism development and planning process (e.g. Aas *et al.*, 2005; Bramwell & Lane, 2000; Bramwell & Sharman 1999; de Araujo & Bramwell, 1999; Jamal & Getz, 1995; Reed, 1999; Timothy, 1998).

However, an over-riding focus of this literature is the avoidance or amelioration of conflict, which has usually occurred through the overuse and exploitation of a destination's resources. In such cases, visitor management strategies are designed and implemented, albeit with varying degrees of local community involvement and consensus. But in terms of religious tension, its management is much more complex as its origins stem from the development of tourism *per se*, rather than from a particular consequence of tourism that has occurred at a destination. For some, tourism symbolises 'the West', the antithesis of 'the East', as it is defined by characteristics such as capitalism, decadence, corporate tyranny, injustice and oppression, which are repugnant to fundamentalist interpretations of Islam (Atran, 2006; Desker, 2003). Increasingly coastal tourism resorts have been subject to religion-fuelled terrorist acts. Examples of such terrorism include the bombings in Bali's resort of Kuta in 2002 when almost 200 foreign tourists and local people were killed, and more recently, at Egypt's coastal resorts of Taba in 2004 and Sharm el-Sheikh in July 2005. Given the increased susceptibility of coastal resorts to terrorism, how then should religious tension and conflict be tackled, particularly when it is potentially directed at the whole of the tourism industry and all tourists irrespective of nationality and origin? How is the safety and security of those involved with the industry and of those who visit and reside in coastal resorts to be maintained?

There is an increasing body of literature that highlights the consequences of terrorist acts for tourist destinations generally (Coshall, 2003; Feichtinger *et al.*, 2001; Neumayer, 2004; Pizam & Smith, 2000; Sönmez, 1998; Wahab, 1995), which also examines the impact of terrorism on the tourism industry in Bali (e.g. Henderson, 2003c; Hollinshead, 2003; Lewis & Lewis, 2004; Ramakrishna & Tan, 2003) and Egypt specifically (e.g. Aziz, 1995; Wahab, 1996), and focuses on managing the effects of terrorism in resort destinations, including those that have been directly targeted (Bierman, 2002; Henderson, 2003c; Hitchcock & Darma Putra, 2005; Sönmez *et al.*, 1999; Tarlow, 2000). Despite such considerable work, little is known about the effectiveness of strategies that seek to address religious tension and focus on the management of the effects of terrorism in coastal resorts. In addition, with the exception of a few studies (e.g. Dolnicar, 2005), even less is known about the most effective means to tackle tourist fears of travelling to those coastal resorts that are directly and indirectly affected by terrorism, and of the success of such strategies. Furthermore, previous research has focused exclusively on the tourist, and neglects to consider how terrorism affects those who live, and are involved with tourism, within the coastal resorts targeted by terrorists. Given the continued expansion of tourism within the pleasure periphery, combined with the potential for an increase of religious motivated terror missions, there is clearly much scope for further investigation of such issues.

'Coastal Resort Structures: Variation versus Standardisation' comprises the fourth theme of this book, which explores the global diversity of coastal resorts and the implications for the resort product. Chapter 11 (Preston-Whyte and Oelofse) provides a spatial interpretation of coastal resort development in South Africa, with an examination of the drivers behind the development of different forms of resorts. In contrast, Chapter 12 (Weaver) utilises Dependency Theory to examine the structural characteristics of resorts in Southern Carolina and Antigua, whilst Chapter 13 (Agarwal and Shaw) explores the tensions created by the coexistence of mass tourism and eco-tourism resorts within the context of Mexico.

An emerging issue within these chapters, as well as those chapters in the preceding section, concerns the implications of new tourist spaces for tourism destinations. As these contributions demonstrate, coastal resorts vary in form and cater for an increasingly fragmented market divided into a variety of niches, each with their own clientele and associated impacts. Mass tourism holidays to coastal resorts may encompass cleverly packaged and marketed alternative forms of tourism, as Agarwal and Shaw (Chapter 13) demonstrate. It has diversified into multiple trips of varying duration, a wide variety of active and passive activities are now undertaken in a range of environmental settings, and inevitably mass tourism has diverse and sometimes dire consequences for tourism destinations. According to Gotham (2002: 1739), many of these new tourist spaces 'are sites of inequality and struggle'. This contention is reinforced by Jayne (2000: 20), who argues that they are 'shrouded by discourses and issues of enclosure'. As tourism continues to expand, Wall and Mathieson (2006) state that questions concerning associated social, economic and cultural effects will continue to become more pressing.

Although there is a wealth of literature on the impacts of tourism on destinations, many studies are inherently flawed as they are backward-looking and examine the consequences of tourism after they have occurred. In addition, according to Wall and Mathieson (2006: 63) 'there is often inadequate specification of the types of tourism which are involved and of the characteristics of the community in which the impacts occur'. Furthermore, these authors state that many studies fail to specify details of the precise nature of tourists – their numbers, distribution, activities and other characteristics, as well as the settings in which tourism takes place. Thus many questions remain unanswered such as: What are the costs and benefits of tourism development for the economy, society and the environment of coastal resorts? To what extent is the local community within coastal resorts becoming marginalised? Who is responsible for tackling these consequences? To what extent is the local community of coastal resorts able to mediate change? Therefore, understanding the consequences of change whilst it is occurring is crucial to the successful planning and management of coastal resorts.

State intervention in terms of the planning and development of coastal resorts comprises the fifth and final theme addressed by this book. This demonstrates how the nature and extent of state intervention in tourism planning and management varies greatly between coastal resorts globally. Thus, Chapter 14 (Cohen-Hattab and Shoval) provides some explanations for this variation and considers the implications of state intervention for coastal resort planning, development and management in Israel and Egypt. This theme is then developed further in Chapter 15 (Yüksel and Yüksel), which explores the influence of clientelism on the development and management of the Turkish resort of Kusadasi.

Both chapters allude to the failure of the state to effectively plan and manage coastal resort development, an issue that features also in Chapter 4 (Agarwal). Shoval and Cohen-Hattab (Chapter 14), for example, discuss how the absence of planning and supervision has contributed to intensive coastal resort development and subsequent environmental damage. Whilst recognising the difficulties of operating in an unstable political climate, combined with the constant threat of terrorism, they also state that if coastal tourism development continues unchecked, it is likely to have disastrous consequences for the future of Egypt's and Israel's Red Sea resorts. Yüksel and Yüksel (Chapter 15) explore government failure in more detail and contend that the decisions of state institutions are perceived by Kusadasi's local community to be characterised by bribery and corruption. As a consequence, they argue that social networks play an important role in coastal resort development.

Traditionally, most investigations of government involvement in tourism planning and development have focused on 'one visible institution anchored in a single location, situation or site' (Philo & Parr, 2000: 514). An example of such a study is Charlton and Essex's (1996) examination of local authority involvement with tourism in England and Wales. According to Pearce (1997), however, state intervention often transcends the wider environment via exchanges and social relations. Thus, in order to understand the nature and effectiveness of government involvement in coastal resort planning and management, it is important not to view state institutions as a backdrop within which to set the study of the dynamics of tourism development, but to focus on unravelling the complex networks of social relations between individual actors. It is in this respect that coastal tourism research may benefit from the 'institutional turn', an approach derived from the 'New Economic Geography', to examine institutions, their governance and the manner in which they steer economic practices and relations (Amin & Thrift, 1994; MacLeod & Goodwin, 1999; Wood & Valler, 2001). With this in mind, it is perhaps then more appropriate to frame future research of this issue within 'a spidery network of dispersed intentions, knowledge, resources and powers' (Philo & Parr, 2000: 514).

Future Management Issues

This chapter so far has attempted to highlight some important issues that have emerged from all of the book's contributions. What becomes clear from this discussion is that the experiences of coastal resorts globally are extremely diverse. Managing and sustaining tourism is clearly a complex task and one that is likely to become ever more difficult in the future in view of increasing market competition, the changing nature of tourism and the uncertainty caused by the threat of terrorism. Given these challenges, the final part of this chapter attempts to place such issues into a wider management context. Therefore, in order to remain competitive and to keep abreast of changing consumer trends, we discuss the increasing importance of innovation, knowledge transfer and management. In addition, conflict resolution is detailed as a means to curb social and/or religious tension and the uncertainty posed by terrorism, along with highlighting the value of adopting a post-disciplinary perspective to the study of coastal resorts.

Innovation and knowledge transfer and management

As tourism is a dynamic industry, coastal resorts will only remain competitive if they adjust to new customer demands and to new product and service developments initiated by their competitors. Innovation is therefore crucial to their future success and is a term that is used to refer to the implementation of new or significantly improved services, service production or delivery methods (OECD, 1997). In this context it should be recognised that innovations can be either format driven or process driven, as detailed by studies of the retail sector (Shaw & Alexander, 2006). Furthermore, innovations of such types lead to what Schumpeter (1939, 1947) termed innovative or 'disruptive' competition. This, he claimed, is the competition that matters as it introduces new forms of organisation as opposed to 'repetitive' or normal competition, which describes the situation of similar organisations competing with each other (see Bliss, 1960). Within the tourism industry, due to the co-terminality of consumption and production, innovation often focuses on service individualisation by adapting the service provided, to meet customer requirements (Orfila-Sintes *et al*., 2005). Often such innovation involves conveying a wealth of information and must be supported by information and communications technologies (Buhalis, 1998). This is because information technologies are required: firstly, to reach potential customers with the kind of information that enhances their understanding of the service purchased; secondly, to reach the largest share of demand; and thirdly, to obtain and process the information in order to improve business performance (Orfila-Sintes *et al.*, 2005).

The challenge to remain competitive however is not just about the implementation of new developments and services as the generation and use of knowledge to feed innovation is critical for the competitiveness of both tourism destinations and enterprises (Faulkner *et al.*, 1994; Hjalager, 2002). Knowledge management may therefore be used as a competitive tool, as, according to Cooper (2006: 58), 'it addresses the critical issues of organisational adaptation, survival and competitiveness in the face of increasing discontinuous environmental change'. It involves identifying relevant knowledge, capturing it, transferring and sharing it, so that organisations are able to gain competitive advantage by optimising flows and by managing them more effectively (Bahra, 2001). Thus, drawing on Davidson and Voss's (2002: 32) work, Cooper (2006: 59) states that 'knowledge management is about applying the knowledge assets available to [a tourism] organisation to create competitive advantage'.

Research of innovation and knowledge management is sadly lacking within tourism compared with other sectors e.g. retailing (see Shaw & Alexander, 2006), which is surprising as tourist businesses and tourism destinations, including coastal resorts, are competing with each other in an increasingly aggressive way and their future sustainability is questionable (see earlier discussion). Most studies focus primarily on the hospitality sector and seek to either examine innovation in the context of the use and impact of information technologies (Buhalis, 1998; Camíson,

2000; Olsen & Connolly, 1999; Sheldon, 1983), in terms of the determinants of market competitiveness (Go *et al*., 1994; Hassan, 2000), or with regards to the effectiveness of specific competitive strategies (Claver-Cortés *et al*., 2006; Curry *et al*., 2001; Edgar *et al*., 1994; Ingram, 1996). Moreover, only Orfila-Sintes *et al*. (2005) and Claver-Cortés *et al*. (2006) examine innovative activity in the context of coastal environments, with the latter study focusing on Alicante, Spain, whilst the former focuses on the Balearics. In today's dynamic marketplace, it is vital for coastal resorts to obtain and evaluate information about the strategies and advantages developed by their competitors, and to examine their own market competitiveness. Thus, there are many opportunities to apply the philosophy and ideals behind innovation and knowledge transfer and management, to the study of coastal resorts. Of particular interest therefore, are studies that investigate the diffusion of innovation and knowledge management ideas across resorts, which assess the determinants of their market competitiveness, or which examine barriers to competitiveness.

Conflict resolution

A number of researchers suggest that tourism plays an important role in fostering international peace and facilitating understanding between countries and communities that have traditionally been hostile to each other (e.g. D'Amore, 1988; Mings, 1988; Pizam *et al*., 2002; Var *et al*., 1994; Yu, 1997). This is because 'contact between foreign visitors and local communities of diverse and even conflicting groups may provide opportunities in which perceived notions and stereo-types are broken down and ultimately replaced with mutually positive perceptions of one another' (Sönmez & Apostolopoulos, 2000: 36). Indeed, Kim and Crompton (1990: 353) state that potentially, tourism 'offers a non-threatening apolitical way of tentatively initiating closer relationships and creating an environment which could facilitate more formal political negotiations'.

Despite these claims, there is also a considerable body of literature that disputes the notion that tourism may be a positive force that is able to reduce tension and conflict (e.g. Kim & Crompton, 1990; Kim & Prideaux, 2003; Milman *et al*., 1990). This is perhaps because 'tourism by itself, neither leads to automatic prejudice reduction, nor facilitates improvements in social relationships ... [it] simply provides the opportunity for social contact to occur' (Anastasopoulos, 1992: 641). Conflicts can emerge in any society when disagreements, differences, annoyances, competition or inequities threaten something of importance to one or more groups or individuals. Usually, according to D'Amore (1988: 37), 'It is the separation from other nations and cultures that creates the psychological distance and mind set conducive to nurturing fears and suspicions and contributes subsequently to the potential for destructive conflict'. The development of tourism within countries and communities whose culture and religion are very different to that of the tourists may also generate conflict as Chapters 8 (King), 9 (Henderson) and 10 (Gill and Welk) have demonstrated. Moreover, as many studies have shown, such conflict may even occur despite community participation and collaboration in decision and policy-making (e.g. Bramwell & Sharman, 1999).

Thus, dialogue amongst cultures is not always sufficient to ameliorate conflict. More recently, conflict resolution or management has been heralded as a means through which to seek lasting resolutions that create a balance among the differing parties, the situation and the consequences of actions to be taken. It works on the basis that it acknowledges that conflict is part of any human society or activity, and conflict resolution (or conflict management) seeks to convert conflicting interests into constructive co-operation. If properly managed, conflicts can be catalysts to achieving more sustainable means of development through consensus building and joint action. When viewed as a process, conflict management includes: (1) the holding of preliminary conversations to build trust and understanding; (2) deepening these conversations to identify and define the issues; (3) turning the issues inside-out, upside-down, redefining and reframing them to better reflect reality from different perspectives; (4) engaging in mutual problem solving; (5) agreeing on actions that help all parties meet their needs and preserve their dignity; and (6) following up to assure the results that were expected have been achieved.

To date, conflict resolution has been used extensively within the international relations and business management arenas, as a means to resolve conflict occurring within and between countries in the case of the former, and within the work-place with regards to the latter. Consequently, there has been virtually no application of the construct to tourism, and little is known about its value to resolving religious or culture-based conflicts which occur in tourism destinations, including coastal resorts. To what extent is conflict resolution able to reduce the religious tension which Henderson (Chapter 9) documents as occurring in Malaysia's coastal resorts? Which conflict resolution mechanisms are the most effective in bringing about win–win solutions and encouraging peaceful coexistence within contemporary political, social and economic realities? Who should act as facilitator? These questions remain unanswered and require urgent in-depth study if coastal resorts are to be more effectively planned and managed.

Post-disciplinary perspectives

Many of this book's contributions highlight the need to break free from tourism-centric thinking and a narrow disciplinary focus, and instead either call for the adoption of holistic frameworks to the study of coastal resorts, or couch their studies in broader disciplinary perspectives. For example, Gale (Chapter 2) attempts to demonstrate how critical realism can enhance understanding of the causes and consequences of decline, whilst Agarwal (Chapter 4) highlights how use of the 'institution turn', an ideal derived from the 'New Economic Geography', may aid understanding of coastal resort restructuring. In addition, Bramwell (Chapter 5) argues for a more holistic integrative framework to be adopted for the study of the sustainability of coastal resorts, whilst Sharpley (Chapter 7) discusses how a political economy approach may aid the planning and management of tourism growth in mass tourism coastal resorts.

Clearly, the issues affecting mass tourism coastal resorts, globally, are wide-ranging and consequently, their future planning, development and management must be predicated on research that follows holistic, critical, innovative and radical lines of enquiry. This contention is not new, and thus this book adds to the growing number of publications that call for tourism studies to shift to multi-, trans- and most recently, post-disciplinary ways of thinking. For example, Shaw and Williams (2004) call for tourism studies to be more critical and diverse and argue that the contribution of different strands of research should be recognised. Furthermore, Coles *et al*. (2005) discuss the merits of a post-disciplinary approach, with the latter defined as 'when scholars forget about disciplines and whether ideas can be identified with any particular one; they identify with learning rather than with disciplines' (Sayer, 1999: 5). These views are also echoed by Botterill (2001), Farrell and Twining-Ward (2004), Phillimore and Goodson (2004) and Tribe (2006), with Smith (1998: 311) perhaps most eloquently arguing that post-disciplinarity, 'requires even more flexible and creative approaches to investigating and defining objects than inter-disciplinary approaches, by further stripping away the inhibitions associated with disciplinary parochialism'. Thus, if coastal resort research is to effectively contribute to debates surrounding future management, it is essential that it breaks free from disciplinary boundaries.

Conclusion

This book has attempted to address a gap in the current literature by providing a set of theoretically connected worldwide case studies that examine aspects of coastal resort planning, development and management. In particular, it incorporates a detailed analysis of a range of economic, sociocultural, political and environmental issues that are being experienced, to differing extents, by coastal tourism resorts that are at different stages of development. Given the wealth of coastal resort research that has been undertaken within Britain and Southern Europe, it is therefore hoped that this book provides some unique insights into some of the management issues that coastal resorts are experiencing globally. By doing so, we would argue that this book is more than a mere amalgamation of existing literature, but rather that it advances our conceptual understanding of resort evolution and change at a global level.

References

AAAS Atlas (2000) *AAAS Atlas of Population and Environment*. American Association for the Advancement of Science. Berkeley: University of California. On WWW at www.aaas.org/international. Accessed 5.6.06.

Aas, C., Ladkin, A. and Fletcher, J. (2005) Stakeholder collaboration and heritage management. *Annals of Tourism Research* 32 (1), 28–48.

Abdullah, S. (1992) Coastal erosion in Malaysia: Problems and challenges. In H.D. Tija and S.M.S. Abdullah (eds) *The Coastal Zone of Peninsular Malaysia* (pp. 80–92). Kuala Lumpur: UKM.

Adaman, F. and Carkoglu, A. (2001) Engagement in corruptive activities at local and central governments in Turkey: Perceptions of urban settlers. Paper presented to the *Poverty in the Mediterranean*, third annual conference of Euro-Mediterranean Forum of Economic Institutes, Marseille, 30–31 March 2001.

ADB (1996) *Coastal and Marine Environmental Management: Proceedings of a Workshop*. Bangkok: Asian Development Bank.

Agarwal, S. (1997a) The resort cycle and seaside tourism: An assessment of its applicability and validity. *Tourism Management* 18 (2), 65–73.

Agarwal, S. (1997b) The public sector: Planning for renewal? In G. Shaw and A.M. Williams (eds) *The Rise and Fall of British Coastal Resorts* (pp. 137–158). London: Pinter.

Agarwal, S. (1999) Restructuring and local economic development: Implications for seaside resort regeneration in Southwest Britain. *Tourism Management* 20 (4), 511–522.

Agarwal, S. (2002) Restructuring seaside tourism. The resort lifecycle. *Annals of Tourism Research* 29 (1), 25–55.

Agarwal, S. (2005) Global–local interactions in English coastal resorts: Theoretical perspectives. *Tourism Geographies* 7 (4), 351–372.

Agarwal, S. and Brunt, P. (2006) Social exclusion and English seaside resorts. *Tourism Management* 27 (4), 654–670.

Agarwal, S., Rahman, S. and Shepherd, D. (2006) *Measuring the Determinants of Relative Economic Performance of Rural Areas – A Working Paper*. Plymouth: University of Plymouth.

Aguiar, L., Tomic, P. and Trumper, R. (2005) Work hard, play hard: Selling Kelowna, BC, as year-round playground. *The Canadian Geographer* 49 (2), 123–139.

Ainul, R.H.A. (2003) *Integrating Tourism Management into Biodiversity Conservation in Marine Protected Areas.* Centre for Coastal and Marine Environment, Maritime Institute of Malaysia. On WWW at www.mima.gov.my. Accessed 23.4.05.

Akama, J. (1996) Western environmental values and nature-based tourism in Kenya. *Tourism Management* 17 (8), 567–574.

Alder, J., Hilliard, R. and Pobar, G. (2000) Integrated marine planning for the Cocos (Keeling), and isolated Australian atoll (Indian Ocean). *Coastal Management* 28 (1), 109–146.

Allen, G. and Brennan, F. (2004) *Tourism in the New South Africa: Social Responsibility and the Tourist Experience*. London: I.B. Taurus.
Amadiba Adventures (2005) On WWW at www.coastingafrica.com/Client.asp?ClientID = 304&Level = 2. Accessed 16.01.06.
Amar, P. and Associates (2005) Scoping report for proposed small craft harbour. Unpublished manuscript. Durban: Durban Point Development Company.
American Express (2005) V&A Waterfront. *The American Express Magazine: Expressions* 6–7.
Amin, A. (2002) Spatialities of globalisation. *Environment and Planning A* 34 (3), 385–399.
Amin, A. and Thrift, N. (1994) *Globalisation, Institutions and Regional Development in Europe*. Oxford: Oxford University Press.
Amin, S. (1976) *Unequal Development: An Essay on the Social Formations of Peripheral Capitalism*. New York: Monthly Review Press.
Amiran, D., Shachar, A. and Charney, J. (1995) Eilat and the Aravah settlements – a geographical study. In Y. Aviram (ed.) *Eilat: Studies in the Archaeology, History and Geography of Eilat and the Aravah* (pp. 335–367). Jerusalem: The Israel Society in cooperation with The Israel Antiquities Authority.
Anastasopoulos, P.G. (1992) Tourism and attitude change: Greek tourists visiting Turkey. *Annals of Tourism Research* 19 (4), 629–641.
Andronikou, A. (1987) *Development of Tourism in Cyprus: Harmonisation of Tourism with the Environment*. Nicosia: Cosmos.
Anon (2003) Into Spring. *Malta Independent* 7 April.
Anpudia, R. (1997) Subsecretario de promocion y formento, Secretaria de Turismo. *El Economista* 27 January.
Apostolides, P. (1995) Tourism development policy and environmental protection in Cyprus. In *Sustainable Tourism Development*, Environmental Encounters No. 32 (pp. 31–40). Strasbourg: Council of Europe.
Apostolopoulos, Y., Loukissas, P. and Leontidou, L. (eds) (2001) *Mediterranean Tourism: Facets of Socio-Economic Development and Cultural Change*. London: Routledge.
Aranzadi, C. (1992) Plan marco de competitividad del turismo Español. *Estudios Turísticos* 115, 3–10.
Archer, M. (1998) Realism in the social sciences. In M. Archer, R. Bhaskar, A. Collier, T. Lawson and A. Norrie (eds) *Critical Realism: Essential Readings* (pp. 189–205). London: Routledge.
Ashley, C. and Roe, D. (2002) Making tourism work for the poor: Strategies and challenges in southern Africa. *Development Southern Africa* 19, 61–82.
Ashworth, G. and Tunbridge, J. (2005a) Moving from blue to grey tourism: Reinventing Malta. *Tourism Recreation Research* 30 (1), 45–54.
Ashworth, G. and Tunbridge, J. (2005b) Move out of the sun and into the past: The blue–grey transition and its implications for tourism infrastructure in Malta. *Journal of Hospitality and Tourism* 3 (1), 19–32.
Atran, S. (2006) The moral logic and growth of suicide terrorism. *The Washington Quarterly* 29 (2), 127–147.
Audit Commission (1999) *A Life's Work: Local Authorities, Economic Development and Economic Regeneration*. Abingdon: Audit Commission Publications.
Auyero, J. (1999) From the client's point(s) of view: How poor people perceive and evaluate political clientelism. *Theory and Society* 28, 297–334.
Ayala, H. (1991) Resort hotel landscape, as an international mega-trend. *Annals of Tourism Research* 18 (4), 568–587.

Ayers, R. (2000) Tourism as a passport to development in small states: The case of Cyprus. *International Journal of Social Economics* 27 (2), 114–133.
Azaryahu, M. (2005) The beach at the end of the world: Eilat in Israeli popular culture. *Social and Cultural Geography* 6 (1), 117–133.
Aziz, H. (1995) Understanding attacks on tourists in Egypt. *Tourism Management* 16 (2), 91–95.
Bagguley, P., Mark-Lawson, J., Shapiro, D., Urry, J., Walby, S. and Warde, A. (1990) *Restructuring Place, Class and Gender*. London: Sage.
Bahra, N. (2001) *Competitive Knowledge Management*. Basingstoke: Palgrave.
Bailey, K.D. (1987) *Methods of Social Research* (3rd edn). New York: Free Press.
Bajaquest (2006) *History and Overview – Loreto and La Paz*. On WWW at www.bajaquest.com/loreto/l_p_history.htm. Accessed 05.06.06.
Baldwin, J. (2000) Tourism development, wetland degradation and beach erosion in Antigua, West Indies. *Tourism Geographies* 2 (2), 193–218.
Baldwin, J. (2005) The contested beach: Resistance and resort development in Antigua, West Indies. In C. Cartier and A. Lew (eds) *Seductions of Place: Geographical Perspectives on Globalization and Touristed Landscapes* (pp. 222–241). London: Routledge.
Bang, N.D. (1971) The southern Benguela current region in February 1966. Part 2: Bythythermography and air–sea interactions. *Deep Sea Research* 18, 209–224.
Barett, J.A. (1958) The seaside resort towns of England and Wales. Unpublished Ph.D. thesis, University of London.
Barke, M. and France, L. (1996) The Costa del Sol. In M. Barke, J. Towner and M.T. Newton (eds) *Tourism in Spain: Critical Issues* (pp. 265–308). Wallingford: CAB International.
Barke, M. and Towner, J. (2004) Learning from experience? Progress towards a sustainable future for tourism in the central and eastern Andalucían littoral. In B. Bramwell (ed.) *Coastal Mass Tourism: Diversification and Sustainable Development in Southern Europe* (pp. 157–175). Clevedon: Channel View Publications.
Barke, M., Towner, J. and Newton, M.T. (1996) *Tourism in Spain. Critical Issues*. Wallingford: CAB International.
Barr, T. (1990) *No Swank Here? The Development of the Whitsundays as a Tourist Destination to the Early 1970s*. Townsville: James Cook University.
Basiron, M.N. (1995) *The Significance of the Coastal Environment to Malaysia: Economic, Environmental and Sociological Perspectives.* Centre for Coastal and Marine Environment, Maritime Institute of Malaysia. On WWW at www.mima.gov.my. Accessed 23.4.05.
Basiron, M.N. (1997) *Marine Tourism Industry: Trends and Prospects*. Centre for Coastal and Marine Environment, Maritime Institute of Malaysia. On WWW at www.mima.gov.my. Accessed 23.4.05.
Basiron, M.N. (2004) *Development of Marina in Tioman: Food For Our Thoughts.* Centre for Coastal and Marine Environment, Maritime Institute of Malaysia. On WWW at www.mima.gov.my. Accessed 23.4.05.
Bastin, R. (1984) Small island tourism: Development or dependency? *Development Policy Review* 2 (1), 79–90.
Baud-Bovy, M. and Lawson, F. (1998) *Tourism and Recreation: Handbook of Planning and Design* (2nd edn). Oxford: Architectural Press.
Baum, T. (1998) Taking the exit route: extending the tourism area life-cycle model. *Current Issues in Tourism* 1, 167–75.
Baum, T. (2006) Revisiting the TALC: Is there an off-ramp? In R.W. Butler (ed.) *The Tourism Area Life Cycle* (Vol. 2) (pp. 219–233). Clevedon: Channel View Publications.

BBC (2005) Malaysia's consumer culture. *Assignment*. BBC World Service broadcast, 7 April.

Beatty, C. and Fothergill, S. (2003) *The Seaside Economy: Final Report of the Seaside Towns Project*. Sheffield: Centre for Regional Economic and Social Research, Sheffield Hallam University.

Beatty, C. and Fothergill, S. (2004) Economic change and the labour market in Britain's seaside towns. *Regional Studies* 38 (5), 459–478.

Beck, U. (2000) *What is Globalisation?* Cambridge: Polity Press.

Beckford, G.L. (1972) *Persistent Poverty: Underdevelopment in Plantation Economies of the Third World*. New York: Oxford University Press.

Beeton, S. (2001) Smiling for the camera: the influence of film audiences on a budget tourism destination. *Tourism, Culture and Communication* 3 (3), 15–25.

Bennett, M., King, B. and Milner, L. (2004) The health resort sector in Australia: A positioning study. *Journal of Vacation Marketing* 10 (2), 122–137.

Bernama News (2005) Malaysia targets 16.7 million arrivals this year. *Bernama Daily Malaysian News* 4 February.

Berry, T. (2006) The predictive potential of the TALC model. In R.W. Butler (ed.) *The Tourist Area Life Cycle. Vol. 2: Conceptual and Theoretical Issues* (pp. 254–279). Clevedon: Channel View.

Best, A. (2005) What is driving mountain valley? Ruminations on second homes and other economic drivers. *Mountain Town News* (pp. 1–7) October 14th. Colorado: Arvada.

Bhaskar, R. (1978) *A Realist Theory of Science*. Brighton: Harvester.

Bhaskar, R. (1979) *The Possibility of Naturalism*. Hemel Hempstead: Harvester Wheatsheaf.

Bianchi, R. (2004) Tourism restructuring and the politics of sustainability: A critical view from the European periphery (The Canary Islands). *Journal of Sustainable Tourism* 12 (6), 495–529.

Bierman, D. (2002) *Restoring Tourism Destinations in Crisis: A Strategic Marketing Approach*. Wallingford: CAB.

Bird, B. (1989) *Langkawi: From Mahsuri to Mahatir. Tourism for Whom?* Kuala Lumpur: Insan.

Blamey. R. (1995) *The Nature of Ecotourism*. Occasional Paper No. 21. Canberra: Bureau of Tourism Research, Commonwealth of Australia.

Blázquez Salom, M. (2001) Auditorías ambientales de destinos turísticos. Diagnosis territorial para el desarrollo de Agendas 21 locales. *Cuadernos de Turismo* 8, 39–59.

Bliss, P. (1960) Schumpeter, the "big disturbance" and retailing. *Social Forces* 39, 72–76.

Boissevain, J. (1996) "But we live here!": Perspectives on cultural tourism in Malta. In L. Briguglio, R. Butler, D. Harrison and W. Filho (eds) *Sustainable Tourism in Islands and Small States: Case Studies* (pp. 220–240). London: Pinter.

Boissevain, J. and Theuma, N. (1998) Contested space. Planners, tourists, developers and environmentalists in Malta. In S. Abram and J. Waldren (eds) *Anthropological Perspectives on Local Development* (pp. 96–119). London: Routledge.

Booth, H. (2005) Deep blue sea. *South African Garden and Home* December, 140–143.

Bosselman, F., Peterson, C. and McCarthy, C. (1999) *Managing Tourism Growth: Issues and Applications*. Washington, DC: Island Press.

Botterill, D. (2001) The epistemology of a set of tourism studies. *Leisure Studies* 20 (3), 199–214.
Botterill, D. (2003) An autoethnographic narrative on tourism research epistemologies. *Society and Leisure* 26 (1), 97–110.
Bowermaster, J. (1994) Can ecotourism save the planet? *Condé Nast Traveller* December, 134–143, 156–162.
Bramwell, B. (1990) Local tourism initiatives. *Tourism Management* 11 (2), 176–177.
Bramwell, B. (2003a) Maltese responses to tourism. *Annals of Tourism Research* 30 (3), 581–605.
Bramwell, B. (2003b) Contested discourses around policies for tourism and the environment in Malta. Paper presented at the *ATLAS International Conference: Visions of Sustainability*, Escola Superior de Hotelaria e Turismo de Estoril, Estoril, Portugal, 14–16 November.
Bramwell, B. (ed.) (2004a) *Coastal Mass Tourism. Diversification and Sustainable Development in Southern Europe*. Clevedon: Channel View Publications.
Bramwell, B. (2004b) The policy context for tourism and sustainability in Southern Europe's coastal regions. In B. Bramwell (ed.) *Coastal Mass Tourism. Diversification and Sustainable Development in Southern Europe* (pp. 32–47). Clevedon: Channel View Publications.
Bramwell, B. (2004c) Mass tourism, diversification and sustainability in southern Europe's coastal regions. In B. Bramwell (ed.) *Coastal Mass Tourism: Diversification and Sustainable Development in Southern Europe* (pp. 1–31). Clevedon: Channel View Publications.
Bramwell, B. and Broom, G. (1989) Tourism Development Action Programmes: An approach to local tourism initiatives. *Insights*. London: English Tourist Board.
Bramwell, B. and Lane, B. (2000) (eds) *Tourism Collaboration and Partnerships. Politics, Practice and Sustainability*. Clevedon: Channel View Publications.
Bramwell, B. and Lane, B. (2005) Sustainable tourism research and the importance of societal and social science trends. *Journal of Sustainable Tourism* 13 (1), 1–3.
Bramwell, B. and Meyer, D. (2007) Power and tourism policy networks in transition. *Annals of Tourism Research* 34 (3), 766–788.
Bramwell, B. and Pomfret, G. (2007) Planning for lake and lake shore tourism: Complexity, coordination and adaptation. *Anatolia: An International Journal of Tourism and Hospitality Research* 18 (1) in press.
Bramwell, B. and Sharman, A. (1999) Collaboration in local tourism policy-making. *Annals of Tourism Research* 26 (2), 392–415.
Breener, N. (1999) Globalisation as reterritorialisation: the re-scaling of urban governance in the European Union. *Urban Studies* 36 (3), 431–451.
Brenner, C. and Aguilar, A.G. (2002) Luxury tourism and regional economic development in Mexico. *The Professional Geographer* 54 (4), 500–520.
Briassoulis, H. (2003) Crete: Endowed by nature, privileged by geography, threatened by tourism? *Journal of Sustainable Tourism* 11 (3), 97–115.
Briguglio, L. and Briguglio, M. (1996) Sustainable tourism in the Maltese islands. In L. Briguglio, R. Butler, D. Harrison and W. Filho (eds) *Sustainable Tourism in Islands and Small States. Case Studies* (pp. 162–179). London: Pinter.
Briguglio, L., Archer, B., Jafari, J. and Wall, G. (eds) (1996) *Sustainable Tourism in Islands and Small States: Issues and Policies*. London: Pinter.
British Resorts and Destinations Association (2006) Facts about UK domestic tourism. On WWW at www.britishresorts.co.uk/static/facts.asp. Accessed 5.06.

British Resorts Association (1989) *Perspectives on the Future of Resorts*. Place of publication unknown: British Resorts Association.
British Resorts Association (c.2000) *UK Seaside Resorts – Behind the Façade*. Southport: British Resorts Association.
British Tourist Authority (1976) *British National Travel Survey*. London: British Tourist Authority.
Britton, S.G. (1982) The political economy of tourism in the Third World. *Annals of Tourism Research* 9 (3), 331–358.
Brooke, B. (2005) FONATUR. *The Force Behind Mexican Tourism*. On WWW at www.therealmexico.com/fonatur.htm. Accessed 23.6.06.
Brookes, R. (1989) *Managing and Enabling Authority*. Harlow: Longman.
Brougham, J.E. and Butler, R.W. (1972) The applicability of the asymptotic curve to the forecasting of tourism development. Paper presented to the Research Workshop, Travel Research Association 4th Annual Conference, Quebec, July 1972.
Brown, F. (1998) *Tourism Reassessed. Blight or Blessing?* Oxford: Butterworth Heinemann.
Brunet Estarellas, P.J., Almeida García, F., Coll López, M. and Monteserín Abella, O. (2005) Los Planes de Excelencia y Dinanización Turística (PEDT), un instrumento de cooperación a favor del desarrollo turístico. *Boletín de la Asociación de Geógrafos Españoles* 39, 201–226.
Buchanan, J. (1968) An economist's approach to scientific politics. In M. Parsons (ed.) *Perspectives in the Study of Places* (pp. 77–88). Chicago: Rand-McNally.
Buhalis, D. (1998) Strategic use of information technologies in the tourism industry. *Tourism Management* 19 (5), 409–421.
Buhalis, D. (2003) *eTourism, Information Technology for Strategic Tourism Management*. Harlow: Prentice Hall.
Bui, T.T. (2000) Tourism dynamics and sustainable tourism development: Principles and implications in Southeast Asia. Unpublished PhD dissertation, Nanyang Technological University, Singapore.
Burford, T. (1997) *Tourism vs. Ecotourism in Mexico*. On WWW at www.planeta.com/planeta/97/0297burford.html. Accessed 16.11.05.
Burns, P. (1999) Paradoxes in planning tourism elitism or brutalism? *Annals of Tourism Research* 26 (2), 329–348.
Butler, R.W. (1980) The concept of the tourism area cycle of evolution: Implications for management of resources. *Canadian Geographer* 24 (1), 5–12.
Butler, R.W. (2004) The tourism area life cycle in the twenty-first century. In A.A. Lew, C.M. Hall and A.M. Williams (eds) *A Companion to Tourism* (pp. 159–169). Oxford: Blackwell.
Butler, R.W (ed.) (2005a) *The Tourism Area Life Cycle Volume 1: Application and Modifications*. Clevedon: Channel View Publications.
Butler, R.W. (2005b) *The Tourism Area Life Cycle: Volume 2: Conceptual and Theoretical Issues*. Clevedon: Channel View Publications.
Cabildo de Tenerife (1995) *Estadísticas de Turismo Receptivo 1975–1994*. La Laguna, Tenerife: Patronato de Turismo.
Cabo San Lucas Villas (2006) *History of Cabo San Lucas – Los Cabos, Mexico*. On WWW at www.cabosanlucasvillas.net/history. Accessed 5.6.06.
Camíson, C. (2000) Strategic attitudes and information technologies in the hospitality business: An empirical analysis. *International Journal of Hospitality Management* 19 (2), 125–193.

Campbell, A.J. and Verbeke, A. (1994) The globalisation of service multinationals. *Long Range Planning* 27 (2), 95–102.
Campillo-Besses, X., Priestley, G.K. and Romagosa, F. (2004) Using EMAS and Local Agenda 21 as tools towards sustainability: The case of a Catalan coastal resort. In B. Bramwell (ed.) *Coastal Mass Tourism: Diversification and Sustainable Development in Southern Europe* (pp. 220–248). Clevedon: Channel View Publications.
Cancún Convention and Visitor Bureau (2005) *Cancún- History*. On WWW at http://www.cancun.info/ing/informacion/detalle.jsp?oid = 1166485947195&key = 36197. Accessed 3.6.07.
Cantú, J.C. (2001) *X'Cacel Project Suspended by Environment Ministry*. On WWW at www.turtles.org/xcacel.htm, Accessed 5.6.06.
Cape Times (2005) *Property Times* 28 December, 1–28.
Careless, J.M.S. (1954) Frontierism, metropolitanism and Canadian history. *Canadian Historical Review* 35 (1), 1–21.
Carkoglu, A. (2000) Paper presented to *The Impact of Transition Upon the Poor in the Mediterranean Region*, first annual conference of Euro-Mediterranean Forum of Economic Institutes, Istanbul, 17–18 February 2000.
Carruthers, D., Backus, E., Mertens, M. and Lackey, L. (1997) The lay of the landscape: Mapping the scientific panel's watershed-based recommendations. In Ecotrust Canada (ed.) *Seeing the Ocean Through the Trees: A Conservation-based Development Strategy for Clayoquot Sound* (pp. 32–41). Vancouver: Ecotrust Canada.
Castells, M. (1989) *The Information City*. Oxford: Blackwell.
Cater, E. and Lowman, G. (1994) *Ecotourism: A Sustainable Option?* Chichester: John Wiley and Sons.
Cato, N. (1989) *The Noosa Story. A Story in Unplanned Development* (3rd edn). Milton, NSW: Jacaranda Press.
CBC Radio (1970) Destination Vancouver, draft dodgers head North. *CBC Radio Program: Rule and Revolution* 16 December.
CEHAT (2005) Presidential Inaugural address to the Spanish Confederation of Hotels and Tourist Accommodation, April. Spain.
Chang, T.C. (1999) Local uniqueness in the global village: heritage tourism in Singapore. *The Professional Geographer* 51 (1), 91–103.
Chapman, D. and Cassar, G. (2004) Valletta. *Cities* 21 (5), 451–463.
Charlton, C. and Essex, S. (1996) The involvement of district councils in England and Wales. *Geoforum* 27 (2), 175–192.
Cheshire, P. and Gordon, I. (1996) Territorial competition and the predictability of collective (in)action. *International Journal of Urban and Regional Research* 20 (2), 383–399.
Cilento, R.W. (1923) *Climatic Conditions in North Queensland as they Affect the Health and Virility of the People*. Brisbane: Queensland Government Printer.
City of Cape Town (2003) *Coastal Zone Management Strategy. Integrated Metropolitan Environmental Policy*. Cape Town: City of Cape Town.
Civil Aviation Authority (2005) *Travel and Tourism Market Review*. London: Civil Aviation Authority.
Clancy, M. (1995) Exporting paradise: State, market and the development of the Mexican tourism industry. Paper presented to the *Latin American Studies Association*. Washington, D.C., 28–30 September.
Clancy, M. (1998) Tourism and development: Evidence from Mexico. *Annals of Tourism Research* 26 (1), 1–20.

Clancy, M. (2001) *Exporting Paradise. Tourism and Development in Mexico*. London: Pergamon.
Claver-Cortés, E., Molina-Azorín, J.F. and Pereira-Moliner, J.P. (2006) Strategic groups in the hospitality industry: Inter-group and intra-group performance differences in Alicante, Spain. *Tourism Management* 27 (6), 1101–1116.
Clegg, A. and Essex, S. (2000) Restructuring in tourism: The accommodation sector in a major British coastal resort. *International Journal of Tourism Research* 2 (2), 77–95.
Clements, M. and Giorgio, A (1998) The impact of political instability on a fragile tourism product. *Tourism Management* 19 (3), 283–288.
Cleverdon, R. (2000) Malta. *Travel and Tourism Intelligence Country Reports* 2, 85–101.
Cleverdon, R. (ed.) (2001) Special issue: Fair trade in tourism – applications and experience. *International Journal of Tourism Research* 3, 347–423.
Coast Realty Group (2007) *Ucluelet/Tofino.* On WWW at www.coastrealty.com/UclueletTofino/. Accessed 228.06.07.
Coccossis, H. (1996) Tourism and sustainability: Perspectives and implications. In G.K. Priestley, J.A. Edwards and H. Coccossis (eds) *Sustainable Tourism? European Experiences* (pp. 1–21). Wallingford: CAB International.
Coccossis, H. and Mexa, A. (eds) (2004) *The Challenge of Tourism Carrying Capacity Assessment. Theory and Practice*. Aldershot: Ashgate.
Coccossis, H. and Nijkamp, P. (eds) (1998) *Sustainable Tourism Development*. Aldershot: Ashgate Publishing.
Coccossis, H. and Parpairis, A. (1996) Tourism and carrying capacity in coastal areas: Mykonos, Greece. In G. Priestley, J.A. Edwards and H. Coccossis (eds) *Sustainable Tourism? European Experiences* (pp. 153–175). Wallingford: CAB International.
Cohen-Hattab, K. (2001) The development of tourism infrastructure in Jerusalem during the British rule, 1917–48. Unpublished PhD thesis. The Hebrew University of Jerusalem, Jerusalem.
Cohen-Hattab, K. and Katz, Y. (2001) The attraction of Palestine: Tourism in the years 1850–1948. *Journal of Historical Geography* 27 (2), 178–195.
Cohen-Hattab, K. and Shoval, N. (2004a) The decline of Israel's Mediterranean resorts: Life-cycle changes versus national tourism master planning. *Tourism Geographies* 6 (1), 59–78.
Cohen-Hattab, K and Shoval, N. (2004b) The tourism life-cycle model: The rise and decline of Netanya. *Horizons in Geography* 62, 19–32 (in Hebrew).
Coles, T.E. and Shaw, G. (2006) Tourism property and the management of change in coastal resorts: Perspectives from southwest England. *Current Issues in Tourism* 9 (1), 46–68.
Coles, T., Hall, M. and Duval, D. (2005) Mobilizing tourism: A post-disciplinary critique. *Tourism Recreation Research* 30 (2), 31–41.
Collier, A. (1994) *Critical Realism: An Introduction to Roy Bhaskar's Philosophy*. London: Verso.
Condé Nast (2004) *Readers Travel Awards.* On WWW at http://www.cntraveller.com/ReadersAwards/2004/Cities/. Accessed 3.6.07.
Conlin, M. and Baum, T. (1995) *Island Tourism: Management Principles and Practice*. Chichester: John Wiley & Sons.
Conway, D. (1997) Pursuing an appropriate development model for Caribbean small islands: can past experience help subvert the Neo-Liberal agenda? Paper presented in the ECO17 session at the *Neoliberal Theory and Practice in Latin*

America and the Caribbean conference, Latin American Studies Association, XX International Congress, Guadalajara, Mexico, 17–19 April 1997.

Cooke, P. (1987) The changing urban and regional systems in the UK. *Regional Studies* 20, 243–251.

Cooke, P. (1989) *Localities*. London: Unwin Hyman.

Cooke, P. (1990) *Back to the Future*. London: Unwin Hyman.

Cooper, C. (1990) Resorts in decline – the management response. *Tourism Management* 11 (1), 63–67.

Cooper, C. (1997) Parameters and indicators of the decline of the British seaside resort. In G. Shaw and A.M. Williams (eds) *The Rise and Fall of British Coastal Resorts* (pp. 79–101). London: Cassell.

Cooper, C. (2006) Knowledge management and tourism. *Annals of Tourism Research* 33 (1), 47–64.

Cope, R. (2000) Republic of Cyprus. *Travel & Tourism Intelligence, Country Reports* 4, 3–21.

Corbin, A. (1992) *The Lure of the Sea*. Cambridge: Cambridge University Press.

Coshall, J.T. (2003) The threat of terrorism as an intervention on international travel flows. *Journal of Travel Research* 42 (1), 4–12.

Council for the Environment (1989) *A Policy for Coastal Zone Management in the Republic of South Africa – Part 1. Principles and Objectives*. Pretoria: Joan Lotter Publications.

Council for the Environment (1991) *A Policy for Coastal Zone Management in the Republic of South Africa – Part 2*. Pretoria: Academica Publications.

Courtney, P., Agarwal, S., Rahman, S., Errington, A. and Moseley, M. (2004) *Determinants of Relative Economic. Performance of Rural Areas.* London: Defra.

Crang, M. (1999) Globalisation as conceived, perceived and lived spaces. *Theory, Culture and Society* 16 (1), 167–177.

Creel, J.E., Bezauary, C.L., McCann, J., Molina Islas, C., Carranza, J., Rubinoff, P., Goddard, T., Robadue, D. and Hale, L. (1998) Participatory coastal and marine management in Quintana Roo, Mexico. Paper presented at the *International Tropical Marine Ecosystems Management Symposium*, Townsville, Australia, 23–26 November.

Cronin, L. (1990) A strategy for tourism and sustainable developments. *World Leisure and Recreation* 32 (3), 12–18.

Crouch, H.A. (2001) Managing ethnic tensions through affirmative action: The Malaysian experience. In N.J. Colletta, T.G. Lim and A. Kelles-Viitanen (eds) *Social Cohesion and Conflict Prevention in Asia: Managing Diversity through Development* (pp. 225–262). Washington: The World Bank.

CTO (1990) *Annual Report*. Nicosia: Cyprus Tourism Organisation.

CTO (2000) *Tourism Strategy 2000–2010*. Nicosia: Cyprus Tourism Organisation.

Curry, B., Davies, F., Phillips, P., Evans, M. and Moutinho, L. (2001) The Kohenen self-organisation map: an application to the study of strategic groups in the UK hotel industry. *Expert Systems* 18 (1), 19–31.

Curtis, S. (1997) Rejuvenating holiday resorts – a Spanish case study. *Travel and Tourism Analyst: Occasional Studies* 2, 77–93.

D'Amore, L. (1988) Tourism: The world peace industry. *Journal of Travel Research* 27 (1), 35–40.

Danielson, M.N. (1995) *Profits and Politics in Paradise: The Development of Hilton Head Island*. Columbia, SC: University of South Carolina Press.

Dann, G. (1998) The Pomo Promo of Tourism. *Tourism, Culture and Communication* 1 (1), 1–16.

Dardis, G.F. and Grindley, J.R. (1988) Coastal geomorphology. In B.P. Moon and G.F. Dardis (eds) *The Geomorphology of Southern Africa* (pp. 141–172). Johannesburg: Southern Book Publications.

Darling, C. (1991) *In Search of Consensus. An Evaluation of the Clayoquot Sound Development Task Force Process*. Victoria: University of Victoria Institute for Dispute Resolution.

Datzira-Masip, J. (1997) Tourism policy in Spain. *Revue de Tourisme – The Tourist Review* 1, 41–50.

Davidson, C. and Voss, P. (2002) *Knowledge Management*. Auckland: Tandem.

Davidson, J. and Spearritt, P. (2000) Tourism, post-modernism and Australia. In *Holiday Business: Tourism in Australia since 1870*. Carlton: The Miegunyah Press.

Davies, J. (2001) *Partnership and Regimes: The Politics of Urban Regeneration in the UK*. Aldershot: Ashgate.

de Albuquerque, K. (1991) Conflicting claims on the Antiguan coastal resources: The case of the McKinnons and Jolly Hill salt ponds. In N. Girvan and D. Simmons (eds) *Caribbean Ecology and Economics* (pp. 195–205). Kingston, Jamaica: Caribbean Conservation Association.

de Araujo, L. and Bramwell, B. (1999) Stakeholder assessment and collaborative tourism planning: The case of Brazil's Costa Dourada Project. *Journal of Sustainable Tourism* 7 (3&4), 356–378.

Debbage, K. and Ioannides, D. (1998) *The Economic Geography of the Tourist Industry: A Supply-Side Analysis*. London: Routledge.

DGCAC (Demarcació de Girona del Col.legi d'Arquitectes de Catalunya) (2005) *Debat Costa Brava: un Futur Sostenible*. Girona: DGCAC.

Department of Environmental Affairs and Development Planning (2004) *Rapid Review of Golf Course and Polo Field Developments: Draft Report*. Cape Town: Provincial Government of the Western Cape.

Department of Parks, Recreation and Tourism (2005) *Research Reports*. On WWW at www.discoversouthcarolina.com/agency/researchreports.asp. Accessed 25.7.05.

Department of Statistics Malaysia (2001) *Population Distribution and Basic Demographic Characteristics Report: Population and Housing Census 2000*. Press Report. 6 November.

de Sausmarez, N. (2003) Malaysia's response to the Asian financial crisis: Implications for tourism and sectoral crisis management. *Journal of Travel and Tourism Marketing* 15 (4), 217–231.

Desker, B. (2003) Islam in Southeast Asia: The challenge of radical interpretations. *Cambridge Review of International Affairs* 16 (3), 415–428.

Destan, I.(1998) Development: Consensus or conflict? *IDS Bulletin* 28 (4), 24–45.

Díaz-Varela, M. (2004) El gobierno espera un nuevo récord de turistas y de ingresos en el 2004. *La Vanguardia* 21 July.

Dicken, P. (1998) *Global Shift* (3rd edn). London: Paul Chapman Publishing Ltd.

Din, K. (1989) Islam and tourism: Patterns, issues and options. *Annals of Tourism Research* 16 (4), 542–563.

Din, K. (1997) Tourism and cultural development in Malaysia: Issues for a new agenda. In S. Yamashita, K. Din and J.S. Eades (eds) *Tourism and Cultural Development in Asia and Oceania* (pp. 104–118). Selangor: Penerbit Universiti Kebangsaan Malaysia.

Dinan, C. (2002) Sea changes. Making a difference – from strategy to implementation. Paper presented to *'Turning the Tide: Renewing the UK's Coastal Destinations'*, 9 January. London: Locum Destination Consulting.

Dolnicar, S. (2005) Understanding barriers to leisure travel: Tourist fears as a marketing basis. *Journal of Vacation Marketing* 11 (3), 197–208.

Donmez, M.(1999) Resource and responsibility allocation between central and local government. *Yerel Yonetim* 4 (6), 27–56.

Dorst, A. and Young, C. (1990) *Clayoquot: On the Wild Side*. Vancouver: Western Canada Wilderness Committee.

Doswell (1997) *Tourism: How Effective Management Makes the Difference*. Oxford: Butterworth-Heinemann.

Doxey, G. (1975) A causation theory of visitor-resident irritants. Methodology and research inferences. In *Travel and Tourism Research Association*, sixth annual proceedings (pp. 195–198). Salt Lake City: University of Utah.

Doxey, G.V. (1976) When enough's enough: The natives are restless in Old Niagara. *Heritage Canada* 2, 26–27.

Dreher, A., Kotsogiannis, C. and McCorriston, S. (2004) *Corruption Around the World: Evidence from a Structural Model.* Exeter: Department of Economics, School of Business and Economics, University of Exeter.

Dresner, S. (2002) *The Principles of Sustainability*. London: Earthscan.

Durie, A. (1994) The development of the Scottish coastal resorts in the central lowlands, c.1770–1880: From gulf stream to golf stream. *Local Historian* 24, 206–216.

Earthtrends (2005) On WWW at http://earthtrends.wri.org/pdf_library/country_profiles/coa_cou_710.pdf. Accessed 3.6.07.

EcoClub (2003) *International Ecotourism Club.* On WWW at www.ecoclub.com. Accessed 7.6.06.

Eco Tropical Resorts (2006) *Ecotourism Directory of Eco Resorts and Eco Lodges in the Tropics*. On WWW at www.eco-tropicalresorts.com. Accessed 23.6.06.

Edgar, D., Littlejohn, D. and Allardyce, M. (1994) Strategic clusters and strategic space. The case of the sort break market. *International Journal of Contemporary Hospitality Management* 6 (5), 20–26.

Eidsvik, H. (1995) Ethically, environmentally and economically sustainable tourism. In *Acts of World Conference on sustainable tourism: Tourism of the 21st century, Lanzarote 1995* (pp. 21–25). Santa Cruz de Tenerife: World Conference on Sustainable Tourism.

Egyptian Hotel Association (2005) On WWW at www.egypttourism.org/. Accessed 15.7.05.

EIU (2004) *Malaysia Country Profile 2004*. London: The Economist Intelligence Unit.

EIU (2005) *Malaysia Country Report 2005*. London: The Economist Intelligence Unit.

English House Condition Survey (2001) *English House Condition Survey: Key Facts 2001.* Wetherby: Office of the Deputy Prime Minister Publications Centre.

English Tourism Council (2001a) *Sea Changes: Creating World-Class Resorts in England*. London: English Tourism Council.

English Tourism Council (2001b) *A Time for Action: A Strategy for Sustainable Tourism in England*. London: English Tourism Council.

English Tourist Board (1991) *The Future for England's Smaller Seaside Resorts.* London: English Tourist Board.

English Tourist Board (1993) *Making the Most of the Coast.* London: English Tourist Board.

English Tourist Board (1995) *Revitalizing the Coast.* London: English Tourist Board.

Ergul, A., Tunc, B. and Yuksel, A. (2002) *Kusadasi Commercial Action Plan*. Kusadasi: Kusadasi Chamber of Commerce Publication.

Erisman, H. (1983) Tourism and cultural dependency in the West Indies. *Annals of Tourism Research* 10, 337–61.

Esposito, J. (ed.) (1999) *The Oxford History of Islam*. New York: Oxford University Press.

Essex, S.J. and Brown, G.P. (1997) The emergence of post-suburban landscapes on the north coast of New South Wales: A case study of contested space. *International Journal of Urban and Regional Research* 21 (2), 259–286.

Esteve Secall, R. (2001) Nuevo segmento emergente de turismo: los parques temáticos. *Cuadernos de Turismo* 7, 35–54.

Euromonitor (2005) *Travel and Tourism in South Africa*. On WWW at www.euromonitor.com. Accessed 16.1.06.

Euromonitor (2006) *Travel and Tourism in Mexico*. On WWW at www.euromonitor.com/Travel_and_Tourism_in_Mexico. Accessed 17.8.06.

European Commission (2000) *Towards Quality Coastal Tourism. Integrated Quality Management (IQM) of Coastal Tourist Destinations*. Brussels: European Communities.

Evans, N.G. and Stabler, M.J. (1995) A future for the package tour operator in the 21st century. *Tourism Economics* 1 (3), 245–263.

Evans, N., Campbell, D. and Stonehouse, G. (2003) *Strategic Management for Travel and Tourism*. Oxford: Butterworth-Heinemann.

Even-Zur, I. and Yovel, E. (2004) Reefs, divers and money: An assessment of the monetary worth of diving tourism in Eilat. *Horizons in Geography* 62, 5–18 (in Hebrew).

Farrell, B. and Twining-Ward, L. (2004) Reconceptualizing tourism. *Annals of Tourism Research* 31 (2), 274–295.

Farrell, B. and Twining-Ward, L. (2005) Seven steps towards sustainability: Tourism in the context of new knowledge. *Journal of Sustainable Tourism* 13 (2), 109–122.

Faulkenberry, L., Coggeshall, J., Backman, K. and Backman, S. (2000) A culture of servitude: The impact of tourism and development in the South Carolina Coast. *Human Organization* 59, 86–95.

Faulkner, B. (2002) Rejuvenating a maturing tourist destination: The case of the Gold Coast. *Current Issues in Tourism* 5 (6), 472–517.

Faulkner, B. and Russell, R. (2001) Turbulence, chaos and complexity in tourism systems: A research direction for the new millennium. In B. Faulkner, G. Moscardo and E. Laws (eds) *Tourism in the 21st Century* (pp. 328–349). London: Continuum.

Faulkner, W., Pearce, P., Shaw, R. and Weiler, B. (1994) Tourism research in Australia. In *Proceedings for the Tourism Research and Education Conference* (pp. 3–25). Brisbane: CAUTHE.

Featherstone, M. (ed.) (1990) *Global Culture, Nationalism, Globalization and Modernity*. London: Sage.

Feichtinger, G., Hartl, R.F., Kort, P. and Novak, A. (2001) Terrorism control in the tourism industry. *Journal of Optimization Theory and Applications* 108 (2), 283–296.

Fennell, D. (2003) *Ecotourism: An Introduction*. New York: Routledge.

Ferradás Carrasco, S. (2001) La relevancia del turismo náutico en la oferta turística. *Cuadernos de Turismo* 7, 67–80.

Finney, B.R. and Watson, K.A. (1975) *A New Kind of Sugar. Tourism in the Pacific*. Honolulu: East-West Centre.

Fishbein, M. and Ajzen, I. (1975) *Belief, Attitude, Intention and Behavior. An Introduction to Theory and Research*. Reading, MA: Addison-Wesley.
Fisher, S. (ed.) (1997) *Recreation and the Sea*. Exeter: University of Exeter Press.
Fletcher, A. (1993) The role of landowners, entrepreneurs and railways in the urban development of the North Wales coast during the nineteenth century. *Welsh History Review* 16 (4), 515–541.
FONATUR (1994) Infonatur. Mexico City. *Fondo Nacional de Fomento al Turismo* 1 (4), 2A.
Foreign Policy (2003) The 2003 Globalisation Index. On WWW at www.foreign-policy.com/wwwboard/g-index.php. Accessed 1.6.07.
Frank, A.G. (1967) *Capitalism and Underdevelopment in Latin America*. New York: Monthly Review Press.
Franklin, A. (2003) *Tourism: An Introduction*. London: Sage.
Freitag, T.G. (1994) Enclave tourism development: For whom the benefits roll? *Annals of Tourism Research* 21 (3), 538–554.
Fuertes Eugenio, A.M., Bengochea Morancho, A. and Rubert Nebot, J.J. (1999) Turismo y disponibilidad de recursos hídricos: el caso de Benidorm. *Papers de Turisme* 26, 29–47.
Fullana, P. and Ayuso, S. (2002) *Turismo sostenible*. Barcelona: Rubes ed.
Fuller, C., Bennett, R. and Ramsden, M. (2004) Local government and the changing institutional landscape of economic development in England and Wales. *Environment and Planning C: Government and Policy* 22 (3), 317–347.
Fussell, R. (1965) Recreation and the South Carolina coast. *Southeastern Geographer* 5, 48–56.
Gale, T. (2005) Modernism, post-modernism and the decline of British seaside resorts as long holiday destinations: A case study of Rhyl, North Wales. *Tourism Geographies* 7 (1), 86–112.
Gale, T. and Botterill, D. (2005) A realist agenda for tourist studies, or why destination areas really rise and fall in popularity. *Tourist Studies* 5 (2), 151–174.
García Sánchez, A., Artal Tur, A. and Ramos Parreño, J.M. (2002) El turismo del Mar Menor: predominio de la segunda residencia. *Cuadernos de Turismo* 9, 33–43.
Garland, G. and Oelofse, C. (2005) Review of monitoring and reporting on the state of the coast in South Africa. Unpublished manuscript. Pretoria: Department of Environmental Affairs and Tourism.
Garrod, B., Wornell, R. and Youell, R. (2006) Re-conceptualising rural resources as countryside capital: The case of rural tourism. *Journal of Rural Studies* 22 (1), 117–128.
Geddes, D. (2002) The last resort: Why the UK's traditional seaside destinations must rethink their long-term strategy. *Locum Destination Review* Autumn, 68–70.
Getz, D. (1998) Developing rural tourism: The potential of beach resort hinterlands. In B. Faulkner, C. Tidswell and D. Weaver (eds) *Progress in Tourism and Hospitality Research, Proceedings of the 8th Australian Hospitality and Research Conference* (pp. 700–714). Canberra: Bureau of Tourism Research.
Getz, D. (1999) Resort-centred tours and development of the rural hinterland: The case of Cairns and the Atherton Tablelands. *The Journal of Tourism Studies* 10 (2), 23–34.
Gibbs, D., Jonas, A., Reimer, S. and Spooner, D. (2001) Governance, institutional capacity and partnerships in local economic development: Theoretical issues

and empirical evidence from the Humber sub-region. *Transactions of the Institute of British Geographers* 26 (1), 103–119.
Giddens, A. (1999) *Runaway World: How Globalisation is Reshaping our Lives*. London: Profile Books.
Gil, S. (2003) Tourism development in the Canary Islands. *Annals of Tourism Research* 30 (3), 744–777.
Gilbert, E.M. (1954) *Brighton: Old Ocean's Bauble*. London: Methuen.
Gilbert, E.W. (1939) The growth of inland and seaside health resorts in England. *Scottish Geographical Magazine* 55 (1), 16–35.
Gilbert, E.W. (1949) The growth of Brighton. *Geographical Journal* 114 (1–3), 32–52.
Gill, A. (2004) Tourism communities and growth management. In A. Lew, M. Hall and A. Williams (eds) *A Companion to Tourism* (pp. 569–583). Oxford: Blackwell.
Gill, A.M. and Reed, M. (1997) The re-imaging of a Canadian resource town: Postproductivism in a North American context. *Applied Geography Studies* 1 (2), 129–147.
Gill, A.M. and Reed, M. (1999) Incorporating postproductivist values into sustainable community processes. In J. Pierce and A. Dale (eds) *Communities, Development and Sustainability Across Canada* (pp. 166–189). Vancouver: UBC Press.
Gill, A.M., Kriwoken, L., Dobson, S. and Fallon, L. (2003) The challenge of integrating tourism into Canadian and Australian coastal zone management. *Dalhousie Law Journal* 26 (1), 85–147.
Girling, R. (2006) No, we don't like to be beside the seaside. *The Sunday Times Magazine* 23 April, 16–26.
Gladstone, D.L. (2006) The international formal sector. In D.L. Gladstone (ed.) *From Pilgrimage to Package Tour* (pp. 51–91). London: Routledge.
Go, F., Pine, R. and Ricky, Y (1994) Hong Kong: Sustaining competitive advantage in Asia's hotel industry. *Cornell Hotel and Restaurant Administration Quarterly* 35 (5), 50–61.
Godfrey, K. (1996) The evolution of tourism planning in Cyprus: Will recent changes prove sustainable? *The Cyprus Review* 8 (1), 111–133.
Golding, P. (2005) Chintsa Golf Estate. *The American Express Magazine: Expressions* 74–75.
Gonen, A. (1981) Tourism and coastal settlement processes in the Mediterranean region. *Ekistics* 290, 378–381.
González, P. and Moral, P. (1996) Analysis of tourism trends in Spain. *Annals of Tourism Research* 23 (4), 739–754.
Gordon, B.M (1998) Warfare and tourism: Paris in World War II. *Annals of Tourism Research* 25 (3), 616–638.
Gordon, I. and Goodall, B. (2000) Localities and tourism. *Tourism Geographies* 2 (3), 290–311.
Gormsen, E (1981) The spatiotemporal development of international tourism: Attempts at a centre-periphery model. In *La Consommation d'Espace pour le Tourism et sa Preservation*. Aix en Provence: Centre des Hautres Etudes Touristiques.
Gotham, K. (2002) Marketing Mardi Gras: Commodification, spectacle and the political economy of tourism in New Orleans. *Urban Studies* 39 (10), 1735–1756.
Govern de les Illes Balears (2002, 2003, 2004, 2005) *Dades informatives. El turisme a les Illes Balears*. Palma de Mallorca: Conselleria de Turisme.

Goymen, K. (2000) Tourism and governance in Turkey. *Annals of Tourism Research* 27 (4), 1025–1048.

Goytia Prat, A. (1996) Back to a sustainable future on the Costa Brava. In B. Bramwell, I. Henry, G. Jackson, A. Goytia Prat, G. Richards and J. van der Straaten (eds) *Sustainable Tourism Management: Principles and Practices* (pp. 121–145). Tilburg: Tilberg University Press.

Gozo Tourism Association (2000) *Gozo Tourism. Review and Framework for Future Development*. Gozo: Gozo Tourism Association/Stevens and Associates.

Greater St Lucia Wetland Park Authority (2005) Roots. *Wetland Wire News Flash* 11, November.

Greater St Lucia Wetland Park Authority (2004) Praise for park. *Wetland Wire News Flash* 4, October.

Greenpeace (2005) *Destrucción a toda costa 2005*. Madrid: Greenpeace.

Günes-Ayata, A. (1994a) Clientelism: Premodern, modern and postmodern. In L. Roniger and A. Günes-Ayata (eds) *Democracy, Clientelism and Civil Society* (pp. 19–28). London: Lynne Rienner Publishers.

Günes-Ayata, A. (1994b) Roots and trends of clientelism in Turkey. In L. Roniger and A. Günes-Ayata (eds) *Democracy, Clientelism and Civil Society* (pp. 49–63). London: Lynne Rienner Publishers.

Gupta, A.K. and Govindarajan, V. (2000) Knowledge flows within multinational corporations. *Strategic Management Journal* 21 (4), 473–476.

Hall, C.M. (1994) *Tourism and Politics: Policy, Power and Place*. Chichester: Wiley.

Hall, C.M. (1997) *Tourism in the Pacific Rim: Developments, Impacts and Markets*. Melbourne: Longman.

Hall, C.M. (2000) *Tourism Planning. Policies, Processes and Relationships*. Harlow: Pearson Education Limited.

Hall, C.M. and Lew, A.A. (1998) *Sustainable Tourism: A Geographical Perspective*. Harlow: Longman.

Hall, C.M. and Muller, D.K. (eds) (2004) *Tourism, Mobility and Second Homes: Between Elite Landscape and Common Ground*. Clevedon: Channel View Publications.

Hall, C.M. and Page, S.J. (1999) *The Geography of Tourism and Recreation: Environment, Place and Space*. London: Routledge.

Halseth, G. (1998) *Cottage Country in Transition: A Social Geography of Change and Contention in the Rural-Recreational Countryside*. Montreal: McGill-Queen's University Press.

Hanlan, J. and Kelly, S. (2005) Image formation, information sources and an iconic Australian tourist destination. *Journal of Vacation Marketing* 11 (2), 163–177.

Hardy, R. (2005) *Malaysia: Islam and multi-culturalism*. On WWW at http://news.bbc.co.uk/1/hi/world/asia-pacific/4232451.stm. Accessed 1.6.07.

Harper, T.N. (1998) *The End of Empire and the Making of Malaysia*. New York: Cambridge University Press.

Harrigan, N. (1974) Legacy of Caribbean history and tourism. *Annals of Tourism Research* 2, 13–25.

Harris, R. (1988) The Gullahs: An upside-down world. *Los Angeles Times* 28 August, 1, 26, 28.

Harrison, D. (2001) Tourism in small islands and microstates. *Tourism Recreation Research* 26 (3), 3–8.

Hart, K. (2002) Discussion of papers by Abraham/Platteau and Harragin. Paper presented to *Culture and Public Action* conference, Washington DC, World Bank, June 30–July 1, 2002.

Harvey, D. (1996) *Justice, Nature and the Geography of Difference*. Oxford: Blackwell.

Harvey, D. (1989) *The Condition Of Postmodernity: An Enquiry into the Origins of Cultural Change*. Oxford: Blackwell.

Hassan, S. (2000) Determinants of market competitiveness in an environmentally sustainable tourism industry. *Journal of Travel Research* 38 (3), 239–245.

Hauck, M. and Sowman, M. (2003) *Waves of Change*. Cape Town: University of Cape Town Press.

Hawkins, D., Lamoureux, K. and Poon, A. (2002) *The Relationship of Tourism Development to Bio-Diversity and the Sustainable Use of Energy and Water Resources: A Stakeholder Management Framework*. Report to the United Nations Environment Programme. Paris, France.

Hawkins, R. (1994) Ecotourism: Opportunities for developing countries. In W. Theobald (ed.) *Global Tourism: The Next Decade* (pp. 261–273). Oxford: Butterworth Press.

Hayter, R. (2000) *Flexible Crossroads: the Restructuring of BC's Forest Economy* Vancouver: UBC Press.

Hayter, R. and Soyez, D. (1996) Clearcut issues. German environmental pressure and the British Columbia forest sector. *Geographische Zeitschrift* 84, 143–156.

Haywood, K.M. (1986) Can the tourist area life-cycle be made operational? *Tourism Management* 7 (3), 154–167.

Haywood, K.M. (1988) Responsible and responsive tourism planning in the community. *Tourism Management* 9 (2), 105–116.

Healey, P. (1997) *Collaborative Planning: Shaping Places in Fragmented Societies*. London: Macmillan.

Healy, R.G. (1997) Ecotourism in Mexico: National and regional policy contexts. Paper presented at the *Annual Meeting of the Latin American Studies Association*. Guadalajara, Mexico, 16–19 April.

Hemming Information Services (2003) *Municipal Year Book 2003*. London: Hemming Information Services.

Hendee, J.C., Stankey, G.H. and Lucas, R.C. (1978) *Wilderness Management*. Miscellaneous Publication No. 1365, Washington: US Department of Agriculture, Forest Service.

Henderson, J.C. (2003a) Tourism Promotion and Identity in Malaysia. *Tourism, Culture and Communication* 4 (2), 71–82.

Henderson, J.C. (2003b) Managing tourism and Islam in Peninsular Malaysia. *Tourism Management* 24 (4), 447–456.

Henderson, J.C. (2003c) Terrorism and tourism: Managing the consequences of the Bali bombings. *Journal of Travel and Tourism Marketing* 15 (1), 41–58.

Henry, P.I. and Nassis, P. (1999) Political clientelism and sport policy in Greece. *International Review for the Sociology of Sport* 34 (1), 43–58.

Hiernaux-Nicolas, D. (1999) Cancún bliss. In D.R. Judd and S.S. Fanstein (eds) *The Tourist City* (pp. 124–142). New Haven, CT: Yale University Press.

Hiernaux-Nicolas, D. and Rodriguez Woog, M. (1990) *Tourism and Absorption of the Labour Force in Mexico*. Working Paper No. 34. Washington D.C: Commission for the Study of International Migration and Co-Operative Economic Development.

Hill, B. (2004) *The Enduring Rip. A History of Queenscliffe*. Melbourne: Melbourne University Press.

Hills, T. and Lundgren, J. (1977) The impact of tourism in the Caribbean: A methodological study. *Annals of Tourism Research* 4 (5), 248–267.

Hilton-Barber, B. (2005) Country roads: Take a loan. *Sawubona Magazine* November, 83–88.

Hirst, P. and Thompson, G. (1999) *Globalization in Question* (2nd edn). Cambridge: Polity Press.
Hitchcock, M. and Darma Putra, I. (2005) The Bali bombings: Tourism crisis management and conflict avoidance. *Current Issues in Tourism* 8 (1), 62–76.
Hjalager, A.M. (2002) Repairing innovation defectiveness in tourism. *Tourism Management* 23 (5), 465–474.
Hofmann, N. (1979) *A Survey of Tourism in West Malaysia and Some Socio-Economic Implications*. Singapore: Institute of Southeast Asian Studies.
Hollinshead, K. (2003) Symbolism in tourism: Lessons from "Bali 2002" – lessons from Australia's dead heart. *Tourism Analysis* 8 (2), 267–295.
Holm, C. and Holm, F. (2003) Thesen Islands. *Leading Architecture and Design* July/August, 45–47.
Holmes, D. (2001) Monocultures of globalization. Touring Australia's Gold Coast. In D. Holmes (ed.) *Virtual Globalization. Virtual Spaces/Tourist Spaces* (pp. 175–191). London: Routledge.
Holt, S. (2005) Luna Park. Lower Esplanade (18 Cavell Street), St Kilda. *A Place of Sensuous Resort: Buildings of St Kilda and Their People*. Melbourne: St Kilda Historical Society Inc.
Honey, M. (1999) *Ecotourism and Sustainable Development: Who Owns Paradise?* Washington, DC: Island Press.
Hong, E. (1985) *See the Third World While it Lasts: The Social and Environmental Impact of Tourism with Special Reference to Malaysia*. Penang: Consumers' Association of Penang.
Horwath and Horwath (1989) *Maltese Islands Tourism Development Plan*. London: Horwath and Horwath.
Hotel Eco Paraiso (2006) On WWW at www.ecoparaiso.com. Accessed 23.6.06.
Hotel Rey Caribe (2006) On WWW at www.reycaribe.com. Accessed 23.6.06.
House of Commons (2005–06) Office of the Deputy Prime Minister: Housing, Planning, Local Government and the Regions Committee. *Coastal Towns – Volume II: Written Evidence* (Session 2005–06). London: The Stationary Office Limited.
Howlett, M., and Brownsey, K. (2001) British Columbia: Politics in a post-staples political economy. In K. Brownsey and M. Howlett (eds) *The Provincial State in Canada* (pp. 309–334). Peterborough, Ontario: Broadview Press.
Hudson, B. (2003) Waterfall attractions in coastal tourism areas: The Yorkshire Coastland Queensland's Gold Coast compared. *International Journal of Tourism Research* 5 (4), 283–293.
Hudson, R. (2001) *Producing Places*. New York: Guildford Press.
Hunter, C. (1995) On the need to re-conceptualise sustainable tourism. *Journal of Sustainable Tourism* 3 (3), 155–165.
Hunter, C. (1997) Sustainable tourism as an adaptive paradigm. *Annals of Tourism Research* 24 (4), 850–867.
Hunter, C. and Shaw, J. (2007) The ecological footprint as a key indicator of sustainable tourism. *Tourism Management* 28 (1), 46–57.
IDESCAT (Institut d'Estadística de Catalunya) (2005) *Anuari estadístic de Catalunya 2005*. Barcelona: IDESCAT. On WWW at www.idescat.net/cat/idescat/publicacions/anuari/aec_pdf. Accessed 17.5.06.
INE (Instituto Nacional de Estadística) (2005) *Encuesta de ocupación en alojamientos de turismo rural*. Madrid: INE. On WWW at www.ine.es/inebase/cgi/um?M = %2Ft11%2Fe162eotr&O = inebase&N = &L = . Accessed 1.6.07.

Ingram, P. (1996) Organisational form as a solution to the problem of credible commitment. The evolution of naming strategies among US hotel chains 1896–1980. *Strategic Management Journal* 17, 85–96.
Innes, H. (1930) *The Fur Trade in Canada.* Toronto: University of Toronto Press.
Instituto Canario de Estadística (2005) On WWW at www.gobiernodecanarias.org/istac. Accessed 17.8.06.
Ioannides, D. (1992) Tourism development agents: The Cypriot resort cycle. *Annals of Tourism Research* 19 (4), 711–731.
Ioannides, D. and Debbage, K. (1997) Post-Fordism and flexibility: The travel industry polyglot. *Tourism Management* 18 (4), 229–241.
Ioannides, D. and Holcomb, B. (2001) Raising the stakes: Implications of upmarket tourism policies in Cyprus and Malta. In D. Ioannides, Y. Apostolopoulos and S. Sonmez (eds) *Mediterranean Islands and Sustainable Tourism Development. Practices, Management and Policies* (pp. 234–258). London: Continuum.
Ioannides, D. and Holcomb, B. (2003) Misguided policy initiatives in small island destinations: Why do up-market tourism policies fail? *Tourism Geographies* 5 (1), 39–48.
Ioannides, D., Apostolopoulos, Y. and Sonmez, S. (eds) (2001) *Mediterranean Islands and Sustainable Tourism Development: Practice, Management and Policies*. London: Continuum.
Ionised, D. and Apostolopoulos, Y. (1999) Political instability, war, and tourism in Cyprus: Effects, management, and prospects for recovery. *Journal of Travel Research* 38 (1), 51–56.
Irwin, A. (2004) *Trade and Transport Ministry Briefing: Parliamentary Monitoring Group, South Africa*. On WWW at www.pmg.org.za/briefings. Accessed 16.1.06.
Jafari, J. (2001) The scientification of tourism. In V.L. Smith and M. Brent (eds) *Hosts and Guests Revisited: Tourism Issues of the 21st Century* (pp. 28–41). New York: Cognizant.
Jamal, J.B. and Getz, D. (1995) Collaboration theory and community tourism planning. *Annals of Tourism Research* 22 (1), 186–204.
Jasper, A. (2002) *The Economic Impact of the Eden Project 1st April to 1st October 2003*. Report produced for The Eden Project in association with Geoff Broom Associates. St. Austell: Eden Project.
Jayne, M. (2000) The cultural quarter: (Re)locating urban regeneration in Stoke-on-Trent – a 'city' in name only. In T. Edensor (ed.) *Reclaiming Stoke-on-Trent: Leisure, Space and Identity in the Potteries* (pp. 19–41). Stoke-on-Trent: Staffordshire University.
Jenkins, T.N. (2000) Putting postmodernity into practice. Endogenous development and the role of traditional cultures in the rural development of marginal regions. *Ecological Economics* 34, 301–314.
Jenner, P. and Smith, C. (1992) *The Tourism Industry and the Environment* (Special Report No. 2453). London: Economic Intelligence Unit.
Jessop, B. (1997) Capitalism and its future: Remarks on regulation, government and governance. *Review of International Political Economy* 4 (2), 561–581.
Johnston, R. (1983) *Philosophy and Human Geography. An Introduction to Contemporary Approaches*. London: Arnold.
Jones, M. (1986) *A Sunny Place for Shady People: The Real Gold Coast Story*. Sydney: Allen and Unwin.

Jones, M. (2001) The rise of the regional state in economic governance: 'Partnership for prosperity' or new scales of state power? *Environment and Planning A* 33 (7), 1185–1211.
Jones, M. and MacLeod, G. (1999) Towards a regional renaissance? Reconfiguring and rescaling England's economic governance. *Transactions of the Institute of British Geographers* 24 (3), 295–313.
Jordon, P. (2001) Restructuring Croatia's coastal resorts: Change, sustainable development and the incorporation of rural hinterlands. *Journal of Sustainable Tourism* 8 (6), 525–539.
Journey Malaysia (2005) *Pulau Langkawi*. On WWW at http://www.journeymalaysia.com/MI_langkawi.htm. Accessed 1.6.07.
Kayat, K. (2002) Power, social exchanges and tourism in Langkawi: Rethinking resident perceptions. *International Journal of Tourism Research* 4, 171–191.
Kearney, A.T. and Foreign Policy (2002) The 2001 Globalisation Index. *Foreign Policy* Jan/Feb, 1–6.
Kersten, A. (1997) Tourism and regional development in Mexico and Chiapas after NAFTA. *Planeta.com – Bridging Borders Across the Americas*. On WWW at www.planeta.com/planeta/97/0597lacandon2.html. Accessed 5.6.06.
Kessler, C.S. (1992) Archaism and modernity: Contemporary Malay political culture. In J.S. Kahn and K.W. Loh (eds) *Fragmented Vision: Culture and Politics in Contemporary Malaysia* (pp. 133–157). Sydney: Allen and Unwin.
Kester, J.G.C. and Carvao, S. (2004) International tourism in the Middle East and outbound tourism from Saudi Arabia. *Tourism Economics* 10 (2), 220–240.
Khalifah, Z. and Tahir, S. (1997) Malaysia: Tourism in perspective. In F. Go and C.L. Jenkins (eds) *Tourism and Economic Development in Asia and Australasia* (pp. 176–196). London: Cassell.
Kim, S.S. and Prideaux, B. (2003) Tourism, peace and ideology: Impacts of the Mt. Gumgang tour project in the Korean Peninsula. *Tourism Management* 24 (6), 675–685.
Kim, Y.K. and Crompton, J.L. (1990) Role of tourism in unifying the two Koreas. *Annals of Tourism Research* 17 (3), 353–366.
King, B. (1997a) *Creating Island Resorts*. London: Routledge.
King, B. (1997b) Developing a regional concept for a resort destination area. Challenges and opportunities in the Whitsundays. In R. Teare, B.F. Canziani and G. Brown (eds) *Global Directions: New Strategies for Hospitality and Tourism Development* (pp. 357–382). London: Cassell.
King, B. (2001) Resort-based tourism on the pleasure-periphery. In D. Harrison (ed.) *Tourism and the Less Developed World: Issues and Case Studies* (pp. 175–190). Wallingford: CAB International.
King, B. and McVey, M. (2006) Hotels in Australia 1988–2003. A tale of booms and busts. *Tourism Economics* 12 (2), 225–246.
King, B. and Whitelaw, P. (2003) Resorts in Australian tourism: A recipe for confusion. *Journal of Tourism Studies* 14 (1), 59–66.
King, R., Warnes, A. and Williams, R.A. (1998) International retirement immigration in Europe. *International Journal of Population Geography* 4 (2), 91–111.
King, V.T. (1993) Tourism and culture in Malaysia. In M. Hitchcock, V.T. King and M.J. Parnwell (eds) *Tourism in South-East Asia* (pp. 99–116). London and New York: Routledge.
Kneafsey, M. (2001) Rural cultural economy: Tourism and social relations. *Annals of Tourism Research* 28 (3), 762–783.

Knowles, T. and Curtis, S. (1999) The market viability of European mass tourist destinations. A post-stagnation life-cycle analysis. *International Journal of Tourism Research* 1 (4), 87–96.

Kocdemir, K. (1998) Impossibility of restructuring without administrative reform. *Yerel Yonetim ve Denetim* 3 (5), 15–28.

Korzay, M. (1994) Turkish tourism development. In A.V. Seaton, C.L. Jenkins, R.C. Wood and P.U.C. Dieke (eds) *Tourism: The State of the Art* (pp. 85–99). Chichester: Wiley.

Koutoulas, D. (2006) The market influence of tour operators on the hospitality industry. In A. Papatheodorou (ed.) *Corporate Rivalry and Market Power – Competition Issues in the Tourism Industry* (pp. 148–164). London: I.B. Tauris.

Kuentzel, W.F. and Ramaswamy, V.M. (2005) Tourism and amenity migration: A longitudinal analysis. *Annals of Tourism Research* 32 (2), 419–438.

Lambsdorff, G. (2004) *Global Corruption Barometer*. On WWW at www.transparency.org/working_papers/lambsdorff/lambsdorff_eresearch.html. Accessed 7.6.06.

Langeni, P. (2005) Buy in May ... and stay. *Sawubona Magazine* November, 99–100.

Langer, V. (2003) Echoes of Clayoquot Sound. *Briarpatch* 32 (6), 19–22.

Larsen, S.C. (2004) Place identity in a resource-dependent area of Northern British Columbia. *Annals of the Association of American Geographers* 94 (4), 944–960.

Lash, S. (1991) *Sociology of Post-modernism*. London: Routledge.

Laws, E. (1997) *Managing Packaged Tourism: Relationships, Responsibilities and Service Quality in the Inclusive Holiday Industry*. London: Thompson Business Press.

Lazare, A., Antoine, P. and Samuel, W. (2001) *RNM/OECS Country Studies to Inform Trade Negotiations: Antigua and Barbuda*. On WWW at www.crnm.org/documents/studies/OECS/RNM%20Study%20-%20Antigua.pdf. Accessed 25.7.05.

Leach, M., Mearns, R. and Scoones, I. (eds) (1997) Community-based sustainable development: consensus or conflict? Editorial. *IDS Bulletin* 28 (4), 1–3.

Lead International (2004) *Coastal Water Along the Yucatán Peninsula: Common Pool Resources*. On WWW at http://casestudies.lead.org/index.php?csid = 14. Accessed 3.6.07.

Lee, T. and Balchin, N. (1995) Learning and attitude change at British Nuclear Fuel's Sellafield Visitors Centre. *Journal of Environmental Psychology* 15, 283–298.

Leiper, N. (1990) *Tourism Systems: An Interdisciplinary Perspective.* Occasional Papers No. 2, Department of Management Systems, Business Studies Faculty, Massey University, Palmerston.

Lencek, L. and Bosker, G. (1998) *The Beach: A History of Paradise on Earth*. London: Secker and Warburg.

Levitt, T. (1983) The globalization of markets. *Harvard Business Review* 61 (3), 92–102.

Lewis, R. (1980) Seaside holiday resorts in the United States and Britain. *Urban History Yearbook* 7, 44–52.

Lewis, J. and Lewis, B. (2004) The crisis of contiguity: Communities and contention in the wake of the Bali bombings. *First International Sources of Insecurity Conference*, 17–19 November 2004. Melbourne: Globalism Institute, RMIT University.

Li, W. (2004) Environmental management indicators for ecotourism in China's nature reserves. A case study of Tianmushan nature reserve. *Tourism Management* 25 (5), 559–564.
Life Healthcare (2005) *Life Knysna private hospital.* On WWW at www.knysnaprivatehospital.co.za. Accessed 16.1.06.
Lockhart, D. (1997) Tourism to Malta and Cyprus. In D. Lockhart and D. Drakakis-Smith (eds) *Island Tourism. Trends and Prospects* (pp. 152–178). London: Pinter.
Lockhart, D. and Drakakis-Smith, D. (eds) (1997) *Island Tourism: Trends and Prospects*. London: Routledge.
Loizidou, X. (2004) Land use and coastal management in the Eastern Mediterranean: The Cyprus example. On WWW at www.iasonnet.gr/abstracts/loizidou.html. Accessed 17.8.06.
Lorah, P. (1995) An unsustainable path: Tourism's vulnerability to environmental decline in Antigua. *Caribbean Geography* 6, 28–39.
MacLeod, G. (2001) Beyond soft institutionalism: Accumulation, regulation and their geographical fixes. *Environment and Planning A* 33 (7), 1145–1167.
MacLeod, G. and Goodwin, M. (1999) Reconstructing an urban and regional political economy: On the state, politics, scale and explanation. *Political Geography* 18 (6), 697–730.
MacNaught, T. (1982) Mass tourism and the dilemmas of modernization in Pacific island communities. *Annals of Tourism Research* 9 (3), 359–381.
Mader, R. (1996) *Conservation in Sian Ka'an*. On WWW at www.planeta.com. Accessed 5.6.06.
Mahalli İdareler (2003) *Local Authorities in Turkey – Overview*. On WWW at http://www.mahalli-idareler.gov.tr/Home/Home.aspx. Accessed 3.6.07.
Máiz Suárez, R. and Requejo, F. (2002) *Democracy, Nationalism and Multiculturalism*. London: Routledge.
Malaysia Hotels (2005) *Pangkor Island*. On WWW at www.malaysiahotels.cc/pangkor.html. Accessed 1.11.05.
Malta Environment and Planning Authority (2002a) *Coastal Strategy Topic Paper. Final Draft*. Floriana: MEPA.
Malta Environment and Planning Authority (2002b) *Rural Strategy Topic Paper. Volume 1. Draft for Public Consultation*. Floriana: MEPA.
Malta Tourism Authority (2004) *Malta Tourist Arrivals*. Valletta: Strategic Planning and Research Malta Tourism Authority. On WWW at www.mta.com.mt. Accessed 23.2.05.
Manchado, A. (dir.) (1997) *Calvià Agenda Local 21. ATC sistema territorial y urbano*. 13 vols. Palma de Mallorca: Gabinet d'Anàlisi Ambiental i territorial (GaaT) and Ajuntament de Calvià.
Manente, M. and Pechlaner, H. (2006) How to define, identify and monitor the decline of tourist destinations: Towards an early warning system. In R.W. Butler (ed.) *The Tourist Area Life Cycle. Vol. 2: Conceptual and Theoretical Issues* (pp. 235–253). Clevedon: Channel View Publications.
Mansfeld, Y. (1996) Wars, tourism and the "Middle East" factor. In A. Pizam and Y. Mansfeld (eds) *Tourism, Crime and International Security Issues* (pp. 265–278). Chichester: Wiley.
Mansfeld, Y. (2001) Acquired tourism deficiency syndrome: Planning and developing tourism in Israel. In Y. Apostolopoulos, P. Loukissas and L. Leontidou (eds) *Mediterranean Tourism: Facets of Socioeconomic Development and Cultural Change* (pp. 159–178). London and New York: Routledge.

Manthorp, N. (2005) Par excellence. *The American Express Magazine: Expressions* 67–68.
Marín, C. (2000) New tourism challenges on islands: Resources, risks and possibilities in the information society. The Canary Islands experience. *Insula: Biodiversity and Tourism Symposium.* Port-Cros: France.
Markwick, M. (1999) Malta's tourism industry since 1985: Diversification, cultural tourism and sustainability. *Scottish Geographical Journal* 115 (3), 227–247.
Markwick, M. (2000) Golf tourism development, stakeholders, differing discourses and alternative agendas: The case of Malta. *Tourism Management* 21 (5), 515–524.
Marsden, G. (2003) The last resort? *Locum Destination Review* 13 (Autumn): 54–57.
Mason, J. and Studsholt, A.B. (2001) *Analysis of the Present Situation and Planning Strategies. Documentation and Development of Seaside Tourism in the North Sea Region*. Sweden: Halland County Council.
Mason, P. (2003) *Tourism Impacts, Planning and Management.* Oxford: Butterworth-Heinemann.
Massey, D. (1978) Regionalism: Some current issues. *Capital and Class* 6 (1), 106–125.
Massey, D. (1999) *Power-Geometrics and the Politics of Space and Time*. Hettner Lecture 1998, Department of Geography, University of Heidelberg.
Matthews, H.G. and Richter, L.K. (1991) Political science and tourism. *Annals of Tourism Research* 18 (1), 120–135.
McCarthy, J.J., Fynn, M. and Davies, K.R. (2000) *The Likely Developmental Consequences of a Point Marine Park and Waterworld*. Durban: Moreland Developers.
McElroy, J.L. (2004) Global perspectives of Caribbean tourism. In D. Duval (ed.) *Tourism in the Caribbean: Trends, Development, Prospects* (pp. 39–56). London: Routledge.
McLain, R. and Lee, R. (1996) Adaptive management: Promises and pitfalls. *Environmental Management* 20 (4), 437–448.
McNutt, P. and Oreja-Rodríguez, J. (1996) Economic strategies for sustainable tourism in islands: The case of Tenerife. In L. Briguglio, R. Butler, D. Harrison and W. Filho (eds) *Sustainable Tourism in Islands and Small States – Case Studies* (pp. 262–280). London: Pinter.
MCT (Ministerio de Comercio y Turismo) (1994) *Plan Marco de Competitividad del Turismo Español (Plan Futures)*. Madrid: Ministerio de Comercio y Turismo.
McVey, M. (2001) Malaysia. *Travel &Tourism Intelligence Country Reports* 1, 62–79.
McVey, M.J. and King, B. (2003) Hotels in Australia. *Travel and Tourism Analyst* 3, 1–26.
Meyer, D. (2003) *Outbound UK Tour Operator Industry and its Implications for Pro Poor Tourism in Developing Countries*. London: Pro Poor Tourism Working Paper No 17.
Meyer, G. (1996) Tourism development in Egypt overshadowed by Middle East politics. *Applied Geography and Development* 48, 69–84.
Middleton, V.T.C. (1989) Seaside resorts. *Insights* 1, B1–13.
Middleton, V. and Hawkins, R. (1998) *Sustainable Tourism: A Marketing Perspective*. London: Butterworth-Heinemann.
Miller, G. (2001) The development of indicators for sustainable tourism: Results of a Delphi survey of tourism researchers. *Tourism Management* 22 (4), 351–362.
Milman, A., Reichel, A. and Pizam, A. (1990) The impact of tourism on ethnic attitudes: The Israeli-Egyptian case. *Journal of Travel Research* 29 (2), 45–49.

Milne, R.S. and Mauzy, D.K. (1998) *Malaysian Politics under Mahatir*. London: Routledge.
Milne, S. (1992) Tourism and development in south Pacific microstates. *Annals of Tourism Research* 19 (2), 191–212.
Milne, S. (1997) Tourism, dependency, and south Pacific microstates. Beyond the vicious circle? In D. Lockhart and D. Drakakis-Smith (eds) *Island Tourism: Trends and Prospects* (pp. 281–301). London: Pinter.
Milne, S. and Ateljevic, I. (2001) Tourism, economic development and the global-local nexus: Theory embracing complexity. *Tourism Geographies* 3 (3), 369–393.
Mings, R.C. (1988) Assessing the contribution of tourism to international understanding. *Journal of Travel Research* 27 (2), 33–38.
Ministerio de Economía (2004) *25 años del turismo español en cifras. 25 aniversario Constitución Española 1978–2003*. Madrid: Instituto de Estudios Turísticos.
Ministry of Culture, Arts and Tourism (1992) *Malaysian Tourism Policy Study: Sectoral Report.* Kuala Lumpur: Ministry of Culture, Arts and Tourism.
Ministry of Tourism (1999) *Carrying Capacity Assessment for Tourism in the Maltese Islands. Survey Draft*. Valletta: Malta Ministry of Tourism.
Ministry of Tourism (2001) *Carrying Capacity Assessment for Tourism in the Maltese Islands*. Valletta: Malta Ministry of Tourism.
Mintel (2001) *Long Haul Holidays.* London: Mintel International Group.
Mintz, S.W. (1971) The Caribbean as a socio-cultural area. In M.M. Horowitz (ed.) *Peoples and Cultures of the Caribbean* (pp. 17–46). Garden City, New York: The Natural History Press.
Miossec, J.M. (1976) *Eléments pour une Théorie de l'Espace Touristique.* Aix-en-Provence: Les Cahiers du Tourisme, C36 CHET.
Morah, E.U. (1996) Obstacles to optimal policy implementation in developing countries. *Third World Planning Review* 18 (1), 79–105.
Morgan, N. and Pritchard, A. (1999) *Tourism, Promotion and Power: Creating Images, Creating Identities*. Chichester: John Wiley.
Morris, B. (2001) Architectures of entertainment. In D. Holmes (ed.) *Virtual Globalization. Virtual Spaces/Tourist Spaces* (pp. 205–219). London: Routledge.
Mowforth, M. and Munt, I. (1998) *Tourism and Sustainability: New Tourism in the Third World*. London: Routledge.
Mowforth, M. and Munt, I. (2003) *Tourism and Sustainability: Development and New Tourism in the Third World*. New York: Routledge.
Mullins, P. (1990) Tourist cities as new cities: Australia's Gold Coast and Sunshine Coast. *Australian Planner* 28 (3), 37–41.
Musa, G. (1999) Tourism in Malaysia. In C.M. Hall and S. Page (eds) *Tourism in South and Southeast Asia: Issues and Cases* (pp. 144–156). Oxford: Butterworth Heinemann.
Nagata, J. (1987) The impact of the Islamic revival (dakwah) on the religious culture in Malaysia. In B. Matthews and J. Nagata (eds) *Religion, Values and Development in Southeast Asia* (pp. 37–50). Singapore: Institute of Southeast Asian Studies.
Nagata, J. (1994) How to be Islamic without being an Islamic state: Contested models of development in Malaysia. In A.S. Ahmed and H. Donnan (eds) *Islam, Globalisation and Postmodernity* (pp. 63–90). London and New York: Routledge.
Nagata, J. (1997) Religious correctness and the place of Islam in Malaysia's economic policies. In T. Brook and H.V. Luong (eds) *Culture and Capital: The*

Shaping of Capitalism in Eastern Asia (pp. 79–101). USA: University of Michigan.

Nash, R. (1967) *Wilderness and the American Mind*. New Haven: Yale University Press.

Navarro de Vega, A. (1999) Plan de Calidad Turística Española: antecedentes, desarrollo y puesta en marcha. *Estudios Turísticos* 139, 5–13.

Neto, F. (2002) Sustainable tourism, environmental protection and natural resource management: Paradise on earth? Paper presented at the *International Colloquium on Regional Governance and Sustainable Development in Tourism-Driven Economies*. Cancún, Mexico, 20–22 February.

Neumayer, E. (2004) The impacts of political violence on tourism: Dynamic cross national estimation. *Journal of Conflict Resolution* 48 (2), 259–281.

Newman, J. (2001) *Modernising Governance: New Labour, Policy and Society*. London: Sage.

Newton, M.T. (1996) Tourism and public administration in Spain. In M. Barke, J. Towner and M.T. Newton (eds) *Tourism in Spain. Critical Issues* (pp. 137–166). Wallingford: CAB International.

Nielson, J., Shelby, B. and Haas, J.E. (1977) Sociological carrying capacity: The last settler syndrome. *Pacific Sociological Review* 20 (4), 568–581.

Niiler, P.P. (1992) The ocean circulation. In K. Trenberth (ed.) *Climatic System Modelling* (pp. 117–148). Cambridge: Cambridge University Press.

Nuryanti, W. (1996) Heritage and postmodern tourism. *Annals of Tourism Research* 23 (2), 249–260

Oakes, T. and Minca, C. (2004) Tourism, modernity and postmodernity. In A.A. Lew, C.M. Hall and A.M. Williams (eds) *A Companion to Tourism* (pp. 166–192). Oxford: Blackwell.

O'Dell, T. and Billing, P. (eds) (2005) *Experiencescapes: Tourism, Culture and Economy*. Copenhagen: Copenhagen Business School Press.

OECD (1993) *Country Reports on Economic Practice and Trade Reports: Turkey*. Paris: OECD.

OECD (1997) *The Measurement of Scientific and Technological Activities*. Proposed guidelines for collecting and interpreting technological innovation data, Oslo Manual. Paris: OECD.

OECD (1999) *Buying Power of Multiproduct Retailers*. Paris: CLP Committee, OECD.

OECD (2004) *Economic Surveys: Turkey*. Paris: OECD.

Olsen, M.D. and Connolly, D.J. (1999) Antecedents of technological change in the hospitality industry. *Tourism Analysis* 4 (1), 29–46.

Oelofse, C. (2005) *Environmental spaces and their associated discourses: The shaping of the environment in Knysna.* Workshop on Environmental Decision-making in South Africa. Mimeo, University of KwaZulu-Natal.

Oelofse, C., Scott, D., Oelofse, G. and Houghton, J. (2006) Shifts in ecological modernization: Innovation, deliberation and institutional change. *Local Environment* 11 (1), 61–78.

Office of the Deputy Prime Minister (2006) *Memorandum (CT54).* On WWW at www.publications.parliament.uk/pa/cm200506/cmselect/cmodpm/1023/1023we72.htm. Accessed 1.6.07.

Ommer, R. and Newell, D. (eds) (1999) *Fishing Places, Fishing People: Issues and Traditions in Canadian Small-Scale Fisheries*. Toronto: University of Toronto Press.

Oppermann, M. (1993) Tourism space in developing countries. *Annals of Tourism Research* 20 (3), 535–556.

Oreja-Rodríguez, J., Parra-López, E. and Yanes-Estévez, V. (2004) The sustainability of insular coastal destinations: The case of Tenerife. Conference proceedings (CD-Rom). *Tourism: State-of-the Art II Conference*. Glasgow: Strathclyde University.

Orfila-Sintes, F., Crespí-Cladera, R. and Martínez-Ros, E. (2005) Innovation activity in the hotel industry: Evidence from Balearic Islands. *Tourism Management* 26 (6), 861–865.

O'Riordan, T., Preston-Whyte, R.A., Hamann, R. and Manqele, M. (2000) The transition to sustainability: A South African perspective. *South African Geographical Journal* 82 (2), 1–10.

Ortega Martínez, E. (2003) La internacionalización del turismo de golf en España: Una puerta al turismo sostenible. In E. Ortega (coord.) *Investigación y Estrategias Turísticas* (pp. 1–36). Madrid: Thomson.

Ortega Martínez, E. and Loy Puddu, G. (2003) Calidad y satisfacción en el sector turístico. In E. Ortega (coord.) *Investigación y Estrategias Turísticas* (pp. 233–260). Madrid: Thomson.

Owen, C. (1990) Better days at the seaside – can UK resorts learn from the European experience? *Tourism Management* 11 (3), 190–194.

Page, S.J. (2003) *Tourism Management: Managing For Change.* Oxford: Butterworth-Heinemann.

Palazzo Versace (2005) On WWW at www.lhw.com/Property.aspx?propertyid = 520&ext = Gpzvrcc&gclid = CL6soZGMu4wCFRcGEgodcDR2aQ. Accessed 1.6.07.

Parliament of Queensland (1985) *Sanctuary Cove Resort Act*. Brisbane: Government Printing Office.

Parliament of Queensland (1987) *Integrated Resort Development Act*. Brisbane: Government Publishing Office.

Paternoster Properties (2006) http://www.myproperty.co.za/town_property.asp?province = western%20cape&town = PATERNOSTER. Accessed 1.6.07.

Pearce, D. (1981) *Tourism Development*. London: Longman.

Pearce, D.G. (1989) *Tourism Development* (2nd edn). Harlow: Longman.

Pearce, D. (1995) *Tourism Today: A Geographical Analysis* (2nd edn). London: Longman.

Pearce, D. (1997) Tourism and the autonomous communities in Spain. *Annals of Tourism Research* 24 (1), 156–177.

Pearce, D.G. and Priestley, G.K. (1998) Tourism in Spain: A spatial analysis and synthesis. *Tourism Analysis* 2, 185–205.

Peck, J. (2000) Doing regulation. In G. Clark, M. Gertler and M. Feldman (eds) *A Handbook of Economic Geography* (pp. 61–80). Oxford: Oxford University Press.

Perkin, H.J. (1976) The "social tone" of Victorian seaside resorts in the North-West. *Northern History* 11, 180–194.

Pezula (2006) *Pezula Private Estate.* On WWW at www.pezula.com. Accessed 16.1.06.

Phillimore, J. and Goodson, L. (2004) *Qualitative Research in Tourism: Ontologies, Epistemologies and Methodologies*. London: Routledge.

Philo, C. and Parr, H. (2000) Institutional geographies: Introductory remarks. *Geoforum* 31, 513–521.

Pierre, J. and Peters, B. (2000) *Governance, Politics and the State*. Basingstoke: Macmillan.

Pilotfish (2006) *Zimbali Coastal Resort.* On WWW at www.zimbali.co.za. Accessed 16.1.06.

Pine, B.J. and Gilmore, J.H. (1999) *The Experience Economy: Work is Theatre and Every Business a Stage.* Cambridge, MA: Harvard University Press.
Pine, R. (1992) Technology transfer in the hotel industry. *International Journal of Hospitality Management* 11 (1), 3–22.
PIO (1997) *The Almanac of Cyprus 1997*. Nicosia: Press and Information Office.
Pizam, A and Mansfeld, Y. (eds) (1996) *Tourism, Crime and International Security Issues.* Chichester: Wiley.
Pizam, A. and Smith, G. (2000) Tourism and terrorism: A quantitative analysis of major terrorist acts and their impact on tourism destinations. *Tourism Economics* 6 (2), 123–138.
Pizam, A., Fleischer, A. and Mansfeld, Y (2002) Tourism and social change: The case of Israeli ecotourists visiting Jordon. *Journal of Travel Research* 41 (2), 177–184.
Pizzorno, A. (1992) Introduzione: La corruzione nel sistema político. In D. Della Porta (ed.) *La Scambia Occulto. Casi di Corruzione Politica in Italia* (pp. 3–9). Bologna: Il Mulino.
Planning Authority (2000) *Structure Plan for the Maltese Islands. Tourism Topic Study. Final Draft*. Floriana: Planning Authority.
Pleumaron, A. (1992) Course and effect: Golf tourism in Thailand. *Ecologist* 22 (3), 104–110.
Plog, S.C. (1974) Why destination areas rise and fall in popularity. *Cornell Hotel and Restaurant Administration Quarterly* 14 (4), 55–58.
Pollacco, J. (2003) *In The National Interest. Towards a Sustainable Tourism Industry in Malta.* Valletta: Fondazzjoni Tumas Fenech Ghall-Edukazzjoni Fil-Ġurnaliżmu.
Pollard, J. and Rodriguez, R.D. (1993) Tourism and Torremolinos: Recession or reaction to environment? *Tourism Management* 12 (1), 247–258.
Ponce Sánchez, M.D. (2004) La calidad ambiental como factor competitivo de los destinos tradicionales de sol y playa. *Cuadernos de Turismo* 13, 91–105.
Poon, A. (1993) *Tourism, Technology and Competitive Strategies*. Wallingford: CAB International.
Poria, Y., Butler, R. and Airey, D. (2003) The core of heritage tourism. *Annals of Tourism Research* 30 (1), 238–254.
Porter, M.E. (1986) *Competition in Global Business.* Cambridge, MA: Harvard University Press.
Prats, F. (dir.) (1995) *Calvià Agenda Local 21. Desarrollo y Sostenibilidad en Los Destinos Turísticos Maduros del Litoral Mediterráneo: El Caso de Calvià en Mallorca (Islas Baleares)*. Calvià: Ajuntament de Calvià, Plan de Excelencia Turística, Turespaña, Ministerio de Comercio y Turismo.
Prats, F. (dir.) (1998) *Calvià Agenda Local 21. La Sostenibilidad de un Municipio Turístico. Plan de Acción. 10 líneas de acción estratégicas y 40 iniciativas*. Calvià: Ajuntament de Calvià.
Prats, F. (dir.) (1999) *Calvià Agenda Local 21. La Sostenibilidad de un Municipio Turístico*. Calvià: Ajuntament de Calvià.
Preston-Whyte, R.A. (1999) Restaurant trends in Durban. *Tourism Geographies* 1 (4), 443–459.
Preston-Whyte, R.A. (2001) Constructed leisure space: The seaside at Durban. *Annals of Tourism Research* 28 (3), 581–596.
Prideaux, B. (2000) The resort development spectrum – a new approach to modelling resort development. *Tourism Management* 21 (3), 225–240.

Prideaux, B. (2004) The resort development spectrum: The case of Gold Coast Australia. *Tourism Geographies* 6 (1), 26–58.

Priestley, G.K. (1995a) Evolution of tourism on the Spanish coast. In G.J. Ashworth and A.G.J. Dietvorst (eds) *Tourism and Spatial Transformations* (pp. 37–54). Wallingford: CAB International.

Priestley, G.K. (1995b) Problems of tourist development in Spain. In H. Coccossis and P. Nijkamp (eds) *Sustainable Tourism Development* (pp. 153–165). London: Avebury.

Priestley, G.K. (1995c) Sports tourism: The case of golf. In G.J. Ashworth and A.G.J. Dietvorst (eds) *Tourism and Spatial Transformations* (pp. 205–224). Wallingford: CAB International.

Priestley, G.K. (1996) Structural dynamics of tourism and recreation-related development: The Catalan coast. In G.K. Priestley, J.A. Edwards and H. Coccossis (eds) *Sustainable Tourism? European Experiences* (pp. 99–119). Wallingford: CAB International.

Priestley, G.K. and Mundet, L. (1998) The post-stagnation phase of the resort cycle. *Annals of Tourism Research* 25 (1), 85–111.

Priestley, G.K., Edwards, J.A. and Coccossis, H. (eds) (1996) *Sustainable Tourism? European Experiences*. Wallingford: CAB International.

Prosser, B. (1999) Societal change and the growth in alternative tourism. In E. Cater and G. Lowman (eds) *Ecotourism: A Sustainable Option?* (pp. 19–39). Chichester: Wiley.

Ramakrishna, K. and Tan, S. (2003) (eds) *After Bali: The Threat of Terrorism in Southeast Asia*. Singapore: World Scientific.

Raramuridesign (2006) *Paternoster: Along the West Coast of South Africa*. On WWW at http://www.paternoster.co.za/. Accessed 3.6.07.

Redang (2005) *Redang Island*. On WWW at www.redang.org. Accessed 1.11.05.

Redclift, M. (1997) *Sustainable Development: Exploring the Contradictions*. London: Routledge.

Reed, M. (1997) Power relations and community-based tourism planning. *Annals of Tourism Research* 24 (3), 266–591.

Reed, M. (1999) Collaborative tourism planning as adaptive experiments in emergent tourism settings. *Journal of Sustainable Tourism* 7 (3&4), 331–355.

Reed, M. (2000) Collaborative tourism planning as adaptive experiments in emergent tourism settings. In B. Bramwell and B. Lane (eds) *Tourism Collaboration and Partnerships. Politics, Practice and Sustainability* (pp. 247–271). Clevedon: Channel View Publications.

Reed, M.G. and Gill, A.M. (1997) Tourism, recreational and amenity values in land allocation: An analysis of institutional arrangements in the post-productivist era. *Environment and Planning A* 29, 2019–2040.

Reid, D. (2003) *Tourism, Globalization and Development. Responsible Tourism Planning*. London: Pluto.

Republic of Cyprus Statistical Service (2005) On WWW at www.mof.gov.cy/mof/cystat/statistics.nsf/index_en/index_en?OpenDocument. Accessed 17.8.06.

Resource Assessment Commission (RAC) (1993) *Coastal Zone Inquiry: Southern Australian Case Study, Coastal Management and Decision-Making Processes in the Yorke Peninsula Area*. Canberra, Australian Capital Territory: Australian Government Publishing Service.

Richardson, J.I. (1995) *Travel and Tourism in Australia. The Economic Perspective*. Melbourne: Hospitality Press.

Richardson, J.I. (1996) *Marketing Australian Travel and Tourism. Principles and Practice*. Melbourne: Hospitality Press.

Richins, H. and Pearce, P. (2000) Influences on tourism development decision-making: Coastal local government areas in eastern Australia. *Journal* of Sustainable Tourism 8 (3), 207–231.

Richter, L.K. (1980) The political use of tourism: A Philippine case study. *The Journal of Development Areas* 14, 237–257.

Richter, L.K. (1993) Tourism policy-making in South-East Asia. In M. Hitchcock, V.T. King and J.G. Parnwell (eds) *Tourism in South-East Asia* (pp. 179–199). London and New York: Routledge.

Richter, L.K. and Waugh, W.L. (1986) Terrorism and tourism as logical companions. *Tourism Management* 7 (4), 230–238.

Rico Amorós, A.M. (1997) *Recursos hídricos y desarrollo regional en la Comunidad Valenciana*. Alicante: Universidad de Alicante.

Ritzer, G. and Liska, A. (1997) McDisneyization and post-tourism: Complementary perspectives on contemporary tourism. In C. Rojek and J. Urry (eds) *Touring Cultures: Modern Transformations in Leisure and Travel* (pp. 96–109). London: Routledge.

Robadue, D., Hale, L., McCann, J. and Rubinoff, P. (1997) *Conservation of Critical Coastal Ecosystems in Mexico*. Project Proposal 1998–2003. Rhode Island: University of Rhode Island, Coastal Resources Centre.

Roberts, P. and Benneworth, P. (2001) Pathways to the future? An initial assessment of RDA strategies and their contribution to integrated regional development. *Local Economy* 16 (2), 142–159.

Robinson, K. (1999) Happy New Year KZN. *The Independent on Saturday* 2 January, 1.

Rodney, W. (1972) *How Europe Underdeveloped Africa*. London: Bogle-L'Ouverture Publications.

Rogerson, C.M. and Visser, G. (2004) Tourism development in post-apartheid South Africa: A ten-year review. In C.M. Rogerson and G. Visser (eds) *Tourism and Development Issues in Contemporary South Africa* (pp. 2–25). Johannesburg: Africa Institute of South Africa:

Rojek, C. (1995) *Decentring Leisure*. London: Sage.

Roniger, L. (1994) Conclusions: The transformation of clientelism and civil society. In L. Roniger and A. Günes-Ayata (eds) *Democracy, Clientelism and Civil Society* (pp. 207–215). London: Lynne Rienner Publishers.

Rosado-May, F.J. (1994) The Sian K'an Biosphere Reserve Project. In G.K. Meffe and C.R. Carroll (eds) *Principles of Conservation Biology.* Sunderland, MA: Sinauer Associates.

Rose-Ackerman, S. (1987) Bribery. In *The New Palgrave: A Dictionary of Economics*. London: Macmillan.

Rubinoff, P. and Tobey, J. (2006) *Voluntary Guidelines for Sustainable Coastal Tourism Development in Quintana Roo, Mexico*. The Coastal Resources Centre, University of Rhode Island.

Rudney, R. (1980) The development of tourism on the Côte d'Azure: An historical perspective. In D. Hawkins, E. Shafter and J. Rovestrad (eds) *Tourism Planning and Development Issues* (pp. 213–224). Washington DC: George Washington University Press.

SABC TV (2004) Till the well runs dry – Garden Route. *50/50 Environmental Television Programme* 25 July.

Sack, R.D. (1992) *Place, Modernity and the Consumer's World*. Baltimore: The John Hopkins University Press

Sadi, M. and Bartels, F. (1997) The rise of Malaysia's tourism industry. *Cornell Hotel and Restaurant Administration Quarterly* October, 88–95.

Sadi, M.A. and Henderson, J.C. (2001) Tourism and foreign direct investment in Vietnam. *International Journal of Hospitality and Tourism* 2 (1), 67–90.
Sadler, J. (2004) Sustainable tourism planning in northern Cyprus. In B. Bramwell (ed.) *Coastal Mass Tourism. Diversification and Sustainable Development in Southern Europe* (pp. 133–156). Clevedon: Channel View Publications.
Sanders, D. (2000) Holiday towns in the Leeuwin-Naturaliste region: Another Gold Coast? *The Journal of Tourism Studies* 11 (1), 45–55.
Sastre, F. and Benito, I. (2001) The role of transnational tour operators in the development of Mediterranean island tourism. In D. Ioannides, Y. Apostolopoulos and S. Sonmez (eds) *Mediterranean Islands and Sustainable Tourism Development: Practices, Management and Policies* (pp. 69–86). London: Continuum.
Saudi Arabian News Digest (2004) Arab tourists to Malaysia up 70.5% y/y Jan–July 2004, 8 September.
Sayer, A. (1999) *Long-Live Postdisciplinary Studies! Sociology and the Curse of Disciplinary Parochialism/Imperialism*. Lancaster: Department of Sociology, Lancaster University.
Schembri, P. (1994) The environmental impact of tourism in Gozo. In L. Briguglio (ed.) *Tourism in Gozo: Policies, Prospects and Problems* (pp. 50–56). Msida: University of Malta and Foundation for International Studies.
Schumpeter, J. (1939) *Business Cycles.* New York: McGraw-Hill.
Schumpeter, J. (1947) *Capitalism, Socialism and Democracy*. New York: Harper and Bros.
Scott, K. (2006) Environmental decision-making process of the small-craft harbour, Durban. Unpublished MA dissertation, University of KwaZulu-Natal, Durban.
Scott, K. and Oelofse, C. (2005) The environmental politics of the scoping phase of the development of a small craft harbour, Point Waterfront, Durban. *Proceedings of 11th Annual Conference of the International Association of Impact Assessment*, South African Chapter, 29–31 August.
SECTUR (2003) *Mega-projects*. Mexico: SECTUR.
Seguí, M. (2003a) De l'impact des politiques touristiques. L'exemple des Baléares. *Espaces* 200 (janvier), 15–28.
Seguí, M. (2003b) Les implicacions socials d'un projecte de turisme sostenible. *Territoris* 4, 31–42.
Serrano Fernández, J.M. (2003) Las viviendas de segunda residencia en la sociedad del "bienestar". El caso de un país turístico: España. *Cuadernos de Turismo* 12, 53–75.
Sezer, H. and Harrison, A. (1994) Tourism in Greece and Turkey: An economic view for planners. In A.V. Seaton, C.L. Jenkins, R.C. Wood and P.U.C. Dieke (eds) *Tourism: The State of the Art* (pp. 74–84). Chichester: Wiley.
SGT (Secretaría General de Turismo) (1990) *Libro Blanco del Turismo Español*. Madrid: Secretaría General de Turismo.
Shaalan, I.M. (2005) Sustainable tourism development in the Red Sea of Egypt: Threats and opportunities. *Journal of Cleaner Production* 13 (2), 83–87.
Shackley, M. (1999) Tourism development and environmental protection in southern Sinai. *Tourism Management* 20 (4), 543–548.
Shamsul, A.B. (1996) Nations-of-intent in Malaysia. In S. Tonnesson and H. Antlov (eds) *Asian Forms of the Nation* (pp. 323–347). London: Curzon Press.
Sharpley, R. (2000a) Tourism and sustainable development: Exploring the theoretical divide. *Journal of Sustainable Tourism* 8 (1), 1–19.

Sharpley, R. (2000b) The influence of the accommodation sector on tourism development: Lessons from Cyprus. *International Journal of Hospitality Management* 19 (3), 275–293.

Sharpley, R. (2001a) Tourism in Cyprus: Challenges and opportunities. *Tourism Geographies* 3 (1), 64–85.

Sharpley, R. (2001b) Sustainability and the political economy of tourism in Cyprus. *Tourism* 49 (3), 241–254.

Sharpley, R. (2002a) Sustainability: A barrier to tourism development? In R. Sharpley and D. Telfer (eds) *Tourism and Development: Concepts and Issues* (pp. 319–337). Clevedon: Channel View Publications.

Sharpley, R. (2002b) Tourism management: Rural tourism and the challenge of tourism diversification: the case of Cyprus. *Tourism Management* 23 (2), 233–244.

Sharpley, R. (2003) Tourism, modernisation and development on the island of Cyprus: Challenges and policy responses. *Journal of Sustainable Tourism* 11 (2+3), 246–265.

Sharpley, R. (2005) The accommodation sector: Managing for quality. In L. Pender and R. Sharpley (eds) *The Management of Tourism* (pp. 14–27). London: Sage.

Shaw, G. (2006) Lifestyles and changes in tourism consumption: The British experience. In P. Reuber and P. Schell (eds) *Postmoderne Freizeitstile an Freizeiträume* (pp. 21–45). E. Schmidt verlag: Berlin.

Shaw, G. and Alexander, A. (2006) Interlocking directorates and the knowledge transfer of supermarket retail techniques from North America to Britain. *International Review of Retail, Distribution and Consumer Research* 16 (3), 375–394.

Shaw, G. and Williams, A.M. (1997a) *The Rise and Fall of British Coastal Resorts*. London: Cassell.

Shaw, G. and Williams, A. (1997b) The private sector: Tourism entrepreneurship – a constraint or resource? In G. Shaw and A. Williams (eds) *The Rise and Fall of British Coastal Resorts. Cultural and Economic Perspectives* (pp. 117–136). London: Cassell.

Shaw, G. and Williams, A.M. (2002) *Critical Issues in Tourism: A Geographical Perspective* (2nd edn). Oxford: Blackwell.

Shaw, G. and Williams, A.M. (2003) From lifestyle consumption to lifestyle production: Changing patterns of tourism entrepreneurship. In R. Thomas (ed.) *Small Firms in Tourism: International Perspectives* (pp. 93–113). Oxford: Elsevier.

Shaw, G. and Williams, A.M. (2004) *Tourism and Tourism Spaces*. London: Sage.

Sheldon, P.J. (1983) The impact of technology on the hotel industry. *Tourism Management* 4 (4), 269–278.

Shleifer, A, and Vishny, R.W. (1993) Corruption. *Quarterly Journal of Economics* 108 (3), 599–617.

Si Mexico (2006) *Hotel and Resort Travel Guide*. On WWW at http://www.si-mexico.com/cities/huatulco.htm. Accessed 3.6.07.

Skolimowski, H. (1995) In defence of sustainable development. *Environmental Values* 4, 69–70.

Smith, M. (1998) *Social Science in Question. Towards a Post-Disciplinary Framework*. London: Sage.

Smith, M.K. (2004) Seeing a new side to seasides: Culturally regenerating the English seaside town. *International Journal of Tourism Research* 6 (1), 17–28.

Smith, R. (1992a) Conflicting trends of beach resort development: A Malaysian case. *Coastal Management* 20, 167–187.
Smith, R. (1992b) Review of integrated beach resort development in Southeast Asia. *Land Use Policy* July, 209–217.
Smith, R. (1992c) Beach resort evolution: Implications for tourism planning. *Annals of Tourism Research* 19 (2), 304–322.
Snow, R. and Wright, D. (1976) Coney Island: A case study in popular culture and technological change. *Journal of Popular Culture* 9 (4), 960–975.
Soane, J. (1992) The origin, growth and transformation of maritime resorts since 1840. *Built Environment* 18 (1), 12–26.
Sonck, T. (2004) Marketing Director, SPET (Promoción Exterior de Tenerife): personal communication.
Sönmez, S.F. (1998) Tourism, terrorism and political instability. *Annals of Tourism Research* 25 (2), 416–456.
Sönmez, S.F. and Apostolopoulos, Y. (2000) Conflict resolution through tourism co-operation? The case of the portioned state of Cyprus. *Journal of Travel and Tourism Marketing* 9 (3), 35–48.
Sönmez, S.F. and Graefe, A.R. (1998) Influence of terrorism risk on foreign tourism decisions. *Annals of Tourism Research* 25 (1), 112–144.
Sönmez, S.F., Apostolopoulos, Y. and Tarlow, P. (1999) Tourism in crisis: Managing the effects of terrorism. *Journal of Travel Research* 38 (1), 13–18.
Sorkin, M. (1992) See you in Disneyland. In M. Sorkin (ed.) *Variations on a Theme Park: The New American City and the End of Public Space* (pp. 205–232). New York: Hill and Wang.
South Africa (1989) *Environmental Conservation Act 72 of 1989.* Pretoria: Department of Environmental Affairs and Tourism.
South Africa (1996) *White Paper on the Development and Promotion of Tourism in South Africa.* Pretoria: Department of Environmental Affairs and Tourism.
South Africa (1998a) *Coastal Policy Green Paper: Towards Sustainable Coastal Development in South Africa*. Cape Town: Department of Environmental Affairs and Tourism.
South Africa (1998b) *Tourism in GEAR Tourism Development Strategy: 1998–2000*. Pretoria: Department of Environmental Affairs and Tourism.
South Africa (1998c) *National Environmental Management Act 107 of 1998.* Pretoria: Department of Environmental Affairs and Tourism.
South Africa (2000) *White Paper for Sustainable Coastal Development in South Africa*. Pretoria: Department of Environmental Affairs and Tourism.
South African Airways (2005a) South African Tourism Welcome Awards. *Sawubona Magazine* November, 160.
South African Airways (2005b) Pearl Dawn. *Sawbona Magazine* November, 152.
South African Airways (2005c) Pezula. *Sawbona Magazine* November, 125.
South African Airways (2004a) Lagoon Bay. *Sawubona Magazine* November, 125.
South African Airways (2004b) Pezula. *Sawbona Magazine* November, 133.
South African Airways (2004c) Simbithi eco-estate. *Sawbona Magazine* November, 150.
Southern Explorer Association (2005) The exploration guide to the treasures of the south coast. *Southern Explorer* 1–34.
Souty F. (2002) *Passport To Progress: Competition Challenges For World Tourism and Global Anti-Competitive Practices in the Tourism Industry*. Madrid: World Tourism Organisation.
Stabler, M.J. (1997) *Tourism and Sustainability: Principles to Practice*. Wallingford: CAB International.

Stanton, J. and Aislabie, C. (1992) Up-market integrated resorts in Australia. *Annals of Tourism Research* 19 (3), 435–449.
State of Israel Central Bureau of Statistics and the Governmental Company for Tourism. Various editions 1957–1970. *The Tourism in Israel: A Statistical Review*. Jerusalem.
State of Israel Central Bureau of Statistics and the Ministry of Tourism. Various editions 1971–2005. *Tourism and Hotel Services Statistics Quarterly*. Jerusalem.
State Planning Department (1997) *Decree Law No: 540, Decree Law on the Establishment and Duties of the Department*. Ankara: State Planning Department.
Statistics South Africa (2001) *Census 2001*. Pretoria: Government Printer.
Stoker, G. (1995) Governance as theory: Five propositions. *International Social Science Journal* 155. Oxford: UNESCO/Blackwell.
Stoker, G. (1999) *New Management of British Local Governance*. Basingstoke: MacMillan Press Ltd.
Stonehouse, G.H., Harrill, J., Campbell, D. and Purdie, A. (1999) *Global and Transnational Business – Strategy and Management*. London: Wiley.
Sunar, D. (1999) STDs including HIV/AIDS as a public policy issue: The paradigmatic case of Turkey – Part I. *Bogaziçi Journal* 13 (1–2), 27–40.
Sunday Tribune (2005a) *Property Guide* 4 December, 58.
Sunday Tribune (2005b) *Property Guide* 4 December, 16.
Sunday Tribune (2005c) *Property Guide* 4 December, 1–64.
Surin, K. (1998) Dependency Theory's reanimation in the era of financial capital. *Cultural Logic* 1 (2). On WWW at http://clogic.eserver.org/1-2/surin.html. Accessed 1.6.07.
Sutherland, J. (1999) Hug this tree. *Canadian Business* 72 (8), 48–54.
Swarbrooke, J. (1999) *Sustainable Tourism Management*. Wallingford: CABI Publishing.
Swinscoe, A. (1999) Egypt. *Travel & Tourism Intelligence* 4, 23–45.
Swinscoe, A. (2000) Cairo. *Travel & Tourism Intelligence* 2, 11–27.
Syrett, S. (1997) The politics of partnership: the role of social partners in local economic development in Portugal. *European Urban and Regional Studies* 4 (2), 99–114.
Taclan, T. (2004) *Turkey Tourism Sector Report*. Ankara: Economic and Commercial Department, British Embassy.
Tarlow, P. (2000) Creating safe and secure communities in economically challenging times. *Tourism Economics* 6 (2), 139–149.
Tatoglu, E., Erdal, F., Ozgur, H. and Azakli, S. (2002) Resident attitudes toward tourism impacts: The case of Kusadasi. *International Journal of Hospitality and Tourism Administration* 3 (3), 79–100.
TED (Trade and Environment Database) (1998) *Cancún: Mexican Tourism*. Washington, DC: American University.
Teo, P. and Li, H. (2003) Global and local interactions in tourism. *Annals of Tourism Research* 30 (2), 287–306.
Tessler, M. and Altinoglu, E. (2004) Political culture in Turkey: Connection among attitudes toward democracy, military and Islam. *Democratisation* 11 (1), 22–51.
The Business Times (2005) Double forex income seen. 25 August.
The Nature Conservancy (2002) *Yucatán Coastal Wetlands*. On WWW at www.nature.org/wherewework/northamerica/mexico/work/art8624.html. Accessed 5.6.06.
The New Straits Times (2004) Back on the resort route. 6 November.
The New Sunday Times (2004) The Arabs have arrived. 15 August.

Theroux, P. (1983) *The Kingdom by the Sea. A Journey Around the Coast of Great Britain*. Harmondsworth, Middlesex: Penguin Books.
The Straits Times (2005a) Desaru déjà vu. 18 May.
The Straits Times (2005b) Clerics hit out at lobby against moral police. 16 April.
The Unofficial Guide (2005) *Mexico's Best Beach Resorts*. On WWW at www.travel.msn.com/Guides/article.aspx?cp-documentid = 257200. Accessed 5.6.06.
Thomas, G. and Fernandez, T.V. (1994) Mangrove and tourism: Management strategies. *Indian Forester* 120 (5), 406–412.
Thomas, H. and Thomas, R. (1998) The implications for tourism of shifts in British local governance. *Progress in Tourism and Hospitality Research* 4 (4), 295–306.
Thomas, J.M. (1977) Blacks on the South Carolina Sea Islands: Planning for tourist and land development. Unpublished PhD Dissertation, University of Michigan.
Thomas, J.M. (1980) The impact of corporate tourism on Gullah blacks. *Phylon* 41 (1), 1–11.
Thomlinson, E. and Getz, D. (1996) The question of scale in ecotourism: Case study of two small ecotour operators in the Mundo Maya Region of Central America. *Journal of Sustainable Tourism* 4 (4), 183–200.
Thrift, N. (1999) Steps to an ecology of place. In D. Massey, J. Allen and P. Sarre (eds) *Human Geography Today* (pp. 295–322). Cambridge: Polity Press.
Timothy, D.J. (1998) Co-operative tourism planning in a developing destination. *Journal of Sustainable Tourism* 6 (1), 52–68.
Tinley, K.L. (1985) *Coastal dunes of South Africa.* South African National Scientific Programmes Report 109. Pretoria: Council for Scientific and Industrial Research.
TNS Travel & Tourism (2004) *Great Britain Day Visits Survey 2002–03*. Edinburgh: TNS Travel & Tourism.
Toerisme Recreatie Nederland (1997) *Sea of Culture Action Plan*. The Netherlands: Toerisme Recreatie Nederland.
Toledo, J.V. (1985) Tourism development in Turkey. MSc thesis, Bilkent University.
Tomljenovic, R. and Faulkner, B. (2000) Tourism and older residents in a sunbelt resort. *Annals of Tourism Research* 27 (11), 93–114.
Torres, R. (2002) Cancún's tourism development from a Fordist spectrum of analysis. *Tourist Studies* 2 (1), 87–116.
Tosun, C. (2000) Limits to community participation in the tourism development process in developing countries. *Tourism Management* 21 (6), 613–633.
Tosun, C. (2002) Host perceptions of impacts: a comparative tourism study. *Annals of Tourism Research* 29 (3), 231–245.
Tosun, C. and Timothy, D.J. (2001) Defects in planning approaches to tourism development in developing countries: The case of Turkey. *International Journal of Contemporary Hospitality* 13 (7), 352–359.
Tosun, C., Timothy, D. and Ozturk, Y. (2004) Tourism growth, national development and regional inequality. In B. Bramwell (ed.) *Coastal Mass Tourism. Diversification and Sustainable Development in Southern Europe* (pp. 85–113). Clevedon: Channel View Publications.
Tourism Alliance (2003) *Priorities For Tourism: First Year Review.* London: Tourism Alliance.
Tourism Malaysia (2004) *Your Diving Paradise*. Kuala Lumpur: Tourism Malaysia.
Tourism Malaysia (2005) *Tourism Statistics*. On WWW at www.tourism.gov.my. Accessed 1.11.05.
Tourism Penang (2005) General information. On WWW at http://www.tourism penang.gov.my. Accessed 1.11.05.

Tourism Research Group (1989) *Tourism in Cornwall: A Summary of Recent Research Funded by Cornwall TDAP.* Exeter: Tourism Research Group, University of Exeter.
Towner, J. (1996) *An Historical Geography of Recreation and Tourism in the Western World 1540–1940*. Chichester: John Wiley.
Town of Hilton Head Island (2005) A history timeline of Hilton Head Island. On WWW at www.hiltonheadislandsc.gov/Island/history.html. Accessed 25.7.05.
Travis, J. (1992), *The Rise of Devon Seaside Resorts, 1750–1900*. Exeter: University of Exeter Press.
Tribe, J. (2006) The truth about tourism. *Annals of Tourism Research* 33 (2), 360–381.
Troitiño Vinuesa, M.A., de Marcos García-Blanco, F.J., García Hernández, M., del Río Lafuente, M.I., Carpio Martín, J., de la Calle Vaquero, M. and Abad Aragón, L.D. (2005) Los espacios protegidos en España: Significación e incidencia socio-territorial. *Boletín de la Asociación de Geógrafos Españoles* 39, 227–265.
TTF Australia (Tourism Task Force Australia) (2003) *Resorting to Profitability Making Tourist Resorts Work in Australia.* Sydney: TTF Australia.
TTG Daily News (2005) Malaysia unveils tourism plan for next decade. TTTGTravelHub.Net, 18 February.
Tuan, Y. (1974) *Topophilia: A Study of Environmental Perceptions, Attitudes and Values*. Englewood Cliffs, NJ: Prentice-Hall.
Tunc, B. (2005) *Report of Local Development, Kusadasi*. Ankara: Kosgeb.
Tunstall, S.M. and Penning-Roswell, E.C. (1998) The English beach: Experiences and values. *The Geographical Journal* 164 (3), 319–332.
Tuppen, J. (1998) France: Tourism comes of age. In A. Williams and G. Shaw (eds) *Tourism and Economic Development. European Experience* (3rd edn) (pp. 243–268). Chichester: Wiley.
TURESPAÑA. Instituto de Turismo de España (1998) *El turismo náutico en España, 7° Symposium sobre Puertos Deportivos. Gijón 13–15 May 1998*. Gijón: G.M.M. Consultores Turísticos, S.L. Estudio.
Turner, A. (1996) Water world. *Leisure Management* 16 (8), 66–69.
Turner, F.J. (1962) *The Frontier in American History.* New York: Holt.
Turner, L. and Ash, J. (1975) *The Golden Hordes: International Tourism and the Pleasure Periphery*. London: Constable.
Twining-Ward, L. and Baum, T. (1998) Dilemmas facing mature island destinations: Cases from the Baltic. *Progress in Tourism and Hospitality Research* 4 (2), 131–140.
Twining-Ward, L. and Butler, R.W. (2002) Implementing STD on a small island: Development and use of sustainable tourism development indicators in Samoa. *Journal of Sustainable Tourism* 10 (5), 363–387.
TYD (1992) *Economic Contribution of Tourism Investment*. Istanbul: TYD.
Tyson, P.D. and Preston-Whyte, R.A. (2000) *The Climate and Weather of Southern Africa* (2nd edn). Cape Town: Oxford University Press.
Unal, T.(1992) Local government and tourism. *Anatolia* 3 (25/26), 5–7.
UNCTAD (1998) *International Trade in Tourism – Related Services: Issues and Options For Developing Countries.* Geneva: UNCTAD.
UNDP (2004) *United Nations Human Development Report 2004*. On WWW at http://hdr.undp.org/reports/global/2004/pdf/hdr04_HDI.pdf. Accessed 1.6.07.
Ungerleider, M. (1995) *Tofino: The Road Stops Here Video*. Vancouver: Moving Images Distribution.

United Kingdom Tourism Survey (2005) South West Facts 2004. On WWW at www.star.uk.org//defaultasp?ID = 741&parentid = 469. Accessed 15.8.06.
United Nations (1999) *The Science, Technology and Innovation Policy Review – Jamaica*. New York: United Nations.
United Nations Development Programme (2003) *The Challenge of Sustainable Development in South Africa: Unlocking People's Creativity*. Cape Town: Oxford University Press.
Urry, J. (1987) Some social and spatial aspects of services. *Society and Space* 5 (4), 5–26.
Urry, J. (1990) *The Tourist Gaze. Leisure and Travel in Contemporary Societies*. London: Sage.
Urry, J. (1994) Cultural change and contemporary tourism. *Leisure Studies* 13, 233–238.
Urry, J. (1995) *Consuming Places*. London: Routledge.
Urry, J. (1996) Post modern society and contemporary tourism. In W. Nuryanti (ed.) *Tourism and Culture: Global Civilisations in Change?* (pp. 83–90). Yogyakarta: Gadjah Mada University Press.
Urry, J. (1997) Cultural change and the seaside resort. In G. Shaw and A.M. Williams (eds) *The Rise and Fall of British Coastal Resorts* (pp. 102–113). London: Pinter.
Urry, J. (2002) *The Tourist Gaze* (2nd edn). London: Sage.
Vader, J. and Lang, F. (1980) *The Gold Coast: An Illustrated History*. Milton, NSW: Jacaranda Press.
Vancouver Island (2005) *Tofino*. On WWW at www.vancouverisland.com. Accessed 23.11.05.
Van den Berghe, P.L. (1994) *The Quest for the Other: Ethnic Tourism in San Cristobal, Mexico*. Seattle: University of Washington Press.
van de Weg, H. (1982) Trends in design and development of facilities: Revitalization of traditional resorts. *Tourism Management* 3 (4), 303–307.
Van Teylingen, K., McLachlan, A., Rickard, C. and Kerley, G. (1993) *Conservation Status of the Vertebrate Fauna of Coastal Dunes in South Africa* (Biodiversity Series Report No. 1). Pretoria: Department of Environmental affairs and the Foundation for Research Development.
Var, T., Ap, J. and Van Doren, C. (1994) Tourism and world peace. In W. Theobald (ed.) *Global Tourism: The Next Decade* (pp. 27–39). Oxford: Butterworth-Heinemann.
Vassallo, H. (2003) NUTS about Gozo. *Times of Malta* 16 February.
Venturoni, L., Long, P. and Perdue, R. (2005) The economic and social impacts of second homes in four mountain resort counties of Colorado. Paper presented at the *Annual Meeting Association of American Geographers*, 7 April, Denver, Colorado.
VisitBritain (2003) Implications of an ageing population in Britain. *Foresight* (November), 4–6.
VisitBritain (2005a) The Day Visit Market. *Foresight* 22 (August), 4–8.
VisitBritain (2005b) *What is the Future of Domestic Tourism to 2015*. London: England Research.
VisitBritain (2006) *The Short Break Market – An Analysis*. London: England Research.
Von Meyer, H., Terluin, I.J., Post, J.H. and Van Haeperen, B. (1999) *Rural Employment Dynamics in the EU: Key Findings for Policy Consideration Emerging from the RUREMPLO Project*. The Hague: LEI-DLO.

Wahab, S. (1995) Terrorism – a challenge to tourism. In *Security and Risks in Travel and Tourism Conference Proceedings* (pp. 84–108). Ostersund: Mid-Sweden University.

Wahab, S. (1996) Tourism and terrorism: Synthesis of the problem with emphasis on Egypt. In A. Pizam and Y. Mansfeld (eds) *Tourism, Crime and International Security Issues* (pp. 175–186). Chichester: Wiley.

Wahab, S. and Pigram, J.J. (eds) (1997) *Tourism, Development and Growth: The Challenge of Sustainability*. Routledge: London.

Wall, G. and Mathieson, A. (2006) *Tourism: Change, Impacts and Opportunities* (2nd edn). London: Pearson Education Limited.

Wallerstein, I. (1979) *The Capitalist World-Economy*. London: Cambridge University Press.

Walton, J. (1983) *The English Seaside Resort: A Social History, 1750–1914*. London: Longman.

Walton, J. (1997) The seaside resorts of England and Wales, 1900–1950: Growth, diffusion and the emergence of new forms of tourism. In G. Shaw and A.M. Williams (eds) *The Rise and Fall of British Coastal Resorts* (pp. 21–48). London: Cassell.

Walton, J.K. (2000) *The British Seaside: Holidays and Resorts in the Twentieth Century*. Manchester: Manchester University Press.

Warner, J. (1999) North Cyprus: Tourism and the challenge of non-recognition. *Journal of Sustainable Tourism* 7 (2), 128–145.

Watts, D. (1987) *The West Indies: Patterns of Development, Culture and Environmental Change since 1492*. Cambridge: Cambridge University Press.

Weaver, D. (2004) Tourism and the elusive paradigm of sustainable development. In A. Lew, M. Hall and A. Williams (eds) *A Companion to Tourism* (pp. 510–521). Oxford: Blackwell.

Weaver, D.B. (1988) The evolution of a 'plantation' tourism landscape on the Caribbean island of Antigua'. *Tijdschrift voor Economische en Social Geografie* 79, 319–331.

Weaver, D.B. (1992) Tourism and the functional transformation of the Antiguan landscape. In C. Fleischer-van Rooijen (ed.) *Spatial Implications of Tourism*. (pp. 161–176). Groningen, The Netherlands: GeoPers.

Weaver, D.B. (2005) The 'plantation' variant of the TALC in the small island Caribbean. In R.W. Butler (ed.) *The Tourism Area Life Cycle: Applications and Modifications* (pp. 185–197). Clevedon, UK: Channel View Publications.

Weaver, D.B. and Lawton, L.J. (2006) *Tourism Management* (3rd edn). Brisbane, Australia: John Wiley & Sons Australia.

Webb, J. (2005) *Tourists trick or treat*. On WWW at www.carteblanche.co.za. Accessed 16.1.06.

Weiner, T. (2001) On tourism, Mexico now thinks green. *The New York Times* 31 August.

West Coast Tourism (2006) *Cape West Coast*. On WWW at www.capewestcoast.org. Accessed 16.1.06.

Wheeller, B. (1994) Ecotourism, sustainable tourism and the environment – a symbiotic or symbolic relationship. In A.V. Seaton (ed.) *Tourism: The State of the Art* (pp. 647–654). Chichester: John Wiley and Sons.

White, B.P. (1999) Authoring the tourism landscape of Clayoquot Sound. Unpublished PhD dissertation, Simon Fraser University, Burnaby.

Wickaninnish Inn (2005a) *Storm Season.* On WWW at www.wickinn.com. Accessed 23.11.05.

Wickaninnish Inn (2005b) *History of the Inn*. On WWW at www.wickinn.com. Accessed 24.11.05.

Wiese, P. (2000) *Environmental Impact of Urban and Industrial Development: A Case History of Cancún, Quintana Roo.* On WWW at www.unesco.org/csi/wise/cancun1.htm. Accessed 5.6.06.

Wikipedia (2005) *Tioman Island*. On WWW at www.en.wikipedia.org/wiki/Tioman_Island. Accessed 2.11.05.

Wilkinson, P. (2001) Tourism development in Anguilla. *Tourism Recreation Research* 26 (3), 33–41.

Willems-Braun, B. (1997) Buried epistemologies. The politics of nature in (post)colonial British Columbia. *Annals of the Association of American Geographers* 87 (1), 3–31.

Williams, A.M and Shaw, G. (1988) Tourism – candy floss industry or job generator? *Town Planning Review* 59 (1), 81–104.

Williams, A.M. and Shaw, G. (1997) Riding the big dipper: The rise and decline of the British seaside resort in the twentieth century. In G. Shaw and A.M. Williams (eds) *The Rise and Fall of British Coastal Resorts* (pp. 1–18). London: Pinter.

Williamson, J. (1990) What Washington means by policy reform. In J. Williamson (ed.) *Latin American Adjustment: How Much Has Happened?* (pp. 7–20). Washington: Institute for International Economics.

Wilson G.A. (2001) From productivism to post-productivism and back again? Exploring the (un)changed natural and mental landscapes of European agriculture. *Transactions of the Institute of British Geographers, New Series* 26, 77–102.

Wolfe, R.I. (1982) Recreational travel: The new migration revisited. *Ontario Geography* 19, 103–122.

Wong, P.P. (1986) Tourism development and resorts on the east coast of Peninsular Malaysia. *Singapore Journal of Tropical Geography* 7 (2), 152–162.

Wong, P.P. (1990) Coastal resort management: Tourism in Peninsular Malaysia. *ASEAN Economic Bulletin* 7 (2), 72–85.

Wong, P.P. (1993) Island tourism development in Peninsular Malaysia: Environmental perspective. In P.P. Wong (ed.) *Tourism vs Environment: The Case for Coastal Areas* (pp. 83–97). The Netherlands: Kluwer.

Wood, A. and Valler, D. (2001) Turn again? Rethinking institutions and the governance of local and regional economies. *Environment and Planning A* 33 (7), 1139–1144.

Wood, R. (1984) Ethnic tourism, the state and cultural change in South East Asia. *Annals of Tourism Research* 11 (3), 353–374.

Worden, N. (2001) Where it all began: The representation of Malaysian heritage in Melaka. *International Journal of Heritage Studies* 7 (3), 199–218.

World Tourism Organization (2004) *International Tourist Arrivals by Country of Destination – Americas*. On WWW at www.world-tourism.org/facts/menu.html. Accessed 25.7.05.

World Tourism Organization (2005) *World Overview and Tourism Topics*. On WWW at www.unwto.org/facts/menu.html. Accessed 5.6.06.

Wrangham, R. (1999) Management or domination? Planning tourism in the Banda Islands, Eastern Indonesia. *International Journal of Contemporary Hospitality Management* 11 (2/3), 111–115.

WTO (World Tourism Organization) (1993) *Sustainable Development Guide for Local Planners*. Madrid: WTO.

WTO (World Tourism Organization) (2004) *Inbound Tourism in the Middle East and North Africa* (Special Report No. 23). Madrid: World Tourism Organization.

WTTC (2004) Economic Research, Country League Tables. On WWW at www.rea.ru/hotel/TourMaterials/WTO/2004%20League%20Tables.pdf. Accessed 1.6.07.

www.iet.tourspain/es. Accessed 1.5.06.

www.golfresidencial.com. Accessed 1.5.06.

www.villaixtapa.com/ixtapa_zihuatanejo.htm (undated) *The Past of Zihuatanejo and the future of Ixtapa.* Accessed 23.6.06.

Yalcindag, H. (1997) *Local Government and Problems.* Ankara: Amme Idaresi.

Yeoh, B. and Teo, P. (1996) From Tiger Balm Gardens to Dragon World: Philanthropy and profit in the making of Singapore's first cultural theme park. *Geografiska Annaler* 78B, 27–42.

Yeter, E. (1993) Local government autonomy in the European Union and Turkish Constitution. *Cagdas Yerel Yonetimler* 5 (1), 12–19.

Yeung, H. (2005) Rethinking relational economic geography. *Transactions Institute of British Geographers, New Series* 30, 37–51.

Yip, G.S. (1992) *Total Global Strategy: Managing for Worldwide Competitive Advantage*. New Jersey: Prentice Hall.

Young, B. (1983) Touristisation of traditional Maltese fishing-farming villages. A general model. *Tourism Management* 4 (1), 35–41.

Yu, L. (1997) Travel between politically divided China and Taiwan. *Asia Pacific Journal of Travel Research* 2 (1), 19–30.

Yüksel, A. and Yüksel, F. (2005) Managing relations in a learning model for bringing destinations in need of assistance into contact with good practice. *Tourism Management* 26 (5), 667–679.

Yüksel, F. (2002) Inter-organizational relations and central–local interactions in tourism planning in Belek, Turkey. PhD thesis, Sheffield Hallam University.

Yüksel, F., Bramwell, B. and Yüksel, A. (1999) Stakeholder interviews and tourism planning at Pamukkale, Turkey. *Tourism Management* 20 (3), 351–360.

Zakai, D. and Chadwick-Furman, N.E. (2002) Impacts of intensive recreational diving on reef corals at Eilat, northern Red Sea. *Biological Conservation* 105 (2), 179–187.

Zanetto, G. and Soriani, S. (1996) Tourism and environmental degradation: The northern Adriatic Sea. In G. Priestley, J.A. Edwards and H. Coccossis (eds) *Sustainable Tourism? European Experiences* (pp. 137–152). Wallingford: CAB International.

Index